C0-AUL-455

HARRIET MARTINEAU
A RADICAL VICTORIAN

Harriet Martineau, *c.* 1835

HARRIET MARTINEAU

A Radical Victorian

by

R. K. WEBB

Associate Professor of History
Columbia University

NEW YORK: COLUMBIA UNIVERSITY PRESS
LONDON: WILLIAM HEINEMANN LTD
1960

Library of Congress Catalog Card Number: 59-11698

MANUFACTURED IN GREAT BRITAIN

To the memory of

JOHN BARTLET BREBNER

Contents

Abbreviations used in the footnotes

Works of Harriet Martineau most frequently referred to:

Auto.	*Harriet Martineau's Autobiography*, with Memorials by Maria Weston Chapman. 2 vols., Boston, 1877
Biog. Sketches	*Biographical Sketches.* New York, 1869
EL	*Eastern Life, Present and Past.* New edn. London, 1875
HE	*Household Education.* London, 1849
Hist.	*The History of the Thirty Years' Peace*, with an introductory volume, 1800–1815. 3 vols. London, 1849
Letters	*Letters on the Laws of Man's Nature and Development* (with Henry G. Atkinson). London, 1851
Misc.	*Miscellanies.* 2 vols. Boston, 1836
RWT	*Retrospect of Western Travel.* 2 vols. New York, 1838
SA	*Society in America.* 2 vols. New York, 1837

Periodicals most frequently cited:

ASS	*National Anti-Slavery Standard*, New York
DN	*Daily News*
ER	*Edinburgh Review*
MR	*Monthly Repository*
WR	*Westminster Review*

Libraries:

BM	British Museum
BPL	Boston Public Library
DWL	Dr. Williams's Library
LC	Library of Congress
MCO	Manchester College, Oxford
MHS	Massachusetts Historical Society
NLS	National Library of Scotland
NYHS	New York Historical Society
NYPL	New York Public Library
PHS	Pennsylvania Historical Society
UCL	University College, London

List of Illustrations

The author and publishers wish to thank the following for their kind permission to reproduce illustrations: The Trustees of the British Museum, for the engraving on the jacket; The Daily News Limited (Proprietors of the *News Chronicle* and *The Star*), for Plates VI and IX; and Radio Times Hulton Picture Library, for Plate VIII.

Preface

HARRIET MARTINEAU was an eccentric. Her opinions ranged from penetrating judgments and superb common sense to almost unbelievable dogmatism and just plain silliness. At times her astonishing energy was turned to serious causes of great importance, at other times to momentary enthusiasms of no importance at all. She could write beautifully; she could be inflated and pompous. But her personality was seldom less than fantastical. Her biographers have succumbed either to the causes or to the eccentricities; none of them has really studied or understood her opinions or their origins in her times. As biographers, not historians, they have seen her only as unique (which she was) and not as symptomatic and even typical. It is that untried course which I have taken.

This book can serve as a biography. There is much new material in it which reveals a picture somewhat different from the usual one and which permits some informed speculation and detached generalization impossible a hundred years ago and ignored since. But much biographical detail has necessarily been passed over. Miss Martineau's autobiography is still the best narrative of her life; it can be repeated but not bettered. This book, rather, is intended to answer two questions: what forces in the early nineteenth century formed and were reflected in this singular woman, and what can a study of her amazingly consistent attitudes tell us about early Victorian society? In the end, it comes down to an attempt to define Victorian radicalism.

The difficulties involved in writing on Harriet Martineau are considerable, many of them of her own making. She proclaimed shifts and changes when in reality she was standing still. She combined astonishing candour with a resolute concern for a public image. She could be vague when one wants her to be concrete. I have taken seriously the image she wanted to create, and, relying on other sources, I have supplied some candour where it was most needed. There still remain some gaps and ambiguities in sources and difficulties in interpretation; these are discussed in the bibliographical note, but here I must indicate my gratitude to those persons who helped to smoothe out difficulties.

Sir Wilfrid Martineau most graciously allowed me to see his collection of cuttings of his great-great aunt's leading articles in the *Daily News*; I am very grateful for his sympathetic support. For help in locating manuscripts and for permission to use them, I am indebted to the Marchioness of Crewe, Lady Hermione Cobbold, Mr. George Howard, Viscount and Lady Lambton, Miss E. N. Lawson-Tancred, Mr. John Martineau, Mrs. Sydney Martineau, Mr. C. W. Borlase Parker, Mr. James Pope-Hennessy, and the Rev. H. L. Short. Any scholarly enterprise, and particularly a transatlantic one, makes particular demands on the aid and comfort of friends and strangers who become friends. I should like to mention especially Mr. and Mrs. H. L. Beales, Professor W. H. B. Court, Mr. S. Mervyn Herbert, Mr. O. R. McGregor, Professor Austin Robinson, Mr. Joseph W. Scott, Mr. E. K. Timings, Mr. David Wightman, Mrs. Cecil Woodham-Smith, and Miss Rachel Young.

In the United States, I owe a great and unusual debt to Mr. William S. Coloe, who undertook with remarkable ingenuity and despatch the enormous labour of transcribing the shorthand abstracts made by James Martineau of a long series of letters from his sister. Drs. Lawrence S. Kubie and C. R. Wise were both helpful and indulgent in reviewing my speculations about medical questions, for which, of course, I take final responsibility. My colleagues at Columbia University were always at hand with advice and sympathetic interest; it will hardly be invidious if I single out those most deeply concerned. David Donald, Richard Hofstadter, and James P. Shenton guided my search for materials in the United States; and Jacques Barzun, Peter Gay, Walter Metzger, and Fritz Stern patiently and critically read what I wrote, either in manuscript or in galleys. The Council for Research in the Social Sciences at Columbia generously assisted with grants for research and travel, and the Vice-President of the University, Dr. John A. Krout, through his research funds, helped to make possible the shorthand transcriptions. My wife was of great assistance in preparing the index.

The obligations to librarians must be acknowledged generally; a list of the libraries I used will be found in the bibliography. But special mention must be made of the help of Miss W. D. Coates and her staff at the National Register of Archives and of the great assistance and kindness of Mr. Moorfield Storey and Miss Margaret Munsterberg, whose indexing of the Weston and

Garrison papers in the Boston Public Library not only saved me weeks of work but made it possible to find references otherwise inaccessible or illegible.

One final word: my first work on Harriet Martineau was done in a seminar under J. B. Brebner, Gouverneur Morris Professor of History at Columbia. From that time a dozen years ago until his death late in 1957, I could count on his criticism, his insights, and his friendship. He was able to read most of the manuscript before he died. It owes more to him than to any one else.

R. K. W.

New York City
1959

CHAPTER I

"One of the Strangest Phenomena"

She is one of the strangest phenomena to me. A genuine little Poetess, buckrammed, swathed like a mummy into Socinian and Political-Economy formulas; and yet verily alive inside of that! "God has given a Prophet to every People in its own speech," say the Arabs. Even the English Unitarians were one day to have their Poet, and the best that could be said for them too was to be said. I admire this good lady's integrity, sincerity; her quick, sharp discernment to the depth it goes; her love also is great; nay, in fact it is too great; the host of illustrious obscure mortals whom she produces on you, of Preachers, Pamphleteers, Antislavers, able Editors, and other Atlases bearing (unknown to us) the world on their shoulders, is absolutely more than enough.

THOMAS CARLYLE TO RALPH WALDO EMERSON
June 1, 1837

WHEN Harriet Martineau moved from Norwich to London in 1832, she was twenty-nine years old and famous. Her tales to illustrate political economy had driven Lord Brougham to the exasperated remark that a deaf girl in Norwich was doing more good than any man in the country,[1] and anyone who could exasperate the Lord Chancellor by stealing a march on his Society for the Diffusion of Useful Knowledge deserved the lionizing she got. When she sailed for America two years later, the tales had multiplied and her reputation had grown. Less accustomed then than now to visiting celebrities, the Americans who saw her noted and noted down everything, including much that London took for granted. To find out what she was like, then, we can begin mostly with Americans.

A New York lawyer, Robert Sedgwick, saw Miss Martineau in church on a Sunday morning in September, 1834, and recognized her at once "by the singular ear-trumpet with which she was drinking in Mr. Furness's sermon". She was, he wrote to his

[1] Lucy Aikin to Channing, October 15, 1832, *Corr.*, p. 148. *Auto.*, i,133.

wife, thirty-one and very plain. "I escorted her to Jas. King's to tea the other evg. . . . I afterwards took Mr. Gallatin to see her so that I have first & last seen a gt deal of her & like her extremely maugre her entire neglect to return any part of my admiration. . . ." Mrs. Sedgwick, on holiday in Newport, wished him all the pleasure he could get from the visitor before she came back: "It is not at all likely that the friend of the Lord Chancellor would be tenderly disposed towards an American Counsellor who numbered at least two score summers." The plainness could be taken less gently than in this domestic joke. The wife of a former governor of Louisiana, visiting in Baltimore in January, 1835, went down to the harbour one afternoon to watch the skating, "and to her dismay, was taken to be Miss Martineau, whom Mrs. Grimes thinks the ugliest woman in the world. The boys probably had grounded their supposition upon Mrs. G's wearing a very remarkable cloak, which they in their wisdom thought would suit the authoress." [1]

Plain is a juster word than ugly. She was of average height, perhaps taller than most American women; and when Henry Clay tried to guess her weight, he was very close to the correct figure, 116 pounds. Her complexion, recalled her friend Mrs. Chapman, was neither fair nor sallow, rather "the hue of one severely tasked, but not with literary work". Her hair, low on the forehead, was brown and abundant. Her eyes were "grayish greenish blue". Her head was small—one phrenologist later wondered how so small and ordinary-looking a head could have done so much.[2] The features too were small and set in a characteristically Victorian square-jawed frame. Studying a portrait carefully, one can scarcely fail to be impressed by her confidence, determination, and tradition.

As she grew older, she gained weight. " . . . A large, robust (one might almost say bouncing) elderly woman," Hawthorne found her, "very coarse of aspect, and plainly dressed; but withal,

[1] Elizabeth to Robert Sedgwick, [September, 1834]; Robert to Elizabeth, September 26, 1834, MHS, Sedgwick. A. H. Brune to Eleanor Shattuck, February 2, 1835, MHS, Shattuck. Francis Jeffrey in England wrote to Jane Carlyle that he had seen Miss Martineau and disliked her: "firstly because she is most excessively ugly; and secondly, because there is nobody good enough for her to admire." Jane Carlyle to Miss Stodart, March, 1833, *Early Letters of Jane Welsh Carlyle*, pp. 231–32.

[2] Colton, *Life of Clay*, iv, 390–92. Mrs. Chapman's description is in *Auto.*, ii, 259. Mrs. Charles Bray to S. S. Hennell, April 19, 1845, *George Eliot Letters*, i, 188–89. HM to Elizabeth Barrett, July 11, [1844], Wellesley.

so kind, cheerful, and intelligent a face that she is pleasanter to look at than most beauties. Her hair is of a decided gray; and she does not shrink from calling herself an old woman. She is the most continual talker I ever heard; it is really like the babbling of a brook. . . ." [1] To judge from the crayon portrait done in her old age, she was almost handsome. One can see in it her extraordinary kindness and good humour without in any way losing the strength and conviction. It is easy to imagine the smile gone, the mouth set, the eyes hard—to match the severity of her judgments.

On another point the Americans were agreed. She was very pleasant, not at all so formidable as they had expected. She dressed well and quietly, and spoke in a low voice, rather rapidly. She was, to borrow their adjectives, womanly, vivacious, pleasant, unaffected, affable, courteous, communicative. She was "entirely aware of her eminence & entirely free from self-exaggeration", wrote Robert Sedgwick. Philip Hone, the New York diarist, reported that she was not, as he had expected, "a little too blue to be agreeable", but an excellent talker, fond of laughing, and an engaging companion.[2] This was a first impression common to most of her English acquaintances too. Crabb Robinson was pleased on a first meeting to find her cheerful, sensible, and unassuming. "She pleased us far beyond expectation," wrote Carlyle, and though she was unhappily stone deaf, he found her full of talk, intelligent-looking, and "really of pleasant countenance". And even after that demanding household became aware of her limitations, when as an invalid she moved to Tynemouth, Carlyle told Emerson that he would miss her "blithe, friendly presence". George Eliot, though troubled for a time by the "vulgarity" of her looks and gestures —the same coarseness Hawthorne had noted—found her "quite one of those great people whom one does not venerate the less for having seen". And after Miss Martineau died, she recalled her silvery voice, charming talk, and perfect manners as a hostess.[3]

[1] *English Notebooks*, p. 77.

[2] C. M. Sedgwick to Louisa Minot, September 24, 1834, MHS, Sedgwick. *Philip Hone Diary*, April 5, 1836, i, 206. Deborah Logan Diary, pp. 106–108, PHS. *Life and Letters of C. M. Sedgwick*, p. 241.

[3] Crabb Robinson Diary, October 29, 1833, DWL. *New Letters of Thomas Carlyle*, i, 42. Carlyle to Emerson, December 8, 1839, in unpublished edition of the correspondence by J. L. Slater. George Eliot to Martha Jackson, April 21, 1845; to

The most arresting feature to a person meeting her for the first time was, as it was for Robert Sedgwick, the ear trumpet. At that time, she had two, one the usual kind, the other an ivory cup and earpiece joined by a flexible tube which could be tossed across a table in a charming if disconcerting ritual. In time she came to rely entirely on the former.[1] Miss Martineau herself was certain that her trumpet, "of remarkable fidelity", exerted some kind of winning power, "by which I gained more in *tête-à-têtes* than is given to people who hear general conversation. Probably its charm consists in the new feeling which it imparts of ease and privacy in conversing with a deaf person". Hawthorne, some years later, agreed: " . . . it becomes quite an organ of intelligence and sympathy between her and yourself", seeming "like a sensitive part of her, like the feelers of some insects".[2] But the trumpet was a trial to most people. For Mary Russell Mitford it always cast a pall on conversation, and a Philadelphia man observed to Fanny Kemble that one felt so like a fool saying "How do you do" into a trumpet in the middle of a drawing-room. Another Philadelphian, Deborah Logan, found Miss Martineau's rapid low speech difficult to catch, and since she could not bring herself to ask through the tube for a repetition, she gladly gave up her seat next to the visitor. Besides, she didn't understand what was being talked about.[3]

James Payn, the novelist and editor, has left some bright if not very reliable reminiscences about Miss Martineau, whom he knew in Ambleside. He recalled that her offering the trumpet was "like a churchwarden stopping with his collecting plate in front of one at church, where one would like to be generous in the face of the congregation, but cannot find one's purse". He was sure that the trumpet was not a defence against argument as some sceptics insisted, but he told a local story (not confirmed by her) about its serving literally for defence. In a dispute over the right to a footpath across a field, Miss Martineau determined to stand for the public against the owner; so with trumpet and

Sara Sophia Hennell, January 21, 1852; to Mrs. Charles Bray, March 20, 1877, *George Eliot Letters*, i, 189, ii, 4–5, vi, 353–54.

[1] Creevey to Miss Ord, February 24, [1834], *Creevey's Life and Times*, p. 380. Robinson, *Fifty Years of Fleet Street*, p. 201.

[2] *SA*, i, xiii–xiv. Hawthorne, *English Notebooks*, p. 77 (August 26, 1854).

[3] M. R. Mitford to C. M. Sedgwick, n.d. [1835], MHS, Sedgwick. Frances Anne Kemble to H——, November 27, [1835], *Records of Later Life*, pp. 10–11. Deborah Logan Diary, PHS.

umbrella she took her walk as usual. When a young bull, turned into the field by the owner, prepared to attack,

> . . . the indomitable lady faced him and stood her ground. She was quite capable of it, for she had the courage of her own opinions (which was saying a good deal), and at all events, whether from astonishment at her presumption, or terror of the ear-trumpet (to which of course he had nothing to say), the bull in the end withdrew his opposition (drew in his horns) and suffered her to pursue her way in peace. I wish I could add that she had the good-fortune of another patriotic lady "to take the tax away", but I am afraid the wicked lord succeeded in his designs. More than once, however, I have had pointed out to me over the wall—for the bull was still there—the little eminence wherefrom, with no weapon but her ear-trumpet (for she had her umbrella over her head all the time to keep the sun off), this dauntless lady withstood the horrid foe.

The story is probably apocryphal or at any rate embroidered, although the reference to Godiva's heroism sounds authentic—at least twice Miss Martineau cited the lady as an example of self-sacrifice. But we have recently been reminded by Sir Winston Churchill that to throw out a good story on the ground that it probably did not happen is to ruin history, so I felt that this anecdote should be included. It shows the rather awed respect in which she was held in the neighbourhood, and it helps to commemorate the trumpet, so much a part of her that once, through force of habit, Payn found himself addressing it, as it lay on a table, instead of its owner who was sitting some distance away.[1]

I choose one further observation on the trumpet, because it gives such a pleasant picture. At Newport, Elizabeth Sedgwick found herself seated next to Miss Martineau with no one else very near.

> So I seized the dreaded cup in a fit of desperation—and what was put into it will never be recorded in my chronicle. To my astonishment, however, I felt quite easy—and we promised to go out after dinner. . . . My first impressions of Miss M. are very agreeable. She has a vivacity and love of fun about her that was wholly unexpected. I thought to see her gravely wise and solemnly sensible, and that apples of gold would be dropped for me to feed on—but lo—in the place she sends forth—like any other woman—delicate titbits—pleasant gossipings—and those little nothings—which gracefully uttered are the charms of conversation. She is

[1] James Payn, *Some Literary Recollections*, pp. 83, 87–88. For a Godiva reference, see below, p. 230.

> strictly feminine—and for this, most of all, I like her—She has not thought it necessary with the lion's strength to put on his skin—which is certainly in good taste.

The sequel, though, is odd: "I dreamed the whole night of Miss Martineau's death—and having her heart presented in a nice little box. . . ."[1]

The "love of fun" perhaps calls for comment, because Miss Martineau has so often seemed forbidding and because the efforts at humour in her writings are usually so lamentable. If, as Payn says, she could not create humour, she could appreciate it. He gives instances of domestic jokes (which, of course, do not travel), and a good many others can be extracted from her letters. She was a welcome guest in America, a bright and amusing companion in London, and her household in Ambleside was a merry one. "I doubt," wrote Mrs. H. B. Ker to Mrs. Chapman, "whether in her own family they knew how merry she could be; how well she told laughable stories, and how much she liked to hear them," and Samuel Rogers, the poet, said she had the freshest laugh that could be heard outside a nursery.[2]

To anyone whose acquaintance with Miss Martineau went beyond the casual, another aspect would soon impress itself: her health was, to say the least, unusual. To begin with, she was without a sense of smell and so had a defective sense of taste. From the age of twenty she was deaf. The deafness fluctuated in severity, sometimes with surprising results. She could hear Malthus perfectly, in spite of his cleft palate. When she climbed the Great Pyramid, she left the trumpet behind to avoid breaking it and never missed it until some three hours later, proof, as she saw it, of the engrossing interest of the visit. Some of the variation was due to the nature of the complaint. When the deafness first started, she could hear music by pressing her shoulder blades against the back of the bench. She objected to sleighing because of the incessant jangle of the bells. And once she tried putting a musical snuff-box on her head and fainted from the pleasure of hearing music; after that, she clapped every musical snuff-box she could find on her head. Given these characteristics and the age at which the trouble began, we might venture to diagnose it as otosclerosis, a common form of deafness easily corrected today by a hearing aid and for which a trumpet

[1] Elizabeth to Robert Sedgwick, September 10, [1835], MHS, Sedgwick.
[2] *Auto.*, ii, 583–84.

would be helpful. Ability to hear, as in much deafness, would vary with attention and circumstances. Some variation seems to have occurred in the other senses too. Only once, she recalled, did she taste mutton, and she found it delicious; yet she paid considerable attention to food in Ambleside. In her worst periods, she got comfort and strength from game, oysters, turtle, and champagne; taste and smell must have helped.[1]

It is tempting, but insufficient, to look for a psychosomatic origin of all her troubles. In her youth she showed obvious forms of hysteria, and her digestive difficulties undoubtedly originated in mental stress, as she asserted her illness in the forties did. But the deafness was made worse by an unspecified accident, and she suffered other physical difficulties not easily tied to her mental state. Whatever the cause, she was frequently in bed. From 1839 to 1844 she was an invalid, one of that company of Victorian sofa-dwellers of whom Mrs. Woodham-Smith has recently reminded us.[2] From 1855 she was again an invalid, fearing to die from heart disease (which she did not have), and refusing to go out of her house for fear that she might drop dead in the street. Like so many Victorians, she revelled in illnesses which were painful and distracting, though usually not quite so bad as she made them out. One need only turn over the correspondence between Miss Martineau and Miss Nightingale to become aware of the distinction presumably mortal illness conferred.

Miss Martineau commented in the *Autobiography* on the difficulty of being amused or diverted when the senses are defective, but it was a difficulty that never seemed to get the upper hand. Her activity is amazing—again a Victorian characteristic. Much of the political economy series was written in bed, yet her London life was a round of lionizing. She was certainly one of the most indefatigable travellers the North American continent ever saw; and after her spectacular cure by mesmerism in 1844, she astonished her friends by tramping great distances in the Lake District and by going off on an expedition to Egypt and the Near East, riding camels and donkeys into remote places, climbing Mount Sinai, and feeling no fatigue at all. Perhaps even more astonishing than the physical exertion of her active

[1] Payn, *Recollections*, p. 88. *Auto.*, i, 247. *Letters*, pp. 121–22, 162. *EL*, p. 196. HM to Reeve, January 1, 1863, May 31, 1869.

[2] "They Stayed in Bed", *Listener*, February 16, 1956.

periods are the numbers of books, pamphlets, reviews, magazine articles, leaders, and letters she turned out, well or ill. Her pen went on and on, producing a steady stream of cool, even prose in a most beautifully legible hand. In her worst periods, one of her nieces sometimes wrote letters for her, but when she wrote them herself, the faltering handwriting for which she occasionally apologized is unapparent today.

Much of her time must have been taken up by her generosity. Some of this was public; much of it was private and personal, so the glimpses we have can indicate only a small portion of what she did. Crabb Robinson was a continual target for appeals for money to support her projects: for example, two little Polish girls who had lost their mother and whose father's efforts were not enough to keep them in a proper school and to save them from "utter loss & degradation". They were put to a good school in Hackney, but needed a hundred pounds a year for seven or eight years. In 1844 there was Christina, another little girl to be kept in school. A widow from Norwich who fell on hard times was set up at school-keeping. She collected a purse for another Norwich woman and got her an appointment as matron at University College Hospital. When a housemaid from a tyrannical household came to tea, Miss Martineau made her stay for a good night's sleep and hoped that the example touched the mistress's conscience. She employed the lame school-teacher who lived at her gate in Ambleside to do copying and recommended him to other people. Although she was opposed to Irish nationalism, a fiery young Irishman who wrote to her roused her sympathy; she raised funds for him, found him a literary job in London, and got her London friends to look after him in his last illness. She wrote charming letters to a young Kendal linen-draper gone to work in London, letters full of chit-chat, affection, and friendly advice.

Concerns like these were part of her creed; the mixture of generosity, sentiment, and principle was characteristic; and there is no better example than Ailsie. When one of her New Orleans hosts, a Mr. Newbreen, read what she wrote about the beautiful mulatto slave child in his family, he determined (being an Irishman, recently widowed, and never reconciled to the "peculiar institution") to send the child to England. Miss Martineau, delighted, proposed to adopt her and to train her as her own servant or for some "equivalent independent industrial lot". The master agreed to provide twenty pounds a year for the child's schooling. In the event, the plan came to nothing. Miss Martineau, never able to discover what became of Ailsie, could only suspect the worst. It was a great disappointment, because the experiment would have proved so much. The idea was more than a passing fancy—some years later, Ailsie was the name she chose for her favourite cow.[1]

Her generosity and sympathy were full and without condescension. Those who benefited from it felt a real affection for her, as did, so nearly as I can tell, all the poorer people whom she had anything to do with, whether the wives of the garrison at Tynemouth, the guests at the Christmas parties in Ambleside, or the workmen who built her house so rapidly that Mrs. Wordsworth thought she must have mesmerized them. Her servants worshipped her, and they were repaid with the utmost in loyalty and affection. It must have been a singularly satisfying household to work in.[2]

The generosity and the fun also made her a favourite of young people. Her letters to children are charming. The letters to young men and women are gay and utterly lacking in the pomposity and stuffiness of age; advice, when it is given, is dispensed with a light touch and was surely gratefully received, even when it was not followed. It is pleasant to think of the house at Ambleside full of nieces and nephews from Birmingham and Liverpool, there not simply because they had an aunt with a convenient house in the Lake District, but because they enjoyed themselves. "I put on my spectacles to read by lamp light," she wrote to Emerson, "& try in that act, to remember to avoid assuming the airs of age, & looking down upon the generation of nephews & nieces who are now my friends." [3] There are compound advantages to being clear of Evangelicalism.

In this glowing picture of a kindly and active, if somewhat odd, literary lady there may already have been detected a few

[1] HM to Crabb Robinson, December 4, [1837], August 25, [1844], November 14, [1837], January 7, [1842], DWL. Anne to Deborah Weston, January 31, 1839, BPL, Weston. HM to Reeve, February 24, 1862. HM to Kay-Shuttleworth, January 9, n.y., Harvard. The correspondence of the forties is full of references to the Irishman, Langtree; see below, p. 335. The Arthur Allen correspondence is in the Yale University Library. On Ailsie, *Auto.*, i, 435–46, HM to James, July 29, 1838. On the cow, see below, pp. 259–60.

[2] Mrs. Wordsworth to Crabb Robinson, September 16, 1845, DWL.

[3] HM to Emerson, February 25, [1852], Harvard. There are some delightful letters to a young girl, Spring Brown, in the National Library of Scotland.

indications of flaws. I have thought it necessary to stress her good qualities by placing them first, because the usual conception of her is so forbidding and because these genial qualities will be overshadowed in the rest of this book. Most people may have been considerably and often unexpectedly impressed on meeting Miss Martineau; but if the acquaintance became an extended one, they very quickly began to have second thoughts. Admiration could turn to toleration, near-worship to dislike or distrust; and those few people, like John Stuart Mill, who never liked her, found it easy to justify their hostility.

Deborah Logan, the Philadelphia dowager, was told by her sister, that the visitor was cheerful and agreeable, and that she conversed without pedantry. After she met Miss Martineau, Mrs. Logan added at the bottom of the page, "not quite".[1] Certainly Harriet Martineau set herself up as an authority on English ways and politics in America, as she was expected to do. But her manner was always oracular, and a great many people resented it, particularly when she was merciless in her preaching (to the Americans during the Civil War, for instance) and utterly unaware of grounds for disagreement. She was accused repeatedly of rushing into print with partial information, of credulity and presumption. To be sure, such accusations were often made by people who had been hard and truly hit; but they were made more generally and with caution and regret—which sometimes deepened into annoyance—by responsible, sober, and sympathetic judges. When Carlyle lamented her removal to Tynemouth and the loss of her "blithe, friendly presence", he found some consolation in knowing that he would no longer be troubled by her "meagre didacticalities".

Then, too, she was very likely to talk too much. She knew about the failing and laid it to her deafness. It was not necessarily annoying. People on both sides of the Atlantic were impressed by the ease and style of her conversation. Macready, the great actor, apparently loved it. For example, "Called on Miss Martineau—on the arrival of the carriage drove her home, talking the whole way. After dinner heard the dear children's prayers, &, with the exception of one walk round the garden, talked away the whole evening."[2] Others found the habit less

[1] Deborah Logan Diary, p. 103, PHS.

[2] Macready, *Diaries*, i, 398–99. *Auto.*, i, 491. See also Hawthorne, *English Notebooks*, p. 77.

tolerable. It was the object of one of Sydney Smith's celebrated jokes. Asked how he had spent the night, he replied: "Oh, horrid, horrid, my dear fellow! I dreamt I was chained to a rock and being talked to death by Harriet Martineau and Macaulay." When Hans Christian Andersen visited London in 1847 and was introduced to her at a garden party, he had to lie down for the rest of the afternoon.[1]

Nor was it only the volume of her talk that troubled. There is no escaping it: she was a gossip. John Stuart Mill, who disliked her intensely, accused her of gossiping about his relationship with Mrs. Taylor, and one occasion on which she must surely have done so was the good gossip with Jane Carlyle about literary figures, noted in her journal. George Eliot—a perfect target—wrote to John Chapman that zeal for the reputation of others was not among Miss Martineau's good qualities. "She is sure to caricature any information for the amusement of the next person to whom she turns her ear-trumpet." Crabb Robinson was distressed by an "interesting but uncomfortable" chat about persons he thought highly of, with his hostess making some "most unwarrantable & indeed incomprehensible statements. . . ." Her host when she visited Dublin in the fifties reported similarly that

> she talked with a degree of freedom about others before perfect strangers which I thought likely to lower their estimate of her judgment and discretion. That happened more than once while she was here. All she said might have been quite true and probably was true but I knew that some of her hearers were not at all prepared to accept her statements.[2]

To some people, she seemed inordinately conceited. Here is Robert Browning writing to Elizabeth:

> What a visitation! Miss Martineau is the more formidable friend, however—Mrs. Jameson will be contented with a little

---

[1] Fanny Kemble, *Records of Later Life*, p. 65. A variant version, linking her somewhat differently, is reported by Crabb Robinson (Diary, December 27, 1844); Smith said he dreamed he was in a madhouse and shut up with him were Harriet Martineau and the Bishop of Exeter, the redoubtable Phillpotts. Rumer Godden, *Hans Christian Andersen*, p. 176.

[2] M. St. John Packe, *Life of John Stuart Mill*, pp. 350, 321. HM to Reeve, October 18, 1866, August 8, 1865. She also comments most pointedly on Mill and Mrs. Taylor in letters to James, January 2, 1834, December 21, 1837, and March 2, 1839. George Eliot to John Chapman, October 30, [1854], *George Eliot Letters*, ii, 180. Crabb Robinson Travel Journals, July 11, 1842, DWL. R. D. Webb to Mrs. Chapman, January 9, 1852, BPL, Weston.

> confidence, you see, and ask no questions—but I doubt if you can arrange matters so easily with the newcomer. Because no great delicacy can be kept alive with all that conceit—and such conceit! A lady told me a few weeks ago that she had seen a letter in which Miss M. gave as her reason for not undertaking *then*, during the London season, this very journey which empty London is to benefit from now, "that at such a time she would be *mobbed to death*": whereupon the lady went on to comment, "Miss M. little knows what London is, and how many nearly as notable objects may be found to divert its truculence from herself"—Tom Thumb, and Ibrahim Pacha, to wit.[1]

Certainly Miss Martineau thought highly of herself and was accustomed to being paid court to. One of Mrs. Chapman's sisters expected strained feelings between her and George Thompson, the abolitionist crusader.

> They are both accustomed to be the suns of their respective firmaments. They have both been accustomed to receive great attention in the very diverse world in which they have moved, & neither of them have much intention of spending their time in the burning of incense, having been much more accustomed to play the parts of recipients. They may both be very capable of *loving* other people, but when one is accustomed to play the chief part one's self it is not so easy to appreciate another filling that same position.[2]

If the conceit is understandable, especially as Miss Martineau grew older and lived in the country observing the world from the outside, there was a more serious charge—that she behaved as she did because she wanted notoriety. It was an allegation made at the time of her celebrated cure by mesmerism and the subsequent controversy with the medical profession; it was revived when she proclaimed to the world her conversion to free-thought. Publicity-seeking and notoriety-hunting are of course common accusations when there is only emotion to fall back on—and in both cases passions flamed high. I do not myself believe that they apply to her. Conceit I will grant; she was partial, often ill-informed, appallingly quick to make judgments and resolute in sticking to them. But she had more important ends to serve than self-aggrandizement. Elizabeth Barrett put it neatly:

> She may have acted inexpediently and imprudently,—but her high intentions in doing so, do appear to me above these suspicions.

[1] August 24, 1846, *Browning Letters*, ii, 459–60.
[2] Anne Weston to Mary Estlin, February 15, 1852, BPL, Estlin.

> She may love notoriety—I have no personal means of knowing whether she loves it or not. But I do not see the proof of such a love in this act [the letters on mesmerism], nor in any previous act of her life which ever came to my knowledge. Her *love of truth* is proverbial among her friends, and even among such as are averse from her present views. One friend says, "I was always of opinion that Harriet Martineau was at once the most veracious and the most credulous person of my acquaintance" . . . and a chorus takes up the chaunt. . . .[1]

If one will make an omelette, they say, one must break eggs. Miss Martineau broke friendships. Her servants and lesser people, her nieces and nephews remained fervently loyal, but of her own class and generation she seems to have quarrelled with or drifted away from almost everyone. Some friendships were short and intense. The American writer Catherine Sedgwick, after Miss Martineau's visit to Stockbridge, wrote to Mary Russell Mitford, who had introduced the visitor, "full of Miss Martineau . . . who seems to have delighted them much". But a candid review of Miss Sedgwick's novels in the *Westminster* called forth a hurt lament about Miss Martineau's haste and carelessness which damaged her reputation and impaired her influence in America. Her zeal, Miss Sedgwick told Mrs. Follen, wanted tempering with wisdom and gentleness. The feeling rankled, and when Crabb Robinson spoke to Miss Sedgwick about Miss Martineau in 1839, she replied hastily, "I do not know Miss M." [2]

Elizabeth Barrett, with whom Miss Martineau carried on a long, intimate correspondence in the forties—one invalid to another—thought her the "noblest female intelligence between the seas", accepted some rather pointed criticism of her poetry, and even half, or more than half, believed in mesmerism. Yet she received a letter from Tynemouth in 1844—"the most singular letter I ever received"—in which Miss Martineau suggested that Miss Barrett had been flattering her as Miss Sedgwick had done, and implied that if the fault were not corrected, she might have to cut her off. To Miss Barrett this was humiliating and unjust.

> I write the truth (as far as I can perceive it) even to friends, whom I love dearest and most blindly. I seek the truth myself, and seek

[1] January 15, 1845. *Barrett-Mitford Corr.*, pp. 233–34.

[2] Miss Mitford to Miss Jephson, September 20, 1835, *Life of Mary Russell Mitford*, ii, 168. C. M. Sedgwick to Mrs. Follen, November 20, 1837, MHS, Sedgwick. Crabb Robinson Diary, June 22, 1839, DWL.

> it earnestly. I am not fond of using too strong language, and of dealing in the common commerce of compliment. And yet, you see!

The friendship survived this aberration—undoubtedly due to the morbid introspection which went on from time to time in Tynemouth—but it did not survive the elopement with Browning and the removal to Italy. And Miss Martineau did not easily forget; she intended to have the last word. In 1860 Mrs. Browning wrote: "Oh! and did anyone tell you how Harriet Martineau, in her political letters to America, set me down with her air of serene superiority? But such things never chafe me—never. They don't even quicken my pulsation." [1] But, obviously, they did.

George Eliot was similarly proscribed: the Lewes connection, a rivalry over Comte, and a review in the *Leader* of the book on free-thought were causes enough. Miss Evans tried to overlook things reported to her:

> Whatever may have been her mistakes and weaknesses, the great and good things she has done far outweigh them, and I should be grieved if anything in her memoir should cast a momentary shadow over the agreeable image of her that the world will ultimately keep in its memory. I wish less of our piety were spent on imaginary perfect goodness, and more given to real *im*perfect goodness.

But so Christian an attitude was not reciprocated. Almost the only deliberately nasty thing I have found in a Martineau letter was about George Eliot: "Do you know that Lewes is likely to die? 'All but hopelessly ill,' Matt. Arnold told me the other day: What will she do? Take a successor, I shd expect." W. R. Greg, too, could live to write an appreciation of Miss Martineau, but their friendship—the closest of her new connections in Ambleside, thanks to Greg's belief in mesmerism—could not withstand a difference about slavery and the Civil War; after that Greg was, so far as she was concerned, insolent, unbalanced, and a vulgar philanderer. [2]

Other friendships withered more slowly. We have already seen the affection which the Carlyles felt for her. Again, Jane:

> Of all these ornamental human creatures the one I take most delight in is Harriet Martineau. The horrid picture in *Fraser* with the cat

[1] Browning Letters, Yale, note on p. 5b. September 28, 1844, *Barrett-Mitford Corr.*, pp. 222–23. Letter to Mrs. Martin, August 21, [1860], *Letters of Elizabeth Barrett Browning*, ii, 403.

[2] George Eliot to S. S. Hennell, February 25, [1856] and November 14, 1859; to Charles Bray, November 3, [1853], *George Eliot Letters*, ii, 229–30, 122, iii, 201–2. HM to Reeve, November 17, 1868.

> looking over its shoulder was not a bit like; and the Artist deserved to have been hanged & quartered for so vile a calumny. Neither does the idea generally formed of the woman merely from her reputation as a *Political Economist* do her more justice than that picture! They may call her what they please, but it is plain to me & to everybody of common sense . . . that she is distinctly good-looking, warm-hearted even to a pitch of romance, witty as well as wise, very entertaining & entertainable in spite of the deadening & killing appendage of an ear-trumpet, & finally . . ."very fond of ME".

There was ideological sympathy too in the thirties. But the Negro intervened—both Greg and Carlyle could be shown, she said, Negroes considerably less savage than themselves in their insolent moods. Carlyle could not take her vagaries of the forties—mesmerism, atheism, pension-refusing, and letter-destroying—but he never quite forgot the friendship. When he was asked in the fifties for an estimate, he replied, "Miss Martineau had been extremely kind to me"; then he paused and continued slowly: "Well, she is the sort of woman that would have made a good matron in an hospital." His interviewer suspected later that this was a compliment.[1]

Macready, who so enjoyed her talk and company, she called "one of the first men in every way. In scholarship, in manners, in politics (for he is a Republican) and in virtue, public or private, a perfect hero." When he visited her in Tynemouth, she seemed a heroine—"her fine sense & her lofty principles, with the sincerest religion, give her a fortitude that is noble to the best height of heroism". The Macreadys named a child after her. But the free-thought was too much, and the friendship came to an end. Poor old Crabb Robinson, so faithful in visiting her on his Christmas pilgrimages to the Lakes, felt the same way.

> I had a letter from H: Martineau today—Civil but with nothing personal—full of praise of Mrs. Chapman, no mention of Emerson —nor any reference to my letter. Our correspondence need not go on. She leaves Ambleside on the 29th—I care not to be there before.

He saw her a few times after, but it was an increasingly unprofitable relationship. She could not resist hitting back. Years

[1] Jane Carlyle to Mrs. Aitken, March 6, 1837, *Early Letters of Jane Welsh Carlyle*, pp. 286–87. HM to Reeve, November 17, 1868. David Alec Wilson, *Carlyle to Threescore-and-Ten* (London, 1931), p. 289.

later she recalled that though she liked and respected him, she was bored by his repeated stories and felt he talked and read much that he failed to understand.[1]

Mesmerism and free-thought were important agencies in precipitating breaks with old friends, as often on the one side as on the other. So were her rigid moral standards. So was her radicalism—perhaps the most notable instance of its action was the sudden rupture of a close collaboration with Seymour Tremenheere, the schools and mines inspector who had broken ground for her house at Ambleside.[2] Remonstrance or wavering on fundamental matters she could not tolerate, and the definitive excommunication was usually her doing. At the time of her conversion to free-thought, she wrote, "My genuine friends did not change; and the others, failing under so clear a test, were nothing to me." [3] Nor was she likely to be charitable later: a judgment, once passed, stood and tended to turn to bitterness.

Having drawn this grim picture, we must look at the friendships that lasted. Here I think it right to exclude those friendships of the late fifties and sixties with men like Henry Reeve, the editor of the *Edinburgh*, or the editors of the *Daily News*, who so deeply admired her, kept alive the legends which still persist in the paper's offices, and visited her from time to time usually bringing a box of the cigars she enjoyed. In her journalistic work, Miss Martineau was at her most responsible, and she was so much in agreement with her editors that quarrels would have been unthinkable. Rather, the friendships I want to pursue are those which had to survive the troublesome shifts in her enthusiasms.[4]

Of the women who remained close to her, like Julia Smith or

[1] HM to George Bancroft, August 22, 1843, MHS, Bancroft. *Macready's Reminiscences*, pp. 423, 497. Crabb Robinson Diary, July 8, 1850, DWL. HM to Reeve, December 10, 1869. [2] See below, p. 267. [3] *Auto.*, ii, 45.

[4] One important friend was never put to the test—Charles Follen, the German refugee who became a professor at Harvard only to lose his post because of his uncompromising abolitionism. To Miss Martineau, he was the "greatest & most exquisite human being" she ever knew; and between him, his wife, and herself there was "the most extensive agreement that I have ever known to exist between three minds". Follen was killed in a steamer accident. The friendship with Mrs. Follen did not survive the conversion to free-thought. Perhaps the same thing might have happened with her husband; but he must be mentioned because of the high place he held in her personal pantheon—his portrait hung with Atkinson's and Garrison's above her fireplace. In view of what I shall have to say later, it is perhaps worth recording Emerson's opinion of Follen: ". . . a brave, erect man, of a singularly barren & uninteresting intellect, who always baulked any inquiry for an

Mrs. Henry Turner, a cousin near Nottingham, the closest and most remarkable was Mrs. Reid. She was a daughter of William Sturch, ironmonger and theological writer; the widow of a doctor; an enthusiastic Unitarian who had followed W. J. Fox out of the faith; and one of the founders of Bedford College. She was a faithful visitor and substitute nurse, yet from Miss Martineau's own description, she hardly sounds like an acceptable person. She was remarkably absent-minded, lacked quickness and dexterity, often said stupid things, and was amazingly awkward. She did not know a royal baby was expected, when everyone was talking about it; she had never heard of the electrotype process; she forgot to put tea into the teapot and hot water as well. Yet Miss Martineau, who said she never spilled, broke, or lost a thing, put up with all this awkwardness for the sake of what Mrs. Reid had to offer—the cleverest letters she received, her thoughts on life, her moral insight, her "wandering angels of thought". And, one might add, the quality noted by Mary Mohl, that this excellent person would "push on womankind when womankind is unpushable".[1]

Another unknown was Richard D. Webb, a Dublin abolitionist printer. A Quaker who left the Society when he found that they did not welcome "disturbers", he was a close friend of William Lloyd Garrison and an indefatigable (and illegible) correspondent of Mrs. Chapman and her sisters—indeed he said he had a "perfect passion for Westons". His letters show him a curiously diffident man, continually emphasizing his own insignificance, yet he was capable of some very good analyses of political situations—to Lucretia Mott he was the "best delineator of character I ever met with"—and we shall see much of him in this book. Webb was a Martineau enthusiast: Mrs. Browning may have been the greatest poetess of any age, but for him Harriet Martineau was much more wonderful and admirable and a much greater woman.

---

opinion or for a spiritual fact, by a quotation. He vexed & surprised me by his ignorance of all that I wished to know of his country & his countrymen. But his self-respect commanded respect, & I can well believe that when something was to be chosen or done, he never baulked anybody." HM to Elizabeth Barrett, May 15, [1845], Yale. HM to Crabb Robinson, February 11, [1843], DWL. *SA*, ii, 203–4. *RWT*, ii, 58. Emerson to Theodore Parker, July 17, 1842, *Letters of Ralph Waldo Emerson*, iii, 71. But compare Channing's high opinion, *Memoirs*, iii, 315–16.

[1] HM to Elizabeth Barrett, postmarked August 9, 1844, Wellesley. Crabb Robinson, September 3, 1842, DWL. *Letters of Julius and Mary Mohl*, p. 162. Margaret Tuke, *A History of Bedford College*, pp. 3–17.

They worked together in the anti-slavery cause, collaborated in some journalistic enterprises, and held common views on the Irish situation, he being her host when she visited Ireland in 1852. She liked his family, respected his knowledge and his life of "sublime charity", and put in a good word for him when Carlisle went to Dublin as lord lieutenant. Yet Webb was rebuked severely when he was not up to the mark or when she misread him in such a way as to find a "want of judgment". He wrote to Mrs. Chapman:

> I have never been so mortified by any letter I ever got—partly that I should have impressed so unfavourably one I honour so highly & partly that I should have in some degree implicated you by providing you with such an unfit travelling companion to Ambleside. I would as soon have put my finger in the fire as enter her house if I had in any degree suspected what I now know—so I hope you will excuse me. It was a great comfort to hear your sister Caroline say that Miss Martineau had no right to be very particular if she looked to her own remarks upon others.

Almost a rupture? No, Webb was too modest; he examined himself, forgave her brusqueness, and continued to be tolerated. He knew his status, however: " . . . I think she is tremendously clever—and that she looks a little scornfully on a large portion of those on whom her fame depends." [1]

She did not look scornfully on Richard Monckton Milnes. This placid relationship, which began in the thirties and culminated with Milnes's special eulogy of her in his presidential address at the Norwich meeting of the Social Science Association in 1873, is best understood in terms of Milnes's own temperament and the role in which he cast himself. She, like others, appreciated his kindness and his indifference to opinion. Observant, supple, he was a perfect foil, able to adjust himself to the most varied and contradictory commitments and interests—of his friends and, be it said, of himself. In short, he was not demanding, intellectually or morally, so he could be the only point of tangency for some oddly assorted circles, including that circle—all centre and no circumference—which was Harriet Martineau.[2]

[1] There is a memoir of Webb by Samuel J. May, published in a Boston periodical called *Old and New*. There is a copy in the Friends' Historical Library in Dublin. See also *Life of Garrison, passim*. *James and Lucretia Mott*, pp. 303, 325. Webb to Mrs. Chapman, November 28, 1858, September 24, 1848; Webb to Caroline Weston, March 25, 1849, BPL, Weston. HM to Carlisle, January 4, 1856.

[2] HM to Bulwer Lytton, April 27, [1844]. Pope-Hennessy, *Milnes*, i, 43.

Then there is the problem of Henry G. Atkinson. Atkinson and Harriet Martineau were brought together through the Basil Montagus at the time of her mesmeric cure. The friendship of a motherly woman in her middle forties for a young man just turned thirty developed rapidly into an intimate intellectual collaboration, some effects of which we shall have in time to examine. The rather embarrassing overtones of devotion which appear in Miss Martineau's eulogies of this insignificant man may be read, with some justification, in a venial but compromising sense by a generation more aware than the Victorians that the unconscious has its reasons. In an annoyingly pompous letter written to G. J. Holyoake after her death, Atkinson said he could not wonder that some persons suggested that she was in love with him; but he denied it. She was not in love with him "as a man", he said, quoting Charles Bray, but "only in the highest sense", a statement easier for the nineteenth century to grasp than for the twentieth.

Atkinson was unquestionably attractive. Margaret Fuller, another susceptible female, met him in Westmorland in 1846, just after he had met Miss Martineau.

> He is sometimes called the "prince of English mesmerisers"; and he has the fine instinctive nature you may suppose from that. He is a man of about thirty; in the fullness of his powers; tall, and finely formed, with a head for Leonardo to paint; mild and composed, but powerful and sagacious; he does not think, but perceives and acts. He is intimate with artists, having studied architecture himself as a profession; but has some fortune on which he lives. Sometimes stationary and active in the affairs of other men; sometimes wandering about the world and learning; he seems bound by no tie, yet looks as if he had children in every place.

George Eliot, some years later, was also deeply impressed. Pleasant and intelligent, she reported to Miss Hennell, though she added, "if one could feel ill naturedly towards him there is occasion if not matter for ridicule". But somehow one had to like him, "good, clear-eyed Mr. Atkinson", "who wrinkles up his forehead horizontally and draws in his lips—has a good anterior lobe, but I should think it is not well fed with blood".

Atkinson belonged to a type which will always be with us, at least as long as sufficient fortunes can be inherited. He had only to become a dilettante, and it seems unlikely that he could have done more. He was the second son of William Atkinson, an architect and speculative builder, who died in 1839. He was elected a fellow of the Geological Society in 1836 and remained a member until 1877, but the Society has no more information about him, so that connection (though it appears proudly on the title page of the book he and Miss Martineau wrote in 1851) can be dismissed as a young intellectual plunging into a fashionable science. He served on the governing committee of the Art Union, a body devoted to popularizing the fine arts—more dilettantism. He remained a bachelor, living in London at 61, Upper Gloucester Place. His last years he spent in Boulogne, a circumstance which would convey a whole covey of doubts to a respectable Victorian, though he was not there for one of the usual reasons—insolvency—for when he died in 1884, he left some ten thousand pounds. He was very probably a homosexual. The suspicion grows out of his circumstances, his friendships, and the mysterious visits abroad; it seems confirmed by the frantic moral relativism of his writings, a relativism which sat oddly on Miss Martineau, when she adopted it in their collaboration.[1] If I am right in this conjecture, the friendship with a mature and relatively sexless woman, who could be no kind of threat, is intelligible, if, of course, it is not to be dismissed (on the basis of his letters to Holyoake) as part and parcel of his dilettantism.

To Miss Martineau, Atkinson was very important. She sent him over a thousand letters, which he thought he might one day publish but never did. She willed him her head to pursue his phrenological researches with, but he never claimed the legacy. She embarrassed more than one visitor to the Ambleside house by asking them to agree that his portrait was Christ-like.[2]

He was shrewd and upright, she said in a letter to Charles Kingsley, and of an insight (one recalls Mrs. Reid) unknown to those to whom he had not opened himself as he had done to her. His integrity amounted to romantic honour. He was tender as a guardian angel and patient with those who (like herself) tried

[1] See below, pp. 292–99.

[2] Early in 1833 she had made her brother James her executor and instructed him, should she die, to have her body dissected by Southwood Smith, the eminent physician who had just performed a similar rite on his friend Jeremy Bentham; these, presumably, were the instructions superseded by the gift to Atkinson. For her views on Atkinson's portrait, James Payn, *Recollections*, p. 85; L. E. O. Charlton, ed., *Recollections of a Northumberland Lady*, pp. 217–18.

him most. He suffered only from the sins of men to each other and from the sorrows of others which he saw could be prevented. "An old sage of 80" told her that he had known all the great thinkers of Europe in the past sixty years and knew no mind to compare with Henry Atkinson's—a remark that can be read two ways, but which was probably intended and certainly accepted in only one. Her friend Dr. Samuel Brown told her that Atkinson combined the knowledge of Humboldt and Comte with the strength and delicacy of expression of Carlyle and Tennyson, and she agreed.

Yet amid all this adulation there was a curious detachment. She told Lord Morpeth that Atkinson's mind was not logical, and that he held oddly incompatible opinions. She assured Kingsley that, though Atkinson was the soul of honour and *too* silent about what he heard, she would not show him Kingsley's letters. When she read Margaret Fuller's remark that Atkinson was not a thinker, she was amused but said she could easily understand how Margaret Fuller could feel that way.

He was hardly her master, as was alleged in an attack on the free-thinking book they wrote. Nor did he serve, except in a limited way, "la fonction d'un révélateur", to borrow the phrase he himself quoted from a French review of the *Autobiography*. Since the whole development of her free-thought is foreshadowed in her earlier career, helped on by some deep thinking at Tynemouth, he could have been little more than a catalyst. But she was everlastingly grateful for that and dependent on him for intellectual companionship. As W. R. Greg put it, Atkinson's influence stemmed from "his *full* sympathy in her new *isolating* views". To judge from their book and the letters printed in the *Autobiography*, the subjects they discussed endlessly all belong to the same area of fourth- or fifth-rate philosophizing, which had the virtue of setting the shallow religious world by the ears, but which could produce only derision in the sensible. With such philosophizing, as we shall see, she was deeply concerned; it provided foundation and goal for her faith and her life. Necessarianism, materialism, perfectibilism never found more rhapsodic expression than in Henry Atkinson and never more thrilling response than in Miss Martineau. But in the regions where she was truly competent—politics, economics, society—Atkinson had little or no effect. At any rate, she told Reeve that Atkinson was in some ways immensely conservative and was amused in looking over her shoulder while she wrote a good radical letter on the labour problem.[1]

This catalogue will have provided the reader with certain clues. For one thing, all of the intimate friends who stayed intimate friends were no more than second-rate minds, if that. Atkinson as a philosopher was contemptible; it is most unlikely that anyone today or very many people a hundred years ago would have found Mrs. Reid's "wandering angels of thought" or moral insight overwhelming. On the other hand, the friends with whom Miss Martineau quarrelled, though some like Crabb Robinson or Tremenheere were ordinary men unable to find the flexibility for the extremities of her radicalism, numbered among them a high proportion of first-class intellects. Had Miss Martineau been a Monckton Milnes, she might have continued a friend of Carlyle and avoided the abuse of Dickens; had she been a Mrs. Reid, she might have stuck by George Eliot. But Miss Martineau was a prima donna. And she was also a second-rate mind. She recognized this, in an obituary she wrote for herself:

> Her original power was nothing more than was due to earnestness and intellectual clearness within a certain range. With small imaginative and suggestive powers, and therefore nothing approaching to genius, she could see clearly what she did see, and give a clear expression to what she had to say. In short, she could popularize, while she could neither discover nor invent. She could sympathize in other people's views, and was too facile in doing so; and she could obtain and keep a firm grasp of her own, and, moreover, she could make them understood. The function of her life was to do this, and, in so far as it was done diligently and honestly, her life was of use, however far its achievements may have fallen short of expectations less moderate than her own. Her duties and her business were sufficient for the peace and the desires of her mind. She saw the human race, as she believed, advancing under the law of progress; she enjoyed her share of the experience, and

---

[1] On Atkinson, the will in Somerset House, HM's *Autobiography*, information from the Royal Geological Society, the Art Union Minute Book in the British Museum, Theodora Bosanquet's *Harriet Martineau*, *passim*. In addition, the following letters: Atkinson to Holyoake, June 20, 1877, BM, Add. MSS, 42,726. Margaret Fuller to Catherine Sedgwick, 1846, *Memoirs*, ii, 79–80. George Eliot to the Brays, June 5, 1852, *George Eliot Letters*, iii, 33; to Bessie Rayner Parkes, July 12, 1853, *ibid.*, ii, 109; to S. S. Hennell, January 21, 1852 and September 2, 1852, *ibid*, ii, 4–5, 54. HM to Charles Kingsley, July 7 (n.y.), Princeton, Parrish Collection. HM to Emerson, February 25, [1852], Harvard. HM to Reeve, September 19, 1859. HM to Philip Carpenter, n.d., MCO. HM to Morpeth, July 4, 1845. W. R. Greg, *Nineteenth Century*, ii, 108.

had no ambition for a larger endowment, or reluctance or anxiety about leaving the enjoyment of such as she had.[1]

This extraordinary self-estimate, so typical of her and so like the perceptive obituaries she wrote of others, is not entirely correct. We have already seen instances of an acute lack of sympathy, or what we might interpret as such. On the other hand, there is no question about her keeping a firm grasp of her own views. "Earnestness and intellectual clearness within a certain range"—to that, sympathy, when it did operate, had to give way, and the clarity was reinforced by the conceit of conviction. No wonder she quarrelled. The wonder is that those friends or former friends who were her intellectual superiors (and half-consciously but never admittedly recognized as such) should have retained such favourable opinions as some of them did. Lucy Aikin told Channing that Miss Martineau's "remarkable and fearless sincerity" made her fear for her sometimes in London.[2] Harriet Martineau was the perfect example of the limited intellect secure enough in its convictions to challenge its betters. The phenomenon has always existed and will always exist, the bane of genius—and perhaps its salvation.

This fundamental consideration stated, we must move on to examine her two most significant friendships, for they will illustrate and amplify what I have said. These friends differ from the others I have listed. Both of them were as securely second-rate as Harriet Martineau herself, but in both instances she considered herself the lieutenant, not the chief. Interestingly enough, both were Americans. They were William Lloyd Garrison and Maria Weston Chapman.

Miss Martineau was a thorough-going partisan of the Garrisonian wing of abolitionism, that is, of a particularly vocal minority of the movement, a minority far gone in radicalism—uncompromisingly denunciatory (until success was imminent), pro-women's rights, anti-church, anti-political, and, above all, anti-deviationist. The deviationists were the non-Garrisonians; they were, and still are, legion. The logic of Miss Martineau's commitment will be developed later; for the moment it is enough to say that she identified herself with them when they were persecuted, agreed thoroughly with their likes and dislikes,

[1] *Daily News*, June 29, 1876, reprinted *Autobiography*, ii, 572–73.

[2] Lucy Aikin to W. E. Channing, June 12, 1836, *Corr.*, pp. 297–98. See also W. R. Greg, *Nineteenth Century*, ii, 102–3.

especially the anti-political bias, and considered them the only abolitionists who stuck by principle. The others, who could not see with equal clarity and who fell over into Liberty-Partyism or Free-Soil movements, were not exactly beneath contempt because they were repeatedly visited with it. Garrison was to her, as he insisted on being to the movement, the hero. She found fault with his tone, yet she saw why he used it.

> He considers his task to be the exposure of fallacy, the denunciation of hypocrisy, and the rebuke of selfish timidity. He is looked upon by those who defend him in this particular as holding the branding-iron; and it seems true enough that no one branded by Garrison ever recovers it. He gives his reason for his severity with a calmness, meekness, and softness which contrast strongly with the subject of the discourse, and which convince the objector that there is principle at the bottom of the practice.

When she described his being dragged through the streets in the great anti-slavery riots in Boston, she seized on Mrs. Garrison's exclamation: "I think my husband will be true to his principles. I am sure my husband will not deny his principles." That was to her his greatest virtue.[1]

Her admiration was so great that she told him in 1867 not to visit her for fear she would suffer heart-failure from the emotion. And Garrison returned the admiration. He wrote to Mrs. Chapman, after the *Autobiography* appeared:

> The result is a higher appreciation, if possible, of the intellectual strength, solid understanding, conscientious integrity, fearless independence of thought and expression, courageous "heretical" nonconformity, far-reaching humanity, intuitional grasp, varied knowledge, and literary fertility of that extraordinary woman. . . . It is not doing any injustice to the eminent women of the world to place her at the head, in comprehensiveness of mind and devotion to the general welfare, working through numerous channels, and discussing with masterly ability questions and measures which for ages have been exclusively assigned to the male sex. Then, privately and socially, how admirable her characteristics! [2]

Since such a meeting of minds allows us to extrapolate from one to the other, here is Anne Weston, Mrs. Chapman's sister, summing up Garrison:

> It is difficult for him as regards religious doctrine to place himself on another's standpoint. Somebody or other speaks of Goethe's [sic] "fatal German *many sidedness*." Now I don't call it a fatal gift,

---

[1] *RWT*, ii, 219. *SA*, i, 127.

[2] Garrison, *Life of Garrison*, iv, 268–69.

> but whether it be so or not, it is not one that Garrison possesses. His views on all subjects are matters of most serious & earnest conviction & there is nothing of indifferentism in his character, or that strong sense of the picturesque or artistic that so essentially modifies if not our religious opinions, at least our power of toleration. As a virtuous and sensible man he would include all creeds in the scope of his *toleration*, but very few I apprehend in the scope of his *sympathy*. Some dim remembrances of the early creed of his childhood (as I believe his mother was a rigid Baptist) occasionally hang about him, but there is much about him, heretical as he may be, analogous to the same position & absolute assertion of opinion that is generally found only in the more rigid sects.[1]

Maria Weston Chapman was one of Garrison's high command. She was a fanatical admirer of Harriet Martineau, and the ineptitude of the *Memorials* which she added to the *Autobiography* serves only to obscure the fervour of that admiration. To Miss Martineau, Mrs. Chapman was the greatest woman on record, one whose name would stand beside Washington's as the deliverer of her country the second time.

> She seems to me to have reasoning powers which can never be baffled; learning & literary *fullness* I cannot fathom or compass; & knowledge of the world wh the worldling cannot surpass; & withal, the noblest martyr spirit (because the most enlightened) of our time. And all this is pervaded with the sweetest womanly tenderness that woman ever manifested,—at home, among friends, & wherever there is weakness or woe. If I adopted the old notion of heaven, I should wonder whether she is to take her place among the Seraphs or the Cherubs;—among those who *know* & *can*, or those who *love* & *can*.

She told R. D. Webb that she would be afraid to live with Mrs. Chapman lest through relying absolutely on her sagacity and good sense she lose all reliance on herself. This, said Webb, "was much from a thoroughly direct and sincere woman like Miss M".[2]

Mrs. Chapman was a remarkable woman. Crabb Robinson, when he met her in Paris in 1850, thought her a pretty, middle-aged woman who did credit to the cause. Webb spoke of the "mingled dignity, capacity, & strength" which set her apart from all the other women he had known. Lydia Maria Child told Lucretia Mott—one abolitionist to another—that she considered Mrs. Chapman one of the most remarkable women of

[1] [Anne Weston] to Mary Estlin, November 11, 1851, BPL, Estlin.

[2] HM to Crabb Robinson, July 6, 1850, DWL. Webb to Anne Weston (?), August 12, 1851, BPL, Weston.

the age, with a large and magnanimous heart (certainly an over-generous comment) and a clear, vigorous, and brilliant intellect. Mrs. Chapman had been active in the abolitionist cause from the beginning. Samuel May, another Garrisonian lieutenant, recalled how effective her pen was in the cause—*Right and Wrong in Boston*, *Songs of the Free*, the annual *Liberty Bell*, the anti-slavery bazaars, all testify to the extraordinary activity of which she was capable. She also on occasion took over the editing of *The Liberator* and was closely associated with the *National Anti-Slavery Standard*, the New York paper for which Harriet Martineau wrote for a time, with disastrous results. Her letters are most impressive—again the editing of the *Memorials* is a miserably unfair standard for judging her—dashing, witty, careless effusions of a supremely confident and competent woman, but one without the essentially masculine nature of Miss Martineau.[1]

She was a perfect lieutenant for Garrison, and her taste for controversy and excommunication was as high-spirited and intense as his, if not more so. She was thoroughly radical. When Dr. Estlin, the Bristol abolitionist, died in 1855, she wrote to her sister that "poor dear pa Estlin" was "grit to the back bone", and had the same consolation in his views as Harriet Martineau had in hers:

> Which gives me to know that people are as they *are* & not as they *behave*. *I* am consoled by the idea that what I can't help 'taint no matter. *Eternity* & *infinity* come in like a flood of consolation for *any* thing, whenever I open the gates, although *God* & *immortality* never were much to me,—or rather I don't discriminate, not having, really, selfishness enough to enable me to draw my lines distinctly in *those* regions.

How responsive to Miss Martineau's positivism and Garrison's vague but passionate heterodoxy! If one wants an exultation in confidence:

> Without any self-esteem, but merely as a psychological fact demonstrable to every philosophical investigator, how can we help seeing

[1] Crabb Robinson to Thomas Robinson, June 8, 1850, DWL. Webb to S. H. Gay, December 25, 1849, Columbia University, Gay. L. M. Child to Lucretia Mott, *James and Lucretia Mott*, p. 137. Samuel J. May, *Some Recollections of our Antislavery Conflict*, pp. 231–32. There are large numbers of Mrs. Chapman's letters in the Gay collection at Columbia, the May papers at Cornell, and in the voluminous Weston papers in the Boston Public Library. The *D.A.B.* sketch is ridiculously inadequate.

> that our views are larger, & our souls steadier than those of many —of most of the good & true friends of the cause: to whom it would pain us to deny the highest degree of devotedness & intelligence. Probably to some educational & worldly advantages it is owing, & not to better heads or hearts, but we are really wiser than our constituents, & must bear the penalty of it, which is no hard matter after all. Let us serve them for the cause's sake. . . . Our duty seems to be, to be brain & blood to our good *members* whom we know how to value though they don't know how to value us.

The echoes from Ambleside were deafening.

But Mrs. Chapman was not always so generous with defaulters. To stray from the party line was the worst of sins, to deny credit to the American Anti-Slavery Society (the Garrisonians) was to commit the sin against the Holy Ghost. She would remonstrate with their European agent, Elliot Chesson, keep Richard Webb up to the mark, denounce the caution and duplicity of that "great hypocrite" Joseph Sturge, the English Quaker radical and abolitionist. And as to "our dear & invaluable coadjutor" George Thompson, the English abolitionist who dared to dally with Sturge, well—"magnanimity is his greatest fault". No fatal many-sidedness about her either.[1]

Finally, to her son-in-law about Miss Martineau:

> I have never asked you to like her, though her trust to her own convictions is all that prevents the whole world from liking her. But *that* is the very thing I approve of in her. . . . I do not agree with her often times, for I am a "non resistant," though not in the Xn but the philosophical meaning. The military method is not mine [HM could be very blood-thirsty during the war], and I consider it a great misfortune, in one sense, when a war breaks out as I do that it is a blessing, often times, in another. There are two sides to every shield.[2]

There is the crucial metaphor. Let us see some other examples. Of disturbers of abolitionist meetings:

> Free speech is one thing—overt attempts to destroy us are another. They'd call the dirk or the hemlock-cup freedom; & they may be the day of Judgment. They cant have our sword-of-the-spirit to make dirks of, I trust.

Of a meeting at Framingham, Massachusetts:

> There is certainly an unfortunate irritability at work, however. It

[1] Mrs. Chapman to Anne Weston, n.d. [1855], BPL, Weston; to S. H. Gay, May 19 [1846], January 21, 1854, February 4, 1855, March 4, 1855, Columbia University, Gay.

[2] Portion of a letter, probably to Laugel, Cornell, May.

> seems no collision of principle, but little faults of individual temper & character, which would not even be visible on a less bright surface; but being where they are show like rust-spots on shining sword-blades. I trust they will not injure the weapons—which are, however, it is very painful to see—worn with terrible service of battle.

The same figure of speech sprang to the mind of her grandson in his charming recollections of her:

> She was always handsomely dressed, smiling, dominant, ready to meet all comers. She entered a room like a public person. She was a doughty swordswoman in conversation and wore armour. There was something about her that reminded me of a gladiator, and I sometimes wondered how she had ever borne children at all and whether she had nursed them, or had just marched off to the wars in Gaul and Iberia, while the urchins were being cared for by a freed-woman in the Campania.[1]

A swordswoman! The sword-of-the-spirit! How could she be troubled with the shifts of the politicians? How could she be tempted by power or compromise? It made no difference to her how many subscribers the *Standard* had—fifty thousand or none, for

> . . . its importance is quite other than subscriptional. As the organ of the Am. Soc. it is the only representative on Earth, the *only* one, —of tolerance—union to do justice—*Respect for right.* The world goes straight because of it, as the great ship sails by the beacon light. It is small & rough & scantily fed, but while it blazes, all's safe.[2]

She had found what Miss Martineau called "the true philosophy of ease"—to take a stand on principles and to be thus prepared "for all consequences, meekly and cheerfully defying all possible inflictions of opinion".[3]

Like Garrison, like Maria Chapman, Harriet Martineau stood on principle. In 1856 she wrote :

> Ours is an age when personal qualities are much less concerned in the influence and popularity of public men than they were in a prior stage of civilization; and ours is a country in which men of mark become so, generally speaking, as representatives of some social principle or phase, rather than through their idiosyncrasy.[4]

---

[1] Mrs. Chapman to S. H. Gay, [February 1846], to Mrs. Gay, July 9, 1857, Columbia, Gay. John Jay Chapman, *Memories and Milestones*, p. 211.

[2] Mrs. Chapman to S. H. Gay, January 10, 1856, Columbia, Gay.

[3] *SA*, ii, 161.

[4] "Father Mathew", *Biog. Sketches*, p. 265.

That generalization, increasingly inappropriate after 1867, probably had more relevance between 1832 and 1867 than at any other time. But historically sound or not, relevant or not, it sets out Miss Martineau's basis of judgment. For her *everything*, public or private, had to be done and judged by the fundamental principle involved, and, for all practical purposes, her views of principle were fixed by the time she reached the public eye in the thirties.

This is not to say that she took a line and stuck to it like grim death. Indeed, she was open to impressions and enthusiasms, major and minor, which, if the ground was properly prepared, often developed with alarming luxuriance. To some people, as a result, she seemed appallingly mercurial. For example, Miss Mitford:

> Miss Martineau is a person of great singleness of mind, sincere and truthful; but I have always thought that she did not very well know her own mind. She is so one-sided that I never should be astonished to find her turn short round and change her opinions plump. And this, I suppose, must have been the case here, for really it does not seem possible that the two books [*Crofton Boys* and *Principle and Practice*] could have been written by the same person, unless upon such a theory.[1]

But consistency, wrote Miss Martineau, "(in the sense of immutability of opinion) is not the greatest of virtues in our age of progress". She could comment sadly on earnest men who saw the right on their own side without being able to see that the other side was not necessarily wrong, and she cautioned against stirring great questions "which, while they are the roots of our growing and flourishing Constitution, are incapable of definition and circumscription". Or, here she is on Lord Lansdowne:

> Consistency is, from the character of the time, not only so out of fashion, but for most people so out of the question, that any one signal instance of it fixes as much attention at the present day as conversion and innovation did in a former one. Lord Lansdowne remained steadfast while the Wellingtons and Peels were changing on the one hand, and the Burdetts and the Broughams on the other; and everybody is interested in seeing how this happened. The first suggestion in the case is, that it could not have happened if he had not been of high and ancient family. It could not have happened if his early course had not been determined in a liberal direction;

[1] To Elizabeth Barrett, July 23, 1842, *Life of Mary Russell Mitford*, ii, 253.

nor if he had not been of sound reputation; nor if he had been a man of genius, or of any vigorous ability.[1]

To recall these remarkably reasonable utterances of her maturity—they all date from the fifties and sixties—is to wonder how she could so consistently have violated their precept. The answer is that in her own terms she did not. She admired Peel and Canning above all politicians for conforming to these admirable canons. And if she denounced other politicians or writers who would seem eligible for similar indulgence, it was for their departure from other principles which her infallible method had discovered. The central security of principle amid change is made clear in a striking passage from an essay of 1830, a passage that must be quoted at length:

> The truth is, and we have gospel authority for our conviction, that all influences must be modified to suit the changes of the thing influenced. There were divine and eternal principles involved in the institutions of Judaism; yet those institutions have long been outgrown. There are divine and eternal principles involved in the theism of many savage nations, in the first religious notions of a child, in the various forms of civil government, and in the obscure dawn of every science. Yet all these things are destined to overthrow or decay. The principles, being divine and imperishable, remain; but renovated, expanded, embellished. And so it is with the principles of spiritual philosophy. Our reverence must be given to their essence, not to their forms,—forms often changed, and ever perishable. It has ever been a benevolent employment of moral philosophers to frame systems of ethics for the information and guidance of inferior minds. In their day, such systems are the instruments of important good; but if they could be rendered permanent they would be rendered injurious. The most exalted philosophy of one age is too mean for the capabilities of another. Let the principles of morals be, as they undoubtedly are, destined to outlive the heavens and the earth, still they must, like all other principles, be perpetually modified by the results of experience, expanded so as to occupy the growing faculties, and embellished, that they may stimulate the exertions of religious hope; embellished, not by earthly decorations, but by growing manifestations of that celestial beauty which is ordained to be gradually revealed, lest our weak vision should be "blasted with excess of light".
>
> It cannot be for an instant supposed that we are advocating laxity of principle, or independence of its guidance. It is because we wish the principles of spiritual philosophy to be strict and undeviating in their operation that we contend for their being

[1] "Lord Herbert", *Biog. Sketches*, p. 320; "Lord Denman", *ibid.*, pp. 237–38; "Marquis of Lansdowne", *ibid.*, p. 329. See also *Hist.*, i, 317–18.

allowed full and free scope. We would disentangle them from fetters; we would pull off whatever mask may disfigure them, and beseech them to show us the way of life; and having done so, we would follow them, cheerfully and undeviatingly, delighted to watch their growing radiance, and not afraid to recognize them amidst the glory of their successive transfigurations.[1]

It helps to refer to another writer who dealt with this problem at a somewhat more sophisticated level:

> Principle is a better test of heresy than doctrine. Heretics are true to their principles, but change to and fro, backwards and forwards, in opinion; for very opposite doctrines may be exemplifications of the same principle. Thus the Antiochenes and other heretics sometimes were Arians, sometimes Sabellians, sometimes Nestorians, sometimes Monophysites, as if at random, from fidelity to their common principle, that there is no mystery in theology. Thus Calvinists became Unitarians from the principle of private judgment. The doctrines of heresy are accidents and soon run to an end; its principles are everlasting.[2]

Had Newman ever thought about Harriet Martineau, he most certainly would have considered her a heretic. And nothing would have pleased her more.

W. R. Greg, in applying the remark that her mind was wax to receive and marble to retain,[3] said at once too much and too little. A better, if less felicitous, metaphor is the template, a template of certain fundamental assumptions and procedural rules by which a succession of secondary templates of substantive principles can be derived, much as a machine tool makes dies, which can in turn form articles for use or sale. Development is necessary that adherence to principle might be strict and undeviating, so that once principles had shown the way to life, they could be followed cheerfully and without looking back or to the side. Principles, as we shall see, are induced from observation of facts, but once induced they become the criteria by which facts must be organized. This essential and elaborate proceeding —so thoroughly anti-romantic—is brought out neatly in a criticism of Godwin's *Thoughts on Man:*

> There is great charm in variety of development, as long as there is a uniformity in the principles of the philosophy; but a mere

---

[1] "Essay on the Proper Use of the Prospective Faculty", *MR*, iv, 669–73, reprinted *Misc.*, i, 227–28.

[2] J. H. Newman, *Essay on Development*, p. 39.

[3] *Nineteenth Century*, ii, 102–3. Leslie Stephen borrowed it for his article in *DNB*.

> assemblage of facts and observations, whether they relate to human nature or anything else, leaves but an unsatisfactory impression. Whatever may be the pleasures of a coasting excursion where we see the same shore under all the varieties of aspect,—the pebbly beach, the reedy margin, the rocky promontory, the pastures, the glades, the creeks, successively presented, but finally blending themselves into one landscape,—it is a very different thing to be led through the mazes of an Archipelago where we are swept past now a volcano, and then a vine garden, here an abode of civilized man, and there a haunt of goats and monkeys. In the one case, we can return to our starting point, rich with the results of our survey: in the other, we know not at last how far we have been, or what we have gained; and moreover, it requires good management to get home again.[1]

It is not fanciful to note that whenever she visited a strange city, she went at once to the highest point to see the city laid out as a living map. "It is scarcely credible," she wrote, "how much time is saved and confusion of ideas obviated by these means." [2]

The method was doubly necessary because for her all principles had to issue in action.

> Wherever there is a principle to be acted upon, however minute may be the occasion of daily business which calls it up,—there God is. Wherever there is a truth to be set forth and vindicated, there God is acting with us. Wherever there is a human right to be asserted and maintained, there our filial sympathies unite with our fraternal as entirely as in our Elder Brother, when he gave thanks for all of us who were to be admitted into his joy. Indeed, it is only by regarding our fellow-beings in the light of God's truth and love, that we can have any permanent sympathies with them at all. It is only by taking our stand on principles, and keeping ourselves free to act, untrammelled by authority, that we can retain any power of resolving and working as rational and responsible beings.[3]

The injunction held for small matters and great. The deaf should fix upon the principle of giving the least possible pain to others—it was in applying it that she gave up music, against her inclination and the entreaty of friends, for she knew they would suffer, and never admit it, from a wrong bass in her playing or a false note in her singing.[4] And, macrocosmically, what could

[1] *MR*, v, 433–40, reprinted, *Misc.*, ii, 119.

[2] *RWT*, i, 228.

[3] "On Moral Independence", *Misc.*, i, 182. See also her advice to Arthur Allen to stop looking in upon himself and to employ his thoughts on the interests of others. November 8, n.y., Yale.

[4] "Letter to the Deaf", *Misc.*, i, 251.

she be but a Radical in politics, a Radical in the literal, etymological sense of the word, carrying everything back to the root, to first principles?

Principles were to be found and acted upon in every field—religion, morals, art, and politics—and the corollary obligation to criticize or denounce, if necessary, was inescapable. Hence the preaching to the Americans in the *Anti-Slavery Standard* which the Americans, strangely enough, resented. "The lesson that we hope your countrymen will learn is not that of understanding us better but of proceeding upon some sort of principle in your political enthusiasms, and distrusting, instead of being proud of, impulses which may lead to disappointment and mortification." [1] Hence her attitude to politicians. Palmerston was the worst:

> He never inspired, in any sort of mind, any belief in him, beyond confidence in his ability to avert evil, or to get out of mischief. The more important the principle involved in any affair, the more airy and jocose was he . . . .This was a small matter, however, compared with the feeling which was growing up against him as the man who, so far from using his popularity to restore and establish the principle and method of government by parties, employed his influence in weakening all political principle, and melting down the whole substance of political conviction, by his treatment of all great questions, and his tone in regard to the gravest, as well as the most transient interests which lay under his hand. By his levity he made many things easy; by his industry he accomplished a vast amount of business; by his gay spirits he made a sort of holiday of the grave course of the national life. But he has done nothing to fit his country, or his party, or even his nearest associates, for a wise conduct of national affairs in the time to come.

There was reason to lament his death, for one could only be apprehensive as to what would come next.[2] And what did come she felt was what should have been expected in his train. She liked neither Gladstone nor Disraeli.

Again, Bishop Blomfield, whose skilfulness and political tact enabled the Church of England to survive as an establishment, came under attack for having muddled views at exactly the time when clarity was needed. He was inadequate to his charge because "he strove to take a middle course on a subject which does not admit of it; and he had no principle to assign". Arthur Stanley, in his Broad Churchmanship and desire for comprehension, was a man totally devoid of any sense of the difficulty

[1] *ASS*, July 18, 1859.
[2] "Lord Palmerston", *Biog. Sketches*, pp. 390–91.

of profession or non-profession of opinion and without any instinct which could lead him to appreciate the difficulties of others: in short he had no principles in his religion.[1]

Finally, and most significantly, John Stuart Mill. Shocked by the relationship with Mrs. Taylor, an attachment of the sort she had never experienced, she found his intellectual position thoroughly unsatisfactory.

> My prepossessions have been strongly in his favour; & I believe I appreciate his many fine qualities & accomplishments; but my impression is, & has been for 20 years, that he is an enormously overrated man. I feel afraid to say it,—he is so deferred to by men of good quality on all sides; but I cannot refuse to see signs of fundamental weakness which destroy him as an authority. . . . A strong man might change his opinions to the extent that he has; but there must be some weakness *in a thinker* whose compound change—of kind & degree together,—is so great as J.S.M.'s.[2]

The very qualities which some of us now find most admirable in Mill are the very ones she rejects, and in the name of principle.

It is a high calling. Let us see it once more, this time through the eyes of Matthew Arnold. "What an unpleasant life and unpleasant nature," he said after her death; but in 1855 he had written to his mother in a different vein. He knew nothing of Miss Martineau's works, he said, and could find no applause for her creed, only for her boldness in avowing it.

[1] "Charles James Blomfield", *Biog. Sketches*, pp. 164 ff. See also Olive J. Brose, *Church and Parliament*. On Stanley, HM to Reeve, May 7, 1861. See below, pp. 357-58.

[2] HM to Reeve, February 21, 1859. See also her letters after Mill's death, *Auto.*, ii, 503, 522, and especially 505: "The Managers of the Mill memorial put my name, without even leave asked, on their executive committee. I wrote a remonstrance, desiring it to be withdrawn. It was reason enough to assign that age and illness incapacitated me for any duty of the sort. But there are other reasons. I do not wish to implicate myself with his repute. I have a great admiration for his intellect, and a strong regard for his heart, and a full belief in his innocence of intention. But he was deplorably weak in judgment, with the weakness, so damaging to a man, of being as impressionable as a woman." This whole attitude is strikingly reminiscent of a passage from one of Miss Martineau's early literary and philosophic guides. "You will observe, that no respect is attached to this Proteus of opinion, after his changes have been multiplied. . . . One, or perhaps two, considerable changes, will be regarded as signs of a liberal inquirer, and therefore the party to which his first or his second intellectual conversion may assign him, will receive him gladly. But he will be deemed to have abdicated the dignity of reason, when it is found that he can adopt no principles but to betray them; and it will be perhaps justly suspected that there is something extremely infirm in the structure of that mind, whatever vigour may mark some of its operation, to which a series of very different and sometimes contrasted theories, can appear in succession demonstratively true. . . ." John Foster, *Essays*, p. 70.

The want of independence of mind, the shutting their eyes and professing to believe what they do not, the running blindly together in herds, for fear of some obscure danger and horror if they go alone, is so eminently a vice of the English, I think, of the last hundred years—has led them, and is leading them into such scrapes and bewilderment, that I cannot but praise a person whose one effort seems to have been to deal perfectly honestly and sincerely with herself, although for the speculations into which this effort has led her I have not the slightest sympathy. I shall never be found to identify myself with her and her people, but neither shall I join, nor have I the least community of feeling with, her attackers. And I think a perfectly impartial person may say all in her praise that I have said.[1]

Her judgments were often twisted. Sydney Smith complained that she took seriously half the things he said as "mystifications", and Greg pointed out that later in her life she aggravated the handicap of her deafness by laying down the trumpet before a sentence or paragraph was completed or when she decided what was being said was not worth hearing or was taking an unwelcome turn.[2] Many of her judgments too were masks of principle for more natural if sometimes less creditable impulses. Jealousy, resentment, and frustration can easily be read into them, and one can speculate about motivation from deeper psychological sources such as her unhappiness as a child or her attachment to her brother. But the conscious forms, the rhetoric, and the image are infinitely more important for the historian. In that light, principle must provide the main clue to interpretation: her concern about it and the actions it dictated make the theme of this study. But before we can go on to examine her career in these terms, a few more subsidiary characteristics must be dealt with, attitudes or talents which she brought to the service (and sometimes disservice) of principle.

For one thing, she was an enthusiast. In 1847 Crabb Robinson saw her, just back from Egypt.

She is unchanged only a little browner—The pyramids and Jerusalem have not put clairvoyance's nose out of joint. I wish they had and indeed I expected to apply the line "and old impertinence expel by new" which was the case as to our friend's *American* zeal. She is a woman of considerable talent, has an excellent prose style, observes shrewdly, as far as the want of physical senses admits and

---

[1] *Arnold Letters*, i, 51, ii, 158.

[2] *Nineteenth Century*, i, 103.

> is both generous and conscientious; but she is not blessed with a sound & safe judgment—But who has all the gifts?[1]

And so Richard Webb:

> I had a friendly note from Miss Martineau yesterday begging me to assist in promoting the knowledge of some new discovery she has heard of (what is not new at all) for the preservation of Indian meal, and making it palatable to those who don't like the meal as sometimes made. I believe it is a process of kiln drying. . . . She is a wonderfully compulsive woman and very often gets laughed at for hasty enthusiasms which take their course unattended with sufficient judgment and deliberation. I think she is a good woman whom I greatly respect and I will do all I can to help her whether in the matter of the meal she has any thing new to offer.[2]

She could remind Florence Nightingale in the sixties that the *Notes on Nursing* omitted an important precautionary measure, the placing of beds north and south, head to the north, to align the patient, or any sleeper, with the earth's magnetic field. For several years, she said, whenever she visited a hospital or a lunatic asylum, she always carried a pocket compass. No doubt she issued commands on this subject as firmly to the superintendents as she did to her nephews who were about to marry.[3]

My favourite example shows her in a temple along the Nile.

> A new hieroglyphic sign on the faces of these pillars engages the eye; which is then led on to distinguish bands of colour; and presently to perceive that the walls have been divided into compartments by margins of colour, and rows of hieroglyphic signs. Some dim appearance of large figures, under the films of dust and mould, is next perceived; and in the inner chamber, it was plain, as Mr. E. pointed out to me, that one figure had been washed. There were the tricklings of the water, from the feet to the ground; and the figure was, though dim, so much brighter than everything else that I felt irresistibly tempted to try to cleanse a bit of the wall, and restore to sight some of its ancient paintings.—We sent down to the boat—about half a mile—for water, tow, soap, and one or two of the crew; and while the rest of my party went to explore the great modern temple, I tucked up my sleeves, mounted a stone, and began to scrub the walls, to show the boy Hassan what I wanted him to do. I would let no one touch the wall, however, till I had convinced myself that no colour would come off. The

---

[1] Crabb Robinson to Thomas Robinson, June 18, 1847, DWL.

[2] Webb to Miss Weston, April 4, 1851, BPL, Weston.

[3] The notion of aligning beds is by no means dead. Miss Martineau's authority was Baron von Reichenbach's book on magnetism. HM to Florence Nightingale, January 7, 1860, BM.

colours were quite fast. We might scrub with all our strength without injuring them in the least. It was singularly pleasant work, bringing forth to view these elaborate old paintings. The colours came out bright and deep as the day they were laid on. . . . It began to grow dusk before we finished two figures: and indeed I cannot say that we completely finished any; for a slight filminess spread over the paintings as they dried, which showed that another rubbing was necessary. I did long to stay a whole day, to clean the entire temple: but this could not be done. I was careful to give a dry-rubbing to our work before we left it, that no injury might afterwards arise from damp: and I trust our attempt may yet be so visibly recorded on the walls as to induce some careful traveller to follow our example, and restore more of these ancient paintings.[1]

It was the character of her mind, as Miss Aikin said, "to adopt extreme opinions on most subjects, and without much examination".[2] When something excited her, big or small, she threw herself into it unreservedly. Sometimes she was ludicrous, but on many important subjects she is revealing and significant. When she was full of political economy, so was nearly everyone. She came back from the United States, able to talk of little else, when the reviews were fighting major battles on the subject. In the forties, mesmerism was a marvel to many, and a deeply disturbing one at that. She travelled to the Near East when it was the thing to do. Her enthusiasm for abolitionism and her predictions in the fifties that a crisis was coming proved right. Tiresome as she must have been at times to her friends, she reflected and magnified some powerfully symptomatic contemporary concerns. That is why she was so much talked about and why she is so useful to historians.

Moreover, she wrote books and articles about her enthusiasms. Significantly, she asked Webb to help her in *promoting the knowledge* of the way to make corn meal palatable, and hoped that her example in Egypt would lead other travellers to wall-washing. Enthusiasm can be merely temperamental, but in Harriet Martineau it was related to a wider cultural pattern: her whole career was didactic. Biography was to teach. Like Miss Edgeworth, she wrote tales to teach. She wrote leading articles and open letters to Americans to expound right principles. She gave courses of lectures to the poor in Ambleside. She backed every attempt at national education, except Forster's (the one that

[1] *EL*, pp. 114–15.
[2] Lucy Aikin to W. E. Channing, June 13, 1833, *Corr.*, p. 176.

worked), because she thought it a miserable compromise. She published a book called *Household Education* and another called *Health, Husbandry, and Handicraft*—both collected from magazine writing—and she wrote *Our Farm of Two Acres*, to keep elderly ladies from falling into the trap set by wrong statements in a little book called *Our Farm of Four Acres*. She was an incurable teacher.

Nothing could make this clearer than her views on literature and the arts. Writing on Scott, when she was a young woman, she said:

> If the office of casting new lights into philosophy, and adding new exemplifications and sanctions to morals, be not the "business" of literary genius, we know not what is. It is the "business," the first business of every man to deduce those very lessons from actual life; and we can conceive of no more important occupation than his who does the same thing for many, while doing it for himself. . . . That dark passions are introduced, and have excited an interest, is a sufficient basis for the argument, that their exhibition constituted an important part of the business of his life, who conceived and portrayed their workings.[1]

The feeling remained and grew. To her, Harriet Beecher Stowe's *Dred* was so much a work of genius that English novelists might as well give up altogether, for, after *Dred*, no one would have patience with anything but didactic writing. She became more and more disgusted with contemporary literature. Some Browning she admired; others of "his sayings" she could make nothing of; Tennyson delighted her, but the delight was qualified by a lack of simplicity, the curse of modern poets. Coventry Patmore had the greater fault of coarseness.[2]

The coarseness of the novelists was even more distressing. She admired *Esmond*; but *Vanity Fair* was "a raking up of dirt and rotten eggs". Dickens, with whom she had quarrelled and collided in print (over factory legislation), sank deeper and deeper into squalour—she rushed to read Michelangelo Titmarsh to "sweeten her mind" after reading *Martin Chuzzlewit*.[3] Even James Payn, whose short tales she found exquisite, put his great abilities into novels which she found downright disagreeable. It was George Eliot who called forth the severest

[1] "Characteristics of the Genius of Scott", *Misc.*, i, 19–20.

[2] HM to Mrs. Stowe, September 18, 1856, Chicago Historical Society. HM to Elizabeth Barrett, July 11, [1844], Wellesley. HM to Miss Clough, n.d., Women's Service Library, London.

[3] HM to Helen Martineau, n.d., MCO.

criticism. The moral squalour of "Janet's Repentance" in *Scenes from Clerical Life* was as bad as Dickens's physical ugliness. *Adam Bede* she wished had never been written, or that the secret of the authorship had never come out, or that she could have done something to have caused it to be written by someone other than Miss Evans, whose abilities she admired but whom she never respected or *liked* (she underlines this). *Felix Holt* was immensely able, but again the all-pervading coarseness vexed and oppressed her.[1]

She was of course far more representative of ordinary intelligent Victorian opinion than we might like to think. The French *feuilletons* and the Salisbury Square School were considered highly dangerous. Bulwer-Lytton was universally attacked for *Lucretia*, a crime novel in which he was accused of being unnatural; and he had to publish a pamphlet in reply. The license of modern novelists was a recurring theme in criticism.[2] Much of this attitude was podsnappery, but in Miss Martineau it was more than that. Novels were not, she wrote in her journal, to be judged by their fitness for children. "I object to no real subjects into which pure moral feelings of any kind can enter. Whether they are, when finished, moral or immoral, depends on the way in which they are treated; whether in a spirit of purity and benignity, with foul gusto, or with a mere view to delineation."[3] Mere delineation was not enough. When George Eliot told her that true delineation was good art—they were standing before a disagreeable picture of a stork killing a toad (a good Victorian subject)—Miss Martineau replied by asking whether it would also be good art to show men on a raft eating a comrade, and Miss Evans was silent.[4]

The end of art for Miss Martineau was quite different. Scott was great because, though his style was not sermon-like, his effect was; the callings of novelist and preacher in her view are identical. Why could Charlotte Brontë escape the condemnation visited on George Eliot? Because

> her moral strength fell not a whit behind the intellectual force manifested in her works. Though passion occupies too prominent

---

[1] George Eliot to Mrs. Bray, [May 19, 1854], *George Eliot Letters*, ii, 157. HM to Reeve, December 25, 1859, August 1, 1859, May 7, 1861.

[2] *ER*, vol. 106, pp. 124–56 (July, 1857) and its review of her *Billow and the Rock*, vol. 85, pp. 461–76 (April, 1847). HM to Reeve, September 12, 1858.

[3] October 2, 1837, *Auto.*, ii, 313.

[4] HM to Reeve, May 7, 1861.

> a place in her pictures of Life . . . it is a true social blessing that we have had a female writer who has discountenanced sentimentalism and feeble egotism *with such practical force*. . . . Her heroines love too readily, too vehemently, and sometimes after a fashion which their female readers may resent; but *they do their duty through everything, and are healthy in action*, however morbid in passion.[1]

She could not abide the "Epicureanism" she found in people like Anna Jameson. Like Cudworth in theology, so George Eliot in fiction—both in their various ways sinned against action, the one considering it unworthy of the Divine, the other not considering it. Action Miss Martineau defined as improving. To show things as they are, to delineate faithfully, was not enough. We can see the mid-Victorian novelists as powerful and subtle critics of their age, but not even Dickens could gain this commendation from Miss Martineau, for his principles were wrong, and his methods misguided. Novels were to show what man could be, not what he is, and so how he could be made better. This was the Victorian analogue to "socialist realism".

A final consideration to be kept always in mind in reading Harriet Martineau is that she was a professional writer. Although everything she wrote—and I think I am right to be all-inclusive—fell into the didactic pattern and served a particular cause, she also wrote to live. From the time at the end of the twenties when the family fortune disappeared, she lived by her pen, and lived fairly comfortably. She never made what a popular novelist made, of course, but she invested (on the whole) wisely and she lived simply; so she did better than most free-lance writers do today. She did not write what she did merely to capture a market which a sharp eye had discerned; her moral and didactic intentions save her from charges of mere professionalism. It is always important, however, to remember the way in which she had to write.

Elizabeth Barrett's early estimate—"an eloquent writer & lucid thinker . . . possessing singular powers of description & pathos . . . the possessor of an original & originating mind endowed with high logic and imaginative sensibility"—is pretty much sheer nonsense, as Miss Martineau would have been the first to acknowledge; Miss Barrett was caught up sentimentally

[1] "Charlotte Brontë", *Biog. Sketches*, p. 46. Italics mine. Compare Mrs. Jameson's account of a conversation with HM on George Sand in *Letters and Friendships*, pp. 215–16.

in a remarkably intense relationship with a fellow-invalid. But George Eliot told the Brays that Miss Martineau was the only Englishwoman to possess thoroughly the art of writing; and W. R. Greg felt the same way: "No one who worked so quickly or so hard ever worked so well." Charles Darwin met her at dinner at his brother's:

> It was a very brilliant little party, as all his invariably are. I had a very interesting conversation with Miss Martineau—most perfectly authorial—comparing our methods of writing,—it seems wonderful the rapidity with which she writes correctly.—I felt, however, no small gratification to find that she is not a complete [illegible] & knows the feeling of exhaustion from thinking too much. I thought she was quite invincible, but she confesses a few hours consecutively exhausts [sic] every grain of strength she possesses. She never had occasion to correct a single word she writes, which accounts for the marvellous rapidity with which she brings forward her books.[1]

Jane Carlyle was more sceptical and made a vital distinction:

> Harriet Martineau used to talk of *writing* being such a pleasure to her. In this house we should as soon dream of calling the bearing of children "*such* a pleasure"—but betwixt *writing* and *writing* there is a difference, as betwixt the ease with which a butterfly is born into the world and the pangs that attend a man-child.[2]

Within her boundaries, she was excellent. Her manuscripts are extraordinary—superbly neat and legible, with almost no corrections and changes. In fiction she now sounds stilted and affected, though she did not always strike her contemporaries that way, and Miss Barrett's references to her powers of description and pathos were commonplaces with reviewers. Occasionally, when, as all professional writers are likely to do, she wrote a book that should have been an article, there is padding, and some of the periodical writing is subject to it, a common enough fault. On the other hand, she could write fine set pieces, in the perorations of some of her tales or at great moments in the *History*; and she could exploit a startling incident or hit on stunning epigrams, like her characterization of Brougham or her

[1] Charles Darwin to Elizabeth Wedgwood, microfilm from original at Down House, Kent, in American Philosophical Society, Philadelphia.

[2] *Elizabeth Barrett to Mr. Boyd*, October 4, 1844, p. 266. *George Eliot Letters*, ii, 32. W. R. Greg, *Nineteenth Century*, ii, 101–2. Jane Carlyle to Helen Welsh, [December, 1843], *Letters to Her Family*, p. 164. See Miss Martineau's own comments on writing in her journal, October 9 and 10, 1837, *Auto.*, ii, 315.

amused reference to Calhoun's "steam-theorizing".[1] Her best writing, besides her letters, is in the *History* and in her work for the *Daily News*. There the quality of her prose is almost unvarying and thoroughly in accord with the canons of the fine journalistic style of the middle of the century. It is a great if exasperating tribute that, when positive identifications are lacking, it is next to impossible to single out her contributions to the paper on stylistic grounds.

She was, then, a supremely competent journalist. And she had all the virtues and faults of that profession. The enthusiasm, the didacticism, and the point of view all contributed to her success. A journalistic job well done is a satisfying and even an artistic thing within its limitations, but the limitations are important. Speed is gained at the expense of reflection, contemporaneity at the expense of perspective. Clarity steals from qualification, and deadlines preclude mastery. Enthusiasm brings urgency and conviction but destroys balance. Then, besides, she had a mission, which informed and sometimes distorted everything she did. Still, making all the allowances about her writings that have to be made, subtracting everything that must be subtracted, one can agree with her friend Julia Smith in hardly ever wishing to alter their direction.[2] It is easy to disagree with Miss Martineau's views, even to find them repulsive. But one likes them as they are because they tell us so much.

[1] The Brougham story is told below, p. 127. The Calhoun reference is in a letter to Lord Morpeth, April 26, [1844].

[2] To Crabb Robinson, [June 20, 1844], DWL.

CHAPTER II

Norwich: A Manufacturer's Daughter

IN the early parts of her autobiography, Miss Martineau displays an extraordinary power to recall details. But she also presents the reader with a tough problem when he tries to disentangle the actuality of her childhood from judgments insinuated in her maturity. Nor is it easy to get at the state of things from other people, as we can do for the later parts of her life. Children are seen not heard, and little Harriet, of all children, was unlikely to be an exception. With seven brothers and sisters, all of whom (except James) appear to have been normal, gregarious youngsters, Harriet might have been commented on as visitors returned home from the Magdalen Street house, but it was increasingly possible that she would not have been noticed at all, except by her family. She was not, in the American sense, a dreadful child, but she was distinctly—she recognizes this, indeed emphasizes it—a difficult child.

She was born on June 12, 1802, the sixth of eight children of Thomas Martineau, a manufacturer belonging to an old and distinguished Norwich family, and his wife Elizabeth, the daughter of a Newcastle wholesale grocer and sugar-refiner. Certainly, much of Harriet's strangeness and unhappiness was closely tied to the wretched state of her health. She was what the nineteenth century called delicate, which in this case seems to come down to a weak digestion which both affected and was affected by a highly-strung nervous system. Symptoms of hysteria abound in her recollections—the terrors of certain fairly normal childhood dreams, fears of being unable to descend a staircase or cross to the garden, inability to see the water at the seaside, or "bowel complaint" invariably brought on by magic lantern displays. On Guild Day (the Tuesday before Midsummer Day) the wickerwork and canvas dragon which led the procession terrified her, "wagging his abominable snaky head at us children, & snapping his jaws & chasing us".[1] Fears, a sense of inadequacy, guilt, and bad health all contributed to making her withdraw more and more into herself. Her brother James, after her death, called her "one of those natures—and among them some of the most energetic and gifted in the end—which remain through childhood in a kind of *chrysalis* state", only to break forth in their twenties. It is a familiar phenomenon, particularly in highly sensitive children born into families whose demands are ordinary and conventional.[2] But it creates problems with which a conventional family are likely to be poorly prepared to deal.

One solution—a wrong one—was to expect of Harriet what the other children could do. It was an understandable expectation, for she tried to conceal her fears by climbing trees and running along high walls, but such a solution became increasingly impracticable when after the age of twelve her hearing began to trouble her. Another solution—more or less useless—was to send her away to the country or to relatives, an experiment tried several times, with no manifest improvement. Miss Martineau's own retrospective solution, which colours and distorts her whole picture of her family, was that she should have had more understanding and affection. She insists that as a child her ruling passion was for justice, and that she resented the sermons which dwelt on duties of inferiors to superiors and not those of superiors to inferiors. To some extent, this may be reading back a major intellectual assumption; on the other hand, as a piece of amateur psychologizing, it has some value. Certainly in her later life she did have a passion for justice of this rather limited sort, and certainly the books she wrote on the raising of children (and her own attitudes to children and young people) emphasize the importance of affection, understanding, and equality.[3]

It seems to me not only that her retrospective solution was an impossible one, but that some of her most admirable qualities came, directly or by opposition, from her environment, for all its miseries. For example, one of the qualities of which Miss Martineau herself would have been proudest is strikingly sug-

[1] HM to Lord Houghton, October 13, 1873, Wemyss Reid, *Richard Monckton Milnes*, ii, 282. There is a description of the Guild Day Procession in *A General History of the County of Norfolk*, pp. 1196–97. See also her analysis in *HE*, p. 59.

[2] "The Early Days of Harriet Martineau", *Daily News*, December 30, 1884, reprinted in Bosanquet, *Harriet Martineau*, pp. 218–41. This is a very perceptive and helpful article, to which my references here will be continual.

[3] But this is equally a result of psychological theory. See below, pp. 79–81, 271.

gested by James Martineau's corollary to his mother's quickness of sympathy: a quickness of temper "so far as to render her displeasure at wrong emphatic, and to warn us also, if we did not wish to be laughed at, to do nothing awkward or stupid under her eye".

> In old Nonconformist families especially, the Puritan tradition and the reticence of a persecuted race had left their austere impress upon speech and demeanour unused to be free; so that in domestic and social life there was enforced, as a condition of decorum, a *retenue* of language and deportment strongly contrasting with our modern effusiveness.

Though Dr. Martineau went on to place his family rather more in advance of the movement towards geniality than behind it, the impression of conventionality remains.

Thomas Martineau was a mild man, comforting, generous, and sound. He took some part in civic affairs, but was obviously very much in the shade of his brother, Philip Meadows Martineau, the eminent surgeon whose estate at Bracondale was a show-place in the Norwich area.[1] In the household Mrs. Martineau clearly dominated, and about her has raged a rather pointless debate of the biographers. Mrs. Martineau was obviously too ordinary—and that in its best sense—to be the centre of a posthumous fuss; that perhaps was the real quarrel Harriet had with her. She was, notwithstanding, a woman of considerable talent who had profited enough from a limited education and subsequent self-education, that she was able to serve her daughter as a literary confidante, once Harriet had become reconciled to her in the twenties.[2] They maintained a household in Fludyer Street, Westminster, which seems to have been notable for its good spirits—at any rate Miss Martineau's friends paid sincere tributes to her mother's qualities.[3] But what prodigies of

[1] Thomas Martineau was "a man of more tenderness and moral refinement than force of self-assertion. . . ." James Martineau, "Biographical Memoir", quoted in James Drummond, *James Martineau*, i, 3. Thomas Martineau is mentioned from time to time in the *Norwich Mercury*, but never prominently. His distinguished brother, however, received memoirs on his death in all of the papers, rates mention in the *General History of Norfolk* of 1829, was active in the encouragement of the arts, and had an absolute passion for landscape gardening, which he could afford to indulge. Miss Martineau wrote the memoir in the *MR*, n.s., iii, 131–32 (February, 1829); see also Susannah Taylor to Dr. Reeve, June 1, 1804, in Ross, *Three Generations*, p. 30.

[2] Ellen Higginson, the youngest daughter, comments on Mrs. Martineau's education and interests in a passage quoted in Drummond, *James Martineau*, i, 8–9.

[3] There are tributes to her also quoted in *ibid.*, i, 4–6.

imagination or psychological insight could one expect from her when, with a large family and a busy life, she was confronted with what seemed sheer obstinacy. When, for example, she listened to an accusation from her troublesome daughter of partiality for her sister Rachel, Mrs. Martineau sent Harriet to practise her music, then to bed, and left no doubt of her displeasure. It is a more natural reaction than the saccharine one Miss Martineau imagined as an alternative;[1] perhaps it was almost as healthy, because Harriet's morbidity was treated at times with understanding, and at some point it must have become necessary to take a stand.

It should not be thought, however, that the atmosphere in this household was anything like that of the Evangelical families who come so automatically to twentieth-century minds. As Unitarians, the Martineaus kept religion in proportion and had long since left behind the Calvinist distrust of the pleasures of this world. There is a family tradition about James, who, still a small boy, was found one Sunday with the Bible on his knees, proudly proclaiming that he had read from Genesis to Isaiah since Chapel. When he was rebuked for exaggeration, he replied: "Skipping the nonsense, you know, Mamma", something no child of an Evangelical household could have said.[2]

The Martineaus played cards for money—Miss Martineau recalled the avarice early awakened in her by winning twopence—they danced, they went to concerts (in which Norwich was particularly strong) and to the theatre. The holidays were kept, and especially St. Valentine, with presents and verses, a practice supplanted later in the century by a wider celebration of Christmas. There were excitements like great three-day family meetings, or the Guild Days when the children would steal in to see the banqueting tables laid out in St. Andrew's Hall.

[1] "I slept little, and went down sick with dread. Not a word was said, however, then or ever, of the scene of the preceding night; but henceforth, a most scrupulous impartiality between Rachel and me was shown. If the occasion had been better used still,—if my mother had but bethought herself of saying to me, 'My child, I never dreamed that these terrible thoughts were in your mind. I am your mother. Why do you not tell me everything that makes you unhappy?' I believe this would have wrought in a moment that cure which it took years to effect, amidst reserve and silence." *Auto.*, i, 67.

[2] Drummond, *James Martineau*, i, 10. "Amongst [the Unitarians] there was no rigorism. Dancing, cards, the theatre, were all held lawful in moderation: in *manners*, the Free Dissenters, as they were called, came much nearer the Church than to their own stricter brethren. . . ." Lucy Aikin to Channing, December 26, 1828, *Corr.*, pp. 28–29.

Elections provided a kind of excitement we have lost.[1] In short, an important provincial city was a more exciting place to grow up in, even for a morose child, than say, Haworth Rectory. Little pleasures peek through the gloomy account, games played, hoops rolled, birthday parties with hide-and-seek in the warehouse, silkworms raised and gathered, and the malicious childish mimicry of the mannerisms of William Taylor, one of the leaders of literary Norwich.[2] But moments of fun and bursts of affection were exceptions, and Harriet's childhood was unhappy. Until she found her consolation in religion, she followed the usual chain of childish fantasies: suicide, running away, and hoping that angels would come down through the windows in the roof of the Octagon Chapel to take her up to heaven in the sight of the congregation. That, at any rate, would have shown them!

Whatever there is to say about the Martineau household—and I think there is more to be said for than against it—the parents were determined to give their children an excellent education—indeed for the girls an extraordinary one. It was begun at home in the fashion that one might expect from a radical family caught up in the latest fashions: the older children taught the younger—the monitorial system of Bell and Lancaster, with the usual imperfect results. In 1813 Harriet and Rachel were sent to Mr. Perry, who had lost his pulpit and a good many of his pupils by his conversion to Unitarianism, and, after his school failed, to tutors. For a time Harriet was at a school in Bristol.

Even more important than the obviously high quality of Mr. Perry's instruction was the amount of reading which Harriet did, the more extensive because of her deafness. Her diligence, expository technique, and style came from this training and experience; and in conjunction with her religious concerns the reading produced a particularly hardy strain of interests ranging from metaphysics through politics and political economy to

[1] "I went to Mr. Thomas Martineau's yesterday to see the two Mr. Cokes, Sir Jacob Astley, and Mr. Windham pass by. When the first part of the procession had reached this spot, the last had not entered Magdalen gates—so you may judge of its length. . . . To add to the effect, their bare heads were all covered with the snow, which fell very thick just at the time of the chairing." Susannah Taylor to Sarah Taylor, March 5, 1807, Ross, *Three Generations*, p. 34. The excitement could hardly have been lost on a five-year-old.

[2] These glimpses appear in the *Autobiography* and in the Reeve Letters, e.g., November 12, 1863; HM to Crabb Robinson, March 8, [1844], DWL; and in the letter to Lord Houghton, October 13, 1873, Wemyss Reid, *Monckton Milnes*, ii, 282. HM to Milnes, February 9, [1844].

literature and poetry. She was also taught music—by no less a person than John Beckwith, the terrifying organist of the Cathedral—and music, at which she was very good except during the ordeal of lessons, remained a real resource until her deafness deprived her of it and turned her to literature.

Moreover, the girls were taught to cook and sew and superintend a house, though not, she says, to purchase or deal with butchers or set a table, tasks left to the servants. Sewing was her principal diversion: she made her own clothes, and her woolwork remained a steady source of relaxation and of gifts. If she was awkward in performing household chores when someone was watching her, she could claim with justice in later life to be an excellent manager, neat, efficient, and demanding—as her mother had been neat, efficient, and demanding. Servants in the Magdalen Street house knew their position (Miss Martineau recalled the agony of being sent with rebukes to them); in Norwich or Ambleside there was apparent that characteristic which Beatrice Webb lighted upon as the true distinction of the upper middle class—the habit of giving orders. Mrs. Webb, said G. K. Chesterton, ordered the citizens of the state about as she might order her servants about the kitchen.[1]

Harriet Martineau was in a less strategic postition to have her orders put into effect on a national scale, but the style was the same. Other people's little mistakes of fact she could never abide: she set Mr. Perry straight in front of all his scholars one day about the spelling of Shakespere (as she had it). Her whole life was spent in setting people straight.

> I have always wondered to see the ease and success with which very good people humour and manage the aged, the sick and the weak, and sometimes every body about them. I could never attempt this; for it always seemed to me such contemptuous treatment of those whom I was at the moment respecting more than ever, on account of their weakness. But I was always quite in the opposite extreme;—far too solemn, too rigid, and prone to exaggeration of differences and to obstinacy at the same time. It was actually not till I was near forty that I saw how the matter should really be,—saw it through a perfect example of an union of absolute sincerity with all possible cheerfulness, sweetness, modesty and deference for all, in proportion to their claims. I have never attained righteous good manners, to this day. . . .[2]

---

[1] B. Webb, *My Apprenticeship*, p. 37. *Victorian Age in Literature*, p. 58.
[2] *Auto.*, i, 68.

She was her mother's daughter, and it is odd that, frank as she was about herself, she failed to see that central legacy.

However unhappy Harriet may have been as a child, one derives a pleasanter picture of her circumstances in the twenties. Though James, her closest companion, had gone off to college, there was still much to occupy her with both profit and pleasure. As was inevitable in the large nineteenth-century family, there was a lot of visiting and corresponding. In the first half of the decade, the Martineaus could easily afford not only extended visits to relatives in Newcastle and Bristol but luxuries like a white pony, for Harriet and Rachel, capable of a run to and from Yarmouth in a day. The intellectual tone which characterized the Magdalen Street household became more satisfying now that the children were old enough to take part, indeed to take the lead; and the list of family readings is impressive. Mrs. Martineau had become the best of companions. She tried in every way, Harriet assured James, to broaden her daughter's interests and tastes; their conversations were the kind that Harriet liked; and she constantly invited Harriet's friends to stay with her. Among them, Harriet's closest companion was Emily Taylor, with whom she conversed for hours on the philosophical problems which had come to mean so much, and other members of the Octagon entered in, though Harriet's success at winning converts to her single and insistent necessarian views was not very great.[1]

In spite of this happier general situation, the twenties took a severe toll. In 1824, her eldest brother Tom, so respected by the younger children, died after a year's illness and was buried at sea on a return journey from Madeira. In 1825 the family business was badly caught in the crash, and shortly thereafter her father fell seriously ill and died.[2] In 1826 a most unpleasant family difficulty was precipitated by the engagement of Helen, Tom's widow, to the new Octagon minister, under circumstances that outraged the family and ended in an exchange of the bitterest recriminations. And, as if to test Harriet to the utmost, a new turn in her life, which everyone assumed would most likely lead to her happiness, ended in tragedy.

In 1823 the family had met and been impressed by a college friend of James's, John Hugh Worthington, a highly promising young minister. Worthington visited Norwich on several

[1] These impressions are based on Harriet's letters to James, *passim*.

[2] See below, p. 59.

occasions in the next couple of years, and in late 1825 Harriet felt impelled to deny to James more than mere friendship for the young man. In August of 1826, Worthington again visited Norwich, this time to offer marriage, thus, as James put it, "confirming an intention which everyone but himself had read in his demeanour towards her in Manchester last year". James had some reason to be apprehensive, because Worthington was in miserable health, suffering from depression and proving quite unequal to his duties as minister at Cross Street, Manchester. Harriet was similarly distressed, and (as she says) uncertain of her ability to make him as happy as he believed she could; so she would consent only to a contingent acceptance of his offer, putting the terms to James in rather surprisingly calculating words: "If he proves strong in body and mind, if for six months he can perform his arduous duties with credit and honour, will you with pleasure see me place my hopes of happiness on him? I am yet afraid that the winter should prove such an one as the last; but if it does not, if our friend at length answers to his early promise in all respects, I am sure you will be quieted and easy on my account." [1]

Even this qualified promise had an electric effect on Worthington. He was able to ascribe all his past difficulties to uncertainty about Harriet, and more than one person noted a new spirituality in his preaching: "That young man," said one family friend, "is all spirit; he lifts one up, one knows not where." The family were delighted, and Harriet herself was apparently sufficiently moved by his intensity of spiritual feeling to conquer some of her doubts about him, though by the same token her doubts of her own capacities may well have increased. But her premonition about the winter proved right: in December Worthington suddenly went mad. Mrs. Martineau was away, so Henry took the letters to an aunt who broke the news to Harriet. For a day Harriet was violently ill; the next day she had accepted the blow as the dictate of heaven and wrote to James an extraordinary letter in which she seemed to consider Worthington already dead and asked: "Who that looks on God as the Father of Mercies, on the gospel as true, on the course of Providence as undeviating, can really be miserable?" As we shall see shortly, this attitude is completely in line with her necessarian metaphysics, and it will

[1] This discussion is based entirely on James's abstracts of Harriet's letters; the quoted portions he gives as her own words.

I. Harriet Martineau's Birthplace
Magdalen Street, Norwich

[illegible] shabby to thee till I have got this great business fairly in train. Knight's accounts fire me, — & then again I flag under the labour. I sent such a rouser [illegible] to Mrs Jerningham [illegible] yesterday. Have you got Circulars from Knight's? Lord Morpeth is as eager as I hoped & expected. One capital piece of news on Sat. was of three established Authors, — men who command a good reception — preferring "the immortality of our shilling volume" to a more dignified price & appearance. If this spreads, we are safe, & the greatest boon in the history of the people is secure. — My Traditions are to come out illustrated & with Notes. Think of a million readers of that book! The beginning to be "Caxton", — a lively picture of the rise of the pursuit of Reading, — in wh. all are now henceforth to share. I wish I cd. spare you Knight's detail of Progress, as to the books. He has bought the right of printing Miss Lamb's Shakspere Stories. Do point out where you can the difference between the Chambers' & others' course of perpetual piracy & Knight's scrupulous purchase of copyrights, or right of printing. — He is very flourishing. Last fortnight he sold £10,000 worth of stock, to advantage —

[illegible cross-writing]

II. A Letter from Harriet Martineau, 1844

have strange echoes in her self-conscious insistence on martyrdom later in life.

Through the first weeks of 1827 the reports from Manchester conflicted: Worthington was better, he was worse, the aberration could be accounted for and would not recur, the prognosis was dismal. These contradictory reports hit hard at almost the only point of real weakness in Harriet's personality—her sexual uncertainties. She was afraid, she said in her autobiography, of being unable to justify dependence on herself, as she was afraid of loving her own children too much or of being too devoted to her husband; behind these fears clearly lay more basic insecurities which must inform too her hysterical self-righteousness when she was faced later in life with some instances of sexual attachment among her friends and acquaintances—W. J. Fox, George Eliot, and John Stuart Mill. We shall see as well one almost ludicrous episode involving herself. It would be a guess with more than a little justification that Miss Martineau was latently homosexual.[1]

Whatever may have been the basic cause of her neurotic behaviour, the episode of her engagement is the one point at which panic rather than a frantically maintained façade of duty and rectitude was the response. When she was summoned to Manchester by Worthington's family, she replied, through her mother, refusing to go. It was a difficult action to take, no doubt, and can be explained perhaps by an inability to face what would unquestionably have been an ordeal. But what is one to say to her writing, shortly *before* Worthington died, to demand that his family return her letters to him, lest some wrong use be made of things she had said to him? In her own account, she refers darkly to the interference of others: this hint the biographers have wonderfully embroidered, accusing both Mrs. Martineau and James. Unfortunately, some of the letters to James are missing at precisely this juncture, though he refers in his summary note to what had happened; in one abstract he mentions a letter Harriet had received from Albina, possibly Worthington's sister, begging

[1] For her views on George Eliot and Mill, see above, pp. 14, 34, 39; for Fox and for the episode in Boston, see below, pp. 98–99, 149–51. The suggestion of lesbianism is founded on the peculiar intensity of her friendships with women, on her happy subordination to Mrs. Chapman and her expressed fears of how Mrs. Chapman could dominate her, on her susceptibility to the magnetic influence of Mrs. Wynyard, her mesmerizer, and on the extraordinary passage in which she describes the pleasure of submitting her will to the will of her maid, who had also recently mesmerized her. See below, pp. 227–28.

her not to go to Manchester and to terminate the engagement; but by that time the decision had already been made. The ultimate truth is unravellable; one can only speculate on causes and results. Worthington died in May, 1827, and by June Harriet was writing bright, happy letters to her brother. Worthington is not mentioned in them again, and apart from her wretched health, which only fitfully responded to treatment—galvanism didn't help, bismuth did—one can find no trace of grief. But the illness (digestive troubles) is trace enough, a trace to suggest a sense of guilt, perhaps, or to prove the terrible toll taken by her conquest of her fears or by justification of her failure. It may even have been worth the struggle. At any rate, I am sure she was utterly sincere when she looked back on the episode and wrote:

> My strong will, combined with anxiety of conscience, makes me fit only to live alone; and my taste and liking are for living alone. The older I have grown, the more serious and irremediable have seemed to me the evils and disadvantages of married life, as it exists among us at this time; and I am provided with what it is the bane of single life in ordinary cases to want,—substantial, laborious, and serious occupation. . . . I long ago came to the conclusion that, without meddling with the case of the wives and mothers, I am probably the happiest single woman in England.

Throughout the difficult mid-twenties, she was writing—the conventionally pious devotional works and the first little moral tales that one might expect from a young woman in a provincial circle. Her writing provided the real escape from her personal difficulties—the "substantial, laborious, and serious occupation" —and under the inspiration of Lant Carpenter, and with the advice and tutelage of her brother James and of W. J. Fox, she grew into a writer who crossed the boundaries of her provincial circle. Her sudden celebrity, first in Unitarianism, and then in the world outside those narrow borders, must have surprised the Norwich families who knew her only as a difficult, shy, frowning, and deaf young woman.

Of the three influences outside her own personality and family which produced her characteristic temper and outlook, one was Norwich itself. The reigns of George III and George IV were the great age of the provincial circle. Before the railway came, a visit to London was a rare event; the greater relative scale of the country combined with economic prosperity to reduce the gravitational pull of the metropolis. To be sure, London remained both arbiter and measure, but it was relatively less important—in government, opinion, literature, the arts—than it is today. Londoners, of course, were condescending about the provinces,[1] but London scruples did not weigh heavily in the provincial towns, which had their own standards of snobbery. If pursuit of the intellect sometimes led to pretension and foolishness among the "blue" ladies, it also led to some solid and occasionally startling results. George Eliot came out of Coventry, and that circle was duplicated in every considerable town, sometimes with nearly as much distinction. Then as now, exciting personalities and minds have come from the provinces (or the colonies) to London; but then they were more likely to come already formed by provincial society, instead of as now, fleeing from provincial dullness to be formed in the metropolis.

Norwich was about fourteen hours by coach from London. Its opilation stood at some forty to fifty thousand in the periodn-whpn u concerns us. It had the usual advantages of a county towen itnd cathedral city, and perhaps was better supplied tha most. a The city was host to musical and theatrical artists of in ternational repute, and received the usual round of travelling exhibitions, menageries, performing elephants, and balloonists. There were theatres of distinction, and the Norwich Library boasted that its nine thousand volumes surpassed any similar library outside London.

Norwich was in some ways unique among English cities. Its continental connections had always been close, and the settling there of the Flemish weavers who brought over the New Drapery in the late Middle Ages gave a persistent flavour of the Low Countries. Long after Harriet Martineau's time, there was still a Dutch church, and Walloon French-speaking services were held in St. Mary's the Less once a year. In the early twentieth century one could still see women carrying milk in vessels like those used in Bruges.[2] At the end of the seventeenth century

[1] Here is Lucy Aikin's comment on Samuel Bailey: "You cannot conceive how much the lettered aristocracy of London society disdains to know anything of provincial genius or merit, at least in any but the most popular branches of literature. Montgomery, a Sheffield poet, being also an Evangelical, is tolerably well known in London, and may, in some companies, be slightly mentioned without committing the speaker. But a Sheffield metaphysician!" Lucy Aikin to W. E. Channing, June 1, 1830, *Corr.*, p. 47.

[2] *Gen. Hist. of Norfolk*, pp. 1189–90, 1072–73. C. B. Hawkins, *Norwich, a Social Study*, pp. 10–11.

came the Huguenots, among them the Martineaus. The nonconformist population, then, was relatively large—in 1828 it was estimated at 8,200 out of some 60,000, and of course its influence was out of all proportion to its numbers. Bishop Bathurst (1805–37) was a thorough liberal—Sydney Smith said that he should *touch* for bigotry and absurdity[1]—and the co-operation between Church and Dissent was close: in 1811 the bishop presided over the first meeting of the Norwich Bible Society, an interdenominational body.[2] Dissenters were prominent in city government, the Octagon Chapel of the Unitarians able to boast of several lord mayors before the repeal of the Test and Corporation Acts in 1828. Norwich also displayed a marked radicalism, helped on by a mixture of national strains, perhaps by the separateness which characterized East Anglia from the very early Middle Ages, and certainly by Nonconformity. Though the dissenters were watched during the Napoleonic threat—they had been revolutionary partisans a decade before—and were forbidden to serve in the militia, they were able to take the discrimination lightly and confidently. Later, Norwich Chartism was to prove active, and the authorities indulgent. The city can still cause difficulties for organizers for the Conservative Party.

The great age of Norwich coincides almost exactly with the reign of George III. In it the Unitarians played a large part. Thomas Ivory designed and built the Octagon Chapel in 1754–56, and its pulpit was occupied by a distinguished succession of ministers beginning with Dr. John Taylor and William Enfield. Dr. John Taylor's daughter-in-law, Susannah, was the great lady of the circle in the last years of the century and the first of the new. Not only were her children ornaments to English life, but Mrs. Taylor herself attracted a noteworthy succession of visitors from the capital. There was nothing pretentious about her household—she was not well off—but she was thoroughly charming and highly cultivated, and when the assizes came, her house was crowded with barristers on circuit, among them Mackintosh, Brougham, and Crabb Robinson.

William Taylor, no relative, "was quite as much wondered at for knowing German, as a person would now be for a profound

[1] Lucy Aikin to W. E. Channing, October 15, 1832, *Corr.*, p. 149. Norwich was a relatively poor see, but Bathurst voted in the House as he believed, remarking after one liberal anti-government vote, "I have lost Winchester." He was the only bishop to vote for the Reform Bill.

[2] Brightwell, *Memorials of Amelia Opie*, p. 189.

acquaintance with Russ." [1] He deserves a place for his translations in the van of German influence in England. He was also a periodical reviewer of note, a friend and correspondent of Robert Southey, and a pillar of the Norwich Philosophical Society. By the time Harriet Martineau came to know him he was rapidly declining into a drunken and unattractive old age; but he remained a figure of considerable awe to the children, even when they mimicked his manner. His contemporaries were often shocked, particularly as he gathered young men about him whom Crabb Robinson was certain he would corrupt—by his scepticism perhaps more than his habits.[2] Among other Norwich luminaries were Samuel Parr, the schoolmaster, William Crotch, the organist, Frank Sayers, a poet and writer also important in introducing continental literature, and of course the Norwich school of painters—Crome, Cotman, and the lesser men. This remarkable society could even boast a fabulous eccentric in John Fransham, a self-taught mathematician, free-thinker, marble-player, and performer on hautboy and drum—until he had to burn the hautboy to make some tea. Harriet must often have seen him about the streets, not very clean, with long grey hair, a green jacket, drab breeches and worsted stockings.[3]

By the time Harriet Martineau became fully aware of this society it was in its decline. Many of its great figures were dead or gone. Taylor wrote to Henry Southey in 1812:

> The sunset of Norwich is arrived. Our society is not what it was. By Hudson Gurney's removal to London, and Mr. Trafford Southwell's into the country, the men of wealth and rank who were chiefly hospitable to talent are withdrawn. Some of us are too ill, and some of us are too poor, to convene one another as formerly.[4]

Taylor, to be sure, was just coming out of a severe financial crisis when he wrote this, and there were still to be signs of vigour.

[1] Lucy Aikin to W. E. Channing, January 10, 1842, *Corr.*, p. 414. On Mrs. Taylor, see Ross, *Three Generations*.

[2] One of the young men was George Borrow. On Taylor, J. W. Robberds, *Memoir*. Crabb Robinson Diary, January 14, and August 15, 1824, DWL.

[3] On Fransham, there is a life by William Saint, a memoir by William Taylor in the *Monthly Magazine*, xxxi, and a sketch in the *Gen. Hist. of Norfolk*, pp. 1232–35. That he was a common figure to the young people is indicated in a letter of Mrs. Taylor's to young Henry Reeve, the father of the more widely known editor and translator of Tocqueville: "I rather envy Mr. Fransham [Frenshaw in the text is an obvious misreading] when I see him mending pens and pouring [sic] over small print." Ross, *Three Generations*, p. 24.

[4] Robberds, *Taylor*, ii, 368–69.

The first Norwich music festival was held in 1824; the moving spirit behind it was Richard MacKenzie Bacon, editor of the *Norwich Mercury*, whose daughter was a soprano of some distinction. The Mechanics' Institution, a quite successful one, was set up in 1825. But the economic decline had taken its toll, and the new age was to be very different from anything William Taylor had known or would have appreciated. The Octagon Chapel, too, fell on bad days. "Went with Mottram to Octagon," wrote Crabb Robinson in 1832; "Congregation very small—splendour of the old Octagon is gone—many families are dead or have left N is the explanation given, but why no new ones?" [1]

Harriet Martineau knew chiefly the exhausted and the epigones. That helps to explain her outburst to Henry Reeve about "those silly women who thought themselves literary", whose selfishness and mutual jealousy she found so galling. Yet her estimate of Norwich society in her sketch of Mrs. Opie or in the *Autobiography* is unjust. Norwich was neither so provincial as she made it out, nor so pretentious. Around the fringes it had its faults. It was a society of free and candid exchange of views which could easily degenerate into gossip,[2] a characteristic which may help to explain her own lapses. Certainly, too, the war had helped to isolate Norwich from its contacts with both the continent and London, an isolation made worse by economic decline and—as travellers still know—the railway network. In 1865, Miss Martineau said that she had had a letter from a Norwich cousin asking if John Wilkes Booth was the grandson of old Booth, the music and bookseller.

> Of course, Norwich must have its finger in the pie. I dare say it thinks it was at the bottom of the late eruption of Etna, & of Prince Henry's restoration, & of the death of the Czarewitch, & of the Spanish failure in Santo Domingo. There is always a Norwich man concerned in all great events.[3]

Yet the qualities of that society at its best, which persisted even in its decline, contributed mightily to shaping her.

In part, she was asserting herself against it. Mrs. John Taylor, her relative and neighbour, would never have snubbed

[1] Diary, October 21, 1832, DWL.

[2] Susannah Taylor to Sarah Taylor, November 13, 1814, Ross, *Three Generations*, pp. 46–47. James, in his abstracts (April 4, 1825) suppressed a portion of a letter written jointly by Mrs. Martineau and Harriet, because of remarks about persons.

[3] HM to Reeve, May 25, 1865. HM to Crabb Robinson, Tynemouth, March 8, [1844], DWL. "Amelia Opie", *Biog. Sketches*, pp. 13–21.

the plain, reserved, awkward Harriet,[1] but lesser women probably did. Their selfishness and jealousy must have hurt to be remembered so long. But it was not all negative. Ellen Martineau Higginson, the youngest daughter, recalled the intellectual tone of the Martineau household.

> It is certain that my father and mother knew no language but their own, at least within our memory; yet I cannot remember a time when there was not much reading going on in the family circle, and not only *duty* reading, but discussion and literary talk, and ours was one of the Norwich houses which held in friendship, more or less close, the men and women who bore the names of Taylor, Alderson, Opie, Smith (Sir James E.), Rigby, Enfield, Reeve and Austin; also Houghton and Madge. My father was a plain, business man . . .; he had passed some portion of his childhood under the roof of the Barbaulds, and if he did not bring away much learning from them, I like to indulge the belief that from Mrs. Barbauld he acquired the strong political leanings, and the firm principles of nonconformity, that marked his after citizenship, and certainly descended in no equivocal way to his sons and daughters. . . . I believe that to my mother we must trace the beginnings of literary culture in our household. . . . The love of literature once awakened, my mother seems never to have lost the habit of adding to her store of knowledge, and snatches of reading must have carried her through many trials, from her first being transplanted to what was, to her, the cold and haughty South, through the anxieties of rearing a large family by means of a fluctuating and finally ruinous business. This measure of self-education enabled her to give life to the early lessons of her children, to direct the choice of teachers for them, to collect intelligent people about them, and to give a warm and appreciative sympathy to them in their subsequent literary efforts. So far, it was all Literature—Science was at a discount in Norwich and especially with the Martineaus.[2]

This portrait is confirmed by a memoir of Thomas Madge, the minister at the Octagon, a frequent guest in Magdalen Street. Having finished his duties for the day, Madge (at that time a bachelor) was ready for lively discussion, and he found in the Martineau's house "an ample feast of reason and flow of soul".[3]

Norwich culture helped to form Harriet Martineau's tastes and interests; Norwich radicalism formed her opinions. Her radicalism was, however, more than the affectation or conviction of a literary circle and more than nonconformist. We must turn

[1] See James Martineau's recollection of Mrs. Taylor, Ross, *Three Generations* pp. 38–39.

[2] Quoted in Drummond, *James Martineau*, i, 8–9.

[3] Quoted in *ibid.*, i, 14.

then to the second formative influence: she was a manufacturer's daughter.

Norwich, said Defoe, was "an ancient, large, rich, and populous city". He went on to say that a stranger passing through might think the town uninhabited, while on the Sabbath or a holiday he would wonder where all the people could be held.

> But the case is this: the inhabitants being all busy at their manufactures dwell in their garrets at their looms and in their combing shops, so they call them, twisting mills, and other work-houses, almost all the works they are employed in being done within doors.[1]

According to Arthur Young, the industry of Norwich trebled between 1700 and 1770. Long-staple wool from Lincolnshire and Leicestershire was combed, spun, and woven into kinds of cloth which are now so unfamiliar that it is difficult to arrive at definitions that convey any visual sense. The most important item was camlets, heavy worsted cloth which the East India Company exported. In addition there was a considerable production of lighter fabrics: crapes, which began to be worn about the beginning of the nineteenth century, and bombazines. Bombazines were mixed fabrics of silk and wool, much in demand for dressmaking for their richness of texture and the grace with which they fell. They were made in two sizes: broad bombazines exported chiefly to Spain and Portugal, and the narrow, used in England. Superior Norwich dyeing techniques produced a remarkable black, and as black bombazines seem to have made excellent mourning costumes, the demand for them must have been both heavy and steady, given the sombre enthusiasm with which family deaths were received. Harriet Martineau's father was a manufacturer of bombazines.

Early nineteenth-century Norwich was not, however, in a healthy economic state. Although Lucy Aikin exaggerated in saying that Norwich had been "the melancholy seat of decaying manufactures and redundant population" since her childhood,[2] the remark was true for a good part of her life. The war caused a serious disruption by closing continental markets. An annual value of trade estimated by Arthur Young in 1771 at just under

[1] Quoted in E. Lipson, *History of the Woollen and Worsted Industries*, p. 228. The passage following is based on Lipson, on Hawkins, *Social Study of Norwich*, pp. 1–11, and on *Report of Assistant Commissioners for Handloom Weavers, Parliamentary Papers*, 1840, xxiii, 301–7.

[2] Lucy Aikin to W. E. Channing, January 17, 1836, *Corr.*, p. 261.

a million and a half fell to £800,000 by 1807. War dislocations were temporary; there was a recovery after 1815, but Norwich industry shortly fell victim to more lethal developments: 12,000 looms in 1770, 10,000 in 1818, 5,075 in 1839 and of those 1,021 were unemployed. For one thing, the East India Company lost its monopoly, and the export of Norwich camlets ceased; or rather Norwich was driven out of the field by inferior Yorkshire camlets produced at nearly half the price, a difference Norwich could not overcome by quality. The city was not well located to cope with a decline, given the new economic geography of the country, so costs were necessarily higher than in the north. The West Riding moved ahead by leaps and bounds in the application of machinery, whereas in 1839 Norwich had only a few power looms in its factories. As so often happened, the old-established centre gave way to the brash upstart without preconceptions or vested interests. Asked to explain the Norwich decline, one manufacturer told the commissioners in 1839 that it was party politics; a man who dared to encourage the introduction of machinery would at once run foul of the radicalism of the town. Finally, there was that *deus ex machina* of so many passages in economic history, a change in fashion.

Thomas Martineau's business had felt the burden of the war, and in the crash of 1825–26, the firm was caught with a heavy inventory which dropped to about half its value. He was overdrawn to the limit at the bank, he had to ask the relatives and friends to whom he was in debt for an extension of time, and an order in December 1825 for twenty pieces of goods only momentarily brightened his depression. Miss Martineau recalled his hair turning white and his having to face the sad task of changing his will to reduce his daughters' portions. At the same time, he was found to be suffering from an incurable liver ailment, from which he died in the spring of 1826. After his death, the family kept their money in the firm which had managed to weather the crisis, but it finally failed in 1829, leaving them for a short while close to penniless and throwing Harriet onto her twin resources of needle and pen.[1]

In later years, Miss Martineau would often underline the authority with which she spoke on economics by saying that, as a manufacturer's daughter, she *knew* how things were, and much

[1] HM to James, December 16 and 22, 1825, January 12 and February 7, 1826, MCO. *Auto.*, i, 97–99.

in her later attitude can easily be traced back to Norwich experience. "I remember," she says, "my father's bringing in the news of some of the Peninsular victories, and what his face was like when he told my mother of the increase of the Income-Tax to ten per cent, and again, of the removal of the Income-Tax." [1] Memories of that sort are likely to be very deep. Her brothers teased her about her preternatural wisdom when she lectured the family on the National Debt after having read about it at school. Cobbett came to Norwich and carried on the hustings a series of resolutions to appropriate Church and Crown endowments for paying the debt, to abolish pensions, and, above all, to remit taxation—a series of resolutions which must have been actively discussed in the family, and the true state of the case worked out.[2] The family newspaper, the *Globe*, as she recalled later, taught her political economy long before she knew what it was, and things discussed in the *Globe*, say in 1825–26, were certainly discussed at home, particularly with her brother Henry who took over the settlement of the business.

Moreover, one can never say that she was ignorant or unconscious of working-class problems, as it can be said, for example, of Evangelical families like the Thorntons, who, in the world of high finance, saw almost nothing of the working classes and could not take in what they did see.[3] In 1811–21 the population of Norwich increased from 37,000 to 50,000, with the influx from the surrounding county. Emigration overseas was a long-established East Anglian tradition, and there are a good many instances of long-distance migration. Thomas Cubitt, a Norfolkman originally, recruited labour in Norfolk for London building; weavers went, apparently in one jump, to the West Riding for obvious reasons; and for less obvious ones Norfolkmen turned up in a North Derbyshire colliery in the forties. But migration at first is likely to be short-distance, to the nearest town; so the immediate impact of redundant population on the land was on Norwich itself, with the usual results of overcrowding, sanitary difficulties, educational problems, and disturbances to the peace. When Miss Martineau talked in the forties about working-class conditions as town problems not wage problems, she certainly had some awareness of town problems; it is not surprising that she supported the interventionist work of Chadwick and the

[1] *Auto.*, i, 60. [2] *Hist.*, i, 323.
[3] E. M. Forster, *Marianne Thornton*, pp. 53–54.

sanitary reformers, writing specifically to Norwich to get it publicized there.[1]

Norwich also helped to form her views on questions of wages and trade union activity. The Norwich manufacturer who explained the decline of the city by the refusal of labour and its political allies to accept essential technological innovations, had the full agreement of Miss Martineau. When the first steamboat appeared on the river only to blow up, the weavers looked wise and said that steam could not do all that, while the rest harangued against newfangled inventions. It was the frequency of strikes, as she saw it, that ruined the worsted manufactures there. In this oversimplification she was drawing on recollections from her youth. In 1826, she wrote that

> the unemployed weavers, who could not take work at the wages which the manufacturers could afford, kept a watch at the city gates for goods brought in from the country. They destroyed one cartload in the street, and threw the cart into the river; broke the manufacturers' windows; cooped in a public-house three men from the country who had silk canes about them; and kept the magistracy busy and alarmed for some weeks. About 12,000 weavers in Norwich were then unemployed, and the whole city in a state of depression, the more harassing from its contrast with the activity and high hope of the preceding year.

In 1833 it was the same sort of thing. When some of the manufacturers, worried about soaring poor rates, got with great trouble and difficulty a portion of the East India Company's camlet order for Norwich, the weavers considered the offer of work for several days and a good many declined on the ground that it was not worth giving up their parish pay for. The same answer was given to another manufacturer who introduced a new fabric. Although Miss Martineau came ultimately to a remarkably just view of the aims of trade union activity, memories like these underlay her bitter attacks on strikes, like the Builders' Strike of 1859, which seemed to her misguided and cruel. Interestingly enough, her analysis of the struggle of employer and employed

[1] HM to R. M. Bacon, November 14 [1842], Cambridge, Add. Mss 6247. Norwich poor relief was vested in a Court of Guardians set up by an act of 1712; the whole city was one parish for the purpose of poor relief—an interesting early effort at the kind of reform she was to publicize in 1834. As a result of the rapid rise of expenditure for the poor from an average of £20,000 to over £50,000 in 1826, a new act in 1827 reconstituted the Court of Guardians and abolished the assessment on stocks and personal estates which had hitherto been levied. *Gen. Hist. of Norfolk*, pp. 1314–16.

as an extension of the Saxon-Norman feud is a clear legacy of a radical tradition coming down from the seventeenth century.[1] A sharp distinction must be made, of course, between the radical programme which she inherited and the wider, inchoate, and ominous popular radicalism. Hers was a manufacturer's radicalism, the rationalization of a growing power and the justification of its continuance. It was dogmatic (and to some extent with reason) about the economy; in politics it was liberal. Norwich committed her to both positions.

Mrs. Taylor had danced about the cap of liberty with Dr. Parr in the nineties. When Miss Alderson (later Mrs. Opie) visited London in revolutionary times, she went to Daniel Isaac Eaton's "shop of sedition" and attended the state trials which, had they not issued in acquittals, might well have led her father to emigrate to America. Thomas Martineau, Dr. Reeve, and other dissenters were charged in 1806 with wanting to burn the cathedral as a beacon to guide the invading French. Mr. Madge, the minister at the Octagon, was a great radical.[2]

There is no portion of Miss Martineau's great *History of the Thirty Years' Peace* written with more intensity and conviction than that dealing with the ascendancy of George Canning.[3] To liberal opinion at the time, it was Canning's "adoption of more liberal views", his rejection of the Holy Alliance, and his support of liberal movements on the Continent and in Latin America that marked the turning away from the post-war repression to reform.[4] Canning, too, must have been a rather special hero to the Norwich circle, for when he was a boy at Eton, he used to visit Norwich to stay with an aunt, and Mrs. Opie recalled how a companion of hers had reprimanded the brilliant

[1] *DN*, April 2 and July 23, 1859. *Hist.*, i, 369. HM to Brougham, [February, 1833], UCL. The Saxon-Norman notion appears in *How to Observe*, pp. 196–97 and in her article on domestic service, *WR*, xxxi, 218–32 (July, 1838).

[2] Ross, *Three Generations*, p. 21. Brightwell, *Memorials*, pp. 42–53, 110–14. HM to Reeve, June 24, 1858. Drummond, *James Martineau*, i, 12–14.

[3] She was dispirited by the immensity of the task of writing the *History* until she came to write about a passage of Canning's eloquence, when she knew she was really interested in the job, and her difficulties passed away. *Auto*, ii, 18.

[4] W. E. Channing to Lucy Aikin, June 22, 1831, *Corr.*, p. 71. "Metternich", *Biog. Sketches*, p. 419. That the liberal dissenters were not entirely disinterested in the economic results of his policies is neatly indicated by the investment made by Mr. Madge, the Octagon minister, in Mexican shares. He made £1200 out of it and could have made more had he waited longer before selling. But the taste of success was a dangerous one; he re-invested and lost his money in the crash of 1825. HM to James, February 5, September 11, October 1, and 12, 1825, MCO.

and already famous youngster for talking during a concert.[1] Mrs. Opie and the circle probably let no one forget this, for, even by adoption, "there is always a Norwich man concerned in all great events".

To the dissenters there was one inexplicable mystery about Canning—that with all his enlightenment in foreign affairs, his friendship with Huskisson, and his championship of Catholic Emancipation, he should have stood fast against the claims of the dissenters.[2] It was the one blot on the shield. But to Miss Martineau, Canning seemed the great spokesman for principle—a paragon of intelligent political action, to whose position Peel was successor and Disraeli the worst but far from the only traitor.

> When war is over—(the critical period which admits the rule of the statesman's will)—an organic state succeeds, wherein all individual will succumbs to the working of general laws. The statesman can then no longer be a political hero, over-ruling influences and commanding events. He only can be a statesman in the new days who is the servant of principles—the agent of the great natural laws of society. . . . Amidst the difficulty and perplexity of such changes, a whole nation may be heard calling out for a great political hero, and complaining that all its statesmen have grown small and feeble: but it is not that the men have deteriorated, but that the polity is growing visibly organic; and a different order of men is required to administer its affairs.[3]

Joined with Canning was Huskisson, who also held to principles, even though he had to apply them piece-meal, "to open his hand . . . one finger at a time, because the people or their rulers could not receive a whole handful of the truth about Free Trade".[4] Canning stood for freedom and non-intervention abroad, Huskisson for freedom and non-intervention at home. And he and Robinson lowered taxes. How could they be anything but heroes (of the new order) to the family of a tax-conscious manufacturer who took in the *Globe*?

But Canning and Huskisson were more than wise and new-fashioned statesmen. They were admired not only for what they *did*, but for what they *were*. Both of them were attacked as "new men", who had come from nowhere, slandered as illegitimate, and despised as adventurers. Yet how much better they were than their detractors.

[1] Brightwell, *Memorials*, pp. 363–65.
[2] *Hist.*, i, 393–94.
[3] *Hist.*, i, 317–18. Cf. E. Halévy, *History of the English People*, ii, 174–75, 188, 210.
[4] "George Combe", *Biog. Sketches*, p. 143.

> Canning was one of whom it might be said, according to ordinary notions, that he ought to have been a nobleman. High-spirited, confident, gay, genial, chivalrous, and most accomplished,—he had the attributes of nobility, as they are commonly conceived of: and a nobleman he was,—for he had genius. He held high rank in Nature's peerage. But this was not distinction enough in the eyes of some of his colleagues.[1]

Again, there must have been pride, spoken and unspoken, in Magdalen Street. Miss Martineau in 1832 wrote that the poor were superior to the son of an aristocratic household, for they had a power that came from a knowledge of reality, in contrast to his conventional ignorance of it; yet the poor could make no use of their knowledge—because of ignorance and unpreparedness their power was scanty and unfruitful, forever directed to laying a foundation on which nothing could rise.

> This is better than building pagodas of cards on a slippery surface like the lordling; but it is not the final purpose for which the human intellect was made constructive. . . . The most efficacious experience of reality must be looked for in the class above the lowest, and in individuals of higher classes still, fewer and fewer in proportion to the elevation of rank, till the fatal boundary of pure convention be reached, within which genius cannot live except in the breast of one here and there, who is stout-hearted enough to break bounds, and play truant in the regions of reality.[2]

The manufacturers and their daughters were going to inherit the earth—a prospect that hardly makes for meekness.

[1] *Hist.*, i, 319. *Once a Week*, July 6 and August 17, 1861.
[2] "Genius of Scott", *Misc.*, i, 3–4.

CHAPTER III

Norwich: Priestley's Disciple

NORWICH, then, provided two conditions of her radicalism, one stemming from its economy and the social problems it engendered, the other arising from her position in the liberal, educated, and ambitious manufacturing middle class. The third condition lies in Unitarianism. Here Miss Martineau as a commentator in the fifties is not much help. She acknowledged a debt, but she was so impressed by her rejection of revelation and Unitarian doctrine that her ultimate obligation was not entirely clear to her. It could easily seem to her that her new outlook grew from the spirit of the times or from the incontrovertible facts of the constitution of the universe and the human mind. But spirit and incontrovertible facts came to her through Unitarianism.

Religion was the consolation and joy of her childhood. She made a book of biblical precepts when she was eight, and she played at preaching sermons. But when she became a young woman, the childish things were put away, and she became deeply concerned with theology, a natural interest for anyone with an intellectual bent in the early nineteenth century. She devoted herself to her studies with remarkable energy and enthusiasm. Conventional piety and religious emotion, though present, were not enough: she had a tough mind, too tough eventually for her religion, yet fundamentally formed—and toughened—by it.

The Unitarians were, said Priestley, "a sect everywhere spoken against". When he compared them with the early Christians, he had strong personal evidence, for the parallel was drawn in a sermon he preached at the Gravel Pit Meeting House, Hackney, after the Birmingham mob had burned his house and library. Pursued on all sides, excluded from toleration until 1813, the Unitarians had grievances against the civil power which went far beyond those normal to the dissenting interest, while they carried with them certain intellectual qualities which heightened the discrimination. Their ancestry was Presbyterian, but in the confusion following the ejection of the nonconformist divines from the Establishment in 1662, the Presbyterians were deeply affected by the beginnings of modern science and by rationalism, which carried them (like some elements in the Church) through the half-way house of Arianism to a final avowal at the end of the eighteenth century of Christ's simple humanity.[1]

Any beleaguered group develops certain characteristics directly arising from persecution.[2] If the group is composed of intellectuals, the characteristics are likely to be especially striking —and Unitarianism was attractive to a great many intellectuals. Any group excluded from power and prestige is likely in time to make a virtue of exclusion, to find a moral superiority in the socially or politically inferior position they must occupy. Among the Unitarians this phenomenon took several forms, one of which was a strong tendency to political radicalism.

The developing reform movements from the time of John Wilkes and the American Revolution were enthusiastically supported by dissenters. Priestley predicted in 1789 that Pitt would lose the dissenters to Fox, and he was right. It was a Unitarian, Dr. Richard Price, whose sermon touched off the magnificent fireworks of the *Reflections on the Revolution in France*.[3] And the radicalism of the Octagon at Norwich was uncompromising.

> Our pastor was a great radical; and he used to show us the caricas tures of the day (Hone's, I think) in which Castlereagh was alway- flogging Irishmen, and Canning spouting froth, and the Regent insulting his wife, and the hungry, haggard multitude praying for vengeance on the Court and the Ministers; and every Sunday night, after supper, when he and two or three other bachelor friends were with us, the talk was of the absolute certainty of a dire revolution. When, on my return from Bristol in 1819, I ventured to say what my conscience bade me say, and what I had been led to see by a dear aunt, that it was wrong to catch up and believe and spread reports injurious to the royal family, who could not reply to slander like other people, I was met by a shout of derision at first,

[1] This transition is brilliantly traced in Olive M. Griffiths, *Religion and Learning*, a book which was much used in writing this chapter. The development is also sketched in the first chapter of Francis E. Mineka, *The Dissidence of Dissent*. See also Herbert McLachlan, *The Unitarian Movement in the Religious Life of England*.

[2] Some strikingly relevant comment appears in G. Kitson Clark, *The English Inheritance*, p. 128.

[3] Anthony Lincoln, *Some Political & Social Ideas of English Dissent*, pp. 1–65.

and then by a serious reprimand for my immorality in making more allowance for royal sinners than for others.[1]

The moral defence against the enemy in power—particularly among the Unitarians—invariably took the form of an appeal to principles, and the more exasperated the situation became, the more shrill and insistent was the appeal. It was extraordinary, wrote the young Harriet, to look back on the dissenters of a century and a half before. They objected to specific hardships visited upon them, but no "common principle of action" could be derived from their protests. To the Occasional Conformity Act they opposed, not the fundamental wrong of penalties against conscience or the errors of an Establishment, but only the difficulties and desertions of their own sects. Against tyranny they would rebel, but they never investigated the origin of the power that oppressed them or questioned the legitimacy of uniting the civil and ecclesiastical powers.[2] We can see now that it was precisely the narrowness and expediency that allowed the compromises of the eighteenth century to emerge: the annual Indemnity Acts would assuredly never have passed, had fundamentals been questioned. But then we are not now members of a sect everywhere spoken against, and we see things differently.

The exasperation of the dissenting position increased in all directions after 1790. The compromises of the eighteenth century would not do. The political and social claims of Dissent were bound up with wider demands in a society whose internal boundaries were crumbling. The Establishment came under a powerful attack, helped on by the hostility of the Bishops to the Reform Bill. The universities were besieged, when the Dissenting Academies of the eighteenth century would or could no longer serve. Dissenters rioted against church rates and proclaimed "no compromise" on national education. On these scores Unitarians and other nonconformists could join.[3]

This legacy of an excluded and radical Dissent is central in

[1] *Auto.*, i, 61. Hone wrote a number of parodies; the brilliant caricatures which accompanied them were by Cruikshank.

[2] "Calamy's Life", *MR*, v, 90–92 (February, 1830). W. E. Channing to Lucy Aikin, July 10, 1841, *Corr.*, p. 401. But compare Kitson Clark, *English Inheritance*, pp. 116–21.

[3] "A gentleman who had been canvassing Liverpool for your friend Thornely was repeatedly told by Methodists and Calvinistic Dissenters, 'We are willing to vote for a Unitarian because he will be reasonable about the Church.' A fearful sign for the Establishment when foes league against her." Lucy Aikin to W. E. Channing, October 23, 1831, *Corr.*, p. 99.

Harriet Martineau's early periodical writings. When she moves in on the Establishment, the confidence and excellence of the polemic is almost a shock, after the uncertainties and priggishness of her philosophical and moral writings. To abhor Rome and lambaste Canterbury was part of the birthright of every nonconformist. And the Unitarians were particularly concerned with the maintenance of true principles.

In a sermon preached in 1790, the Reverend Thomas Belsham held up truth as sacred and inviolable and declared it the indispensable duty of all "to *bear testimony to it* by diligent enquiry after it, courageous profession of it, faithful adherence to it, and by using every fair and honourable means of promoting its progress in the world".[1] This profession was to be made no matter what the contumely or what the suffering: "... the confessor who voluntarily renounces ease and opulence, and dignity, that he may devote himself to the propagation of truth; and the martyr who with joy embraces the stake rather than renounce his principles" might be objects of stupid wonder to the mob, but they were the examples to follow. To the Unitarians, self-dramatizing out of all proportion, Priestley had suffered in his way as Servetus had done. The sacrifice of everything for truth and the ideal of martyrdom form a natural mode for intellectuals under attack; it had some strange effects on Harriet Martineau.

The notion of martyrdom aside, Unitarians thought themselves better fitted than anyone else resolutely to pursue and proclaim truth. No people were so useless for petty sectarian purposes, said W. J. Fox, none so strong for general good. Their faith, taken positively, consists of the

> great and universally allowed principles of religion and morality. Of these principles, therefore, they are the natural advocates; of these principles in all their boundless and beneficent application to the concerns of public and private life, or national and individual conduct, of politics, literature, art, philosophy, and the condition of society. This advocacy is their mission, and I verily believe that they will flourish or fall, as they ought, in proportion as it is discharged or neglected.[2]

So Harriet Martineau:

> The duty of the Christian teacher is to declare what he apprehends

[1] *The Importance of Truth.*

[2] "A Letter to the Rev. — —", *MR*, vii, 348, quoted in Mineka, *Dissidence of Dissent*, pp. 257–58.

> to be "the whole counsel of God;" not bit by bit, at random;—now a portion of doctrine, and now a piece of practical instruction, separated from the fundamental principles on which all sound doctrine and good practice are founded; but in the first place to ascertain those principles, then to announce them and afterwards to assist his hearers in applying them to the rectification of their souls, to the guidance of their external, and the invigoration of their internal life.[1]

The sunshine itself, she said, "is not more universal in its vivifying influence than the luminary of truth".[2] She could tolerate no compromise, and no institution could stand in the way. There is fire in her discussion of the Establishment and Dissent in the *History*; the conflict remained a central concern to the end of her life; and her opinion on it was fixed firmly by the time she was thirty.

In an article dealing with a book by Archbishop Whately, she set out an attack and a programme. The worst kind of fraud, she said, is the pious fraud, a species the history of which is to be found complete in the annals of every incorporated religious class, whether in Rome, or Scotland, or England. As to the Church of England, she wrote in 1832,

> There is pious fraud involved in her plea for her gains. She connives at pious fraud in all the distinctions she originates between the clergy and the laity, and sets a premium upon it wherever she offers privileges or emoluments which have for their condition a certain profession of faith. Could the minds of our British clergy be laid open as the minds of Christian men should be, how many real churchmen would be found among them? Set aside those who have no opinions on their faith at all, and those who will have none; those who stifle their own instincts after truth, and those who pervert them; set aside the tri-theists, and the Unitarians, (equally condemned by the Athanasian Creed:) set aside the Arians, and Sabellians, and Deists,—set aside those who pledge themselves to the Articles without thinking, or in spite of thought, those who fear to speak heresy, and those who quietly inculcate heresy,—all in short, who would not in God's presence say amen to the Common Prayer Book, from beginning to end, and how many remain? None of these have a right to the privileges of the church on her own conditions; and though we will not say that a large proportion of them are not really blind, we cannot but think that a strong temptation is held out to them to shut their eyes. We will allege against the church, in this particular, only what she herself admits; that there

[1] "Tayler's Sermon", *MR*, iv, 530 (August, 1830).

[2] "Essays on the Art of Thinking", vi, *Misc.*, i, 112–13. Cf. Bailey, *Publication of Opinions*, p. 120, and Paley, *Principles*, book vi, ch. x.

> is a diversity of opinion within her pale, while her emoluments are offered on a supposition of uniformity of opinion. This she will not deny; and this is enough. By her own confession, she sets a premium on hypocrisy. She does not, like the Romish church, cajole the crowd with mummeries, and saints with false promises, and sinners with false threats, and devotees with a jugglery of the imagination. She does not do this because she cannot. But what she can, she does; for she is possessed with her own branch of the family of Legion. She allegorizes, and prevaricates, and mystifies, and coaxes, and frowns, and does every thing but speak out, and make her servants tell the whole truth. There may be some who fathom her meaning, and swear faithfully to it, and do good service accordingly. It is well; let them be rewarded. But there are others who swear to her in one sense, and serve in another. They serve, however, and are rewarded. There are yet others, who shake their heads about her meaning, but do her bidding: they are to be rewarded of course. But what is to be done with the class who neither understand nor serve? Why, if they *say* they understand, let them come in for their share. And this is not encouraging deceit for the credit of the church! What then *is* pious fraud?

If Whately himself would follow out the dictates of his liberal and candid spirit, he should resign his archbishopric "and preach the gospel in a plain coat. . . ." How much more useful he would be out of the Church! For only when the spiritual is severed from connection with the temporal can the glorious office of the Christian teacher be realized. The cotter, "leading the Saturday night's devotions of his family, is greater in his office than the archbishop preaching amidst the state of his thronged cathedral; and the enlightened dissenting minister is more exalted than either", for he combines the rectitude and freedom of the cotter with the privilege of the prelate "of looking back into the records of all religions and tracing the common source of all their abuses. . . ." [1]

Nor was the duty simply to a congregation. Unitarians, she said, following Fox's sentiments, have an ever-widening range of activity open to them, as professors of all truth: they must "in-treat" their religious adversaries, because they are "defamed"; they must develop to their own members "the consequences of the principles to which they assent"; and finally, it is their peculiar duty to make known to "philosophical unbelievers" what

[1] "Romanism and Episcopacy", *MR*, vi, 381–92, *Misc.*, ii, 132–50. "Salem Witchcraft", *MR*, vi, 545–55, *Misc.*, ii, 389–90. This attitude to the problem of subscription is parallel to opinions expressed in Samuel Bailey, *Essay on Opinions*, pp. 72–73, and, interestingly, Paley, *Principles*, book vi, chapter x, though of course his conclusions are different.

Christianity can be when it is rid of superstition, to help them "to a participation in our joy".[1] When in 1830 the Unitarian Association offered prizes for essays to convert Catholics, Mohammedans, and Jews to Unitarianism, it was no accident that Harriet Martineau won all three. It was her first national, if still sectarian, triumph.

This high mission of truth was not directed solely against the Church and unbelievers. The Unitarians were *everywhere* spoken against, even by other dissenters. "Stretch out thine arm, thou Triune God!" sang the Methodists, "*the Unitarian fiend* expel, and chase his doctrines back to Hell." And while, in the eighteenth century, the Unitarians' triumph over Calvinism and its "gloomy doctrines" seemed to presage a wider victory, in the nineteenth century the rationalists were thrown on to the defensive by the resurgence of enthusiasm in the powerful, proliferating Evangelical movement. Unitarians were separated from the Evangelicals in manners, as we have already seen, and even more crucially on intellectual matters.[2] It must have taken all the confident optimism of which they were capable to withstand the dismal conclusion suggested by the "enthusiastical cant" of the Methodists, not to mention the fanaticism of the followers of Joanna Southcott or Edward Irving. Harriet Martineau's anti-Evangelicalism is complete: to her Cowper was a mere slave to God, John Newton, his friend and the inspirer of Clapham, a spiritual tyrant. To a rationalist believing in the inescapable working of natural law, the doctrine of an interruptive providence was contemptible, intellectually and morally; hence her malice against a man like Michael Sadler, who answered Malthus by saying merely that God would take care of his own. Her opposition to such "misguided humanitarians" was grounded as much on religion and philosophy as on political economy. Hence, too, her insistence on the importance of investigating the credentials of the persons proclaiming miracles: miracles remained essential in the Unitarian scheme as a divine proof of God's mission conferred on the human Jesus; but they were not to be expected in the modern world from every Tom, Dick, Harry, or Joanna possessed of a divine mission.[3] Perhaps it would be just to say that

[1] "Aspland's Sermons", *MR*, v, 20–21 (January, 1831).

[2] See above, p. 46. HM's opinions of Wilberforce and Hannah More are in *Hist.*, ii, 131. The Methodist hymn is quoted in Mineka, *Dissidence of Dissent*, p. 19.

[3] "On Nature and Providence to Communities", *Misc.*, ii, 269–75. "Hull's Discourses", *MR*, iv, 590–94 (September, 1830).

it was more against other dissenters than against the Church that Unitarianism asserted its particular system of knowledge.

Although the Unitarians insisted that their theology was derived directly from the Bible, they were far from believing that every minor point of faith or morality, let alone a knowledge of the external world, could be explained from biblical precepts. As Harriet Martineau wrote in 1830, "it is now time to discover what is the essence of that faith and the principle of that practice",[1] something to be done by the exercise of reason. The new light had appeared in the seventeenth century and grew in brilliance. According to Belsham, Bacon and Boyle, Locke and Newton, Clarke and Hartley were "names which will be dear to science and to virtue as long as the world endures".

> We who enjoy the benefit of that resplendent light which their admired and immortal writings have diffused over the philosophical, the political and the moral world, see the errors of our forefathers, we revere these heroes of science, these champions of truth, of liberty and virtue, as the best friends and benefactors of mankind, we are proud of calling them our countrymen, and the latest posterity will pronounce their names with veneration and gratitude.[2]

In this sense, the Unitarians were thoroughly impregnated with the basic convictions of the Enlightenment.

The life of Newton published by the Society for the Diffusion of Useful Knowledge gained the whole-hearted approbation of Harriet Martineau, despite her dim views of biography in general, and in her comments something of the admiration appears:

> It is not probable that equal success would attend the same method [in writing biography] in any other case: for such a subject as Newton can no where else be found. There is no other man whose life approached so nearly to a pure abstraction. No other man was perhaps, so free from the entanglements of various pursuits, from the intricacies of social relations, from the inconsistencies of jarring passions and irreconcilable desires. Every other man's life, external and internal, is a system of checks and counterchecks; and in proportion to the balance of these checks is the happiness of his lot, and the perfection of his soul. But Newton started off almost from his birth into a lofty career where there was neither opposition nor drawback. . . .[3]

[1] "Tayler's Sermon", *MR*, iv, 531 (August, 1830).

[2] *The Importance of Truth*, pp. 6–8. The worship of Locke, so foreign to our order of enthusiasm, is neatly indicated in two letters of Sarah Austin, one to Cousin, one to Guizot, in 1850, on the Austins' visit to Locke's tomb. Ross, *Three Generations*, pp. 250–53.

[3] "Doddridge's Correspondence", *Misc.*, ii, 347. This is also an interesting and

Newton's achievement entranced a great many men of the eighteenth century and sent them scurrying in every direction to apply his methods in fields far removed from mechanics.[1] In the popular triumph of the "Newtonian" approach, the tension-ridden, voluntaristic universe of the Middle Ages gave way to a mechanical universe, moving by inertia not will, and hierarchy was supplanted by a linear succession of cause and effect. In most philosophic minds, wrote Harriet Martineau,

> ideas are classed in the order of Cause and Effect. In this manner alone can the true relations of things be ascertained: by this method alone can our experience be made useful to us, or our present circumstances become conducive to our future good. Though we have no knowledge of the nature of the connexion between causes and effects, and can only reason from the fact that certain antecedents have invariable consequents, it is plain that without a distinct apprehension of this truth, there can be no real knowledge. This distinct apprehension, in the mind of the most ignorant of mankind, will produce rational conduct, in so far as its influence extends: while its obscurity may subject the profound philosopher to error at which he will hereafter stand astonished.[2]

Newton and the scientists provided not only the challenge and the concepts, but the method. The more enthusiastic and less sophisticated devotees of the Enlightenment, including the Rational Dissenters, insisted on an equivalent certainty in other fields of enquiry; the result is that their writings are full of references to observed facts, hypotheses, and the certainty of Euclid's demonstrations. The principles of which they talked in every field were, to them, scientific truths, scientifically derived.

Our fault in the past, Harriet Martineau said, which has led to so many dreadful errors, has been ignorance of the true principles of philosophizing.

> Either explicitly or unconsciously, we form a theory, and (as we all like our own theories) we make all circumstances bend to it, and all our observations go to support it.

---

significant ideal for biography! But to her biography was didactic, and it is easier to teach if adventitious circumstances are out of the way. She wrote a leading article on Newton, *DN*, September 21, 1858.

[1] James was able, before he left the College in York, "to attain the great object of my ambition,—the reading of Newton's 'Principia' ", Drummond, *James Martineau*, i, 34.

[2] " Essays on the Art of Thinking, iii," *Misc.*, i, 78. Cf. Bailey, *Publication of Opinions*, p. 189.

The old philosophers formed theories, searched the facts, and then looked for some place to appeal. Where?

> No one knew; so the philosophical world was divided among jarring factions, till Bacon published the right method of discovering truth, which has caused philosophy to advance with rapid strides, and a new light to dawn on the world of science. This principle is so simple that it seems extraordinary that it should not sooner have been adopted; and yet so vast in its operation, that attempts to estimate its effects are vain. This method is to bring together an accumulation of facts previous to the formation of a theory; and having carefully observed their bearing upon a particular point, to deduce [a slip] from them a principle which may be applied to the explanation of new facts. Had Newton lived before Bacon, he might have formed an erroneous theory of optics, and have been confirmed in it by a partial observation of facts; but he drank deeply of the spirit of the new philosophy, and by it regulated his inquiries. . . . In like manner must science continue to advance, and the mysteries of nature be unravelled. In like manner must we all, if our object be truth, conduct every inquiry. And if tempted to smile at thus comparing great things with small, the researches of a Newton with the feeble efforts of intellects puny as ours, let us remember that if an object be worth pursuing at all, it is worth pursuing in the best way.[1]

Her answer was not less fervent for being over-simple and parochial.

It was necessary to give up what she denounced as empiricism —the unsystematic floundering about amid facts, with outknowing what to do, without a theory as guide.

> When a general principle has been satisfactorily established, it is to be applied to the elucidation of such facts as may admit of an explanation by it. If no general principles were known, the multiplicity of facts which we must register as the materials of knowledge would be too burdensome for any mind. . . . The method of generalization has let in light upon this darkness, and originated a well-founded and animating conviction that the meridian splendour of unclouded truth is not too dazzling for the human intellect.
>
> By reference of a number of facts to one principle, to which they bear a common relation, order is introduced into the midst of confusion, and the understanding is required to entertain a few well-arranged ideas only, instead of a confused multitude. When facts are thus classed under general principles, the memory is relieved, the judgment unfettered, and the imagination rendered duly subservient to the reasoning power. The commander of an army

[1] "Art of Thinking, ii", *Misc.*, i, 71–72.

> would be hopeless of preserving discipline, if the conduct of every soldier were under his unassisted charge. The forces are therefore divided into regiments, battalions, and companies, under their respective officers; and thus unity is established among a multitude of individuals, and a countless host is subject to the control of one man.[1]

It is to Miss Martineau's credit that she saw the dangers in this method.

> It is the tendency of our minds to become too firmly attached to a theory deduced by ourselves, especially when well-founded. We should be on our guard, therefore, to apply it to that class of objects alone to which it relates. To stretch one theory to the explanation of every class of facts is as fruitful a source of error as to apply half a dozen theories to the explanation of so many similar appearances. To this error those are most liable whose range of inquiry is contracted, who love truth, but have little leisure or opportunity for study. . . . While our observation of facts is very limited, a small portion of philosophical knowledge may be sufficient to account for them; but if we seek to extend our range, we must be careful that our minds are so disciplined as to receive new ideas without prejudice, that they are strengthened for the formation of new conceptions, prepared to apply well-known truths in their proper places, and to leave them behind when we enter on unexplored and extended regions.[2]

Hence the highly intelligent remarks we have already noticed on the foolishness of demanding consistency in detail; but on the other hand she denounced John Stuart Mill as a weak thinker because he did not hold fast to a position.[3]

While there is an undeniable truth in the contention that theory is necessary in order to observe, there is also the undeniable danger that a self-conscious concentration on theory and method will lead inevitably to the pitfalls which she so clearly descried and all too seldom avoided. The revelation of a seemingly sovereign method, filtering down from the great minds, had captivated the amateurs. The Rational Dissenters and Miss Martineau were not its only devoted practitioners: it lies behind the dogma of the political economists, the historical laws of Buckle, and the "scientific" analysis of Karl Marx.

Alongside the sovereign method was a thoroughly mechanistic

[1] "Art of Thinking, v", *Misc.*, i, 106. So Whately, lecturing at Oxford on political economy, could urge careful attention to forming right theories, lest the mind be drawn off from truth to classes of facts which would only confuse the issue. *Introduction to Political Economy*, pp. 11–13.

[2] "Art of Thinking, ii", *Misc.*, i, 73–74.

[3] See above, p. 34.

and linear psychology. The sensationalism of Thomas Hobbes—resulting, significantly, from his attempt to reduce the explanation of all phenomena, physical, mental, and political, to motion—was refined by John Locke. Locke insisted that the mind was blank at birth. From the stimulus of external objects conveyed through the senses came simple ideas which the mind formed into compound ideas by the process of association.

Locke seems to have raised more problems for his successors than most seminal thinkers. Of these the most important was the relationship between the mind and the external world. Berkeley, like Descartes earlier, solved this problem by relying on God's intervention. But David Hume was more disturbing. He said that if we know only what comes to us through the senses, then all knowledge is essentially subjective and a certain knowledge of an external world is impossible. With particularly devastating effect, Hume applied his scepticism to the assumptions about the necessity of causality which seemed to these enthusiasts to lie at the base of the whole Newtonian system. The corrosiveness of scepticism extended then to the possibility of a secure science, to the necessary foundation of morality, and perhaps worst of all, to the existence of God. Hume recognized the problems that his relentless if genial mind raised, and found his resource in habit and custom: that is, we have always seen B follow A, and so we act in the expectation that B will follow A tomorrow, though we have no certain knowledge that it will do so. So too morality reduces to what is customary.

It is impossible for us now to realize the awful impact which this criticism had on many of Hume's contemporaries. We are thoroughly imbued with relativism in culture and morality; we are quite accustomed to complementarity and indeterminacy in physics; we are perfectly ready to see current scientific interpretations jettisoned as others have been in the past. The conventional seems remarkably adequate to the twentieth century; to the eighteenth it was not so. The desire for security was as strong intellectually as it was politically. To the radicals and liberals, the security of science was indispensable as a foundation for the new structure they wanted to build; convention smacked too much of Toryism. To the Tories (and many Liberals), on the other hand, the corrosion destroyed the guarantees of their security—faith in God and in an inescapable moral order. Hume wanted literary fame; he at least got notoriety.

There were perhaps three main responses to Hume, all aimed at reintroducing certainty. One was to deny that Lockean assumptions necessarily led to scepticism, that is, to vindicate scientific method by tagging Hume a perverter of it. A second was the product of Scotland, the "common sense" school growing out of the teachings of Hutcheson and Reid, and culminating in the work of Dugald Stewart. This school posited the existence in the mind of a number of "faculties", which might be subsumed under the sovereign faculty of "common sense", which tells us that, whatever doubts might be raised, there is an external world. The Scots, in short, seemed to introduce a fundamental quarrel with the *tabula rasa* of Locke, as it appears to most of his readers. A third solution was provided by Immanuel Kant and his followers, since the chill wind of Hume's criticism had penetrated even to Königsberg. Kant accepted the impossibility of knowledge of things in themselves, and found his security in the forms imposed by the mind on impressions.

The last solution is of no importance to the present study. Kantian influence was slow in coming to England. Thomas Belsham in his work on mental science explained that he would say nothing about Kant, for he had tried him and could make nothing of it.[1] Coleridge did his best, but most people professed to be unable to understand him either, as Peacock's devastating portrait of Mr. Glowry shows. And Channing, although he declared he would be delighted to hear of any irruption of Kantism into England, had no very high hopes of its success.[2] It is manifest that, much as Harriet Martineau admired Channing, his propaganda for the "intellectual philosophy" touched her not at all.[3]

The challenge of the Scottish school was taken seriously, but hardly understood. Using a rollicking critical style he later came to regret, Priestley flayed Reid, Beattie, and Oswald in turn, accusing them of reintroducing the innate ideas which he thought had been effectively thrown out by Locke, and of dethroning reason.[4] This remained basically the attitude of the Rational Dissenters to the Scots.[5] To be sure, the school was recognized

[1] Griffiths, *Religion and Learning*, p. 159,

[2] W. E. Channing to Lucy Aikin, December 31, 1829, *Corr.*, pp. 43–44.

[3] *Auto.*, i, 81.

[4] *Remarks on Dr. Reid's Inquiry, Dr. Beattie's Essay and Dr. Oswald's Appeal*, 1774, *Works*.

[5] See, for example, Speculation V, "Is Human Nature endowed with a Common

to have some virtues, particularly Dugald Stewart. Stewart is quoted extensively and admiringly, for instance, in the *Principles of Education* by Lant Carpenter, the Bristol Unitarian minister who was a chief inspirer of the young Harriet's intellectual and religious career. And in her autobiography she says that she enjoyed the Scotch school in spite of Priestley's contempt, but never believed in it.[1] She found Stewart charming and could not subject him to the pertness with which she treated Reid and Beattie, for "the truth of detail scattered through [his] elegant elucidations, the gentle and happy spirit, and the beautiful style, charmed me so much that I must have been among his most affectionate disciples, if I had not been fortified against his seductions by my devotion to Hartley." [2]

So we are brought to the pertinent defence against Hume. Priestley and his followers thought they could demolish his arguments by following the path cut by David Hartley. To Priestley, Hartley had "thrown more useful light upon the theory of the mind than Newton did upon the theory of the natural world". To Lant Carpenter, he was, repeatedly, "the great Hartley", who combined "the intellectual qualities of the seraphic order with the affections of the cherubic". Little wonder that Harriet Martineau, Carpenter's pupil, came to consider Hartley as her idol.[3]

As a physician, Hartley was particularly interested in the physical basis of mental activity. He found it in a suggestion derived from Newton, which he adapted and extended, that is, that vibrations are transmitted from the sense organs along the nerves to the brain, where lesser vibrations are set up. Hartley himself was not a materialist, for he declared it impossible to discover how physical vibrations were connected with mental phenomena; but his explanation of association is crucial. If a series of sensations are impressed on the brain in the order ABCD, they arouse, by some unknown means, the ideas *abcd*; after a repeated experience of this series, the sensation A, coming singly, will recall not only idea *a*, but *bcd* as well. Like Locke, he was con-

Sense, destined to be the Criterion of Truth. . . ." in Thomas Cogan, *Ethical Questions* (London, 1817), a book of which Miss Martineau was a great admirer.

[1] See her review of Crombie's *Natural Theology*, *Misc.*, ii, 262.

[2] *Auto.*, i, 81–82.

[3] Priestley, *Remarks on Dr. Reid's Theory*, *Works*, iii, 26. Carpenter, *Principles of Education, passim*. *Auto.*, i, 80. It is interesting that Miss Martineau borrows the metaphor of the cherubim and seraphim to describe Mrs. Chapman. See above, p. 25.

cerned with the building up by this means of compound ideas on the basis of sensations. By this simple explanation based on contiguity Hartley managed to include the whole range of human experience and activity.

From the appearance of the *Observations on Man* in 1749, Hartleian psychology was the ruling school in England for over a hundred years. It is basically the psychology of James Mill, John Stuart Mill, Alexander Bain, and a whole host of lesser people. There is no need to cite statements to show its popularity; one need only to turn to any book on education to see its force. It was the stimulus to education that was perhaps its most important result. If man has no innate ideas, a good many ancient notions, like original sin, are less easy to maintain. If man is what he was made by sensations, then by controlling the sensations, man himself can be made whatever is wanted, subject only to limitations imposed by fundamental differences in intelligence. The optimistic, even perfectibilist, possibilities inherent in this view are self-evident.

Harriet Martineau first learned her Hartley at second hand, through Priestley's edition, from which the doctrine of vibrations was excluded, to save space and so effort on the part of readers whom Priestley wanted to convert. She took a contemptuous attitude, later, to the vibration theory, an attitude certainly not that of Priestley, who believed it; she talked too about the "monstrous deficiencies and absurdities" of the system—which is going too far. Yet she said, writing in 1855, "I cannot at this hour look at the portrait of Hartley . . . without a strong revival of the old mood of earnest self-discipline, and devotion to duty which I derived from [him] in my youth. While the one school has little advantage over the other in the abstract department of their philosophy, the disciples of Hartley have infinitely the advantage over the dreaming school [i.e., the Channing-Coleridge approach] in their master's presentment of the concrete department of fact and of action."[1] Certainly her faith in education is Hartleian. As for the self-discipline and devotion to duty, to understand that we must turn to a vital consequence of Hartley's teaching which provided Miss Martineau with the bedrock of her attitude to life from beginning to end—the doctrine of necessity.

Necessarianism is a modern doctrine. It is not, says Priestley,

[1] *Auto.*, i, 80.

what the ancients meant by Fate, or what the Calvinists mean by Predestination, although he admired Jonathan Edwards' necessarian position, provided only that it be shorn of its "gloomy Calvinism".[1] He traced the rise of necessarianism from a celebrated passage in Hobbes's *Leviathan*:

> *Liberty* and *necessity* are consistent. As in the water, that hath not only *liberty*, but a *necessity* of descending by the channel, so likewise, in the actions which men voluntarily do, which, because they proceed from their will, proceed from *liberty*; and yet, because every act of man's will, and every desire and inclination, proceedeth from some cause, and that from another cause, in a continual chain (whose first link is in the hand of God, the first of all causes), proceed from *necessity*.

Locke, Priestley continues, unaccountably obscured this subject by his confused treatment, a confusion cleared to a considerable extent by Collins in his *Philosophical Inquiry concerning Human Liberty* in 1715, while Hartley's *Observations* provided the final confirmation.

The necessarian doctrine does not seem so strange to us as it did to many troubled minds in the eighteenth century. Basically, it contends that all action is done in obedience to motives. Motives in turn are determined ultimately by external impressions brought together by the law of association. If one suspends volition, the very suspension is another act of volition determined by a complex of causes. As all matter operates in obedience to natural laws, so the whole of mental and moral life, being a function of matter, is similarly subject to natural laws and operates as mechanically as the planets. This view, stripped of its insistence on Divine Prescience (demanded by Priestley's religious commitments) is of course little different from the positivistic doctrines which ruled nineteenth-century science, and much of twentieth-century science still obeys them.[2] It was in accordance with assumptions like these that Freud made the discoveries which have done so much to make clear the linear determination of our volitional acts. If the Freudian view of the importance of childhood in forming the personality had been as common in the early nineteenth century as it is now, the Priestleyan school would not have seemed so appalling as it did to its opponents; and it is interesting to observe that the doctrines of child-rearing

[1] The subject is discussed in Priestley's *Disquisitions relating to Matter and Spirit* (1777), and its appendix *The Doctrine of Philosophical Necessity Illustrated*, *Works*, iii.
[2] Griffiths, *Religion and Learning*, p. 89.

based on Hartleian psychology include many points with which modern psychologists would heartily agree.

Of course, materialism was hateful to most early nineteenth-century thinkers; again, they could not easily give up the freedom which Priestley seemed to deny them. No matter how many times Priestley reiterated that he did no such thing, it was difficult to make the point stick. Everything that is granted under the ordinary use of the term freedom, he said, the necessarian allows. It is to *philosophical liberty* that he objected as derogating from the power of God, productive of anarchy, and contrary to reason.

> All the *liberty*, or rather *power*, that I say a man has not, is that of *doing several things when all the previous circumstances* (including the *state of his mind*, and his *views of things*) are precisely the same. What I contend for is, that, with the same state of mind (the same strength of any particular passions, for example) and the same views of things, (as any particular object appearing equally desirable) he would always, voluntarily, make the same choice, and come to the same determination. For instance, if I make any particular choice to-day, I should have done the same yesterday, and shall do the same to-morrow, provided there be no change in the state of my mind respecting the object of the choice.

Two problems in particular had to be dealt with to escape the censure of persons outside the school: the problem of evil and the sanctions of morality.

Did not this doctrine of necessity, it was asked, necessarily make God responsible for all evil? To this, the nature of God and Priestley's optimism provided the answer:

> When it is considered, that the distinction between things *natural* and *moral* entirely ceases on the scheme of necessity, the vices of men come under the class of common evils, producing misery for a time; but, like all other evils in the same great system, are ultimately subservient to greater good. In this light, therefore, every thing, without distinction, may be safely ascribed to God. Whatever terminates in good, philosophically speaking, is good. But this is a view of moral evil, which, though innocent and even useful in speculation, no wise man can or would choose to act upon, himself, because our understandings are too limited for the application of such a means of good; though a Being of infinite knowledge may introduce it with the greatest advantage.

Man, being finite and limited, of course dare not do evil that good may come of it, and so we must govern our conduct by certain inviolable rules; God, however, in his infinite wisdom, may choose devices he would not have chosen *on their own account* for the sake of things with which they have a necessary connection.

> And if he prefers that scheme in which there is the greatest prevalence of virtue and happiness, we have all the evidence that can be given of his being infinitely holy and benevolent, notwithstanding the mixture of vice and misery there may be in it. For, supposing such a necessary connexion of things, good and evil, the most wise, holy and good Being, would not have made any other choice; nor do I see that it is possible to vindicate the *moral attributes*, or the *benevolence* of God, of which they are only modifications, upon any other supposition than that of the necessary connexion, in the nature of things, between good and evil, both natural and moral.

The final result of this solution to the problem is of course highly comforting. The necessity which Hume seemed to Priestley to have destroyed has been reintroduced, and the misery and evil which we see about us have been explained away as part of a larger scheme.

> This being admitted to be the fact, there will be a necessary connexion between all things past, present and to come, in the way of proper *cause and effect*, as much in the intellectual, as in the natural world; so that, how little soever the bulk of mankind may be apprehensive of it, or staggered by it, according to the established laws of nature, no event could have been otherwise than it *has been*, or *is to be*, and therefore all things past, present, and to come, are precisely what the Author of nature really intended them to be, and has made provision for.[1]

On the moral question, Channing accused Priestley of epicureanism, not in the sense of inactivity, but in that "he sought refuge in his optimism from that deep feeling of men's present miseries, that thorough sympathy with human suffering, which, I think, marks those whom God selects as the great benefactors of their race". It is a just remark,[2] but the qualification that it did

[1] *Illustrations*, *Works*, iii, 462. Cf. Southwood Smith, *Illustrations of the Divine Government*, pp. 14–19.

[2] W. E. Channing to Lucy Aikin, December 29, 1831, *Corr.*, p. 111. Miss Aikin wrote to Channing of a conversation with her brother Arthur, who had been Priestley's pupil at Hackney: "He says that certainly in one sense Priestley was *self-satisfied*. He had emancipated himself from the yoke of Calvinism, which was little made for his sunny temper; and with such immovable, such entire conviction he had settled it with himself that all things must at all times be working for the best, because ordained and guided by the wisest and best of beings, that neither any misfortunes of his own, nor any disappointments to those causes which he espoused,

not mean inactivity is crucial. The necessarians had to labour hard to prove the distinction between their activist views and the resignation of fatalism. The necessarian contention was that under their system, every man is the maker of his own fortune. His own actions and determinations are necessary links in the chain of causes and effects.

> . . . the apprehension that their endeavours to promote their own happiness will have a certain and necessary effect, and that no well-judged effort of theirs will be lost, instead of disposing them to remit their labour, will encourage them to exert themselves with redoubled vigour; and the *desire of happiness* cannot but be allowed to have the same influence upon all systems.

Charles Bray, writing a half-century later, put it another way:

> The fatalist believes that everything is written in the book of fate, and must happen as there written, and it is useless therefore taking any steps to avoid it; thus paralysing all effort; on the other hand, the necessarian believes that for every effect there is a cause, which is equal at all times to produce the result desiderated, and that, therefore, the knowledge and use of these causes put fate in his own hands. It is true that what is written in the book of fate must come to pass; since that is no more than saying that what will happen will happen; but if we were permitted to read this book, we should find that the difference of faith in the fatalist and necessarian was itself the efficient cause of an entirely different fate to each believer.
>
> Again. The necessarian must still use motives; and as in practice therefore, it is said, he must praise and blame and love and hate as others do, it is the same thing as if he continued to believe in free will. It is true he must still use motives, but he knows that if he does not use efficient ones, he cannot succeed; whereas the believer in free will thinks it always a chance whether he shall

---

were able to make deep or lasting impressions on his spirits. He was an optimist both by disposition and system, but from *Epicurean* tranquility no one could be further. He was the most active of men; he could not have lived inactive; and to the propagation of this, his great principle, there was nothing he was not ready to sacrifice. My aunt [Mrs. Barbauld] has said of him, with as much truth as brilliancy, that 'he followed truth as a man who hawks follows his sport—at full speed, straight forward, looking only upward, and regardless into what difficulties the chase may lead him'. This sanguine spirit prompted him to adopt the maxim, that no effort is lost; he firmly believed that all discussion must end in the advancement of truth; and hence he could never perceive any mischief or danger in the fullest exposure of any doctrine which he believed. He was constitutionally incapable of doubt; what he held, he held implicitly for the time; but Arthur says he was not tenacious upon anything which did not affect his great principle of optimism—that is, of necessity." Lucy Aikin to W. E. Channing, October 23, 1831, *Corr.*, pp. 93–94.

succeed or not, and if he blames any one, it is generally any one but himself, to whom the fault properly belongs.[1]

It is a shallow enough doctrine, and none of it seems very strange to us. Part of the difficulty with objectors was the uncompromising sound of the word *necessity*. It inevitably made sensitive people see the loss of all freedom of choice, in the ordinary sense, and to envision a necessarian world peopled by Epicureans and Antinomians. Priestley expressed a willingness in one essay to abandon the word, but in another place he ventured the opinion that unless people apply themselves early to the study of necessity and to a regular study of pneumatology and ethics, they will never truly understand it, but be misled by the generality of writers who understand no more about it than themselves. This caution is reminiscent of Miss Martineau's statement in the *Autobiography* that "none but Necessarians at all understand the Necessarian doctrine". Perhaps it is not too far-fetched to suggest that this flaunting an exasperating phrase certain to incur opposition was a part of the Unitarian "candour", part of the martyrdom for truth.[2]

Not all Unitarians were partisans of the doctrine of necessity. Priestley tried to show Price that he was really a necessarian in spite of himself. Channing did not bother to read Priestley. Lucy Aikin, writing to Channing, complained that, while she was unable to answer necessarian logic, she found it increasingly unsatisfying, because its adherents were so earthbound. She hoped that a more lofty philosophy of some sort would serve as a counterpoise to political economy, Bentham, and Paley. Indeed, Mr. Madge and a good many of Harriet's friends, at the Octagon and elsewhere, argued repeatedly with her, Emily Taylor being especially worried about the effect of Hartley on the purity of Harriet's faith.[3]

Harriet was not to be shaken. She put herself through a course of reading Priestley's Hartley, Hartley himself, and, as an exciting confirmation, Southwood Smith's *Illustrations of the*

[1] *The Philosophy of Necessity*, pp. 419–20. This book was first published in 1841. Bray was a member of the Coventry circle which produced George Eliot, whose conversion to free thought was affected by necessarianism. See Humphrey House, "Qualities of George Eliot's Unbelief", *All in Due Time*, pp. 112–14, and *George Eliot Letters*, i, p. lv.

[2] Priestley, *Illustrations*, *Works*, iii, 467, and *Examination of Dr. Reid*, *Works*, iii, 7.

[3] W. E. Channing to Lucy Aikin, December 29, 1831, Aikin to Channing, June 1, 1830, *Corr.*, pp. 111, 45–46. See also William Turner's views, Drummond, *James Martineau*, ii, 261. HM to James, January 6, 1823, March 12, November 14, 1824.

Divine Government. When she read Hume's *Dialogues* she found herself disappointed and confused, but turned at once to Brown on cause and effect and Cogan's *Ethical Questions* for guidance in overcoming what seemed a sophistical argument. She invested thirteen guineas in Rutt's edition of Priestley, and hung an engraved portrait of the great man, given her by a friend, on her bookshelves. The way had been prepared by Lant Carpenter in Bristol, and she needed after that only to open her Priestley to find how all his arguments tended to advance religion, how sublime was Hartley's view of divine government, and how exciting was the prospect, glimpsed in her own awakening, of the perpetual progress which men might attain by a similar indoctrination. Indeed, and her brother saw this, her mind was remarkably akin to Priestley's in its confidence, precipitancy, and optimism. "What can religion be for," asked Margaret in her novel *Deerbrook*, "or reason, or philosophy, whichever name you may call your faith by, but to show us the bright side of everything . . . ?" Miss Martineau had escaped into religion in childhood; it meant promise and happiness for the rest of her life.[1]

She accepted Priestley's materialism completely. Associationism goes without saying: no one would attempt to deny the capacity for pleasure and pain, and the formation of universal principles through the operation of association. The rest followed as a matter of course. An author she was reviewing called necessarianism a doctrine which should never have been heard of beyond the walls of colleges.

> This might be very well if this were a doctrine which did not imperiously demand the attention of every reflecting mind. But whether heard of or not beyond the walls of colleges, it is, and ever will be, pondered by minds who cherish an intelligent desire to compare the agency of Providence with the course of human life. We speak from experience when we say, that the difficulty of reconciling Divine agency with human responsibility perplexes the early operations of the reasoning powers in the youthful mind, and remains a painful subject of doubt, continually recurring, till the difficulty is fearlessly grappled with and overcome. It is not with this doctrine as with many which arise to perplex us, of little consequence whether it be understood or not; nor is it hastily to

[1] HM to James, February 22, 1822, January 6, December 7, 1823, March 12, May 8, June 14, 1824, February 5, October 12, December 22, 1825, MCO. *Deerbrook*, i, 85–86. See also her headshaking comment on Carlyle's pessimism, *Auto.*, ii, 311–12, quoting her journal for 1837; *How to Observe*, pp. 36–37; or her articles on Lessing's *Education of the Human Race*, *Misc.*, ii, 296–343.

be concluded that its difficulties are incapable of solution. As all men are practically Necessarians, it is very well that those whose minds are not importuned with "obstinate questionings" should never know that others suffer from doubts from which they are free. But perplexities having once arisen, as we doubt not they do in the majority of intelligent minds, there is, in our belief, no peace and no safety till the firm ground of conviction, which we believe to be accessible to all, be attained. The result of an enlightened and complete inquiry is, by ample experience, proved to be most satisfactory; viz. that as well might the husbandman desist from his toils until he should learn whether the harvest would rise spontaneously, as an immortal being neglect the care of his soul, because it is subjected to influences over which he has no control.[1]

Since necessarianism, as she understood it, put a premium on enlightened self-discipline and enforced the moral of labouring to bring about the millennium, the life which she foresaw was necessarily an active one.

The perfect adaptation of the external and internal world to each other affords an evidence to which no one can be blind, that a perpetual reciprocation of influences is the purpose which they are designed to fulfil. It is not more certain that the materials afforded by nature are those by which the immortal spirit is to be built up, than that the stirring soul is to exert a reciprocal action upon those outward things which minister pleasure and pain to itself and others. . . . A faculty which moves without producing any result, no more fulfils its general purpose than a sunbeam darted on the eyes of the blind. It is made for action; and exercise is the condition of its health and vigour. This is true of all the intellectual faculties, and of all the moral powers generated by them.[2]

By the use of enlightened reason, principles of action can be derived; once derived, those principles must be put into effect. Common dignity arises, she says, from pride, but a better kind of dignity comes from decision of character, which will be heedless of the fluctuations of the world, make events bend before it and opposition come to nothing. She requires that this decision of character rest on a higher power, for if it rests on mere self-confidence it will be destroyed. But properly based—on a God, whom Priestley defines as an intelligent first cause, who has made the universe to operate within an unfailing causal system—this Christian consistency can enable a man to pursue his course

[1] "Natural History of Enthusiasm", *MR*, n.s., iii, 425 (June, 1829). On materialism, *Misc.*, ii, 207–30; on associationism, the clearest statement of many is in *Misc.*, ii, 265–66.

[2] "Essay on the Proper Use of the Prospective Faculty", *Misc.*, i, 224. There is an excellent statement of the necessarian creed as a programme in *SA*, ii, 92–94.

relentlessly, to die in peace, and to stand "awed but unabashed, in the presence of the Majesty on High."

> This is the dignity which alone can enable the frail child of earth to mingle, without presumption, among the sons of God; which renders him a fit inhabitant of the courts of heaven, and secures him a welcome among the wise, who "shine as the brightness of the firmament, and as the stars for ever and ever." [1]

In writing this passage she was obviously strongly indebted to the essays of John Foster, the Baptist minister who was probably the most widely read essayist of the early nineteenth century. Although Foster was a Calvinist, he was a curious one, deeply influenced by the same canons of the Enlightenment which affected Miss Martineau. There are noteworthy parallels between his views on adherence to principle and Miss Martineau's mature opinions of John Stuart Mill. They were in complete agreement on the proper use of the intellect—on the importance of knowledge, on the necessity for reducing it to general principles, on the authority and conviction which a right method will convey to the thinker. Finally, they are at one on the necessity for action.

> Not only should thinking be thus reduced, [said Foster] by a strong and patient discipline, to a train or process, in which all the parts at once depend upon and support one another, but also this train should be followed on to a full conclusion. It should be held as a law generally in force that the question must be disposed of before it is let alone. The mind may carry on this accurate process to some length, and then stop through indolence, or start away through levity; but it can never possess that rational confidence in its opinions which is requisite to the character in question, till it is conscious of acquiring them from an exercise of thought continued on to its result. . . .
>
> Another thing that would powerfully assist toward complete decision, both in the particular instance, and in the general spirit of the character, is for a man to place himself in a situation analogous to that in which Caesar placed his soldiers, when he burnt the ships which brought them to land. If his judgment is *really* decided, let him commit himself irretrievably, by doing something which shall oblige him to do more, which shall lay on him the necessity of doing all.[2]

---

[1] "On Dignity of Character", *MR*, n.s., i, 785–91 (November, 1827).

[2] John Foster, "On Decision of Character", *Essays*, pp. 163–66. The essays were first published in 1804 and went through eighteen editions during Foster's lifetime. He died in 1843, and Harriet Martineau's later favourable estimate of him can be found in *Hist.*, ii, 697.

Harriet Martineau was continually burning ships.

Historians writing on the emerging characteristics of the Victorian age have always heavily emphasized Evangelicalism, with its insistence on the insignificance of the individual and on the importance of service. This emphasis, while unquestionably important, has been somewhat overdone. I have tried here to point out how the same ideals of activity and service could emerge from a context which bore not a trace of Evangelicalism, and which, far from stressing the insignificance of the individual, raised him to the towering pinnacle of mastery of his own fate through mastery of the laws of the universe. To be sure, the necessarian school, carrying into the nineteenth century the doctrines and conviction of one aspect of the Enlightenment, was not so widespread as the Evangelicals. But, though the Unitarians were a small sect, they were an amazingly powerful one. They insinuated themselves into virtually every corner of English life, and strategic corners too.[1] None of them was more "enlightened," confident, and active than Harriet Martineau.

One final question remains: was Miss Martineau a Benthamite? Contrary to the usual casual opinion, I do not think she was. Nor did she, and there are other reasons than her assertion for believing her. A fortnight before Bentham died in 1832, he gave Mrs. Austin a ring with his portrait and some of his hair let in behind. He kissed her and said, "There, my dear, it is the only ring I ever gave to a woman." [2] In 1859, writing to Henry Reeve, Miss Martineau referred to this incident, saying that many people had wondered when Bentham died why he did not leave her a ring and a lock of his hair, "and it was almost in vain that I disclaimed being a comrade". The Utilitarianism of that coterie, she said, she could never understand. And small wonder. Although Benthamite Utilitarianism and Priestleyan Necessarianism had risen from the same sources—in Hobbes Locke, Hume, and Hartley—although it was from Priestley himself that Bentham got the phrase "greatest happiness of the greatest number", the two streams ran parallel and did not meet.

[1] R. V. Holt, *The Unitarian Contribution to Social Progress.* Cf. G. J. Holyoake, *Reasoner*, i, 129 (July 29, 1846): "Priestley would now be sneered at for debating the abstruse question of philosophical necessity—yet out of it has come the significant 'fashion of the age'—the attempt at ameliorating the external circumstances of the people."

[2] Ross, *Three Generations*, p. 84.

Miss Martineau knew some of Bentham's work and admired it. In her early articles she mentions him twice, once (it can be no one else) as a "regenerator" who held out hope of a rapid advance in political science through "the Novum Organon with which he has furnished us", but which will not be "in full use till his grey hairs have descended to the grave".[1] She could work with Chadwick and admire his single-minded devotion in applying Benthamite forms to the solution of vast social problems. She was impressed by Southwood Smith; at one point she wanted him to dissect her body when she died, as he had done with Bentham. Had she known him, she would probably have got on famously with James Mill. With the practical reforms of the Benthamites she was generally in sympathy, and the criterion of utility was one to which she would naturally respond. But she went beyond them.[2]

Bentham was primarily a reformer. He started by asking himself tremblingly if he had the genius for legislation, and having answered affirmatively, he set out to discover the true principles on which legislation could be drawn. Although his work had ramifications in every field, its typical expression was administrative. Here the felicific calculus and the assumption of equality of pleasures could work well, however defective it was (as Harriet Martineau and John Stuart Mill and Mazzini pointed out)[3] in prescribing individual ethics. But the very nature of such a calculus seems almost to forbid any truly revolutionary action. If one sits down to calculate the results of a course of action, balancing the pleasures and pains likely to result, predicting the probable benefit and usefulness to mankind, the moment of action, in a revolutionary sense, would be gone. And much as Miss Martineau could admire reforming activity, she was a better revolutionist than administrator. Had she been the hospital matron Carlyle suggested she should have been, the institution would soon have been in a turmoil. She was too concerned with fundamentals.

[1] "Theology, Politics, and Literature", *Misc.*, i, 193.

[2] This section owes much to Peter Gay, Mary Peter Mack, and J. L. Talmon, though they bear no responsibility for the full argument.

[3] Miss Martineau was delighted by Mill's criticism of Bentham, a criticism which Mrs. Grote considered ungrateful to radicals and which George Grote called weak and preposterous. HM to James, November 3, 1837, and August 4, 1838. For Mazzini on Bentham, a view which Miss Martineau would clearly have endorsed, see *People's Journal*, ii, 292 (1846).

The true Benthamite, then, was rigorous and precise, a legal and administrative reformer. Harriet Martineau was doctrinaire, utopian, and woolly. For her, reform subserved broader ends. Her instrument was not calculation but principle. Once found, principle had to be acted upon, with no alternatives considered. But, happily for her, she was in a position to use principle to criticize; she seldom had to trouble herself about how to apply it in detail.

In her the assumptions and consciousness of power of the manufacturer were mixed with the self-consciousness of Dissent; but this characteristic English amalgam was informed and changed by something else, an oversimplified near-travesty of the best thought of the Enlightenment. An optimistic perfectibilist, she would enforce and reinforce inevitable change. It was not only that things could be done or should be done, but that they would be done. Because she knew where society was heading—her thinking was teleological not instrumental—she was capable of revolution (or of talking it) in almost the wildest Jacobin sense. Not for nothing is one reminded from time to time in reading her of Karl Marx. Not in programme, to be sure, but in spirit. Hers was a clean manifestation of the radical temper.

CHAPTER IV

London: Teacher of the People

IN 1817, Harriet Martineau was sent to Bristol—one of the periodic efforts to settle her by sending her away—to attend a school kept by her aunt. She stayed for fifteen months, improving not at all in health, suffering for the last part from homesickness, but profiting greatly, she insisted, from the surroundings, the intellectual challenge posed by her cousins, and the warmth and understanding of her aunt. At Lewin's Mead Chapel Harriet came under the spell of Lant Carpenter, the great Unitarian preacher and teacher, who had just come to Bristol from Exeter.

In her autobiography she is particularly savage about Carpenter. She hated to recall the devotion, the fanaticism, which he aroused in her; so she considered him superficial, narrow, and "thoroughly priestly". His power over the young, she wrote, was extraordinary, yet because no essential Christian doctrine permeated his instruction, his pupils, once they left, displayed an amazing diversity of religious opinion—from Catholicism to atheism. This diagnosis, of course, reflects a special view of religion and of Christianity arrived at by a peculiarly constituted mind. A less involved commentator might have seen rather the effectiveness of a teacher who could stimulate his pupils to the pursuit of truth that might, in a narrower view, corrupt.

James Martineau, at any rate, took a very different view. As a result of Harriet's enthusiasm, he was withdrawn from the Cathedral school in Norwich to be sent to Carpenter; and after his training at the Unitarian College at York, he returned to Bristol as Carpenter's assistant. Though James thought him lacking real perception of beauty or experience of aesthetic emotions, except as they might serve some higher moral purpose, he saw too that Carpenter was politically alive and dedicated (to liberalism, of course) and an admirable religious instructor,

> Profound *moral feeling* . . . was the great primary force of his whole mind; transcending and directing not only his intellectual gifts, but (if it is possible to separate and compare what in him were so absolutely blended) even his religious affections. I have never seen in any human being the idea of duty, the feeling of right, held in such visible reverence.

So profound was this combination of pedagogical excellence and moral fervour, that few, James believed, could have left his school who "did not stand upon the threshold of the life then opening before them, with some breathless feeling of its grandeur and awfulness".[1]

Harriet returned home from Bristol filled with a burning religious zeal which, while it led her mother and sisters to make fun of her, gave her considerable comfort. It helped, too, to determine the course of her studies. There is in Manchester College, Oxford, a letter from Harriet to Dr. Carpenter, written in 1819 as soon as she returned home. It is a "fan letter", which makes precisely this point about his guidance, and her letters to James, as she worked her way through Priestley and Hartley, show how well she followed the lines laid down in Bristol. But it was not merely for her intellectual development that she owed a debt to Carpenter's teaching. His text on gospel history aroused interests that led to her little *Traditions of Palestine*, and probably as well to her later exploration of Egypt and the Holy Land. His moral fervour strengthened and stimulated hers, and it must have been wonderfully thrilling to her to learn that he had mentioned her *Devotional Exercises* in a sermon at Lewin's Mead. I think it is as good as demonstrable that the consuming ambition of her youth, which *mutatis mutandis* remained her passion, came as much from Carpenter as from anyone else. In his *Principles of Education*, objecting to certain aspects of Maria Edgeworth's otherwise admirable educational works, he said:

> If any female writer should hereafter come forward to the public, possessing the clearness, simplicity, correctness, and well-stored understanding of an Edgeworth, the brilliant yet chaste imagination and "devotional taste" of a Barbauld, and the energy and high-toned moral principle of a More, divested of bigotry, and founded upon genuine Christian theology, in the scale of utility she will probably stand unrivalled among her contemporaries,

[1] James Martineau to R. L. Carpenter, 1841, Drummond, *James Martineau*, i, 19–20.

however eminent her age may be in every thing great and good.[1]

In a paper setting down her aims and the rules to attain them, in 1829, Harriet Martineau wrote:

> I believe myself possessed of no uncommon talents, and of not an atom of genius; but as various circumstances have led me to think more accurately and read more extensively than some women, I believe that I may so write on subjects of universal concern as to inform some minds and stir up others. My aim is to become a forcible and elegant writer on religious and moral subjects, so as to be useful to refined as well as unenlightened minds. But, as I see how much remains to be done before this aim can be attained, I wish to be content with a much lower degree of usefulness, should the Father of my spirit see fit to set narrow bounds to my exertions. Of posthumous fame I have not the slightest expectation or desire. To be useful in my day and generation is enough for me.[2]

It is impossible to think that Carpenter did not awaken her response to the need and so help her to become what W. J. Fox called a "national instructor". At any rate, service to the "Cause" was the basic reason for her writing, before the financial situation in 1829 made it necessary.[3]

More important than Carpenter was her brother James. His retiring disposition helped to bind them to each other more closely than to other members of the family, so when James went off to school at Bristol and later to college at York, Harriet was desolate. In his abstracts of her letters, James recorded directly some of the things she said about their friendship. Since by 1843 they were already drifting towards the final break, perhaps recording them served some need for encouragement and conviction in James; for us they indicate the intensity of her affection. When she was not quite twenty, she wrote that if she should die, the thought of James's love would always retain its soothing power; she was calm in the knowledge that they would meet again after death, where the pain in her soul would not spoil the enjoyment of that love. Again, in 1823, when she was visiting at Torquay, she went for a walk on the hills: "It is midst scenes like this that the mind feels as if it could do and bear all things, for in those scenes is the present forever made manifest. . . . O! that James was with me [indecipherable] when I am

[1] Pp. 41–42. The mention in his sermon is referred to in a letter from HM to James, May 28, 1824.

[2] *Auto.*, ii, 166.

[3] Garnett, *Fox*, p. 82.

enjoying any pleasure of this kind, for he better than anyone besides can enter into and share my feelings and to him better than to anyone besides can I declare every thought of my heart." Again and again she came back to the certainty that the strongest affections of her earthly heart were given to James, and she could say as late as 1834 that some remarks he had made about the Benthamites and about the growing power of sympathizing with joy and sorrow not only touched her deeply but proved him still and forever her "nearest and dearest friend". [1]

It seems likely that the attachment to James had some effect on her uncertainties about John Worthington; certainly the letters already quoted in that connection indicate a deep concern for James's approval of the engagement. But if the guess I have made about her psychosexual make-up has any validity, the relationship with James, posing no threat, could rest on and draw an undiluted strength from the identity of their intensely held intellectual positions, just as the similarly unthreatening friendship with Atkinson rested on the bedrock of common conviction.

Through the letters of the twenties, her dependence on James is modified by an habitual assumption of the role of elder sister. When he announced his decision to abandon engineering for the ministry, she carefully stated the case against the change and urged him to abide by his parents' decision; when they decided in favour of his inclination, she was delighted that he could turn himself to the sacred things that meant so much to her. When he became engaged to Helen Higginson of Liverpool, Harriet welcomed the news with clearly sincere congratulation; she was excited by the prospect of meeting Helen; when she met her, she was enchanted; and she served as mediator between her parents and the Higginsons whose permission for the engagement, while James was still a minor, was resented in Magdalen Street. Helen Martineau became a regular correspondent, outlasting the correspondence with James, and there is no trace at all, in any of the letters, of jealousy or resentment.[2]

This free and apparently healthy affection between brother

[1] HM to James, September 1, 1821, April 28, 1823, February 2, 1824, January 30, 1834.

[2] HM to James, June 26, July 15, 1822, October 6, November 30, 1823, February 2, June 14, 1824, January 8, February 5, November 11, 1825, April 28, May 23, August 30, 1826. The letters to Helen Martineau are in Manchester College, Oxford.

and sister permits us to emphasize without complications their joint intellectual enterprise. Though Harriet told James that she found studies the best substitute for his presence, though she asked continually for advice and comment, she seems largely to have taken the lead. In vacations they were able to talk and study together; it was in such a session that her own troubles about problems of foreknowledge and freewill were solved by a suggestion from James. He dropped a hint about the doctrine of necessity, of which he had heard a great deal at York.

> I uttered the difficulty which had lain in my mind for so many years; and he just informed me that there was, or was held to be, a solution in that direction, and advised me to make it out for myself. I did so. From that time the question possessed me. Now that I had got leave, as it were, to apply the Necessarian solution, I did it incessantly. I fairly laid hold of the conception of general laws, while still far from being prepared to let go the notion of a special Providence. Though at times almost overwhelmed by the vastness of the view opened to me, and by the prodigious change requisite in my moral views and self-management, the revolution was safely gone through. . . . Being aware of my weakness of undue sympathy with authors whom I read with any moral interest, I resolved to read nothing on this question till I had thought it out; and I kept to my resolve. When I was wholly satisfied, and could use my new method of interpretation in all cases that occurred with readiness and ease, I read every book that I could hear of on the subject of the Will; and I need not add that I derived confirmation from all I read on both sides.

On a walking tour of Scotland in 1824, brother and sister talked philosophy incessantly. James recalled:

> My sister's acute, rapid, and incisive advance to a conclusion upon every point pleasantly relieved my slower judgment and gave me courage to dismiss suspense. I was at that time, and for several years after, an enthusiastic disciple of the determinist philosophy, and was strongly tainted with the *positivist* temper which is its frequent concomitant; yet not without such inward reserves and misgivings as to render welcome my sister's more firm and ready verdict. While she remained faithful through life to that early mode of thought, with me those "reserves and misgivings," suppressed for a while, recovered from the shock and gained the ascendancy. The divergence led to this result,—that while my sister changed her conclusions, and I my basis, we both cleared ourselves from incompatible admixtures, and paid the deference due to logical consistency and completeness.[1]

[1] Quoted in Drummond, *James Martineau*, ii, 262–63.

The testimony to the whirlwind force of Harriet's conviction is believable, and her concern is oddly reminiscent of the day when she, at the age of five or six, crept into her baby brother's room to show him the sunrise and to talk solemnly to him about religion.

When she visited James and his family in Dublin in 1831, she wrote to Fox that everything in that "blessed household" was bright except for the troubles that James had from the Philistines —for he was about to resign his ministry over his principled refusal to accept the *Regium Donum*, a government grant to Irish Presbyterian ministers. He showed, she said, the soul of a Stephen, so gentle, so forbearing. Again, if only his sermons on necessity could be published, she was sure that all the world must at once become necessarian. In 1832, after she was famous, she suggested to Tait, the Edinburgh publisher, that she hoped James, who held her views and was one of the most accomplished philosophers alive, would join her, he to plead for the people "by lofty appeals to the guides of Soc[iety], I by being the annalist of the poor". No wonder James's subsequent changes of opinion were so painful, an estrangement, says Garnett, unintelligible to the ordinary man, but terrible to those who live in the world of ideas.[1]

It was James who made the suggestion that she turn her hand to writing and send something to the *Monthly Repository*. Through that journal she was brought into touch with the third great influence of her youth, W. J. Fox. Fox, too, came from Norwich, but hardly from the circles in which the Martineaus moved. His father, an unsuccessful small farmer, had come to town, and William was in turn a helper in his father's similarly unsuccessful weaving establishment, an errand boy, and a bank clerk. In 1806, having become religious, he went to London to study at the Calvinist Homerton Academy. Within a few years, just after assuming his first pastorate at Fareham, Hants, he was troubled by doubts; by 1812 he was a Unitarian. He became one of the sect's most celebrated preachers, in effect the founder of the British and Foreign Unitarian Association, and minister of South Place Chapel, Finsbury. In 1827 he became editor of the *Monthly Repository*, purchased by the Association from the Rev. Robert Aspland, who had founded the little journal in 1806. Fox bought the paper from the Association in 1831 and

[1] Garnett, *Fox*, pp. 89–92. HM to Tait, November 10, 1832, NLS.

made it over into a more general periodical, of an uncompromising radicalism in complexion, and of unsurpassed excellence and distinction in its articles and its list of contributors.[1]

Harriet Martineau's first contribution to the *Repository* was an article in 1821 on "Female Writers of Practical Divinity"; a few other articles followed in the period of Aspland's editorship. By 1827, however, she had begun to branch out, though in a very small way. A "solemn old Calvinistic publisher", Houlston, of Wellington, Shropshire, with whom she had been put into touch by a friend, published some of her little tales, paying her a sovereign each; her devotional works had found Norwich and London publishers; but she remained within sectarian bounds and barely a professional writer. When she answered Fox's advertisement for contributors to his recently acquired *Repository*, he replied that he was familiar with her earlier work and admired it, but in response to her inquiry about payment, he regretted that the trustees of the Association would not allow it. So she began to write for him for nothing.

Then in 1829 the family firm which her brother Henry had continued to manage along with his wine and porter business had to be wound up—the doom of Norwich textiles was inescapable. Arrangements were made for paying the creditors fifteen shillings in the pound, terms which Henry had some difficulty in carrying out; consequently the family had to begin to look to their own maintenance. Rachel and Ellen both went out as governesses. Harriet, after toying with a scheme for a correspondence course to educate girls after they left school—on the "easy terms" of twenty-five guineas a year—fell back on her writing. Fox offered, under the circumstances, to pay her fifteen pounds a year; in return she contributed a remarkable series of articles, essays, reviews, tales, and poems, to some of the more important of which reference has already been made.

Her literary ambition was wider still. She was already meditating her autobiography. She wanted to contribute to the reviews, but she had not the connections, and it was probably too early in her career in any event. She thought about writing a novel. Fox apparently discouraged the project, but since he liked her tale-writing, she went on with that. In 1829, taking up an idea derived from Lant Carpenter, she published

[1] On Fox, see Garnett, *Fox*, and on the *Monthly Repository*, Mineka, *Dissidence of Dissent*.

Traditions of Palestine; or, Times of the Saviour, which had some success on both sides of the Atlantic and which, when she wrote her autobiography, she still regarded with deep affection. Other moral tales followed, and in 1830 she brought off the triumph, already mentioned, of winning three prizes for essays to convert Roman Catholics, Jews, and Mohammedans to Unitarianism.[1]

Even more important than the literary guidance she received from Fox was her introduction to life in London. Fox's friend and collaborator, afterwards his mistress, the beautiful and talented Eliza Flower, took the young Harriet under her wing. "They saw that I was outgrowing my shell," Miss Martineau wrote later, "and they had patience with me till I had rent it and cast it off. . . ." Fox urged that living in London was essential to a literary career, but she could not desert her mother, who was, however, willing to provide for Harriet's spending three months a year in town, while keeping the Magdalen Street house as "the executive workshop for undisturbed writing". When she went to London, she lived with her relatives and worked every day under Fox's direction in his study. In his house she met the most prominent figures of London Unitarianism, including Southwood Smith, whose *Illustrations of the Divine Government* she so respected. Through Fox she could feel close to the centre of excitement about the Reform Bill, for he was a member of the council of the National Political Union and rather expected (or hoped) to be sent to the Tower. In that event, Harriet would probably have become editor of the *Repository*, and she jokingly promised her mentor that if he were hanged, she would provide a splendid obituary. She wrote a couple of reform songs which Eliza Flower set to music, and she had the satisfaction of knowing that they were sung at meetings.

When Harriet wrote to James exulting in the freedom of the Fox household and giving accounts of conversations in which the

[1] See above, p. 71. She looked differently on conversion by the mid-forties. She had seen a new English church for converted Jews being built in the Holy Land, but she did not expect it to attract many converts. "Those who withdraw these converts from their old connections, habits, principles, and intercourses, are, indeed, under an obligation to supply them with new: but it is to be hoped that they consider well what they are doing, and how tremendous a responsibility they are taking on themselves, as regards the *morale* as well as the fortunes of their converts. It is no light matter to subvert a man's habits of mind and life, to isolate him in the midst of his own city and race, and render him wholly dependent on his religious teachers." *EL*, p. 376.

participants said precisely what they thought of each other's experiences and faults and of the relative strength of their temptations, James found the picture unhealthy, repulsive, and not a little indelicate. A free-thinking, high-living clique, he called them, and his sister soon came to share his opinion. Her gratitude could always wait on principle.

In 1834 Fox escaped from his unhappy early marriage by setting up another house with Eliza Flower in Bayswater; thereupon Harriet Martineau refused to see them again. When a correspondence with Fox was revived after her return from America, she found him sophistical and slippery and was happy enough to report that Eliza was unhappy. His refusal to return her letters broke the connection a second time, though they were in touch in the mid-forties when both of them worked for the *People's Journal*; apparently there was some correspondence after. But it could never be the same. Because she thought that love, like other passions, should be guided by duty, Fox seemed to pity her as unfeeling, as a mass of logic, "whereas, if nothing in me were stronger than my logical powers, alas! for me!" [1]

These three men, then, helped to form her career. It was the mission to become a national instructor, drawn from Carpenter, and advice from James and Fox that helped her to the remarkable accomplishment that launched her career on the national scene: the *Illustrations of Political Economy*. The germ of these little stories lay in two tales she had written for Houlston. The theme of the first, *The Rioters*, was suggested by an account in the *Globe* of some machine-breaking; the success of that tale led a group of Nottingham and Derby manufacturers to ask her to write a tale on wages. The result was *The Turn-out*.

> It was in the autumn of 1827, I think, that a neighbour lent my sister Mrs. Marcet's "Conversations on Political Economy". I took up the book, chiefly to see what Political Economy precisely was; and great was my surprise to find that I had been teaching it unawares, in my stories about Machinery and Wages. It struck me at once that the principles of the whole science might be advantageously conveyed in the same way,—not by being smothered up

---

[1] The collaboration with Fox is discussed on the basis of *Auto.*, i, 107, 112–13; Garnett, *Fox*, pp. 76–83, 189–90; HM to James, *passim*, 1829–34 and 1838; HM to Milnes, April 21, [1844]. The Fox-Martineau correspondence has been destroyed, according to information from Mr. David Garnett.

> in a story, but by being exhibited in their natural workings in selected passages of social life. . . . [My] view and purpose date from my reading of Mrs. Marcet's Conversations. During the reading, groups of personages rose up from the pages, and a procession of action glided through its arguments, as afterwards from the pages of Adam Smith and all the other Economists. I mentioned my notion, I remember, when we were sitting at work, one bright afternoon at home. Brother James nodded assent; my mother said "do it;" and we went to tea, unconscious what a great thing we had done since dinner.[1]

The thing they had done made her famous. It did so because the tales appeared at precisely the moment when others besides Norwich Unitarians thought that political economy was important.

In the form we know now as classical economics, political economy stood as orthodoxy throughout the first half of the nineteenth century. To a generation unshaken in its faith in Newtonian possibility, its founders seemed to have provided, if not all the answers, at least the categories and the methods by which the right answers could be reached. The generalizations of that great and rather undisciplined compendium of economic observation, *The Wealth of Nations*, were given a pessimistic turn by Malthus's law of population. J. B. Say, in France, helped to systematize the science, and Ricardo, in good scientific fashion, reduced it to an abstract system.

Social sciences, unlike the physical sciences, are not so readily accepted as sovereign; they trench on more interests and prejudices, and their conclusions seem more malleable. So the science of political economy experienced vicissitudes from which Newtonian mechanics (the obvious analogue in the physical world) was relatively free. The Political Economy Club was livelier than the Royal Society; while Newton might ignore Hooke, Ricardo could not ignore the heresies of Malthus,[2] nor the Ricardians the worse apostasy of the Ricardian Socialists.

The teachings of Adam Smith had received some notice from

[1] *Auto.*, i, 105–6. I suspect the account is a bit over-dramatized—there is no mention of the project or of Mrs. Marcet in the letters to James in 1827—but it is probably essentially true. At one point, Mrs. Marcet's character Mrs. B. suggests tales as a valuable vehicle for economic truths.

[2] Though, as T. W. Hutchison has recently shown, he could simply dismiss economic heresy in Bentham. "Bentham as an Economist", *Economic Journal*, lxvi, 298 (June, 1956).

the intelligentsia by the 1780's; Shelburne and Pitt made efforts to transform his teachings into policy; Smith himself, a pre-industrial writer, doubted that the merchant community could ever be brought out of their narrow prejudices to accept free trade, and the ministers found he was right. By 1820, however, the merchants of London were petitioning for free trade, and in the following decade Huskisson and Robinson began the gradual demolition of the protective structure built around British trade. This liberalization was not the unalloyed triumph of an intellectual system; British industry had so far stolen a march on continental rivals that it could afford free trade. The restrictive system which had been necessary two hundred or even fifty years before, and which was to become necessary again a hundred years later, had become an incubus, a hindrance to expansion. So Adam Smith's neologism *mercantilism*—the merchant's philosophy—within fifty years became a misnomer; the merchants (or most of them) were free-traders.

The great work of political economy as a test for institutions was negative; under its demands outworn regulations and institutions were swept away. By mid-century British trade and industry were freer than they had ever been before or would ever be again, but concurrently the system, so valuable in criticism and destruction, was showing itself notably weak on the constructive side. The state was called in to redress the balance, and the economists went back to their studies to rethink their assumptions.

In the 1820's, however, the work was only beginning. Though some men could see the deficiency already, and could worry about the value of a negative freedom as a foundation for a moral code, they were easily confused, and in many cases rightly, with the defenders of special interests and outworn or sentimental philosophies. But there were other kinds of opposition too, and political economy had to fight for every forward step it took. It was the bullionist controversy of the second decade of the century and the resumption of specie payments in 1819, with its marked deflationary effects, that brought the claims of the new science sharply home to people who had not thought seriously about it before.[1] Up to 1818, said a writer in the

[1] The central position of this step is reflected in a letter of Francis Place to HM, September 9, 1832, BM, Add. MSS, 35,149, ff. 192b–193; and as well in Samuel Bailey, *Essays on Opinion*, p. 116.

Westminster Review, the subject was scarcely discussed outside a small circle of philosophers, and the *Quarterly* agreed:

> From the time in which the bullion question came out of Pandora's Scotch mull, parliament has been wearied with the interminable discussions which they [the political economists] have raised there. Youths who were fresh from college, and men with or without education, who were "in the wane of their wits and infancy of their discretion", imbibed the radiant darkness of Jeremy Bentham, and forthwith set themselves up as the lights of their generation. No professors, even in the subtlest ages of scholastic philosophy, were ever more successful in muddying what they found clear, and perplexing what is in itself intelligible.[1]

As law became the inevitable vehicle of debate in the seventeenth-century struggle between king and parliament, from the third decade of the nineteenth century, political economy was both bone and mode of contention.[2] The most famous writers on the subject, like Malthus or McCulloch, could demand from publishers higher payments than any but the most popular novelists.[3] Chairs were set up in the universities and filled with distinguished theorists—Senior and Whately at Oxford, McCulloch at University College, London, Jones at King's College. The important periodicals retained political economists who could be sent into battle against political rivals—where contributions to economic science were only incidental to contemporary political and intellectual battles. The newspapers took up the cry, and judges began to lecture from the bench.[4] Of course, as the science moved out of the study into parliament, street, and press, it changed its character. Abstractions were converted into rules of action; qualifications disappeared. The "welfare" recommendations of Adam Smith were conveniently forgotten, and some of the unpalatable conclusions of Ricardo were glossed over; even Ricardo spoke differently in parliament on some subjects than he wrote on them. Popularization, in short, had its usual effect. A writer in the *Athenaeum* in 1828

[1] *WR*, iv, 89 (July, 1825); *QR*, xliv, 277 (January, 1831). The *Quarterly's* reviewer was quite wrong about Bentham. See Hutchison, *Econ. Journal*, lxvi, 288–306 (June, 1956).

[2] The point was made succinctly by Bulwer-Lytton, *England and the English*, ii, 104–5.

[3] McCulloch's work on statistics in the thirties was to bring him £950 to £1000. McCulloch to Coates, Society for the Diffusion of Useful Knowledge, Letters, July 20, 1832, UCL. Malthus to J. Thomson, November 27, 1813, BPL.

[4] *The Times*, January 12, 1831, reports the lecture of Mr. Justice Alderson at Dorchester. Hammond, *Village Labourer*, pp. 275–76.

commented on the large degree of attention which the science had attracted,

> but, unfortunately, the languor of the public mind precluded the possibility of that science being studied in its full depth and extent, and imposed on its professors a necessity of supplying the popular demand with essays and treatises, in which the elements and practical results were packed together in the closest and most concise form; and in which a hasty student might provide himself with formulas and classifications enough to heap upon his ignorance the husks of knowledge. Thus, a double wrong was done to those writers whose genius fitted them for exploring the principles of the science, as well as for pursuing with success their practical application and development. They were "cabin'd, cribbed, confined" in the intermediate space allotted them betwixt the beginning and the end of their labours, and compelled to rapid inference from abstractions to realities. And when this too popular method had produced its natural fruits, the whole blame was thrown on the political economists, by critics who would assuredly not have recompensed their labours, had they engaged in more extensive or profound investigations.[1]

The opposition was varied and powerful, particularly among the working classes and their sympathizers. Sadler wrote books against Malthus. Joseph Livesey in his *Moral Reformer* denounced the "cheerless, cold-hearted systems of Malthus and Wilmot Horton". Little socialist papers all over the country pointed to the evils of competition. William Pare, the Birmingham socialist, with a full knowledge of what Ricardo had to say, denied an identity of interests between classes. The Glasgow trade union paper cried "Confound Political Economy for an insolent blockhead", and looked forward to the time when the downtrodden people would rise up to make "the whole of the overgrown capitalists of the country, with the Editor of the Scotsman, and his bald-headed friend, Political Economy, on their backs, topple over, and lie sprawling in the mud, instead of thus scrambling among the branches, while searching for the root of the tree. . . ." As a final example, the most widely circulated and most powerful working-class paper of the thirties, the *Poor Man's Guardian*:

> The juggle of the political economists . . . is now seen through; when translated into plain English, political economy means nothing more or less than this—Give up the whole produce of your labour—fill everybody's cupboard but your own—and then

[1] August 20, 1828. A review of Say's *Cours complet* by Q.

> starve quietly!!! Oh, no, no; the wealth-producers must obtain useful knowledge of a very different description, if they desire to better their condition. . . .

The useful knowledge they recommended was a knowledge of the tactics of street-fighting.[1] The labour theory of value was another double-edged legacy of John Locke.

Whately told his students that vituperation against the science, "which you will be prepared to hear, though, of course, not to answer", was not in itself a bad sign.

> In proportion . . . as any branch of study leads to important and useful results—in proportion as it gains ground in public estimation—in proportion as it tends to overthrow prevailing errors—in the same degree, it may be expected to call forth angry declamation from those who are trying to despise what they will not learn, and wedded to prejudices which they cannot defend.[2]

But it was not easy to remain above the struggle. Vituperation was reinforced by alarming action: rick-burning (which brought Whately himself into the field with a tract), trade unionism, machine-breaking, or simply the kind of sullen resistance which led Andrew Ure to recommend the employment of more tractable children. If political economy was true—and its advocates had no doubt of that[3]—then men had to be brought to accept it. All of the political economists were ardent advocates of education, and their own subject was a primary concern. Malthus was conclusive about its importance. McCulloch said that, with the growing power of public opinion, people could not be left uninstructed, lest they become dupes and "by their misdirected zeal, numbers, and energy [insure] the triumph of such [measures] as were most destructive to themselves".[4] Even the *Quarterly*

[1] *Moral Reformer*, 40–42 (February, 1831). Third Co-operative Congress, *Proceedings*, pp. 56–57. *Herald to the Trades' Advocate*, December 25, 1830. *Poor Man's Guardian*. January 7, 1832.

[2] *Introductory Lectures on Political Economy*, p. 16.

[3] Thus Francis Place: " . . . its principles are to me clear—conclusive—universal and incapable of change; and I believe also that the prejudice which has been raised against the principles of political economy and its advocates is the greatest of all obstacles to the advancement of the multitude". Place to William Carpenter, January 24, 1839, BM, Add. MSS, 35,151, f. 127. Or these words: "These may be called conclusions of political economy, or facts in God's world, I care not which. Facts they are, and it is time that all workpeople thoroughly understood them." Samuel Green, *Working Classes of Great Britain*, pp. 30–31.

[4] T. R. Malthus, *Essay on Population*, ii, 357–60. J. R. McCulloch, *Discourse on the Rise, Progress, Peculiar Objects, and Importance of Political Economy*, pp. 84–85.

Review, little as it appreciated some aspects of the science and its advocates, saw this virtue in it:

> It would be a real blessing if the working classes could be made acquainted with some of the fundamental principles of Political Economy; such as the laws of population; the causes of the inequality of mankind; the circumstances which regulate the market of corn, or the market of labour. They would then perceive that inequality does not originate in the encroachments of the rich or the enactments of the powerful, but has been necessarily coeval with society itself in all its stages; they would learn that the recompense of labour is governed by definite principles—and we are grateful for any measures which may tend to diffuse such knowledge.[1]

To agree on the urgency of teaching political economy did not solve the problem of how to teach it. William Ellis in the forties was to have considerable success in teaching it in schools, but schools, particularly in the twenties and thirties, reached only part of the working classes and even then the pupils were likely to stay only long enough to learn to read imperfectly. The newspapers presented a more likely channel, and Place was particularly active in writing articles for them. He lamented the profusion of small misguided periodicals, but saw that the stamp laws got in the way of answering them in the same form. So he tried discussion groups with what he felt was considerable success for "teaching the people's teachers", that is the forty or fifty men he would have in on a Sunday morning, after the London Working Men's Association was formed in 1836. But it seemed to come down pretty much to a reliance on tracts and pamphlets, which could be sold or given away and perhaps read.[2]

McCulloch himself set out to bring the science to the working man, having already contributed to middle-class education in the subject with his article in the *Encyclopaedia Britannica* and his text-book. Plans for a cheap booklet projected by Constable fell through in the crash of 1825–26, but McCulloch rescued the part already written—on wages—and issued it as a separate shilling pamphlet. Place at once set about calculating the cost for a cheap printing—perhaps at twopence—but the plan came

[1] xxxii, 420–21 (October, 1825).

[2] The Place MSS are full of concern about this problem. BM, Add. MSS, 35,149/120b–123, 35,151/41, 101–101b, diary entries for 1826 in 35,146, *passim*; and cuttings in 35,154.

to nothing, and he contented himself with a strong recommendation to working-class readers:

> If workmen are wise, they will contrive the means of obtaining this little manual, so that every man among them who can read and reason may possess a copy. This may be done in many ways: those who can afford it, may purchase a copy at once; those who cannot, may club their pence with their fellows, as is done in Bible Societies, until every one has his book—a penny a week from twelve men will purchase a copy weekly, two-pence a week two copies weekly. Men in workshops might put down their sixpences, and at a fortnight's end, buy a book for each: and no doubt the publisher would sell them in half-dozens and dozens for less than a shilling a copy. Masters employing a number of workmen could hardly do anything more useful to themselves, as well as to their workmen, than purchase a number of these books, and giving or selling them to their most intelligent workmen. It has been observed that this is a book likely to be as useful to the masters as to the men, and it may be assumed as a circumstance sure to occur, that every master who reads it, as well as every intelligent workman, will recommend its perusal to others.[1]

McCulloch failed to sell half of the edition of two thousand. "I lost my pains and £40 by this effort to improve their Sovereign Majesties. When I commit another *faux pas* of the same sort my friends had better get me shut up."[2]

The Society for the Diffusion of Useful Knowledge had indicated at the outset that tracts on politics and political economy would be among its publications, but internal divisions in a society which, despite radical backing, remained remarkably whiggish, prevented their appearance and so helped to weaken the Society's influence. Charles Knight, the publisher, did, however, write two pamphlets, *Results of Machinery* and *The Rights of Industry*, which were published by the Society, praised and blamed depending on the prejudices of reviewers, distributed through the Society's machinery, sold, and given away.[3] *Chambers's Journal* and similar publications did what they could, and the tracts multiplied. They were intended to teach the science to children or to the working classes, or to the two indifferently, for the problems of style and level of approach were hardly yet analysed, let alone solved. Let us again hear from Richard Whately at Oxford:

[1] BM, Add. MSS, 35,146/10, 35,154/110b.

[2] McCulloch to Coates, July 9, 1831, S.D.U.K. Letters, UCL.

[3] This whole matter is discussed in R. K. Webb, *The British Working Class Reader*, pp. 85–90, 114–22.

There are some very simple but important truths belonging to the science we are now engaged in, which might with the utmost facility be brought down to the capacity of a child, and which, it is not too much to say, the Lower Orders cannot even safely be left ignorant of. One of them I adverted to in a former Lecture. Can the labouring classes (and that too in a country where they have a legal right to express practically their political opinions,) can they safely be left to suppose, as many a demagogue is ready, when it suits his purpose, to tell them, that inequality of conditions is inexpedient, and ought to be abolished—that the wealth of a man whose income is equal to that of a hundred labouring families, is so much deducted from the common stock, and causes a hundred poor families the less to be maintained;—and that a general spoliation of the rich and equal division of property, would put an end to poverty for ever? . . .

Much of that kind of knowledge to which I have been alluding, might easily be embodied, in an intelligible and interesting form, not merely in regular didactic treatises, but in compilations of history, or of travels, or in works of fiction, which would afford amusement as well as instruction. For amusement, of one kind or another, men *will* seek, and find: and it is therefore a great point gained in respect of morality, if the mass of the people can be provided with such as shall be, even merely not hurtful. . . . It is not enough to teach the people to read, and then merely to put the Bible into their hands. Books should be written expressly for their use, (and how can men of education be more laudably occupied?) not merely of grave instruction, but also such as may form in them a taste that shall tend to withdraw them, in their hours of recreation also, from all that is gross and corrupting.[1]

Imagine that view multiplied among thoughtful, concerned people all over England, and it is easy to see what Harriet Martineau set out to do, and why she was so enthusiastically received.[2]

Enough has been said to indicate how neatly political economy fitted in with Miss Martineau's qualifications. Not only did the context provide a challenge and a mission for a fledgling "national instructor", but the science itself was so much a part of her that the moment of illumination she experienced on reading Mrs. Marcet's *Conversations* was little more than the discovery

[1] *Introductory Lectures*, pp. 217–19.

[2] And Mrs. Marcet too. Her *Conversations on Political Economy* of 1817 was a serious and sometimes rather demanding text in the traditional form of a dialogue. But in 1831 she published some simple fairy tales collected in 1833 as *John Hopkins's Notions of Political Economy*, which, said the *Athenaeum*, while they did not rival the Martineau tales "in depth of science or range of fancy", were nonetheless a very creditable attempt. Mrs. Marcet said in a preface that it would be obvious to the reader that the tales were intended primarily for the working classes.

of the name of political economy. The economic problems of Norwich and of the Martineau family provided a personal involvement; I have already suggested that the subjects of political economy must have been discussed again and again in the Magdalen Street house. But even more impressive is the way in which, once she began to study political economy systematically, the science fitted into her fundamental intellectual pattern.

Her periodical writing in the two years before the *Illustrations of Political Economy* was begun shows her concern with it. In 1832 she published an essay in the *Repository* on the duty of studying political economy, obviously to prepare the way for her series. Fraud and circumvention in commercial life, theft and licentiousness among the poor, idleness and deceit in a population unwisely allowed to grow too numerous, wars, commercial jealousy, and national competition—all arose from acts inconsistent with political economy; yet the subject was hardly known, she said, in any class, in government, among the middle classes or the working classes. The philanthropists, instead of devoting themselves to propagating and attaining proper principles, toyed with bettering the consequences of neglect, and so held back the rapid improvement of society. Compare Sadler, she said, who urged the poor to have children on the conviction that God would provide, with Arkwright, who created employment for a million of permanent population. The bit-by-bit reformers like Liverpool, Canning, and Huskisson, though headed in the right direction, did not go far enough; they got lost amid details, even though general principles were clearly evident. The few who really understood political economy were not in the ministry, in parliament, or, with a few exceptions, in the universities and schools. Their sole outlet was the press. Of one thing Miss Martineau was certain. If people wanted a better state of things, if they wanted reform, they had to begin by informing themselves, by learning the principles of political economy so that their interests, governed by those principles, would be properly looked to by government.[1] That was the work to which she would contribute.

Here again the advocacy of principle over empiricism, for political economy was a science. This fact had struck her forcefully on reading Samuel Bailey's *Essays on the Pursuit of Truth.* She quoted him at length on the superb way in which political

[1] *MR,* n.s., vi, 24–34 (January, 1832); *Misc.*, i, 272–88.

economy illustrated the doctrine of necessity: "The principle which is at bottom of all the reasonings of political economy, is in fact the uniformity with which visible or assignable circumstances operate on the human will"—an illustration she thought not only apt but beautiful.[1]

In these comments there is apparent an attitude with which Miss Martineau has not usually been credited. The political economy tales, for reasons which will shortly be apparent, can be read in a way that would seem to issue in so bleak an outlook that Thomas Gradgrind himself could not have improved on it. John Stuart Mill wrote to Carlyle that "she reduces the *laissez-faire* system to absurdity as far as the *principle* goes, by merely carrying it out to all its consequences".[2] That is true enough, but it does not say the final word about Miss Martineau's attitude to political economy. It is so easy to see the issues of political economy and laissez-faire in black and white. To take a good confrontation of views, in 1847 the *Morning Post*, a Tory paper, attacked the theory that leaving each individual to his own devices will produce the good of the whole; this was not only erroneous but anti-social. In good Tory fashion, it continued:

> We had rather see men commanded by the law, and induced by habit, to act continually as members of a community, and to consider not what is best, each for himself, but what is best for the whole society. We do not suppose that the selfishness of human nature is ever to be overcome, but we would have the laws and institutions of society so framed as to give it all possible discountenance.

To this *The Economist* replied that law-making individuals are as liable to err as ordinary individuals, and as there are no instincts directed to promoting social welfare, the probabilities would seem to favour the promotion of public good by leaving ordinary individuals to take care of themselves. Self-love has built up commerce; through commerce, self-love builds peace, and so laissez-faire is in the best sense social.

> The *Post* probably imagines, because laws and institutions are intended to promote the public benefit, that they make society; but a different philosophy represents society as the natural product of the instincts of individuals, to which Tory and protectionist institutions have endeavoured to give a form different from that impressed on it by nature.[3]

---

[1] *Misc.*, ii, 284. [2] April 11 and 12, 1833, *Letters of John Stuart Mill* i, 46.
[3] *The Economist*, January 2, 1847.

Somewhere between these two opposed positions, one (we may say) paternalistic, the other individualistic, stood Harriet Martineau. That Tory and protectionist institutions worked counter to nature she had no doubt; on the other hand, for her, self-love was akin to barbarism. To the Mandevillian paradox of private vices—public virtues, Miss Martineau replied with the morality which lay in necessarianism. That philosophy, it will be remembered, required the utmost exertion on the part of the individual to bring himself into line with the natural laws of society; for the individual to rest sunk in ignorance and selfishness was a sin and one surely to be punished by the necessary operation of the laws. McCulloch and the economists saw ruin as the punishment for miscalculation or improvidence; but the sovereign remedy of education was a part of the total system. Individuals, in good Hartleian fashion, could be so formed as to allow the natural laws to produce a happy and full society; if they were not so formed, the laws would operate anyhow, but the society would not be a happy one.

Political economy, by itself, could be no more than negative. The positive action had to come, not from the state, but from an active diffused morality. After all, the Newtonian model itself was negative, taken alone; positive creative science could arise only by pursuing its implications in accordance with a method which had produced but was external to the model. The moral difficulty that Smith had resolved by postulating the moral sentiment Harriet Martineau solved by necessarianism.

To be sure, many advocates of political economy paid little more than lip-service to this essential qualification; in some, the Gradgrinds and Bounderbys with whom Leonard Horner and his fellow factory inspectors had to deal, there was not even lip-service.[1] For them, it was every man for himself, and devil

[1] "Met Mr. Leonard Horner, Factory Inspector, at the Council office today. He said that since his appointment—in 1833 he had not met six Mill Owners who expressed any sympathy with, or regard for the improvement of, the labouring classes in their employ!" H. S. Tremenheere, Journal, July 13, 1840. See also the distinction between "good" manufacturers and "bad" manufacturers in J. B. Brebner, "Laissez-faire and State Intervention in Nineteenth-Century Britain", *Journal of Economic History, Supplement*, VIII (1948), p. 66, n. 9. Place's comment is relevant: "Our friend Fox is as you say 'a great public benefactor': He is one of the very few persons who will put himself to inconvenience, spend his time and take pains to do good for the sake of those he wishes to serve, and I know very few indeed who will do these things. I have very little respect for mere talkers, scarcely any for foolish benevolent people who go canting about caring little for any thing which is they think not likely to increase the reversionary interest they have

take the hindmost—an attitude for which Miss Martineau could not find sufficient reprobation. "*When the ends of individual life are duly regarded*," she wrote, "the aims of society (which are themselves but means) will be certainly fulfilled." With more equal distribution of labour, it will be easier to distinguish individual capacities, and the rewards of labour will be more secure. "Then the temptations of self-interest would be weakened, as there would be less want, and men could not covet or grasp with impunity." [1] Or, even better to illustrate the point, here is her reply to an author who was indignant at the idea that benevolence could grow out of self-love through the influence of early association, i.e., education:

> We hope we are not "ever anxious to degrade the character of man," yet we avow such to be our belief; and in the whole economy of Providence, there is no process which more powerfully excites our admiration and gratitude than that by which the selfish principle is made subservient to the growth of benevolence. It is a beautiful spectacle to watch the expansion of the affections in the mind of a child; to see how, by pleasurable association, his interests are gradually transferred from himself to others; how, having once felt pleasure and pain for his parents and companions, the association strengthens, till a desire of the good of others renders him unmindful of his own feelings; how, self-denial being once exercised, the exercise becomes more easy and frequent till it is itself the source of as much pleasure to the individual as his benevolence can confer on others; and how the sum of human happiness is thus indefinitely increased, and man is prepared for that state where nothing that defileth can enter. . . . As for the degradation imputed to the process referred to, it is purely imaginary. Man is what he is, by whatever means he became so; and as the choice of those means does not rest with him, the beauty or meanness of the process employed is ascribable not to him, but to his Maker and Guide. Benevolence is venerable and beautiful, and the elements from which it is formed, the influences under which it expands, are created and administered by God. It is the part of man to investigate the nature of those elements, to watch the operation of those influences, in order to use, as he best may, his privilege of co-operating with the univeral Father in the development of mind, and the creation of happiness. If he ventures to doubt the

in heaven. Mr. Fox is not one of these, he is one who would do good, even if he were persuaded there was no heaven at all, he understands the true reasons why he should endeavour to make mankind wiser and better and consequently happier. As for me I almost despair of them, and have always done so, yet I sometimes endeavour to be useful because I know nothing better that I can employ myself about." (Place to HM, September 8, 1832, BM. Add. MSS, 35,149/189b.

[1] "Godwin's Thoughts on Man", *Misc.*, ii, 131. Italics mine.

efficiency, or dispute the existence, of the process, because it is not accordant with his notions of fitness and beauty, it follows that his notions are imperfect, and not that the process is in fault. . . . Where Dr. Crombie sees deformity and apprehends degradation, some other inquirers discern order and dignity: not that they think selfishness desirable in itself, or see anything noble in the perfection of benevolence. But beauty resides in the process, though not in the elements employed; and the dignity of the object imparts significance to the means by which it is attained.[1]

The political economy tales, then, may have overstated the case, for reasons which could hardly be avoided in a rapidly written, simply conceived, didactic work. In some of her associations with manufacturers in later years, she may have seen goodwill and benevolence where we might not. Yet she felt that her primary sympathies lay with the working men against their masters, as we shall see, subject only to the realization (which she firmly believed would come about) *on both sides* of what men could and could not do.

Miss Martineau was to have her views on property considerably modified by her visit to America. In what specific ways she does not say: perhaps in connection with the argument from property rights for the maintenance of slavery, or as a result of conversations with Channing, whose views on property were remarkably heterodox.[2] But whatever the nature of the impact, she was able to see some good in Owenism, to repent the stringency and silliness of some of the tales, and in the late thirties, she reported to her friend Tremenheere that she had dressed down a doctor who spoke to her against the labouring man, assuming that that was what she, as an economist, wanted to hear.

Two problems faced her as she studied political economy: how best to illustrate it, and how to find a publisher. In 1829, Fox, her inevitable adviser, received the two tales written for Houlston, followed shortly by another tale on the enclosure of commons, and replied encouragingly. In 1831, she applied to the Society for the Diffusion of Useful Knowledge, apparently encouraged by the publication of Knight's *Results of Machinery*.

[1] "Crombie's Natural Theology", *Misc.*, ii, 263–64. This same argument is to be found at considerable length in Speculation II, "Is Benevolence a Principle Distinct from Self-Love, or a Modification of It?" in Cogan, *Ethical Questions*, pp. 81–103, esp. pp. 100–103. Miss Martineau was an admirer of this book.

[2] Channing to William Burns, March 31, 1832, *Memoir of William Ellery Channing*, ii, 118. *SA*, ii, 176–87.

She mentioned the two Houlston tales, and indicated that her scheme for a series was only in its earliest stages. She sent the enclosure story, then called *Pemberton*, but later (probably with revisions) the third story in the series, *Brooke and Brooke Farm*. Knight approved the story and the scheme, and she agreed to adopt changes he had suggested, but the project died in committee, rejected, she said later, because of dullness.[1] The planning of the series was done in Dublin in 1831 while she was visiting James and his family. One publishing firm, sounded by mail, asked her to stop in London, then turned her down. Other London firms were similarly disinclined, the cholera and the reform excitement serving as the ostensible reasons.

She was rescued finally by Fox, whose brother was just then setting up as a publisher. Charles Fox consulted James Mill, who, as one might expect, rejected the idea of political economy wrapped up in tales and recommended didactic form. The other reluctant publishers probably agreed with him. Though Miss Martineau might insist that moral sciences were best taught by exemplification, that "dramatists and novelists of a high order have usually the advantage, as moralists, over those whose office it is to present morals in an abstract form",[2] a scheme of twenty-three tales in twenty-five parts was rather a large hostage to proof of the proposition, particularly when the plan came from an unknown young lady in the provinces. Small wonder, too, that Charles Fox insisted on discontinuing the series at the end of the second number, unless a thousand copies were sold within a fortnight. Miss Martineau was expected to find not only enough subscribers to ensure covering costs—Fox never expected the series to pay to the extent of providing her with any income—but ways of handling the distribution. But she accepted the terms, pressed James and the rest of the family into promoting subscriptions, and drew up a prospectus which was sent, at her mother's suggestion, to all the members of both houses of parliament. By February, these efforts had brought only three hundred subscriptions, so Fox must have approached the publication date with considerable uneasiness.

As matters turned out, she was right and the publishing world was wrong. The monthly sale hovered about ten thousand, which Fox calculated to mean about 144,000 immediate readers.

[1] HM to Knight, April and June 1831, S.D.U.K. Letters, UCL.
[2] "Genius of Scott", *Misc.*, i, 28, 52–53.

She was soon released from the subscription clause of the contract, each number was reprinted, and by August there was a profit of £600 to be divided between publisher and author, thus allowing Harriet to make a generous loan to James to help him to move from Dublin to Liverpool.[1] The S.D.U.K. tried to get the series back; a society, projected by Roebuck, Place, and Hume to provide cheap political reading matter, asked for it. In Norwich, Miss Martineau's mail swelled fantastically, as M.P.'s sent her bluebooks, and individuals, official and non-official, tried to persuade her to write about their pet projects. Her first important intuition of what the public wanted had been triumphantly accurate. She was famous.

"I wish I was in London," she wrote to Place, "I want to be doing something with the pen, since no other means of action in politics are in a woman's power." So in November, 1832, she moved permanently to London, lodging first in Conduit Street, then in August, 1833, taking a house in Fludyer Street, just behind Downing Street. There her mother and aunt Lee joined her, the addition of the aunt being a prerequisite since, given her work, Miss Martineau could not commit herself to being her mother's sole companion. It was not, perhaps, an ideal arrangement, but the older women respected her work and her independence, and, limiting her callers to two hours a day, she settled in to work.[2]

Her original notion was that the tales, which average about one hundred and thirty duodecimo pages each, should appear quarterly; her brother and her publisher persuaded her to accept a monthly schedule. That meant a two-year programme of deadlines, doubled later by the addition of the poor law tales, and complicated by occasional bouts of illness and a continual round of lionizing in London society. Under such conditions, the composition of the *Illustrations* was nothing short of a *tour de force*. It required not only determination but rapid and certain methods.

In her autobiography she indicates some of the books on which she relied and some of the efforts she made to ensure the accuracy

[1] HM to James, December 18, 1831, February 16, August 30, and November 18, 1832. HM to Tremenheere, February 23, 1844, Tremenheere Papers.

[2] HM to Place, May 12, 1832, BM, Add. MSS, 35,149/147b. HM to James, March 14, August 1, September 15, 1833. The rent for the house was £50, taxes £25, and furniture was purchased from the previous tenants for £325. Only one attic had to be papered.

III. A Contemporary Opinion

Here is Miss Harriet in the full enjoyment of economical philosophy: her tea-things, her ink-bottle, her skillet, her scuttle, her chair, are all of the Utilitarian model; and the cat, on whom she bestows her kindest caresses, is a cat who has been trained to the utmost propriety of manners by that process of instructions which we should think the most efficient on all such occasions. There she sits cooking—

> " . . . rows
> Of chubby duodecimos;"

certain of applause from those whose praise is ruin, and of the regret of all who feel respect for the female sex, and sorrow for perverted talent, or, at least, industry; doomed to wither in the cold approbation of the political economists; and, after ghosting it about for their hour,

> " . . . thence
> Be buried at the Row's expense."

(*Fraser's Magazine*, November 1833)

IV. Christus Consolator by Ary Scheffer

A print of this painting hung in Miss Martineau's room at Tynemouth. That talisman, she called it, "including the consolations of eighteen centuries!—that mysterious assemblage of the redeemed Captives and tranquillized Mourners of a whole Christendom!—that inspired epitome of suffering and solace!—it may well be a cause of wonder, almost amounting to alarm, to those who, not having needed, have never felt its power. If there were now burnings or drownings for sorcery, that picture, and some who possess it, would soon be in the fire, or at the bottom of a pond. No mute operation of witchcraft, or its dread, could exceed the silent power of that picture over sufferers." (*Life in the Sickroom*, p. 158). In a leading article in the *Daily News*, December 22, 1857, she described it. On the one hand, Christ heals the brokenhearted: the mother and her dead infant; Tasso representing the woes of genius; the aged widow; the young widow, and the young girl representing faith, resignation, and hope, the three phases of trust. The three men behind, the infidel, the recusant, the intending suicide, represent the converse moods of unbelief, rebellion, and despair. On the other hand, He delivers the captives—Mary Magdalen, the maniac, serfs of various nations, and the Negro slave. In the corner are the "beautiful accessories" of the broken sword and spent cannonball. In the article she was angry because a Southern book used the picture with the Negro omitted.

of her settings. The Norwich public library (a large one) provided her with a good many materials. Friends provided her with more. Richard MacKenzie Bacon, editor of the *Norwich Mercury*, was one source. Through Fox she was put into touch with Joseph Hume and Francis Place. Hume sent her reports on fisheries; Place responded with long and enthusiastic letters, pamphlets, and blue-books on population, wages, combinations, poor laws, emigration, and currency. She told him that she would go on troubling him, and he was delighted to help: he thought her bold where others were timid, and the tales not only gratifying but exhilarating.[1]

The writing itself was simple; after a few days of planning, she wrote the tales as she wrote letters, without stopping, and without any correction or revision. The only difficulty was shortage of space, for the doctrines had to be fitted in as if she were packing a trunk, but that, she told Place, she rather enjoyed. One extract from a letter describes the process with the excitement of contemporaneity rather than of memory:

> I am going on swimmingly. Mr. Hume has sent me the Parliamentary Reports I wanted, & truly they give me just what I might have looked for in vain elsewhere. Being willing to put the horse before the cart, I take Popn. before Wages; & as I want all the room I can get, I carry on the same characters as I was grieved to part with at the end of V [*Ella of Garveloch*]. Nothing can suit better, it seems to me. Ella & her brother (in V) establish a Rent on Garveloch, & have only two dwellings for a neighbourhood, & fish in a poor way, & make out with helping & growing a little poor barley. Now (in VI) the British Fisheries being established close by (a fact) they rise & multiply (a fact) till a bad season or two pinches them (a fact) & then comes an epidemic, (a fact) thins them, & helps up the survivors. Here is room for bustle, in contrast to the last, for uncommon scenery & varied incident, & for showing the miseries of the positive check. The society is sequestered enough to exemplify the principle without interruption, & numerous enough to make it a fair example.—With the cooperage & curing establishments, in addition to the finishers & managers, there will be 4 or 500 people on the scene.—Won't this do famously? I did think of having a village at the time of the last plague; but it was too far back to admit easily of the colloquial comments necessary; & people wd complain of its being an extreme case, & wd be put in

[1] HM to Bacon, n.d., Cambridge, Add. MSS, 6244 (35). *Auto.*, i, 149, 176–96. HM to Place, n.d., May 12, 1832, June 1, 1832; Place to HM, September 8 and 9, 1832, BM, Add. MSS, 35,159/146–49, 189–94. Joseph Hume to HM, March 29, 1832, Harvard.

mind of the Cholera. Mr. Hume sent his documents just in time. —Well; next come Coventry Wages; & then two more, before I have done with the mighty subject.[1]

The Wealth of Nations and the *Essay on Population* were of course important sources for doctrine. Smith, however, was the least important of the major writers: he provided some illustrative material—the setting of *Ella of Garveloch* was suggested by a passage in *The Wealth of Nations*—and much of the discussion of practical reforms is Smithian. Malthus's essay was, of course, central; she went no further in her population stories than the Malthusian solution of "moral restraint", but even that gave the *Quarterly* a chance to "tomahawk" her for dealing with forbidden subjects and Place a chance to criticize her in a friendly way for ignoring birth-control.[2]

The clearest and most frequently used source for doctrine was James Mill's *Elements of Political Economy*. She had commended his organization in an earlier article,[3] and an examination of the subjects treated in each of the tales alongside the index to James Mill's text will show that the development is parallel, item by item. The demands of narration varied the proportion, of course; sometimes the immediate political or social importance of a subject (like population) caused her to give more attention to it than Mill did. But his influence went far beyond organization. In a half-dozen of the stories, the summaries at the end, which form the doctrinal skeletons of the tales, are taken practically *verbatim* from Mill or are obvious *précis* of longer discussions, positively identifiable by her use of concepts peculiar to Mill.

The reason for her reliance on Mill is easy to see. His text is a belligerently schematized summary of the principal doctrines of political economy, and, as McCulloch pointed out, the "secondary principles and modifying circumstances, which exert so powerful an influence over general principles, are wholly, or almost wholly overlooked".[4] For the close schedule on which

[1] To W. J. Fox, March 29 [1832], BM, Add. MSS, 35,149/145–145b.

[2] "But I am sure of my point as to the tendency of population to press on the means of subsistence always. Only the *tendency*." HM to E. P. Peabody, October 21, [1835], LC.

[3] *MR*, n.s., vi, 24–34 (January, 1832), *Misc.*, i, 285. As a reviewer put it, "Miss Martineau, who is a disciple of Mill, proposes to become an evangelist of his doctrines." *MR*, n.s., vi, 136 (February, 1832). Mark Blaug, *Ricardian Economics*, is excellent for the context of economic theory in which the tales, as political economy, must be judged.

[4] McCulloch, *Literature of Political Economy*, pp. 17–18.

Harriet Martineau was working, Mill was made to order. But here, as in her writing for the *Monthly Repository*, it is on matters of theory where she relies most heavily on Mill and the other writers. In dealing with applications of theories, with practical reforms, she is less dependent on the authority of the economists and falls back on the more familiar ground of her inbred manufacturer's radicalism.

In the range of educational opinion Harriet Martineau stood well to the left. Education, she thought, cut two ways, up and down; it would teach the lower classes their best interest, to co-operate, if not baldly to obey, and—as I have stressed before—it had to teach the ruling classes to be worthy of that co-operation. That dual purpose is evident in the tales. Take, as an example of the first, *The Hill and the Valley*. Competition forces the manager of the works to install machinery; when a boy is killed through his own carelessness, the anger of the workers rises to such a pitch that they destroy the machinery. Troops are called to restore order, the miscreants are taken off to prison, and the destruction of the factory forces the ironworks to close, depriving the people who had streamed to the valley of their means of support. The tale is reminiscent of her earlier *The Rioters*, but the conclusion there—the wholly moral one of the misery produced by rioting—is now replaced by the assertion that "the interests of the two classes of producers, Labourers and Capitalists, are therefore the same; the prosperity of both depending on the accumulation of CAPITAL". The importance of capital accumulation through saving is a central assumption of Ricardian economics and the ground of an important fight with Malthus; but the optimistic implication of an identity of interests of the classes does not follow logically, for Ricardo held that a rise in wages necessarily meant a decline in profits, and believed that the introduction of machinery, while necessary, often ran counter to the interests of the working classes. But optimism was important amid the attacks of trade unionism and socialism

So too, the problems of wages and population are heavily emphasized—as one might expect when the agricultural risings of 1830 were a recent memory and a Royal Commission was sitting on the poor law. Population theory is explained in the Garveloch tales, the wages fund theory in *A Manchester Strike* (one of the best stories). Then comes *Cousin Marshall*, on poor laws and charity; *Ireland*, an argument against extending the poor law; *Homes Abroad* to urge emigration; while *For Each and For All* refutes socialist theories.

Other tales have a different purpose, the radical one of blasting away at entrenched interests and inherited prejudices. The indictment of slavery in *Demerara*, demands for freedom of the money market in *Berkeley the Banker* and in *Messrs. Vanderput and Snoek*, the impassioned pleas for free trade in *The Loom and the Lugger* and *Sowers Not Reapers*, the accusations against colonial monopoly in *Cinnamon and Pearls* and against privileged trading corporations in *A Tale of the Tyne*—all these are certainly aimed at higher game than working men. If the series were directed solely to the task of convincing the lower classes of the inevitability of the bourgeois industrial order and social morality, if its effect were intended to be entirely conservative, preponderant attention would hardly have been given to the present abuses of the system, and something more on the hygienic order of Mrs. Marcet's fairy tales would have resulted. In the coupled purpose of the series, the radical outweighs the conservative; the clearing away is the greater task; and in the very association of the two appeals is reflected her confidence in the amenability to reason, in the educability, of the audience she was addressing. She could afford to be bold, she told Place, because she had nothing to lose which could stand in comparison with her regard for the people —and she meant it.[1]

Moderation is hardly an outstanding characteristic of the tales. At many points she goes beyond her mentors. Her optimistic conclusion about identity of interests is a case in point; the lengths to which she has her characters carry "moral restraint" is another. J. S. Mill felt it necessary to remonstrate against her entire condemnation of the poor laws, when the poor law commission had clearly pronounced in favour of the principle of a poor rate.[2] Empson, in the *Edinburgh*, protested against her enthusiasm in cutting down private benevolence.[3] The terrible pass to which the people of Garveloch are brought by their uncontrolled reproduction; the successive disasters which come to the people burdened with corn laws; the astounding reformation

[1] March 28, [1834], BM, Add. MSS, 35,149/276.
[2] *MR*, n.s., viii, 321.
[3] lvii, 31–32 (April, 1833). Note too his whiggish alarm at the implication that poverty might be abolished, pp. 18–19.

of the village of Brooke after enclosure—they seem ludicrous and easily support Mill's contention about her reducing the whole science to absurdity by carrying it out logically to all its consequences.

Such extremism is easy to understand. To begin with, as we have seen, she was enthusiastic. Further, her characters were frankly intended to embody principle; they had to stand uncompromisingly for good or bad and had to preach absurdly. But the approach seems to have fitted remarkably well with the demands of most of her readers, and our objections and Mill's are not found generally among the responses I have seen. Again, the speed with which the tales were written had something to do with their crudity. Empson pointed out that the later tales showed the stress of the schedule on which they were composed, and some of the faults and extremities which troubled his Whig conscience he attributed simply—if somewhat incorrectly—to haste and insufficient reflection. The principal consideration, however, is that these tales were a remarkable display of a journalistic talent, that true journalistic talent, as Leslie Stephen put it, "of turning hasty acquisitions to account".[1] They aimed at bringing the science down to an assimilable level for the great mass of people. The books already written did not do that: "they give us its history; they give us its philosophy; but we want its *picture*".[2] And that picture could not be over-subtle. Said Gibbon Wakefield a few years later: "Thinking, to those who are unused to it, is a very disagreeable process; most people can be induced to exercise their reason only by some enticement addressed to their imagination. . . . In order to instruct, it is needful to amuse." [3] The ordinary reader has little patience with qualifications and hedging; a call to action is not footnoted, limited, and cautious. Yet the dangers of such an approach are great. It can caricature what it aims to teach, and the enticement can become an end in itself. Charles Knight was probably right in saying that thousands read the tales for the stories and left the principles quite aside.[4]

[1] *DNB.*

[2] *Illustrations of Political Economy*, Preface, p. xi.

[3] Preface to his edition *The Wealth of Nations* (1843), i, p. vii.

[4] *Popular History of England*, viii, 47. Empson scented the danger too; he saw that the method demanded constant reference from summary to narrative and back again to fix the principles firmly in the reader's mind. *ER*, lvii, 36–37. But compare *MR*, n.s., vi, 137: "This is no attempt to trick the idle into knowledge, by offering

It seems strange today to read the praises which were bestowed on the *Illustrations* for their characterization, depiction, and narration.[1] While the tales do not, perhaps, deserve Leslie Stephen's description as "unreadable", it is not possible to ascribe to them much literary distinction, and it is to the author's credit that she recognized her limitations.[2] Even granting the necessity of some incredibly didactic conversations, her characters are for the most part wooden, the emotion is synthetic, and the rare attempts at humour are hopeless. There is, to be sure, remarkable ingenuity displayed in setting each of the tales, but she was not always successful in tying the story to the doctrine she was trying to teach.[3]

Criteria have changed. The *Norwich Mercury* spoke of "delicacy of perception". Lucy Aikin commented to Channing on the grace, animation and pathos of the stories, "rare even in works of pure amusement". Channing, who dissented from the doctrines, delighted in the stories:

> The Garveloch tales are particularly good. What a noble creature Ella is! To give us in a fishing-woman an example of magnanimity and the most touching affection, and still keep her in her sphere; to make all the manifestations of this glorious virtue appropriate to her condition and consistent with our nature,—this seems to me to indicate a very high order of mind, and to place Miss Martineau among the first moral teachers as well as first writers of our time. Perhaps I may be partial. I feel so grateful to her for doing such justice to the poor and to human nature, that I am strongly tempted to raise her to the highest rank.

But Miss Mitford liked the first story best—"very interesting and Robinson Crusoe-ish",—and the rest she found rather too wise for her. "I have an old aversion to do-me-good books in general,

---

it the semblance of mere amusement. The design is fairly avowed. The object is to impart instruction in the mode best adapted to reach and enlighten the minds of those who have not been accustomed to continued and severe thought. They are previously told the truths of which the nature and proofs are to be evolved by the narrative. Political economy was first learned by the study of history and the observation of facts; why should it not be taught in a similar way, and communicated by tales which are substantially true, though circumstantially fictitious?"

[1] Fox in *MR*, n.s., vii, 379; Empson in *ER*, lvii, 9–10; or Charles Knight's fantastic estimate, *Popular History of England*, viii, 477. Even the *Quarterly's* slashing article admitted some literary merits, although it found many faults, xlix, 130 (April, 1833).

[2] In the autobiographical memoir published after her death, reprinted in *Auto.*, ii, 565.

[3] *French Wines and Politics* is probably the best example of this fault. See also *Spectator*, November 9, 1833, on *Briery Creek* (her tribute to Priestley); or *Athenaeum*, December 28, 1833, on *Cinnamon and Pearls*.

& to political economy in particular—perhaps because I don't understand it." [1]

There were other critics besides the *Quarterly* who attacked Miss Martineau as the representative of a school. John Sterling spoke of her extraordinary zeal and talents, but said her picture of the West Indies was absurd, wrong on cultivation, wrong on the Negroes. ". . . I have seen negroes after a hurricane, and she has not, and I know that it both is a calamity to them, and that they feel it to be so." A member of the Society for the Diffusion of Useful Knowledge urged, during the reconsideration, that the Society decide against the tales. He was doubtful about stories; they needed very careful revision, "or the Society will be lending itself occasionally to the propagation of Benthamism, or Utilitarian notions; and there are various low passages about Religion, and the observance of the Laws, which I should think would be improper, in the hands of youth at least".[2] But in general the response was enthusiastic.

The *Spectator* could hardly contain its excitement about the work of this "benefactor of her species". Brougham urged Napier to see to it that the *Edinburgh* review was a favourable one and that it specifically pointed out how extensively the tales must be used. "She is as prolific as Scott, she reasons as well as A. Smith, and she has the best feelings, and, generally, the most correct principles of any of our political economists"—a remark which does not speak well for Brougham's knowledge of the subject. To the *Athenaeum*, she was learned without being blue, and, unlike the tale-writing part of her sex, capable of writing with feeling and truth without lapsing into sentimentality. Place wanted to distribute the tales widely, particularly the last of them, a kind of summary called *The Moral of Many Fables*. He knew, he told her, of no book so valuable, or so likely to work an instantaneous effect if every master and man would read it. If he were rich, he would see to it that every institution, public library, or book club of any sort, stationary or perambulating, had copies of it.

Thomas Latimer, the Exeter journalist, suggested that the

[1] *Norwich Mercury*, June 2, 1832. Lucy Aikin to W. E. Channing, October 15, 1832, and Channing to Miss Aikin, May 30, 1833, *Corr.*, pp. 148, 172–73. Mitford, *Life*, ii, 140–41.

[2] John Sterling to Sarah Austin, July 9, 1832, Ross *Three Generations*, pp. 86–87. Ward to Coates, December 7, 1832, S.D.U.K. Letters. For criticism from a vested interest, see Oculus, *The Tale of "Cinnamon and Pearls"*.

money used to set the police on some local trade unionists might better have been spent distributing a few sets of Miss Martineau's "admirable treatises". The *Norwich Mercury* urged all those who loved their country to disseminate *The Hill and the Valley* as widely as possible, "not only among those who can read, but even among those who have not yet enjoyed the good effects of the schoolmaster, in order that they may hear read this cheap and unpretending volume, which while it teaches how to spread around the greatest good to the greatest number, inculcates a morality which must lead to the best results". Walter Farquhar Hook, the vicar of Leeds, suggested to a correspondent that *A Manchester Strike* would be "useful to your poor people at Coventry, if the time should come when any such folly should be meditated". These tributes and recommendations could be multiplied, though it is probable that there is none quite so portentous as Herbert Spencer's recollection that, although he probably read them largely for the stories, his letters of the spring of 1835 indicate that he had "gathered something of a solid kind".[1]

There was interest manifested in working-class circles too. John Finch of Liverpool, commenting on the progress of the co-operative principle, remarked that the fact "that every employment is honourable in proportion to its usefulness, has recently been beautifully illustrated in a little work on Political Economy, by Miss Harriet Martineau".[2] John Doherty, the trade unionist, though not assenting to all the principles, commended *A Manchester Strike* very highly for its veracity. "Every incident of the tale is drawn from real life, the characters are accurate and striking, and the whole plot of the story, or rather history of the 'strike' is natural and easy." The sufferings, the quarrels, the jealousies, and all the incidents of the general strike are most accurately drawn, he said, and anyone familiar with the great turnout of 1829 could place several of the characters.[3]

[1] *Spectator*, February 4, March 3, August 4, November 3, 1832, January 4, 1834. Brougham to Napier, July 17, 1832, BM, Add. MSS, 34,615/443–45. *Athenaeum*, May 19, 1832. Place to HM, March 4, 1834, BM, Add. MSS, 35,419/275b. Lambert, *The Cobbett of the West*, pp. 63–64. *Norwich Mercury*, January 14 and March 10, 1832. Hook to W. P. Wood, December 7, 1833, W. R. W. Stephens, *Life and Letters of Walter Farquhar Hook*, i, 257. Herbert Spencer, *An Autobiography*, i, 110–11.

[2] Third Co-operative Congress, *Proceedings*, p. 14.

[3] *Poor Man's Advocate*, September 29, 1832. Place supplied her with information for this tale, and to him she said it was her "most important subject". May 12, 1832, BM, Add. MSS, 35,149/147.

The Manchester and Salford Association for the Spread of Co-operative Knowledge wrote to express their admiration for her undertaking, and they received a reply which deserves quotation:

> Within a short time, and happily before the energy of youth is past, I have been awakened from a state of aristocratic prejudice, to a clear conviction of the *Equality of Human Rights*, and of the paramount duty of society, to provide for the support, comfort, and enlightenment of every member born into it. All that I write is now with a view to the illustration of these great truths; with the hope of pressing upon the rich a conviction of their obligations, and of inducing the poor to urge their claims with moderation and forbearance, and to bear about with them the credentials of intelligence and good deserts.
>
> All of us who agree in these grand principles, must aid one another in their diffusion. I will do what I can through the press; you must help me by assisting the circulation of my volumes. . . . I am not at present backed by the capital or influence of any society; and the success of my series depends therefore on the integrity of its principles, the merits of its execution, and the zeal of its friends. No pains shall be spared on my part.
>
> The two books that you mention are on my list. I have never seen Thomson's [Thompson's] work; the other is familiar to me, "Revolt of the Bees".[1]

She may have said a bit more than she really intended, but the letter makes clear the self-consciousness of her radicalism. The *Poor Man's Guardian*, reprinting this letter, called the *Illustrations* an excellent work, but when she attacked Owenism and advocated Malthusianism, the paper changed its opinion and in 1834 could sneer: "News for Miss Martineau.—The *Portland Courier* (an American paper) says that the young ladies of that town have formed an anti-matrimonial society!"[2] Finally, the *Monthly Repository* reported that at a public meeting in Spitalfields, when a speaker was urging legislative interference to protect the silk-weavers, a voice from the crowd shouted, "We want Harriet Martineau here!" How much one wants to know the source and the tone of voice!

The distribution problem was difficult; eighteenpence monthly for two years was a heavy outlay to expect from a working-man.

[1] *Lancashire and Yorkshire Co-operator*, n.s., March and April 1833; the letter is reprinted in the *Poor Man's Guardian*, May 5, 1832. She wrote to Place, who also recommended Thompson, that she had been unable to get hold of it, June 1, 1832, BM, Add. MSS, 35,149/148b.

[2] February 22, 1834. See also the attack on her Malthusianism in *Cobbett's Magazine*, April, 1833.

Mechanics' Institutions circulated the tales, of course; the committee of one of these organizations had rejected a members' appeal to allow novels in the library, but made an exception in the case of Miss Martineau's stories,[1] set apart from ordinary novels by their purpose. Manufacturers undoubtedly distributed them, particularly *A Manchester Strike*, as the *Spectator* and other papers urged. But though the tales remained on lists in the forties, though William Ellis could still give them as a gift to a teacher whose work in political economy he admired,[2] it is certain that their circulation was almost entirely middle-class. A very neat epitaph may be found in a letter to Mrs. Chapman after Miss Martineau's death. The writer recalled how the political economy series "beautifully bound, used to excite my admiration as a child".[3] Surely it was not beautifully bound tales in a banker's library that did the work that needed doing.

Or did they? *Spectator* pointed out ten years later that the series would not then have met the same success. By a lucky hit, Miss Martineau took the tide at its height, when the world was all agog for political economy.[4] There is the clue. The tales are important, not because they taught political economy, but because they evoked a response. A society in conflict was trying to find a way out through what we might call informal education. It was a mighty faith, this belief in the power of truth. But the problems of diffusing truth were severe, and the popularizers had a lot to learn. Miss Martineau was further along with the lessons than most and her efforts coincided precisely—as they were to do so often in future—with a need that was widely felt. Perhaps it was that work, testimony not conversion, that most needed doing. Austin Robinson, writing about *Life in the Wilds*, has summed it up nicely:

> Its great success, I am sure, rested on the passion to instruct rather than upon the desire to learn. We who suffer from a surfeit of simplified economics, may perhaps underrate the demand of an age that lacked a host of popularizers, and believed more faithfully that the ultimate truths were to be found in the principles discovered by Mr. Ricardo. But Harriet, I am sure, sold ten copies

---

[1] J. W. Hudson, *History of Adult Education*, p. 160.

[2] *Chambers's Journal*, May 24, 1845. Robert Fellowes, *Common Sense Truths, Proposed for the Consideration of the Working Classes*, p. 38. E. K. Blyth, *Life of William Ellis*, pp. 89–90.

[3] Emma Marshall to MWC. April 20, 1877?, BPL, Weston.

[4] December 5, 1840. Cf. Bulwer-Lytton, *England and the English*, ii, 74–75.

of *Life in the Wilds* to those who wished to give it to others for their good for every copy she sold to those who wished to read it themselves. Her tales epitomised the Victorian view of how others should be made to think.[1]

"She has now had a full season of London *lionizing*," wrote Miss Aikin to Channing, "and it is no small praise to say that, as far as we can judge it, it has done her nothing but good. She loves her neighbours the better for their good opinion of her, and I believe thinks the more humbly of herself for what she has seen of other persons of talent and merit." [2] The testimony to her modesty is general. That she carried it off so well is indeed admirable, because the temptations were great. The lionizing was one thing; she described it herself in an article in the *Westminster Review* in 1838, parts of which were reprinted in the *Autobiography*. But the snares and delusions of her position were more subtle and overpowering than that, and she could not resist entirely.

It is a failing common to intellectuals who by one means or another get near the seats of power that they begin to think that they have some effect. Everybody commented on the way in which the great and powerful flocked about Miss Martineau; she, understandably, commented on it herself. To her friend Miss Bacon, in Norwich, she wrote that she moved to London not merely for pleasure, but for the facilities it offered; still more, "the claims of the Govt. work which I have undertaken make it my *duty* to stay where I can work best".[3] And since Miss Bacon was no mousy provincial innocent, but a musician of some repute, this was not merely an effort to impress people at home, though it was certainly partly that.

Again, she wrote to James Tait regretting that she could not send him more for his magazine than she had done, but there she was, overwhelmed with materials and perplexed with a choice of outlets for her work. The series, still in progress, was a chore; moreover, "I have now direct access to the Cabinet, & feel that nothing is so important as to preach my sermons there. The radicalism of a woman does not alarm them, & I learn not a little from them as to how much the aristocracy does actually know of the people." [4] In 1833, she wrote elatedly to a friend

[1] *Economic Journal*, liv, 116–20 (April, 1944).
[2] June 13, 1833, *Corr.*, p. 176.
[3] N.d., Cambridge, Add MSS 6346 (45).
[4] November 10, 1832, NLS.

that she had had a long talk with Mr. Mackintosh, one of the factory commissioners. She was delighted to learn that Southwood Smith had been appointed physician to the central board of factory inspectors at her suggestion. "He is *precisely* fitted for the office, & I am very happy indeed that the appointment has taken place." She had written to Brougham to urge Smith's nomination, and, even though others certainly did so with greater effect, she must have found the choice especially encouraging, for Smith had written *Illustrations of the Divine Government*, the book about which she had been so delighted when her mother gave it to her ten years before. She had put a necessarian philosopher into government! [1]

Yet if she remained modest, we can be gentle with her fantasies. It is difficult to overstate the excitement of her situation —one year to wait excitedly in Norwich for expresses and newspapers with the latest news of the Reform Bill,[2] at the end of the next year to live in a house behind the Prime Minister's and be waited upon by ministers, secretaries, and the Lord Chancellor himself.

One of the most charming and impressive of her regular visitors was Thomas Drummond, already famous for the Drummond light, a source of hitherto unequalled power for lighthouses or microscopy. Drummond had been lured into politics and was to perform superbly as under-secretary for Ireland from 1836 to his death in 1840. In April, 1833, he became private secretary to Lord Althorp, the chancellor of the exchequer. "As his [Drummond's] business then lay in Downing Street, & I lived in the next street, Fludyer Street, he used to come to my study from Lord Althorp or Lord Grey when they wanted my opinion on measures which they were then preparing. . . . Our express business was (commonly) discussion of certain items of Lord Althorp's forthcoming budget, & changes in some of them, & consultations about Lord Grey's tithe measure, now forgotten in the final settlement." [3] Whatever may have been the effect of her advice on government measures, the conversations in her study—it must have been a pleasant and lively place to drop in on in an age when government routine was less demanding than

[1] HM to Brougham, two notes from April, 1833, UCL.
[2] HM to Place, May 12, 1832, BM, Add. MSS, 35,149/147b.
[3] From a letter of 1865, quoted in J. F. McLennan, *Memoir of Thomas Drummond*, p. 176.

it is today—were of great value to her. The continuation of the political economy tales in the five *Illustrations of Taxation* of 1834 profited, and even more, the perceptive and informed chapters on the Reform Cabinet in the *History*.

Miss Martineau was a very useful person to have around. What nowadays would be done by public relations officers then had to be done by private individuals. Charles Knight, for instance, as official publisher to the Poor Law Commission, undertook a number of publications which we would call propagandistic, as well as the printing of circulars, information sheets, and the innumerable printed forms (then something new) required by novel administrative techniques. Similarly, Miss Martineau was to write her *Guide to Service* for Knight and the Poor Law Commissioners in 1838. In 1833 she was chosen to prepare the way for the poor law reform.

Miss Martineau's friends were powerfully impressed by the court paid her by Lord Brougham.[1] In later years, Miss Martineau was one of the ex-Chancellor's most persistent critics, and her characterization of him at the end of an obituary sketch is maliciously accurate.[2] She assured Crabb Robinson that she had never thought well of him, that she had always known the bane of his vanity and the curse of his profligate soul.[3] Her opinion of him was certainly affected, despite her disclaimer, by a business dealing: he had promised, she said, to add twenty-five pounds to the seventy-five promised by the S.D.U.K. for each of the four poor law stories. The Society produced its three hundred pounds promptly, but she never heard from Brougham. Moreover, a visit to Lambton Castle made her a devoted admirer of Lord Durham, who left no doubt with the visitor of his

[1] "Here I pause to welcome Harriet Martineau, with all her blushing honours thick upon her. The Chancellor has sent for her expressly to write tales illustrative of pauperism, and has supplied her for the purpose with an immense mass of documents accessible only to official persons." Lucy Aikin to W. E. Channing, November 19, 1832, *Corr.*, p. 156.

[2] Lord Brougham and a group of guests were sitting for a daguerrotype. "The artist explained the necessity of perfect immobility. He only asked that his Lordship and friends would keep perfectly still 'for five seconds'; and his Lordship vehemently promised that he would not stir. He moved about too soon, however; and the consequence was—a blur where Lord Brougham should be; and so stands the daguerrotype view to this hour. There is something mournfully typical in this. In the picture of our century, as taken from the life by History, this very man should have been a central figure; but now, owing to his want of stedfastness, there will be for ever—a blur where Brougham should have been." *Biog. Sketches*, p. 164.

[3] April 27, 1843, DWL.

unfavourable view of the Lord Chancellor. From that time on, Brougham was "reserved, compromising and negative", whereas Durham was firm in radicalism and invariably calm and noble. She never forgave Brougham for his attacks on Durham or for the mercilessness with which he hounded Durham during and after the Canadian mission.[1]

On the other hand, it is equally clear that when Brougham first came to Fludyer Street, she was delighted. He knew more about the people than she had thought, she wrote to Tait; he was an extraordinary man for details and objected not at all to let others deduce principles from them, though he was not particularly anxious to do so himself.[2] She was a bit uneasy, though, over her association with power. When Brougham told her that she had a legitimate claim on a pension, she was considerably upset, because a pension could lead to misrepresentation. On the other hand, she wanted to travel to educate herself, and it would be cowardly to refuse an earned recompense. Her uncertainty is clear in her letters to James, but finally she decided to override her brother Robert's objections and to accept the money, if it was clearly offered for past services. In the event, nothing came of the proposal;—had the government wanted to offer her a retainer, or had she become too close to Durham?[3]

With *Poor Laws and Paupers Illustrated* it is unnecessary to stop long.[4] She was anxious to undertake the project when Brougham suggested it, partly because she would feel more at home in the material supplied to her by her friends than she was in political economy, "freed from the panic of the idea of stereotyping a hundred blunders with each No.", as she put it. Then, too, like the larger series, the need for the new effort was so great and the hope considerable that it might help to correct the social evils from which the country was suffering. For that she was willing to risk the heavy additional burden the work would place on her. The letters to Brougham about the series are wonderful for their tone. She could be properly respectful to the great man: "I feel too deeply to express very plainly the gratification that it is

[1] HM to James, December 3, 1833. *Auto.*, i, 166–67. *Hist.*, ii, 158–59.

[2] HM to Tait, November 10, 1832, NLS. HM to James, January 18, 1833.

[3] HM to Durham, December 18, [1833], HM to James, August 1 and September 20, 1833. See also Garnett, *Fox*, p. 87.

[4] They are discussed at some length in Webb, *British Working Class Reader*, pp. 126–27.

to a solitary young authoress, who has had no pioneer in her literary path but steadfastness of purpose, to find her exertions approved by yourself." But such gestures interfered not at all with her negotiations. She was to have the time she wanted (she was willing to resign her periodical work if necessary), and the arrangement with Charles Fox was to carry over to the new series. And "I must be secured against any repetition of the somewhat mortifying treatment which I have twice received from your Committee [of the Society for the Diffusion of Useful Knowledge] & also from any alteration being made in my writings *without my consent*".[1] She knew her adversaries, and she won her points.

The tales are based on the material collected by the assiduous assistant commissioners and printed in the vast report; she was given access to it before it was made public. The pictures of the evils of the old law are strikingly drawn, and the recommendations of the report—abolition of outdoor relief, paid overseers, unions of parishes, "less eligibility", a central commission—are set out with the exaggeration of her earlier illustrations of principle. The series attracted considerable attention—it is symptomatic of the importance of her work that the respectable public did not seem to get bored with her—but was not a publishing success, for Charles Fox lost £380 on it.

Still another project, however, deserves some careful attention, since it reveals attitudes which will be important in some later concerns, and because it deals with a pressing social problem. The labour unrest of the early thirties took the form of strikes and continual if not very successful efforts at trade union organization, culminating in the Grand National Consolidated Trades Union in 1834 and the transportation of the Tolpuddle labourers.

Industrialism brought together groups of Englishmen who had hitherto gone their separate ways without the necessity for much thought about a common situation. With the new interdependence in society there came also some filtering down of ideas, radical ideas, with which in many instances the men from the lower classes were unprepared to deal adequately—a fact which helps to explain the spotty, unsuccessful, and quarrelsome picture

[1] HM to Brougham, October 10, 1832, [December, 1832], and two from February, 1833, one misdated 1834. HM to S.D.U.K. Committee, a copy, March, 1833, UCL.

of early working-class organization. But contact between classes did not automatically bring agreement or understanding. Disraeli's metaphor of two nations had a broad application to a conflict of two (or more) cultures. One solution for this cultural estrangement, on the part of the enlightened middle and upper classes and many working-class leaders, was to assimilate the inferior culture to the superior; at the same time, there were leaders (from both classes) who were prepared, either from interest or conviction, to assert the claims of the inferior culture, to stand, if necessary, against the new world and to idealize an older, freer England. Hence the adulation of Cobbett, say, or of Feargus O'Connor, and the rejection of Lovett. The assimilation has made progress, but in the middle of the nineteenth century, the estrangement was almost as great as it had been in 1820, in spite of all the efforts of Place and the London Workingmen's Association and the Society for the Diffusion of Useful Knowledge and the Chamberses and the Christian Socialists and Harriet Martineau.

Lord Durham, whose fortune rested on coal, had been seriously troubled by labour unrest since 1831. His agent, Henry Morton, wrote to him then about a discussion with union leaders who were Ranter Preachers of an intelligence and acuteness which surprised him, so novel was this contact. He told them that he would gladly raise wages, if they would draft 150 or 200 men to be dismissed, and explained that with a redundancy of labour they were in no position to impose their demands. "This last sentence shock'd one of the Ranter preachers," who replied that "providence had not, & wd not send more people into this sinful world than was quite necessary for its purposes." The miners were indignant, and Morton was appalled—a good example of ideological estrangement!

Moreover, even the most sympathetic persons in the upper classes were shocked by the brutality of so many of the lower classes. Lord Durham wrote to Parkes in 1834:

> I am sorry you don't approve of the tone of my unions remarks. You know not the outrages sanctioned *in this* county. . . . Men were *stripped stark naked* & *flogged* thro' the villages, before the eyes of *women* & children—others were waylaid & dreadfully beaten—a magistrate was murdered in cold blood by two unionists—because he was engaged in removing some of them from the houses of the owners.—It is considered here absolutely necessary to denounce the instigators of these outrages—& thus I did in a manner most

friendly to the mass—If I had complimented or shirked the condemnation of the delegates, their influence would not have been shaken. My remarks apply only to the delegates of this part of the country. I know nothing of their proceedings elsewhere. Here they were most careless and dangerous.[1]

And so they were elsewhere. E. C. Tufnell, a civil servant, responded with his attack on the trade unionism and all its works; Gibbon Wakefield wrote an alarmist pamphlet on the dangers of mob violence, understandable and effective when eighteenth-century violence could still be remembered and a revolution in a new kind of society was a momentary expectation. Place and Harriet Martineau and Lord Durham, on the other hand, tried to do something positive. You will see, wrote Durham to Joseph Parkes, "that I have been taking the field agst the unions in the only effectual way—viz, establishing one myself, in which all the ostensible & good objects of unions are attained, without the illegal, disgraceful and dangerous accessories which rendered the others so greatly obnoxious to all who value free labor & good order".[2] It was a scheme for a benefit club, or friendly society, which could serve too as an educational force and as a channel of communication between the owner and the workmen in the pits.

To this work Miss Martineau was asked to contribute. She was invited to Lambton Castle and plied with information about unions, strikes, and delegates to work up into a pamphlet. When she returned to London she wrote to Durham to say that, her health aside, she was anxious to get to work if she could satisfy herself as to form and publishing details. Should it be an address, or a familiar essay? If an address, to whom should it be put, both masters and men? Should it appear in a newspaper or as a tract? The Evangelicals had made tracts and addresses unpopular, but she thought that might be overcome. Should it carry her name or not? And she had plenty of evidence about ill-advised strikes and leaders—the reprehensible ones as well as the heroic ones who found themselves forced into leadership in a direction they did not themselves want to go.[3]

The upshot of the affair was a little tract called *The Tendency*

[1] Morton to Durham, April 6, 1831; Durham to Parkes, January 24, 1834, Durham Papers.

[2] Durham to Parkes, January 18, 1834, Durham Papers.

[3] There is a considerable correspondence on this matter, involving Durham, Parkes, and HM in the Durham Papers.

of Strikes and Sticks to Produce Low Wages, and of Union between Masters and Men to Ensure Good Wages. It was published at Durham in 1834 and widely circulated by Durham's agent. In it, Miss Martineau upheld the idea of union as a means of investigating situations and seeking out remedies. If the men were oppressed, they could resist most effectively by being combined; if the masters were not to blame, the men could help each other through union by refusing to underbid. In the situation in 1834, when competition was severe and profit margins narrow, opposition of interests could only be disastrous, and strikes tragic. All this she was able to document factually with instances of permanent displacement of struck labour by machines and of the expenses and risks of delegates and general unions.

Place was most enthusiastic and distributed the booklet to working-class leaders who came to see him; the argument fitted in neatly with his attack on general unions and his support of what he called "trade clubs". He and Miss Martineau wanted bold, positive, radical measures, and both were strong supporters of the friendly society movement. There might be abuses, to be sure, Miss Martineau wrote, but the recent acts protecting friendly societies were necessary to support them. As to complaints of over-legislation, well, legislation was necessary to protect an exposed class against the oppression of unworthy officers and the frauds of which they might not become aware until they were ruined—another contradiction to the usual view of Miss Martineau as an uncompromising opponent of government intervention.[1]

The Lambton visit and its sequel, then, serve to illustrate something of the positive content of Miss Martineau's concern about the condition of the working classes; it serves also to underline another matter. In his review of the booklet, W. J. Fox criticized her for the tone she adopted. "She claims to be a teacher of the people; and well has her claim been supported by most of her works. But to be the people's teacher she must always show herself the people's friend, not merely for the soundness of her advice, but by the tone and spirit of her admonitions." That was a useful warning, and an important one for the problem of popular writing, but Fox also suggested that the change in tone might be accounted for by her having been taken in by the Whigs, a feeling echoed too in the review in the *Athenaeum.*[2]

[1] Place to HM, March 31, 1834, BM, Add. MSS 35,149/278–279b. HM to Durham, n.d., Durham Papers. [2] *MR*, n.s., viii, 308; *Athenaeum*, May 10, 1834.

This charge struck Miss Martineau to the heart, for it called her radicalism in question, accused her of forsaking principle, and suggested that she had been insufficiently wary, despite her soul-searchings. She could reproach Fox about the matter some years later,[1] and she defended herself against the general charge in letters both to her brother and to Francis Place. Radicals, she told Place, were so illiberal; it was the worst possible compliment to the principles of radicalism that they trusted them in no hands but their own. "I am a radical, & am known to be so, wherever I go; & it is not seldom that I have to lament the absurdity of the mutual distrust of some of the more zealous of our party." She must have found Place's letters to her encouraging. She was bold, he said, where others were timid. "You and I, Miss Martineau, are the only real radicals in the country." [2]

That she was a real radical she never doubted, in a loyalty to principles which, as we have seen, far transcended a barren commitment to free-trade or laissez-faire dogma. Read properly in context, the political economy tales and her other work in London in the thirties display a fundamental concern for the positive creation of a good society. Radical and fundamental can be synonymous, and, in her case, they were. Certain great natural laws governed society; within that framework men had radically and fundamentally to reconstruct themselves and others, to teach them the natural laws on obedience to which their happiness depended. Of course she was impatient of "empiricism"—that grubbing about in political expediency or immediate necessity which characterized the shortsighted in politics, administration, labour, and business.

To repeat a phrase already quoted: she had, she said, nothing to lose which could compare with her concern for the people. To teaching one of the vital imperatives of necessarianism she had devoted three years of work. Then Lord Henley suggested that she go to America. There another side of her radicalism came into play. She wanted to travel, she told Durham, to take a holiday—not for indulgence but improvement. And her American travels *were* a journey for improvement—her own, England's, and America's.

[1] Garnett, *Fox*, p. 190.

[2] HM to Place, March 28 [1834], Place to HM, March 4, 1834, BM, Add. MSS, 35,149/275–77. HM to James, January 18, 1833.

CHAPTER V

America: The New Society

AS Western observers streamed to Russia in the twenties and thirties of this century, so European observers travelled to the United States in the nineteenth century. They went to see a great experiment in action, and, as in the parallel case a century later, their intentions and conclusions were determined less by the country they visited than by their hopes and fears for society at home. The literature of nineteenth-century travel in America is immense, and almost without exception it angered the Americans. Americans, then as now, were painfully concerned about what the rest of the world thought about them, and the visitors seemed condescending, hasty, stuffy, malicious, prejudiced, or blind. But the visitors took back what they had come for: ammunition for a political battle. For many years, wrote John Stuart Mill in 1840, every book by a returned traveller became a party pamphlet.[1] I have already suggested that the quarrels about economic theory can be looked at as subordinate to a purpose in its broadest sense political; America served even more pertinently.

The issue was democracy. To the radicals America was either the land of promise or, more judiciously, the test of their ideals. Many middle-class radicals particularly had fault to find, with slavery, the tariff, or American manners,[2] yet they kept high hopes, admired American institutions (or lack of them), and hoped to copy those they liked in Britain. "Our brethren have the advantage of us in many things," wrote a correspondent to Francis Place, "plenty of room and an admirable government; but for public ignorance look at their tariff and I looked in vain

[1] *ER*, lxxii, 2–3 (October, 1840).

[2] So Parkes to Lord Durham, February 13, 1834: "Mr. Phillips is a Boston man, less of an American icicle in his manners, & very intelligent. That which most amazes me in Yankees is the cold primitiveness of their manners. They seem like Puritan adults of old just emancipated from the process of *dipping* in a Chapel."

for the moral superiority I had hoped to find. Still I love America, which few Englishmen will say."[1]

This detached admiration was not characteristic of the working-class press. William Cobbett had denounced America in his Tory days, but his *Emigrant's Guide* of 1829 bore out the conclusions he had reached in his *Year's Residence in America* of 1817: one would find complete civil and religious liberty, the tax-collector would not annex most of one's income, and there would be "no Wilberforces—think of that—NO WILBERFORCES!" In America there were no laws against trade unions, no police spies. Senate and House were compared to Lords and Commons and both the latter were found sadly wanting. A speaker told a meeting of the National Union of the Working Classes in 1832 that he had looked into an English court "not of justice but law, for justice was banished from the land (hear); he saw there the old women in wigs and gowns, and he thought of America, where there were no wigs and gowns, but justice unmixed and unbiassed (hear)."

Radical editors loved to print comparative tables of government expenditure in the two countries, usually with an injunction to "look on this picture—and on this!" The President's salary was less than the retirement pension of the Lord Chancellor; the total cost of the American executive only a little more than the chancellor's salary and three-quarters of the salary of the Lord Lieutenant of Ireland. The cost of the royal family, not to mention the aristocracy, exceeded the whole expenditure of the American government, civil and military. Someone wrote in Richard Carlile's *Prompter* in 1831:

> In North America, because a Republic and a cheap King, there is [sic] no tax-gatherer, no tithes, no church-rates, no poor-rates. The American ships can fight our ships. The American army has beaten every English army sent against it. The American people have had no "Rock" or "Swing" among them, and there is not a human being among them, but may, if he like, get his stomach well filled with victuals, his body well clothed, bedded, housed.[2]

Nor was it only American government that was superior. American society was or was becoming infinitely better than the British. There were no titled aristocrats. Land was cheap, property-holding was widespread, and the *Poor Man's Guardian* drove

[1] Sidal Howes to Place, January 14, 1831, BM, Add. MSS, 37,950/109b.
[2] *Prompter*, April 2, 1831. *Poor Man's Guardian*, June 9, 1832.

home the threatening lesson, threatening, that is, to the respectable, propertied classes. Jackson's challenge to the Bank of the United States, it said, was a blow by the democrats against the monied aristocracy,

> which if properly followed up will consign it to the bottomless pit. . . . With a power over the law, they can do every thing that is not naturally impossible. They can regain all they have lost, make education universal, and bottom their prosperity on a rock adamant. They can alter the tenures of land, so as to make the soil (what God intended it) the inheritance of the whole people. They can make such changes in the organization of industry, and in the transmission of property, as will render all accumulations impossible, beyond the fair reward of past services.[1]

These were minority opinions, at least among those who counted. To most observers, America was either hypocritical in its pretensions or altogether abhorrent. Americans merely smuggled in an aristocracy—which might not be a true one—instead of honestly recognizing the fact of natural differences in rank. Some states, it was asserted, provided in their constitutions for "Your Excellency" and "Your Honour", terms universally used for and demanded by officials. Incompetent soldiers long cashiered still went by their military titles—this was repeatedly noticed—and every horse-leech insisted on being addressed as "Doctor".[2] An 1819 pamphlet pointed out that the Americans had no annual elections, while all their vaunted wisdom in constructing a constitution did nothing to prevent bribery in every election from the presidency down. Official corruption at all levels was "proved" from the comments of returned travellers and notably from the early anti-American works of Cobbett. As for economy in government, a pamphleteer pointed out (in oddly familiar tones) that while Britain was fighting Napoleon and supporting "on her shoulders the tottering fabric of all Europe . . . America was occupied in the less glorious, though more lucrative, employ of gathering the spoil".[3]

The travellers and their books were vital to this debate. Mrs. Trollope and Captain Basil Hall were widely read and excerpted in improving journals to demonstrate the existence of insubordination, say, or sectarian tyranny in America. The publication of Reeve's translation of Tocqueville's *Democracy in America* (1836

[1] *Poor Man's Guardian*, December 27, 1834.

[2] *Bristol Job Nott*, June 6, August 1, 1833 and *passim*. *Penny Magazine*, November 2, 1839.

[3] *Hints to Radical Reformers*, pp. 11–12.

and 1840) had a great impact on British intellectuals. John Stuart Mill, who was strongly influenced by the book, noted that its practical conclusions, despite its unexampled impartiality, leaned to radicalism. Yet some of Tocqueville's phrases, such as "tyranny of the majority", could be used by Tories, and, after Sir Robert Peel and the booksellers had finished recommending the book, "it has since been the opinion of the country gentlemen that M. de Tocqueville is one of the pillars of Conservatism, and his book a definitive demolition of America and of Democracy". The *Quarterly Review* urged that the translator persuade his publishers to bring the book out in a cheap form "in order that the interesting and practical wisdom with which it abounds may be placed within the reach of those classes where prejudice and error take their firmest stand". H. S. Tremenheere, the schools and mines inspector, included Tocqueville among the authors—the others were Aristotle, Machiavelli, Bacon, Locke, and Burke—from whose works extracts should be taken and worked into ordinary education to set the question of democracy right in men's eyes.[1]

This interest in and concern about America existed at all levels of political life; I have tried here to suggest their wider reaches. One more example should suffice. Here is the *Leeds Times*, thoroughly exasperated:

> The appearance of Dickens's work on America, has been the signal for an attack, by the Tory press, upon Democratic institutions and forms of government. It is discovered that there is a great deal of vice in America, that there is a "universal distrust" of public men, that its press is immoral and licentious, that its people are vulgar and spit horribly, and that they maintain slavery and a great many of the other abominations bequeathed to them by the Old World. All this is set down to the account of Democracy! It is Republicanism which has done it all! It is the Free Institutions of America which are to blame for all this. And accordingly, the inference attempted to be drawn is,—hold fast by the old world system,—stick to monarchy, aristocracy, and class legislation,—and away with all dogmas of a full, fair, and free representation of the people,—or of Presidents, Congress, or Democratic forms of government.
>
> . . . The object of Democratic government is equal liberty, equal laws, and equal justice to all. If the Americans have not yet arrived at this consummation, it is no fault of Democracy; no more

[1] *ER*, lxxii, 2–3 (October, 1840). *QR*, lvii, 162 (September, 1836). Tremenheere, Journal, May 29, 1840.

> than the present misery of England is the fault of its Christianity. The wonder is, not that America is so bad as it is, but that [it] is not a great deal worse. . . . Has not the Democracy of America accomplished sufficient during the last fifty years, to enable us to infer still greater achievements from it in the approaching future? Surely the grumblers ought to be satisfied with America. Monarchy has no instance of national greatness or achievement, to be compared with America, since the beginning of the world. The defenders of the old institutions should be more careful. They provoke comparisons which are exceedingly dangerous to "glorious constitutions." [1]

Into this debate Harriet Martineau stepped at precisely the crucial moment—when the working-class press was at its loudest, when Reform had raised the question of democracy out of the realm of theory, when there was an organized Radical party in Parliament, and when America itself was undergoing an extraordinary test of its claims and accomplishments. "Whatever else may or may not be true about the Americans," Lord Henley told her, "it is certain that they have got at principles of justice and mercy in the treatment of the least happy classes of society. . . . Will you not go, and tell us what they are?" [2]

Miss Martineau had written a life of Howard (for the S.D.U.K., who never printed it) and her poor law tales; she knew that in those fields the Americans had something to offer. The fame of American experimentation in prison management had spread all over Europe—Tocqueville and Beaumont went to inspect prisons, and Dr. Tuckerman, the Boston Unitarian and social worker, had come to Europe in 1833–34.

> It grieves everybody who knows him here [she wrote to Durham] that this singularly benevolent & wise man should be suffered to leave this country without being examined by those who can make the best use of the best communications he can make respecting the management of the poorer classes in all circumstances, & the working of American institutions among the industrious classes of the Union. I do not believe that any man living can teach us more on these subjects. [3]

Tuckerman had, of course, come to her attention through the Unitarians, whose connections with the powerful, if different, Unitarianism of America were close. Nor were the broader questions of the political importance of America absent.

She was, of course, already well-known there. American Uni-

[1] Quoted in *English Chartist Circular*, ii, no. 92.
[2] *Auto.*, i, 203.
[3] January 29, 1834, Durham Papers.

tarians read the *Monthly Repository*; a Boston clergyman, whom we shall meet later in a curious situation, had already republished some of her devotional works. The political economy tales were reprinted at once in Boston, and in early 1834 Henry Ware, a Cambridge minister, wrote to Catherine Maria Sedgwick that he thought a series of tales should set down the principles of religion and improve them by displaying the modes of their operation. "In a word, I fancy that a succession of *Illustrations of Christianity* might be made to do as much for religion as *Illustrations of Political Economy* have done for that science. . . ."[1] Naturally, a great deal was hoped for from a prominent writer whose sympathies were known to be on the liberal side.

Channing thought, however, that she would give more pleasure than she would receive. He tried to explain to Miss Aikin the reasons why travellers received such unfavourable impressions when they crossed the Atlantic. Because subsistence was easy and labour honourable in America, there were no good domestics, and Europeans missed them. Children were subjected to fewer outward restraints, and inner restraints were often neglected, so Englishmen were shocked (then as now) by "domestic insubordination". Again, Americans, thanks to Puritanism, were reserved in nature; the people being king, there was an unattractive wariness and deference to opinion; because everyone had to work, there was not much time to cultivate social graces, and society was less important. The "repulsion of celebrity" would hamper free communication, though genuine affability and self-forgetfulness might overcome that fault. "But let her come," he said, "and let her tell the truth, too, of us. I want that we should know our faults, and if nothing else will do, be scourged out of them; but there is no need of this severity; there is a spirit of improvement at work among us, and a wise philanthropic traveller may do us good." The affability Miss Martineau had; Miss Aikin thought that her dissenting background would have prepared her fully to find warm hearts under cold manners; and as for scourging or encouraging on matters of principle, it would have been difficult to find any traveller better suited to the task.[2]

Miss Martineau's travelling companion was Louisa Jeffrey, a young woman she had known in London, who offered to go with

[1] Henry Ware to C. M. Sedgwick, January 31, 1834; Dewey, *Life and Letters of Catherine Maria Sedgwick*, p. 239.

[2] W. E. Channing to Lucy Aikin, May 5, 1834, June 19, 1834, *Corr.*, pp. 207, 216.

her in return for expenses other than her passage. Miss Jeffrey was a perfect choice, suitably discreet and retiring to allow her friend all the prerogatives of the great lady; pleasant and intelligent, to judge from occasional comments about her or from the single letter I have seen; and invaluable in complementing and reinforcing Miss Martineau's own observations.

They sailed from Liverpool on August 9, 1834. Miss Martineau was fully prepared for the difficulties of the voyage—wadded quilted caps and petticoats, a stone hot-water bottle, and a horsehair glove for rubbing the flesh as a substitute for exercise and a remedy for queasiness. On the fourth day out she gave one of the flowers she had carefully kept to each of the passengers, "very like a message from home". Every morning she withdrew to a quiet corner of the deck to write, to the amazement and intrusive curiosity of the children and one rather stupid man. In bad weather she urged the ladies to go out on deck, to no avail; she was indefatigable in calling attention to sights to be seen, but when she wanted to be alone to watch the colours or the iridescence of the sea, she found an open volume of Shakespeare an infallible device for keeping away unwanted company. When it was calm, she sewed, and when a hurricane presented itself for observation, she got the captain's permission to fasten herself to the post of the binnacle to watch. No wonder the forty-two days of the voyage did not seem a moment too long. It is unlikely that passengers or crew quickly forgot her.[1]

From New York she went up the Hudson. From Stockbridge, Massachusetts, she went to Albany, through New York State to Buffalo and Niagara, then through Pennsylvania to Northumberland, where Priestley had lived and was buried. Six weeks at Philadelphia, three weeks at Baltimore, five weeks at Washington, then to Montpelier to see Madison, to Charlottesville to see the University of Virginia, to Richmond and, after a nine-day journey, to Charleston, South Carolina. She crossed the deep South—Columbia, Augusta, Montgomery, Mobile, New Orleans—steamed up the Mississippi, visited Mammoth Cave and stayed three weeks at Lexington, Kentucky. Ten days in Cincinnati impressed her very deeply. Another steamboat trip on the Ohio

[1] Crabb Robinson calls her description of the voyage in *RWT* "the most animated account of so *dis-animating* a subject I have ever met with". Diary, February 9, 1838. Her advice to ladies on such a voyage is in a letter to Mrs. Macready, December 29 [1840], NLS.

took her back to Virginia—White Sulphur Springs and Natural Bridge. She returned to New York in mid-July, 1835. The autumn she spent in touring New England, again in Stockbridge, then—Miss Jeffrey having gone home—west to Niagara for a second time, to Detroit and Chicago, and on the lakes by way of Mackinaw to Cleveland. Her last journey was through the interior of Ohio—unaccountably missing Oberlin College for which she expressed so great an admiration—to the Rappite settlement at Economy, and through Pennsylvania to New York. She sailed for England on August 1, 1836 and, with commendable opportunism and economy, wrote an article on "A Month at Sea" for the *Penny Magazine*.

Travelling in the United States in the 1830's was strenuous and primitive. It might mean horseback or stage, the airless and dirty canal boats which so appalled Dickens, steamers of various degrees of excellence, or the short, cindery lines of the new railroads. The two ladies stood up to this test remarkably well; they also survived a very active social life when they were stationary. There were only a few minor indispositions, in Baltimore, where one might have expected it with the unusually cold weather they encountered, and in Boston. There had to be equable tempers to put up with bad inns, disgusting food, and occasional exceptions to the general good manners. But there was so much to do and to reflect on—journals to keep and prisons to visit, Niagara to experience and caves to explore, and, above all, there was a new society building itself, with commendable if not wholly satisfactory results.

The local papers noticed her arrival and reported the parties given for her. Local booksellers laid in supplies of the political economy tales, and members of society who had not read them found sufficient curiosity to give them a trial. The *Southern Rosebud*, edited in Charleston by Mrs. Gilman, reprinted her *Letter to the Deaf*. Miss Martineau willingly and cheerfully gave advice to deaf persons who applied to her for information, and Mr. Camp, of Baltimore, must have experienced a rise in the sales of his elastic tubes for ear-trumpets, though they cost ten dollars and were not always perfect.[1]

[1] *Charleston Courier*, March 13, 1835, *Charleston Mercury*, March 14, April 7, 1835, April 9, 1835. *National Intelligencer*, Washington, January 19, 1835, and advertisements from January 21. *Southern Patriot*, Charleston, March 25, 1835. Deborah Logan Diary, p. 118, PHS.

"I was quite taken with the sweet-tempered sensible lady," wrote Emerson to Carlyle, "but what a pitiable life she leads!—in a procession endless of company." [1] It was the lionizing Channing had predicted, and she tried as best she could to get out from under the infliction of the national fault of flattery by changing the subject.[2] Naturally she turned to "those most homelike of our acquaintance", the Unitarians. Where there was a Unitarian minister, he was her natural host, and where there was none he was missed. A "little Unitarian sympathy" mixed delightfully with the ever-present kindness, she wrote to Mrs. Gilman, her hostess in Charleston. At Cincinnati they stayed over Sunday on purpose to hear Mr. Peabody—for they had not been in a Unitarian church since they left Georgia—only to find that Mr. Holland was visiting that day, and she had difficulty in hearing him.[3]

In Washington she sometimes entertained, having taken rooms in Mrs. Peyton's boarding-house on Pennsylvania Avenue. She would not promise, she wrote to J. P. Kennedy, the Baltimore Congressman, but that he would find Calhoun on her stairs, though, of course, it might be Clay.[4] Webster and Judge Story

[1] October 7, 1835, Slater edition.

[2] For a particularly repulsive expression of her "modesty": "I do not mind telling you that [your letter] gave me exquisite pleasure; and the more because I am convinced that the glory & delight wh you have experienced in your intellectual intercourse with me are far more subjective than objective. But your sympathy is precious to me. I am afraid I *have* been ungracious sometimes when praise, mere praise, has been dashed in my face whichever way I turned; but I trust I have never rejected sympathy. You have divined my intents in my works better than I shd have supposed possible from so imperfect a set of performances." HM to E. P. Peabody, October 21, [1835], LC.

[3] *Auto.*, i, 386–87. HM to Mrs. Gilman, February 11, 1835, NYPL. HM to James Freeman Clarke, Cincinnati, June 21, 1835, Harvard.

[4] "This place [Washington] seems the centre of delights,—& no less, of politl knowledge. After breakft, we go to a certain Committee room in the Capitol, where Mr. Osgood paints, & there I sit for my picture just now for an hour daily. Then we go into the Supreme Court, where Judge Story has secured the Reporters' chairs for us, [and] the seven Judges are friends or acquaintances of ours! Then perhaps we go into the Senate, & find plenty to note & look at & listen to. The library & H. of Represves are also haunted by us. Then we come home and dress for dinner at the President's, or at our Envoy's or some other such place; & I have long talks with His Majesty, or Mr. Van Buren, or Webster, Clay, Calhoun, Preston, or dear Judge Story, or some other capital person. Then, to a grand squeeze somewhere, where we meet every body; or else home, to find Mr. Everett, or Judge Story again, or some Senator who is too busy to come at any other time, but who stays till just midnight. This is a pretty life, is it not? I find it not only very entertaining, & prodigiously exciting; but my spirits rise every day from feeling that I am now really getting the knowledge I wanted; & that I am able to form my own notions

came to call, literary ladies would stop by on their way to a ball. But usually it was Miss Martineau who was entertained, and that raised the problems that are usually raised when one is giving a party for a famous intellectual: whom to invite and how to keep things moving. Kennedy wrote to his wife that he wanted to give a party: "I will invite the Seatons and others —Miss Martineau and some beaux if I can find any clever enough." [1] Here is a description of the carrying-on she caused in Stockbridge:

> I have written Miss M. today, & Jane has sent an invitation to her house. Our first thought—our first exclamation was—"What a pity Louisa [Minot] is gone!"—Jane's sudden inspirations as to how she shall entertain her would amuse you. She breathes them out between orders to Annie, lessons to the children, & consultation with Tucker. "Martineau must be lighted—can't we get the lamp up from New York"?—"There's the ginger—ginger must be a treat in England"!—"I have engaged one pair of chickens, and now Brown's dog is going I shall have some chance of keeping them"! —"Oh, my spermacetis are out"! "Brinton must *yallow* wash the parlour for Martineau"! "Oh Heavens & Earth I wish I could get my new fangled stove ready for Martineau"!—"Hal go down to Brinton's early & tell him he must get the nails in my sofa for Martineau"!—& then her plans for moral & intellectual entertainment. She says she'll take her to the Rathbone's & Bettys, & Charles shall give her a Fete at Lenox Jail—What are we to do for mankind? Women guests are hard to entertain without their aid. The Major distrusts her profundity in political economy, & Mr. A. her soundness in radicalism, & both I think are a little shy of a confederate, or rival, in petticoats.[2]

But, after the fuss, what a good guest she was! She was pleasant, lively, transparently sincere, and adaptable. "She never remarks on our conventional manners, and usually adopts them; for instance, she eats her egg out of a glass, holds her fork in her left hand, & eats a hearty dinner without grumbling at one o'clock." [3] For that one could put up, I should guess, with some over-hasty generalizations.

She had barely set foot on land when she was asked the inevitable question: How do you like America? That was, of

of the characters of the great men whose names have been familiar to me for many years." HM to Charles Brooks, Washington, January 25, 1835, LC.

[1] *RWT*, i, 147. HM to J. P. Kennedy [January 1835], Kennedy to his wife, January 26, 27, 29, 1835, Peabody Institute, Baltimore. Deborah Logan Diary, PHS, February 2, 1835 and p. 103, early December.

[2] C. M. Sedgwick to Louisa Minot, September 24, 1834, MHS.

[3] Dewey, *C. M. Sedgwick*, p. 242.

course, a favourite topic everywhere. Then, too, Miss Martineau was English, and there was great eagerness to know about England, a concern she felt it necessary to criticize in her books. But she was apparently quite willing to serve as oracle, for, after all, she was a friend of cabinet ministers. The cabinet crisis resulting from the king's dismissal of Melbourne and the failure of Peel to form a government was a natural subject at the beginning of 1835, and Miss Martineau's predictions were accurate enough to support her reputation. Deborah Logan, in Philadelphia, noted a comment Miss Martineau had made about the change in conversational style in England—no more long disquisitions, but short and rapid, like Brougham's observations—"something to think of"—in an evening where "not much of agreeable conversation was elicited".[1] But primarily Miss Martineau had come to learn. Americans were glad enough to talk about themselves, and she was skilful at directing the conversation. She occasionally reports exchanges, I am sure accurately.

> The first time I met an eminent Southern gentleman, a defender of slavery, he said to me (within the half hour),
> "I wish you would not be in such a hurry away. I wish you would stay a year in this city. I wish you would stay ten years, and then you would change your opinions."
> "What opinions?"
> "Your opinions on slavery."
> "What do you know of my opinions on slavery?"
> "Oh, we know them well enough: we have all read 'Demerara.' "
> "Very well: now we shall understand each other; for I must tell you that I think about slavery exactly as I did when I wrote that story. Nothing that I have seen shows me that I have anything to qualify of what is said there. So now you do know my opinions."
> "Oh yes. I don't want to know anything more of your opinions. I want you to know mine."
> "That is exactly what I want. When will you let me have them?" [2]

She could be cutting too. A lady in Boston:

> "Have you seen Dr. Channing's book [on slavery]?"
> "Yes. Have you?"
> "O no. Do not you think it very ill-timed?"

---

[1] Deborah Logan Diary, pp. 106–108, PHS. Louisa Jeffrey to Henry Clay, July 19, 1835, Colton, *Clay*, iv, 395–97. HM to Durham, February 13, 1835, Durham Papers.

[2] *RWT*, i, 226.

"No; I think it well-timed; as it did not come out sooner."

"But is it not wrong to increase the public excitement at such a time?"

"That depends on the nature of the excitement. But this book seems to have a tranquillising effect: as the exhibition of true principles generally has."

"But Dr. Channing is not a practical man. He is only a retired student. He has no real interest in the matter."

"No worldly interest; and this, and his seclusion, enable him to see more clearly than others, in a case where principles enlighten men, and practice seems only to blind them."

"Well: I shall certainly read the book, as you like it so much."

"Pray don't, if that is your reason." [1]

A traveller gathers information at his own risk, and in Miss Martineau's case, the risk was doubly great, for everyone was sure that she was going to write a book, even though she insisted that she was not committed to it. Ordinary political biases were likely to be emphasized to her, in order to make a good showing to the world. She talked to people at all levels of society, and she was mightily impressed by some conversations she had with people of little formal education and no position. But every traveller is likely to be most deeply affected by the statements of people whose positions approximate his own, and the great majority of her intimate friends belonged to a single political group.

The Federalist party had declined, calamity-howling, into impotence and extinction at the time of the War of 1812; but a new party division was signalized by the overwhelming victory of Andrew Jackson in 1828. The invasion of Washington by the western Jacksonians, raw, crude, and anything but respectable, was a symptom, as she saw it, of democracy on the march. When they trampled the furniture and pulled down the curtains at the inaugural reception, they were trampling and pulling down the claims to supremacy of the respectable and relatively aristocratic Eastern seaboard. Although Miss Martineau was eventually deeply impressed by the openness and promise of the Westerners, her early months in the East found her committed to a contrary position. She would hardly have taken seriously the words of the first gentleman she met in New York: "that I had arrived at an unhappy crisis; that the institutions of the country would be in ruins before my return to England; that the levelling spirit was desolating society; and that the United States

[1] *SA*, ii, 161–62.

were on the verge of a military despotism." [1] But the actual state of things, as she saw them in the next few months, did not seem much more encouraging; and her early Whiggism was cultivated by the Whig politicians. As she had done in preparing the political economy tales, she relied on men in power to provide her with information. "My friends," she wrote to J. P. Kennedy, "can in no way serve me so effectually as by thus putting in my way the materials of that knowledge wh I came hither to obtain; & no pains shall be spared on my part to make the best use of such opportunities". [2] If they served her, they also served themselves, and spared no pains to see to it that she got the right views.

The principal issue of debate when she was in Washington was Calhoun's report on executive patronage. Jackson, on coming into office, had turned out office-holders right and left, to fill their places with good Jacksonians. Moreover, he carried through his long-standing fight against the Bank of the United States—Nicholas Biddle's powerful institution—refusing to renew the Bank's charter and withdrawing Federal deposits which were thereupon lodged in state banks, the so-called "pet banks". Then there was the unprecedented situation of the impending liquidation of the public debt and the possibility of a surplus. Patronage, the possibility of the surplus, and the state bank deposit scheme were obvious sources of executive power. All of these Calhoun attacked, proposing to get rid of the surplus revenue, to cut the President's power over office-holders, and to establish legal control over public funds. [3]

The problem of patronage and its significance in terms of power were not lost on a radical like Miss Martineau; after all, one of the chief points of Whig attack in England from the end of the eighteenth century had been against patronage, and the "decline of influence" from about 1780 was a fact of cardinal importance in the political and constitutional history of England. This question was undoubtedly long and enthusiastically discussed with the great Whigs who gathered by the fender at Mrs. Peyton's, and Harriet Martineau was provided with copies of the report, one of which was sent to Lord Durham. It was something new to Englishmen, she wrote, to hear complaints of a super-

[1] *SA*, i, 8.
[2] HM to J. P. Kennedy, [January 1835], Peabody Institute, Baltimore.
[3] Wiltse, *John C. Calhoun, Nullifier*, pp. 255–60.

abundance of public money, but the report obviously roused echoes of Dunning's famous resolution in 1780 that the influence of the Crown had increased, was increasing, and ought to be diminished. If I thought, she said, that one or two corrupt administrations could ruin the United States, the glory would be gone; but prosperity will preserve the country from convulsion, and exposures like the Report would open the eyes of "low & interested faction", and the virtues of the Opposition leaders will countervail the admiration of "Jackson *the General*".

Indeed, such an Opposition had scarcely been seen in the world.

> Each of these men is a host in himself, & Webster seems fit to be the monarch of the world. Of *our* great men, certain qualities may be predicated, when it is known from what class they proceed. Here, each stands on his own individuality, & no two in the least resemble each other. I wish that there was no sectional prejudice to keep them from heartily uniting; for then no corruption cd stand before them. As it is, they have, I shd think, settled the question raised by some of our English reformers, as to whether there is really any use in the Senate of the United States. The President makes grievous complaints to me of his Senate,—a proof of its utility.[1]

As strangers, she and Miss Jeffrey had to be permitted neutrality, she wrote to Miss Sedgwick, but she could not hide her conviction that there was nothing to be found outside London to compare with the Whig leaders. "Still true to their Jerusalem, every one of these English," commented Miss Sedgwick, and she wondered about the claim to neutrality, for her brother Theodore had been in Washington and had seen Miss Martineau. So strong a preference for Webster, Clay, Preston, and Calhoun would be difficult to conceal. And some of the same attitudes were still present a year and a half later. It was embarrassing to the Sedgwicks, for Theodore was a passionate Democrat; yet he said nothing severe or hypercritical of Miss Martineau, notwithstanding the absurd things she said about Jackson. "I cannot but think it is more prudent for women to abstain from political judgments," mused his sister.[2]

Miss Martineau's Whig enthusiasm was taken seriously in high

[1] February 13, 1835, Durham Papers. "Suffice it now that there is no leadg member of the opposition for whom I do not feel very high respect and regard; & that I cannot say exactly the same for the administration party." HM to Charles Brooks, January 25, 1835, LC.

[2] C. M. Sedgwick to Mrs. H. D. Sedgwick, February 21, 1835, April 3, 1836; C. M. Sedgwick to Louisa Minot, February 26, 1835, MHS.

Democratic circles. W. L. Marcy, governor of New York, and a close associate of Jackson and Van Buren, wrote a letter to George Bancroft, the historian, after her visit to Bancroft in late summer, 1835:

> I can assure you that I was very glad to learn that Miss Martineau had fallen into your hands. She made but a passing visit here and I had but a casual introduction to her. Mr. H. Bleecker saw more of her than any other person here, & accompanied her on her way west as far as Schenectady. She expressed an anxiety to me that her intercourse in this country should be with such persons as would be likely to give her right views of our society and more particularly of our government; but he felt apprehensive that it would be otherwise. In a communication some weeks since with Mr. V. Buren relative to her, he expressed an opinion that she had imbibed erroneous views of our country & considered it unfortunate that she had been so long & so intimately associated with Mr. Clay & his political friends. You have confirmed the justice of his conclusions. I sincerely regret this result because I regard Miss M. as an exceedingly clever writer *whose opinions of us will go far in Europe to give us a character*. You will excuse me for saying that I know of no one more likely than yourself to correct the obliquity of her views, & I much rejoice that you have determined to direct your efforts towards that object. If you should prepare a statement of your views on the principle of our democratic institutions (and I entreat you most earnestly to do so) and should think fit to submit them to my inspection I should be much pleased to have you do so, & if I had an opportunity should by your leave, show them to Mr. V. B. for his judgment & observations thereon, as an act done on my own motion or if you choose with your consent.[1]

I know of no better indication of the seriousness with which her visit was regarded. I have been unable to find a trace of the sequel to this letter; there is however, little question but that Bancroft did what he could when he had Miss Martineau at Northampton. He drove her all around the countryside, and that meant a good many opportunities for Democratic homilies as they visited Amherst or drove up Mount Holyoke, or—especially—as they visited the old graveyard at Northampton to see the graves of some of the original settlers. In the sixties she still remembered the delightful drives, but recalled too that Bancroft had got "into frightful spirits, whooping & waving his handkerchief at the country people we met".[2] Perhaps that was Ban-

[1] September 24, 1835, MHS, Bancroft. Italics mine.

[2] *RWT*, ii, 83–90. HM to Reeve, March 5, 1866. " . . . My feelings count years as nothing and carry me back to the times when you and I taught Miss Martineau to have some knowledge of Jeffersonian Democracy. . . ." George Bancroft to

croft's natural behaviour; perhaps it was an attempt to illustrate democracy at work. In the books she later wrote on America, the Whig bias so apparent during her visit was considerably modified. It may have been Bancroft's doing or the Sedgwicks' talk, but I doubt it. The reasons lay deeper.

The winter spent in Boston was the most important part of Miss Martineau's stay in America. Of Boston in general she was contemptuous enough in her books. She called it the "head-quarters of Cant", and accused Boston women of pedantry and Boston merchants of truckling and worse. Her story about one Boston bluestocking is worth repeating; it has, by the way, all the earmarks of a tale that came from Mrs. Chapman. This good lady exploded about *Society in America*: "She has ate of our bread and drunk of our cup; and she calls dear, delightful, intellectual Boston pedantic!" to which the reply was, "If she thinks Boston pedantic, did you mean to bribe her, by a cup of tea, not to say so?" [1] Boston, as Miss Martineau saw it, suffered from the general fault of cities in America, where there was no metropolis to test ideas. It was provincial, and Norwich must have sprung to her mind. But Boston had its redeeming features, features which the conventional aristocracy did not know: a natural aristocracy comprising a larger number of "peculiarly interesting and valuable persons living in near neighbourhood" not to be matched outside of London.[2] She was at home among the Unitarians and the Abolitionists.

With one of the Unitarians there was, apparently, an extraordinary *contretemps*. There is only Mrs. Chapman's indigant note to support the story—it lies among the materials which she felt should be recorded but which could not be included in the memorials. There are, however, confirmatory circumstances, and besides the story is really too ludicrous and too typical to have been made of whole cloth. Dr. Channing's assistant was Ezra Stiles Gannett. He had served as secretary of the Unitarian Association for six years down to 1831, when he resigned and published some tracts and a little magazine called *The Scriptural Interpreter*. It was Gannett who edited (Mrs. Chapman says "mangled") Miss Martineau's early devotional works and the *Traditions of Palestine* for American publication. Gannett was an

William Marcy, October 27, 1847, in the Hurja collection, Washington, D.C. Dr. James P. Shenton found this reference for me.

[1] *Auto.*, i, 343.

[2] *SA*, ii, 170.

unhappy man. There were, his son records, "certain secret struggles", an unvarying comparison of himself with others, always to his own discredit. He craved approval and could give none to himself. He stood in the shadow of a great man whose gentleness he saw only as forbearance. Slights he magnified; kindnesses became pity. "The mood made him very sensitive and exacting with those few friends who knew his feelings best; and their words rebuking, cheering, jesting, reasoning with him are sad to read." [1] In October 1835 he married, though he was seriously overtired and had contemplated postponing the marriage. Shortly thereafter Miss Martineau came, naturally, as a guest to his house in Hayward Place. I give Mrs. Chapman's account:

> She was obliged to work late,—& so was Mr. Gannett; & one evening very late, when the rest of the household were asleep, he began to bemoan his many sufferings, & for a climax he demanded her sympathy in his ill-assorted marriage, as he said,—& began to say all the things in admiration of herself as his *true* mate, which might properly enough have been said were he unmarried, & paying his court to her. Under the actual circumstances she was much shocked, & began to meditate escape, when his manners were such as to compel the conclusion that if not bad, he was mad: and under the full conviction that he must be the latter, his guest rushed to her own room & secured herself for the night. The next morning she left the house, going to Dr. Channing to tell him that his colleague needed his immediate care to avert insanity; of which the treatment of herself by such a man was sufficient evidence.
>
> Dr. Channing was amazed & incredulous. His colleague was incapable of meaning ill,—& she herself was under a delusion. But while the conversation was going on, a note was handed her from Mr. Gannett expressing love & grief, & repentance for the scene of the last night. "There," said H.M. handing him the note:—"you see your colleague needs immediate care & medical advice. You really must attend to him." Dr. Channing made no reply, but turning to the fire, put the note into it.

She then went to Watertown to the Follens, where she was not yet expected, and fully explained her premature arrival. Of course they refused to believe the tale, and suggested that perhaps her deafness—but she cut them short by saying, "I suppose there is no mistake when a man goes down on his knees to me?" [2]

Poor Gannett had a complete nervous breakdown in the following March and was ordered to the country and then to

[1] W. C. Gannett, *Ezra Stiles Gannett*, pp. 142–56.
[2] BPL, Weston, vol. 6, no. 4.

Europe—without his wife. He visited Miss Martineau in London, where she was apparently very kind to him. The incident is revealing. She saw clearly enough what was wrong, but understanding deserted her completely in a situation of this sort—witness the Fox and Mill *liaisons*—and discretion was never one of her characteristics. It is a testimony either to her own character or to some incomprehensible aspect of nineteenth-century morality that the incident never clouded her friendship with Gannett's close associates.

She produced reactions enough in that strange Boston circle. Margaret Fuller confided to her journal that she desperately wanted an intellectual guide. "I have hoped some friend would do,—what none has ever yet done,—comprehend me wholly, mentally, and morally, and enable me better to comprehend myself."

> I have had some hope that Miss Martineau might be this friend, but cannot yet tell. She has what I want,—vigorous reasoning powers, invention, clear views of her objects,—and she has been trained to the best means of execution. Add to this, that there are no strong intellectual sympathies between us, such as would blind her to my defects.[1]

They remained friends and correspondents until Margaret's sad death by drowning in 1840, but transcendentalist and Priestleyan were a twain which could never meet.

For the chief figures of the transcendentalists, Emerson and Channing, Miss Martineau had a curiously detached admiration. She was certain that Channing was a great man, though she could not forgive his rejection of Priestley, nor accept his German metaphysics. Emerson was a regular correspondent and later a visitor to her house at Ambleside; she admired his essays and rejected his cloudiness. Both men received extended discussion in her American books. She was enthusiastic and emotionally drawn to them; intellectually they were poles apart. Channing, as I have suggested, may have affected her views on property; on radical views of social duty they were in agreement. She remained discriminating and judicious; she could take what suited and leave what fell short.

The transcendentalists may have fallen short; the abolitionists did not. Miss Martineau came to Boston sceptical, and left a convert to Garrisonianism. The history of anti-slavery in the

[1] *Memoirs of Margaret Fuller Ossoli*, i, 197 ff.

United States is enormously complex. The cause of the slave was one of the proliferating reforms of the twenties and thirties, part of the aftermath—benevolent and perfectionist—of the Great Revival of the early years of the century, a revival which began with a generous reinterpretation of Calvinism at Yale, and which was carried west through the "burned-over district" of New York to the Middle West by the great evangelist Charles Grandison Finney.

Under the leadership of Theodore Dwight Weld, one of Finney's disciples, religious anti-slavery grew to enormous proportions in the Middle West. The New York abolitionists, headed and financed by the Tappan brothers, created an extraordinary verbal problem by their advocacy of immediatism, trying to borrow the prestige of the British campaign for immediate emancipation but reinterpreting it to mean "gradual emancipation immediately begun". There were other manifestations of anti-slavery too, which must be summed up in the phrase that G. H. Barnes has used as the title of his study, the anti-slavery impulse. But Barnes is concerned primarily about the organizational responses to this impulse; as a result he is unjust to Garrison. He sees Garrison as a brilliant fanatic, a divisive force who retarded the anti-slavery movement—an attitude which inescapably reminds a British historian of the hostility of historians like Hovell to Feargus O'Connor for disrupting the Chartist movement. But Chartism was not a single movement, nor was anti-slavery.

Garrison had started his anti-slavery career by helping Benjamin Lundy in Baltimore to edit *The Genius of Universal Emancipation*, for which Garrison got himself thrown into jail for libel. He moved to Boston, and with financial help from Arthur Tappan (whose money had got him out of jail) he founded the *Liberator* in 1831. So violent was the language of this extraordinary paper that Garrison was thrust into a remarkable position. Utterly distrusted as a leader by other anti-slavery enthusiasts, with only a small personal following, with a subscription list of only about four hundred white persons and a good many free coloured persons, Garrison became the emblem of anti-slavery, the target of pro-slavery attacks. In 1833, he travelled to England and established his primacy among anti-slavery groups there. At home, baulked more and more by opposition within the ranks of anti-slavery, Garrison moved left into all kinds of unorthodoxy—

feminism, anti-clericalism, anarchism—further alienating the orthodox. To the disaffected and to the general public Garrison was an enemy whose name blighted his cause; to his friends he was a man of austerity and singleness of purpose.

> They knew that the harshness of his writings was derived from his righteous absolutes of faith, never from vindictiveness; and that his intolerance was for the principles that he hated, and not for the men who followed them. For all his "I-ness"—his obsessive self-importance—Garrison was truly what his followers believed him to be, the embodiment of devotion to a cause.[1]

And those were precisely the qualities which committed Miss Martineau to his service. With her lively admiration of martyrs for principle, she could not easily forget that Garrison had been dragged through the streets in 1835 by a Boston mob.

Miss Martineau had arrived in America with her anti-slavery reputation before her. George Thompson, the English anti-slavery orator, came at about the same time. Her captain was questioned before the ship docked to find if Thompson was on board—for New York had just undergone its first slavery riots and had Thompson landed, it was suggested, he would not have survived long. The captain made discreet inquiries about Miss Martineau's own position and was assured that while she opposed slavery, she came to learn, and that satisfied him.

The author of *Demerara* was known in the South. They hoped that they might convert her, as we have seen; but on so vital a principle she could not give in. To be sure, the American books were written after she had become a Garrisonian, but there is no doubt about the purity of her anti-slavery feeling long before she went to Boston.

> The first great question [she wrote to Durham] seems to be whether education can be carried out to the extent of the suffrage;—a difficulty in a country wh is exposed to a vast immigration of ignorant people. The next, whether the North & South can be kept united; & the third, how Slavery is to be extinguished, if they remain united. The far superior intelligence of the North, while it is unable to set up a President, seems to peril the Union; but the utter helplessness of the South, in case of a separation, seems to promise a grumbling submission on her part. Of the prospects of Slavery I shall be better qualified to speak 6 months hence, when I shall have travelled through the South. My present belief is that the case is nearly desperate; & I fear that no colonization

[1] G. H. Barnes, *The Anti-Slavery Impulse*, pp. 98–99.

> plans will work quickly enough to prevent an extensive derangement of society, through either the sudden breaking up, or the attempted continuance of the institution. Our experiment in the West Indies is being watched with intense interest.—I am just going to visit Mr. and Mrs. Madison, who can exhibit to me more than anybody else of the social & domestic effects of the system. I then go through the Southern states, under circumstances wh will ensure my knowing all that can be learned of it. It is utterly detestable, as I see already.[1]

But opposition to slavery and support of the abolitionists—a term which meant Garrison to the enraged South—were not the same thing. Miss Martineau's tact in questioning brought such an unanimity of response on the latter subject that she assumed that Garrison and the abolitionists were an unfortunate and retarding influence.

> When we dined with General H. [wrote Caroline Gilman from Charleston] we were invited an hour before the other guests, that he might give her, at her request, his views on slavery. She studiously avoided arguing on these subjects, but quietly and keenly directed her attentions and questions to gentlemen of all parties in such a manner as to bring out the whole scope of detail of their several opinions. She made no secret of her aversion to slavery. She perceives and acknowledges, however, that the movements of the abolitionists have injured and retarded the cause of slaves here.[2]

It was at Henry Clay's that the Garrisonians moved in on her, through a letter from Mrs. Chapman—one of the fanatics, Clay explained; in August, 1835, she met them in a riotous Boston where their safety was really threatened. The imposing presence of Mrs. Chapman made its mark, for one thing; the seeming reasonableness and good nature, which we can see in the letters of the Garrisonians, if not in their printed work, captivated her. Above all, she liked them because they were dedicated to right principles. She was cautious enough, still, but in November she committed herself. The Ladies' Anti-Slavery Society held a meeting on the 18th under a threat of mob action; she was asked to speak and she did, thus circumspectly:

> I have been requested by a friend present to say something—if

[1] February 13, 1835, Durham Papers.

[2] Caroline Gilman to E. G. Loring, quoted in a letter from Mrs. Gilman to Miss Martineau's mother, 1835, reprinted *Auto.*, ii, 235–36. Miss Martineau's later picture of Mrs. Gilman is anything but attractive, "a northern wife who had rushed into that admiration of *Slavery* which the native ladies do not entertain". *Auto.*, i, 344. *Southern Patriot* (Charleston), December 4, 1835.

only a word—to express my sympathy in the objects of this meeting. I had supposed that my presence here would be understood as showing my sympathy with you. But as I am requested to speak, I will say that what I have said through the whole South, in every family where I have been; that I consider Slavery as inconsistent with the law of God, and as incompatible with the course of his providence. I should certainly say no less at the North than at the South concerning this utter abomination—and I now declare that in your *principles* I fully agree.[1]

Mrs. Chapman was triumphant. A public endorsement by a prominent writer was important to the cause. Its guarded formulation was no serious problem: printing even that would have an effect, and when it appeared in the *Liberator*, it did. Miss Martineau agreed wholly with abolitionist principles, Loring reported to Garrison, but did not know enough of their measures to judge them. Channing, he thought, had converted her to the idea of individual as against associated action, but in the main points she was sound—"creating and exerting a moral influence against slavery in the free states", and if she could do it, bringing emancipation immediately without compensation to owners, which was further than a good many abolitionists would go. They had all winter to work on her about measures. In March, 1836, Garrison reported to his wife that he had had two highly successful interviews with Miss Martineau and had attended an evening party to discuss "some of the great topics of reform". There was no fear, he said, of her printing anything in England or America against the abolitionists or favouring the colonizationists.[2] The battle for Miss Martineau's mind had been won.

Other friends were less happy. They knew that George Thompson had had a narrow escape, and that foreign agitators were not welcome. A good many doors were closed against her. Boston and New York papers attacked her, and the papers of the South pointed the moral. We would like, said one little Carolina paper,

[1] *Auto*, i, 351–52.

[2] Loring to Garrison, December 5, 1835, Garrison to his wife, March 7, 1836, *Life of Garrison*, ii, 55–56, 98. By March, Garrison was hopeful that she would do Channing good. There was reason to be concerned about her attitude to the colonizationists. In *MR*, v, 758–60, November 1831, she had written an article on Liberia which was highly laudatory. "If one African can be made intelligent, virtuous, and refined, the reproach of the Negro ceases. If one African state can be made civilized and free, the question of Slavery is settled forever." And she was sure that the pilgrims to Liberia would one day be honoured as "the heralds of a new era of justice and philanthropy". This article was pointedly omitted from the *Miscellanies* of 1836.

to have the opportunity to send this "Peter Parley dabbler in Political Economy . . . a pair of our old unmentionables". More seriously, a Charleston paper warned that Southerners would be forced to become Tories by the doings of the British liberals.

> Miss Martineau, whether all along an incendiary under the rose, or dissatisfied with the share of *éclat* which accompanied her lionizing through our country, has recently crowned her wanderings with abundant notoriety, by a public Amalgamation with Garrison & Co.—starred it upon the stage of their exhibition room, became an Orator in their Academy—and is now looked up to by them as one of their mothers in Israel. Mrs. Trollope could not have done worse.

This, said another paper, is the way she repays the hospitality of the South.

> Southerners have received repeated warnings as to the free manner in which they receive foreigners, and this is another admonition how, in the frank simplicity of their manners, they extend to persons who visit them those facilities by which these persons expect to gather materials of denunciation, if not defamation and reproach.[1]

She got the usual quota of abusive letters and threats about entering the South when she reached Cincinnati, threats she chose to take seriously enough to alter her plans and undoubtedly to imagine the thrilling weight of the martyr's crown. She was committed to the most important cause of her life.

When Miss Martineau returned to England, the booksellers were waiting, and she has left an amusing account of their solicitations.[2] A contract was closed with Saunders and Otley. She got £900 for the first edition of *Society in America*, £600 for the *Retrospect of Western Travel*, terms which she thought generous enough notwithstanding more liberal offers from other publishers. Both books were successful, the second more so than the first. Her own explanation was that the first book required not only concentration but sympathy and understanding for the Americans, while the second was merely a book of travels. Carlyle told her that he would rather read about Webster's cavernous eyes and arm under his coat-tail, than political speculation suggested by a cut-and-dried system. But it is more than

[1] *Charleston Mercury*, December 18, 1835, which quotes the *Salisbury Carolinian*. *Southern Patriot* (Charleston), December 3, 1835.

[2] *Auto.*, i, 398–405.

that: the *Retrospect* is, flatly, a much better book.[1] It is a superb piece of reporting, lively, anecdotal, and revealing.

Society in America, on the other hand, is a curious affair, badly constructed and at times tedious. It aims at political analysis but periodically, especially in the section on the economy, lapses into a book of travels, with long descriptions, which, while interesting enough in themselves, detract considerably from the force of the argument. She herself found fault with the book when she wrote her autobiography. Its fundamental fault, she said, in good Comtean terms, was its metaphysical framework, a too abstract treatment of a necessarily concrete subject. But, she said, the fault was not entirely hers; it lay rather with the American theory which she had immaturely chosen as her standpoint. Moreover, she was affected by the American method of dissertation or preaching and was, like her American friends, full of Carlyle; so, she said, the book was in the American fashion and far more useful on the other side of the Atlantic than in England. Yet she found a good many personal responses in the form of applications for guidance and counsel, because "of my hearty conviction that social affairs are the personal duty of every individual, and from my freedom in saying what I thought". Immature in conception and American in form the book may have been, but it was thoroughly characteristic of its author. And it is incomparably more important than the second, better book.

Her friends and admirers received *Society in America* well. Miss Mitford dissented from the theories, but found the book ardent, eloquent, earnest, sincere, full of pictures, and full of heart. Mrs. Jameson, who was in America at the time, also dissented from some of the views but considered it "the truest of books". Monckton Milnes coupled it with Carlyle's *French Revolution*, "a threnode of the old world, a Te Deum of the new, blending in chorus", and thought her treatment of slavery far more lofty than was to be expected from her school. To Fox, it was masterly. Dickens, who was no friend, considered it the best book on America.[2]

[1] The reviewer in *Spectator* (February 3, 1838) disagreed with the general view. He found *Society in America* full of important observations, while the *Retrospect* was made up of leavings of little interest or importance. But *Spectator* was a radical paper.

[2] *Life of M. R. Mitford*, ii, 198. Mrs. Jameson to Mrs. Austin, December 27, 1837, Ross, *Three Generations*, p. 136. Wemyss Reid, *Monckton Milnes*, i, 196. Garnett, *Fox*, p. 167. Dickens is quoted in a letter from A. W. Weston to D. Weston, February 4, 1842, BPL, Weston. But see Disraeli's sizzling and remarkably apt review, *The Times*, May 30, 1837.

In America the book met with almost complete condemnation, except from a few friends. Fanny Kemble's comment that most Englishmen who read it at least respected her character, integrity, and courage, found few echoes in America. It was, reported Channing, in as bad odour as Mrs. Trollope's book, perhaps worse; he could hear with perfect composure criticism of her mistakes of fact, but he could not be indifferent to imputations on a character he admired so greatly. "I honoured her reverence for truth; but those who did not know her give her no credit for this."

All of the Americans saw factual errors, which were natural enough; most of them lamented a tendency to generalize too quickly, though few were as bold as Margaret Fuller who wrote to Miss Martineau that a few months of mellowing would have modified the "degree of presumptuousness, irreverence, inaccuracy, hasty generalization, and ultraism on many points"—but then Miss Martineau had criticized Bronson Alcott. Most Americans were too angry to analyse. Mrs. Jameson reported that they would have willingly roasted the author of the book before a slow fire and have eaten her up afterwards. To Thurlow Weed, Miss Martineau was an "ugly, deaf, sour old crabapple". Five years after the book appeared Dickens wrote dolefully to Macready:

> I speak of Miss Martineau, and all parties—Slave Upholders and Abolitionists, Whigs, Tyler Whigs, and Democrats, shower down upon me a perfect cataract of abuse. "But what has she done? Surely she praised America enough!" "Yes, but she told us some of our faults, and Americans can't bear to be told of their faults. Don't split on that rock, Mr. Dickens, don't write about America; we are so very suspicious."

In 1853, Edward Everett (who received some rough treatment) was still sore enough to write in his journal that she was the most ingeniously and systematically mendacious and uncandid of all the tourists, adding to everything else the spite of an old maid. And in 1883 his nephew Edward Everett Hale could still refer to her as a foreign carpet-bagger. These are all northern opinions; there is little point in chronicling the abuse from southerners.[1]

[1] W. E. Channing to Lucy Aikin, September 8, 1837, *Corr.*, pp. 297–98. F. A. Kemble, *Records of Later Life*, pp. 52, 80. *Memoirs of Margaret Fuller Ossoli*, i, 254–58. Miss Martineau claimed that she never got this letter. Mrs. Jameson's comment is in Ross, *Three Generations*, p. 136. G. G. Van Deusen, *Thurlow Weed*, p. 80. *The Letters*

Leaving aside prejudice and touchiness, we must inquire what substance there is in the arguments against her book. A great many people made excuses on account of her deafness, noting that much of the give and take of conversation would have been lost on her. Miss Martineau herself realized this drawback, and I doubt that on the whole it was very serious, particularly with Miss Jeffrey present to compare observations and journal entries.[1] Edward Everett ascribed her attack on him to private pique because he had not taken her hint that she would like to stay with him in Boston.

> I did not like her; & thought I shewed her all the attentions which could reasonably be expected,—more than my means enable me to extend to the majority of respectable travellers who bring letters to me.—She could not probably fail to perceive that I was not disposed to enlist among her idolators. I perceived the plan of "black mail" on which she was travelling & foretold the penalty that awaited me.[2]

But there are more substantial reasons, some worthy, some not, to account for her dislike of Everett. Horace Mann thought the attack on Everett and Peleg Sprague cruelly unjust. In both cases, he said, the men were used to prove what she thought a general truth, as they were important enough to confer dignity on her demonstration; that is, they were used as a physician might use vivisection.[3]

This comment brings us squarely up against her method and her reliability. She was often imposed upon by interested persons, Miss Mitford was told, and when the points bore out her own theories she eagerly swallowed them. So, too, Louisa Minot, the wife of a Boston merchant, who found "marks of credulity & of want of discrimination & delicacy which nothing short of perusing the book with my own eyes would ever make me believe would come from her. What a set of gossips she must have fallen among, & what a ready ear she lent to their tales." Things intended as banter she took as sober truth. "I never knew a person," wrote Catherine Sedgwick, "of half her sagacity whose judgments of character were so fallible & as it seems to me accidental. You cannot guess beforehand who she will particularly

of Charles Dickens, i, 66. Journal of Edward Everett, November 24, 1853, MHS. Edward Everett Hale is quoted in *Life of Garrison*, ii, 57 n.

[1] M. R. Mitford, *Letters*, i, 157–58.

[2] Edward Everett to W. B. O. Peabody, June 19, 1837, MHS, Everett.

[3] To Mary T. Peabody, June 25, 1837, MHS, Mann.

admire & overestimate & for whom she will have a distaste." There is strong internal evidence, said Horace Mann in commenting on her views on slavery, "that she has turned much gossip into history, & has quoted Ellis Gray Loring's fireside talk as an annalist would the records of a government".[1]

The charge of credulity and gossip is, as we have already seen, true enough.[2] She astonished and seriously embarrassed some of her friends. From the moment she went to Boston, said Miss Sedgwick, she was apparently "the general depository of all this base circulating medium". She was a remarkably sympathetic person, so others were communicative; there seemed no harm in telling a foreigner things that had to be kept quiet at home; or, we may add, there might seem to be a great advantage in telling a literary foreigner whose book would justify the ways of some Americans to the world. Her test of authenticity was not very reliable. To the gossip she was given she responded innocently; a frank and generally ingenuous person herself, she treated others as the same. Her informants have much of the blame to bear, of course, but unhappily it was not in her nature to keep her counsel.

She astonished the Sedgwicks by saying that it was common knowledge that Webster and Everett were "licentious", and she supported this contention with details of which the company had never heard. But to a protest from Mr. Minot that he had never heard anything of the sort she replied, "I don't know where Mr. Minot has lived." The allegation of course fitted nicely into her developing awareness of the gulf between principle and practice which was to be the main burden of her book; it was hypocritical that Massachusetts people, who considered themselves the most moral people in the country, should have leading men of so low a level of purity. And so appalling a truth had to be spoken. There is the fact to be considered, too, that there was probably something in what Miss Martineau gossipped about—Miss Sedgwick herself recognized that "the first political men have rarely the average purity of the respectable classes of the com-

[1] M. R. Mitford, *Letters* i, 157–58. Louisa Minot to Jane Sedgwick, July 16, 1837; C. M. Sedgwick to Mrs. H. D. Sedgwick, April 3, 1836, MHS, Sedgwick, Mann to Mary T. Peabody, June 25, 1837, MHS, Mann.

[2] "Miss M's bad habits of judging and talking rashly affect me less on account of their universality. If I give her up on this account, I know not where to stop. As Paul says, 'I must needs go out of the world,' I must stop both ears. What is the staple of conversation but 'personal talk' with little or no foundation?" Channing to E. P. Peabody, March 23, 1838, Peabody, *Channing*, p. 361.

munity". The question was really one of prudence, but, to a person of Miss Martineau's temperament, prudence was out of place when the perfection of a civilization had to be enforced.

The *Westminster Review* commented that her remarks on her friends had an appearance of freedom amounting to asperity—the bad aspect of her greatest quality, her moral courage; her vividly real portraits were intended to enforce an elevated principle. This interpretation must be considered. There was a strong streak of the common scold and gossip in her make-up, but it is also true that from obedience to the highest ends, one can easily be reduced, as she was in Boston, "into the position of a common vulgar-minded person", as Miss Sedgwick put it.[1]

Another charge was that she forced her observations to support *a priori* theories, "having always some theory to establish, or general principle to support, or preconceived opinion to confirm". Disraeli, in reviewing *Society in America*, was brutal about it. With no learning and little reading, he said, "armed only with the absurd axioms of an arbitrary scheme of verbiage which she styles philosophy, and which appears to be a crude mixture of Benthamism, political economy, and sansculotte morality", she rushed through the United States,

> analysing, resolving, defining, dividing, subdividing, and mapping out "the morals" of America, to adopt her own favourite jargon, not as they appear to her or to any other chance speculator, but as they ought to figure according to the principles which she imbibed before her visit, and the crude meditation of which probably amused her outward voyage. There is something infinitely ludicrous in the vanity and presumption with which this lady squares the circle of American morals and discovers the longitude of impending civilization of a new world![2]

He had hit on the core of her intellectual method.

We have already looked at some of her rules for thinking, and have noted the dangers she saw in hypothesizing. She repeated them for travellers. In 1838 Charles Knight published a little book by Miss Martineau called *How to Observe Morals and*

[1] A letter from Mrs. Follen showed Miss Sedgwick that the Everett story had had a monstrous growth; Miss Martineau had never told the Sedgwicks that Everett had attempted to seduce a young woman in Boston. But Miss Sedgwick read Mrs. Follen's letter aloud, and a little girl who was present said later, "Now do tell me aunt Katy all about Mr. Everett seducing Miss M." This emendation, commented Miss Sedgwick, "wd put the *comble* to the gossip". Miss Sedgwick's extraordinarily full and interesting letter is to Jane Minot, May 30, 1836, MHS, Sedgwick. *WR*'s comments are in a review of *RWT*, *WR*, xxviii, 253 (January 1838).

[2] *The Times*, May 30, 1837.

Manners, the second book of a series, the first being *How to Observe Geology*. The argument of this book is not here retroactively applied to her American visit, for it was sketched out on shipboard—Disraeli's intuition served him well—on her way to America: it was originally intended as an article and, when the publisher's scheme was changed, was expanded (or padded) into a book.

Travelling, she maintained, is a serious business. There can be no work more serious than reporting the important things that happen in the world. Hasty and ill-informed generalizations make it impossible to establish the conviction that no one civilized nation is better than another, taking the whole field of morals into account; they can only prevent inspiring in men the spirit of impartiality, mutual deference and love which can enlighten and rectify the understanding. Now, a proper approach to other countries is easy enough to master. The traveller must first know what it is that he wants to know, just as the chemist will make more progress by having an aim and method than he will by empirical dabbling.

Next, the traveller must have an enlightened understanding, and, most important of all, must possess the "principles which may serve as a rallying point for his observations, and without which he cannot determine their bearings, or be secure of putting a right interpretation upon them. A traveller may do better without eyes, or without ears, than without such principles, as there is evidence to prove." Among the principles must be the philosophical belief that men's moral feelings, instead of being inborn, grow up as the result of influences to which they are subjected; but the traveller will know too that there are certain great general influences, so that certain feelings about right and wrong will exist everywhere, as if men were born with them.

> For instance, to torment another without any reason, real or imaginary, is considered wrong all over the world. In the same manner, to make others happy is universally considered right. At the same time, the traveller is prepared to find an infinite variety of differences in smaller matters, and is relieved from the necessity of pronouncing each to be a vice in one party or another. His own moral education having been a more elevated and advanced one than that of some of the people he contemplates, he cannot but feel sorrow and disgust at various things that he witnesses: but it is ignorance and barbarism that he mourns, and not vice.

The traveller, then, judging men only by the law of nature,

must realize that every prevalent virtue or vice results from particular circumstances in the society which he may or may not be able to discover, though it is important that he try. Add to these philosophical requisites a broad sympathy, and the traveller is prepared not only to observe intelligently, but to give a true account of what he sees.

Here then is a specific application of the method she had outlined in her essays on the art of thinking. How well did she carry out her precepts? In her own view, perfectly. Here is Mrs. Chapman, who can stand for her:

> Harriet Martineau has been sometimes called dogmatic and opinionated by incompetent acquaintances and opposition politicians, in both countries; but I think it would be difficult to cite an instance where her preconceived opinions, however warmly cherished (as her high ideas of prominent Americans certainly were), did not immediately yield to facts. Pride of opinion she had not: it was clearness of sight and consequent strength of conviction. But till insight and experience came to justify the conclusions of sight, she held them subject to correction, with a readiness to renounce error that I have never seen equalled.[1]

That is to say, once among the Garrisonians, her prejudices for Calhoun, Clay, and Webster—indeed for any politician—gave way before the facts which the Bostonians mustered so skilfully. I do not mean to imply that the abolitionists took her in; they simply reinforced convictions already present. Certainly their conversations—for they were as unpolitical a group as ever existed—could not unaided have accomplished the shift in her views on Whig measures between her visit to Washington and her book. She had her own principles to apply; she did so rigorously, under an overruling commitment to abolitionism and with the support of like-minded friends. So far, so good. Where she went sadly astray from an intelligent application of her method was in her establishment of the principles and her deductions from them. She said that she was simply applying the principles of the Americans; actually, they were quite of her own creation. Once again, she had fallen into the trap of her method and never knew she was caught.

She disliked the title of her book. She wanted to call it *Theory and Practice of Society in America*, which Saunders and Otley, understandably, would not hear of. It indicates, though, what she wanted to write about. She had little hope of pleasing anyone in

[1] *Auto.*, ii, 287.

either country, she wrote to Clay; it would have been easy enough to do so by merely copying her journal. But the occasion was too serious to be trifled with, and so she risked everything by making "an open avowal of principles which have no chance of being popular". Then a typical flourish: "I am very easy now the thing is done. My conscience is discharged, and I really do not care much what becomes of me in name and fortune, while I cannot live without freedom of speech. This last can never, now, be taken from me."[1]

The book is really a contribution to the British debate on the principles of society, for which America was a relevant experiment.

> The old world naturally looks with interest to the new, to see what point of civilization it reaches under fresh circumstances. The interest may be undefined, and partly unconscious; but it is very eager. The many, who conceive of no other objects of general pursuit than the old ones of wealth, ease, and honour, look only to see under what forms these are pursued. The few, who lay the blame of the grovelling at home upon outward restrictions alone, look to America with extravagant expectations of a perfect reign of virtue and happiness, because the Americans live in outward freedom. What is the truth?

She saw, as we have seen earlier, that both Tories and working-class Radicals were too simple, insufficiently philosophical in their approach to America. What America had done, as she saw it, was to disprove Burke. Even if the whole experiment were to collapse, it would still be held proved that a theory of government can be formed by deduction from the principles of human nature: America had demonstrated the capacity of mankind for self-government.

> It seems strange that while politics are unquestionably a branch of moral science, bearing no other relation than to the duty and happiness of man, the great principles of his nature should have been neglected by politicians—with the exception of his love of power and desire of gain,—till a set of men assembled in the State House at Philadelphia, in the eighteenth century, and there throned a legitimate political philosophy in the place of a deposed king. . . . The *rationale* of the new and "impossible" government is "that all men are created equal; that they are endowed by their Creator with certain inalienable rights; that among them are life, liberty, and the pursuit of happiness; that to secure those rights, governments are instituted among men, deriving their just powers from the consent of the governed." This last recognizes . . . the great

[1] HM to Clay, May 15, 1837, Colton, *Clay*, iv, 413.

principles of indefeasible rights; human equality in relation to these; and the obligation of universal justice.

The Golden Rule had come into politics at last. She found it encouraging that the English were interested in Jefferson and Madison, for they were "men inspired by the true religion of statemanship, faith in men, and in the principles on which they combine in an agreement to do as they would be done by". All that remained for the Americans to do was to prove the other impossible thing—that men could live by that rule.

There were her principles, the specific embodiments of the laws of nature by which, in her terms, it was allowable to judge another people. These principles were enunciated by the Americans themselves; and any American, she was sure, would scorn to have his institutions—or his economy, manners, and religion—judged by any other standard: "He will disdain every test but that furnished by the great principles propounded in the State House at Philadelphia; and he will quarrel with no results fairly brought out by such a test, whether they inspire him with shame, or with complacency. In either case, he will be animated by them."

The Americans exalted the founding fathers; so did Harriet Martineau, but with this difference: the Americans mercifully thought of them as little more than names or symbols; she gave them the qualities of gods and never thought of them as politicians. Where the Americans took the Declaration as a formula and an excuse for raucous piety on the Fourth of July, Harriet Martineau took it literally and, as she had done with political economy, reduced it to absurdity "as far as the *principle* goes by merely carrying it out to all its consequences". She would never have understood Georges Sorel's myth.

How did the United States measure up to this rigorous test of its own rhetoric? It was too early to tell finally, she said, for the United States had not yet had time to develop a national character. The controlling power of prior circumstances—the cause of deviations from principle—had not been broken.

> The principles of truth, and the rule of justice, according to which the Declaration was framed, and that revolutionary struggle undertaken and conducted, should, but for prior influences, have been the spirit inspiring the whole civilisation of the American people. There should then have been the utmost social as well as political freedom. The pursuit of wealth might then have been subordinated at pleasure; fear of injury, alike from opinion and from violence,

> should have been banished; and as noble facilities afforded for the progression of the inward, as for the enjoyment of the outward man. But this was not given. Instead of it there was ordained a mingling of old and new influences, from which a somewhat new kind of civilisation has arisen.

The Constitution of this new civilization, when she brought it to the test, proved bad insofar as it contained compromises of principle, especially the recognition of slavery, the worst anomaly in America. The existence of a Senate too was an anomaly, as it implied a league of states rather then a whole people, so she predicted the eventual realization of a second chamber built on a more consistent principle. The appointment of judges for life removed them from democratic responsibility and was by that principle condemned. But in spite of its shortcomings, the Constitution had, she thought, worked well enough to justify the belief that it was nearer to perfection than any other government and the hope that further advances to an uncompromising democracy would be made.

On the great constitutional issues of the time, she favoured a strict construction—a curious attitude for an admirer of Marshall and a friend of Justice Story, but one which shows how corrosive was her test of principles. A tariff could not be justified by the powers granted to Congress; the nullifiers—defenders of states' rights—were correct as far as their opposition to the tariff went, though their means were wrong and calculated to harm the democratic cause in the world by offering the spectacle of disunion and civil war. The opposition of the majority made a central bank impossible and rightly so, not only in terms of constitutional powers of the central government, but because of the inherent dangers of monopoly and a moneyed power. Nor was there constitutional authority for internal improvements, though the exercise of the usurped power indicated a need for it; hence the constitution should be amended rather than be strained to support any function, however desirable. Quite clearly, she was thinking in terms of the English radical attitude towards state power, an attitude that comes out classically in her brief chapter on revenue and expenditure. Pennsylvania, she reported, spent forty pounds a year for defence and two thousand for education, Massachusetts eighty thousand pounds for schools. "Men who govern themselves and each other with such moderate means, and for such unimpeachable objects, are no more likely to lapse into disorder than to submit to despotism."

Party divisions arose from the natures of individuals; hence they would exist if there were no differences in outward fortunes. The wealthy fear loss by change, the talented fear yielding power to numbers instead of desert, the educated are prejudiced "with doctrines. . . nourished [in] the pride of youth, and prepossessions inwoven with all that has been to them most pure, lofty, and graceful". The aristocratic party, then, is founded on fear. Democracy, on the other hand, contains the rising and aspiring, those whose motive power is hope, the adventurers, the philanthropists, and the small but inestimably powerful class of the geniuses, for all genius is aspiring and democratic. This party distinction existed in America as in Europe, but with this difference: in America there was no need to fear the poor. With property-holding widespread, the poor offered no threat to law and order, a threat more likely to come from above. Nor was there more to fear from ignorance, for the country was better educated than any other, if not yet enough for safety.

The majoritarian principle, an inescapable deduction from the premises, would assure the triumph of democracy. As knowledge, conviction, action come out of ignorance, as the people learn slowly but surely by experience, the majority will be proved to be ultimately in the right. The theory presumes, of course, that the majority would choose not only the best measures but the best men, and in no respect could she find American practice so far behind theory as here. Yet even these mistakes were ultimately remedied or remediable, and bad choices would come to nothing, a neat example of necessarianism. She thought, for instance, that there was nothing to fear from the presidency; Jackson himself had proved that. He came to office with all the possibilities of establishing a despotism, a cry revived at every high-handed act—vetoes, appointments, removal of deposits, the quarrel with the French. Yet here were his eight years nearly done, and the most desponding complaint she heard was not that he had strengthened the central government, not that he had settled matters to his own satisfaction, but that every great question was left unsettled. "But the very fact that these affairs remain unsettled, that the people remain unsatisfied about them, proves that the people have more to learn, and that they mean to learn it."

The implicit wisdom of the majority was brought out again in the attack on freemasonry. Freemasonry, because of its secret obligations, and because it aimed at power which rightly lay with the whole people, was inconsistent with a republic. The incident of Morgan's murder for revealing masonic secrets dramatized the issue; and the anti-masonic party came into being on the basis of true republican principles. "A bad institution is overthrown. The people have learned an important lesson; and they have gone through an honourable piece of discipline in making a stand for the law, which is the life of their body politic." It was an encouraging sign, for worse institutions remained to be cast out, and the world was watching.

America appeared sound in structure and hopeful in policy, but in political spirit it was sadly defective. Negroes were denied their rights, women were politically non-existent, and the fault of majoritarianism was rampant—a too great estimation of opinion resulting in a fear of responsibility and a political apathy absolutely inconsistent with democratic principles. The flattery which public men lavished on their hearers or the condescension of Everett's Bloody Brook address were other sad signs. The way out was clear: "In his political as in his moral life, man should, in the depth of his ignorance and the fallibility of his judgment, throw himself, in a full sense of security, upon principles; and then he is safe from being depressed by opposition, or scared by uncertainty, or depraved by responsibility." In short, the solution lay in education, and American education for democracy was deficient. It might be argued that American children needed no instruction in politics, because they were taught it every day of their lives. But such everyday instruction was only in details, not in the principles by which the details could be judged and transmuted into knowledge. "They come to school with their heads crammed with prejudices, and their memories with words, which it should be part of the work of school to reduce to truth and clearness, by substituting principles for the one, and annexing ideas to the other."

Still more light is thrown on Miss Martineau's social views by her discussion of the economy. The tariff, of course, was an abomination. She saw enough women in New England made poor by the depreciation of stock in factory schemes launched because of promises of the tariff—the innocent sufferers as the entrepreneurs learned salutary lessons about the diversion of resources into unnatural channels. But such self-condemnation of the tariff was not the important thing: it was condemned by the fundamental republican principles to which, lacking constitutional authorization, every man had to appeal.

> It is contrary to all sound republican principle, that the general government of a nation, widely spread over regions, and separated into sections diversified in their productions, occupation, and interests, should use its power of legislating for the whole to provide for the particular interests of a part. . . . Whatever direction and application of industry and capital may be ultimately most beneficial, Congress has, on principle, no more business with it than with the support of what may prove in the end to be the purest religious doctrine.

> If America had been as free, from the beginning, in all respects, as a young country ought to be,—free to run her natural course of prosperity, subject only to the faithful laws which regulate the economy of society as beneficially as another set of laws regulates the seasons, we might never have heard of [Clay's] American system.

Slavery lay at the bottom of it. The South, with an arbitrary tenure of labour, demanded an arbitrary distribution of capital, only to find that matters turned out otherwise than anticipated. The South continued to deteriorate, while manufactures replaced and renovated the commerce of the North. But the South's hatred of the tariff was based not on the reasonable ground of principle, but on the ridiculous allegation that it was the cause of all their troubles. If only America had kept her commerce and labour and capital free, she could have been the pattern and instructress of the whole civilized world. She lacked the knowledge and the requisite faith. But there was still hope.

> It may not yet be too late for her to be in the van of all the world in economical as in political philosophy. The old world will still be long in getting above its bad institutions. If America would free her servile class by the time the provisions of the Compromise Bill expire, and start afresh in pure economical freedom, she might yet be the first to show, by her transcendent peace and prosperity, that democratic principles are the true foundation of economical, as well as political, welfare.

When Miss Martineau turned to consider American attitudes to and institutions of property, she found the picture better. Everyone admitted that great private wealth was inconsistent with republicanism, and though competition and ostentation were everywhere, they did not go beyond the bounds which public opinion placed to them. Large estates were divided, not, as in the absurd and barbarous system in England, transmitted entire by primogeniture. The Americans had made a remote approach to equalization of wealth.

> This method is as yet perceived by only a few: but the many who imitate as far as they can the modes of the Old World, and cherish to the utmost its feudal prepossessions, will only for a time be able to resist the convictions which the working of republican principles will force upon them, that there is no way of securing perfect social liberty on democratic principles but by community of property.

Americans rightly had a horror of a despotism which would equalize property arbitrarily. Public opinion required an approach to the equality of property demanded by justice—no man should encroach on his neighbours to enrich himself, on his younger children to enrich the eldest, or on the present generation for the sake of the future.[1] By the same principle no one should be allowed to take from the industrious to give to the idle, from the strong to give to the weak, from the wise to give to the foolish. "Such aggression upon property can never take place, or be seriously apprehended in a republic where all, except drunkards and slaves, are proprietors, and where the Declaration of Independence claims for every one, with life and liberty, the pursuit of happiness in his own way. There will be no attacks on property in the United States."

Yet sooner or later, a better principle of property would have to be found. The moralists, with Channing in the lead, lamented the greed and competition of society; scholars maundered ridiculously about the necessity of an aristocracy and leisure to overcome the superficiality of scholarship rising from their own shortcomings; professional men were driven into competition; merchants drove themselves mercilessly while their wives lived in useless and ignorant indolence; and the working classes had not the leisure they wanted for higher things. The English, who realized the viciousness of property, were hampered by inherited institutions. In America there was little more to do than to retrace the false steps they had taken in imitation of the Old World; their accumulation of abuses "is too small to be a serious obstacle in the way of the united will of a nation". It might be protested that men would fear such a change, but they would not be deprived of anything needful, if the change in property resulted from a change of tastes.

[1] Edward Hope, the high-minded hero of *Deerbrook* (1838), though in the extremity of poverty, refuses a legacy from a grandfather who failed to divide his wealth among his heirs.

> As for the details of the future economy indicated, it will be time enough for them when the idea which now burns like a taper in scattered minds shall have caught, and spread, and lighted up all into an illumination sufficient to do the work by. Whenever a healthy hunger enables the popular mind to assimilate a great principle, there are always strong and skilful hands enough to do the requisite work.

In other ways too America fell short of her potentialities. If the national mind were judged by legislation, she said, it would be deemed of a very high order; to judge by American literature, the country had no mind at all. But here too the promise lay in the future. Nations are like individuals in the growth of mind; philosophers and poets are possessed by ideas long before they can express them, so America had to wait for the genius who could come to express her national spirit. In reviewing Miss Sedgwick after her return, she made the same point. Miss Sedgwick had passed out of the imitative stage to true description, the department in which Jane Austen excelled; when she was at her best, in her tales rather than her novels, she could give the world a true picture of American manners, but the higher mission of genius escaped her.[1]

In religion the Americans had moved beyond Europe to repudiate establishments, so they had to be judged by their own higher principles of religious freedom and not by the example of societies whose errors they had escaped. By this standard her Unitarian conscience was shocked. What sort of Christianity was it that was adopted almost universally? Asceticism perverted religion to mere performance, the pressure of opinion in the North brought opprobrium on Catholic and atheist, slavery in the South divorced religion from its radical principles of justice and liberty, and the clergy everywhere were aristocratic, craven, and isolated. God was not worshipped; opinion was.

> I doubt whether, among the large "uneasy classes" of the Old World, there is so much heart-eating care, so much nervous anxiety, as among the dwellers in the towns of the northern States of America, from this cause alone. If I had to choose, I would rather endure the involuntary uneasiness of the Old World sufferers, than the self-imposed anxiety of those of the New; except that the self-imposed suffering may be shaken off at any moment.

Of the excrescences to be removed, none was so important as slavery, the greatest crime against American principles. It had

[1] *WR*, xxviii, 22–24.

bred most of the evils of society. The riots to which America was subject at the time were not like most European riots, but riots of opinion, like the Birmingham riots of 1791 which drove Priestley into exile, or the attempts of the Liverpool merchants to push Clarkson into the dock; the mobs were "respectable" men, not from the lower depths. But the poison in the North was nothing to the poison in the South—a society sunk in feudal codes of honour, physical force and overriding fear, an economy, at any rate east of the Alleghenies, steadily deteriorating. Attempts to recover by pushing commerce were hopeful, however, for "the opening of every new rail-road, of every new pier, is another blow given to slavery". And in abolitionism lay not only the great hope but the great symptom that men's minds were on the move against the abomination. Events in Washington—the Gag Rule, the clamour about petitioning, the actions of time-serving politicians—helped to wake the country, and the abolitionists stood selflessly by to help. Never was so reasonable a set of people brought together, informed, devoted, perceptive men and women who overcame their artless weakness in politics by heroism, meekness, and faith.

I have not in this summary showed Miss Martineau's best qualities: a keenness of observation, a sense of significant detail, incisive portraiture, that is, her good reporting. But I have abstracted and illustrated the essence of her view of society, and an extraordinary view it was, limited, naïve, even at times embarrassing. She never grasped the enormous possibilities in economic growth. She never once doubted that education and proper circumstances, in good Hartleian fashion, would produce a whole nation of clear-sighted, selfless, active, benevolent, and dedicated men and women—good (and dreadfully dull) citizens. English presuppositions and radical deductions abound—in her attitude to the state, in her interpretation of religion, and, I think too, in her attitude to wealth and property, for she came from a manufacturing class which was not rich, which ploughed its profits back, and some of whose members welcomed social responsibility.

She was, in fact, not really interested in America at all. She was interested in certain abstract propositions which America could prove. Feudalism, she said in *How to Observe*, had given way to the opposite state of society, whose prevalent virtues and vices were of a vastly different character. Physical force, pride in ancestry, idleness were replaced as standards of judgment by moral power, work, and accomplishment. The old world inclined to the view that man was creator and king, while the new world began to see man as "a creature, a subject, a transparent medium through which the workings of principles are to be eternally revealed". It was becoming clear that the higher honour lay in obeying the natural laws of inward and outward life. And as the servile class rose, increasingly cared for and looked after, it gradually began to exercise its own judgment on legislation. Here then was the critical period when

> a new promise blossoms under the feet of the lovers of truth. There are many of the hand-workers now who are on the very borders of the domain of head-work: and, as the encroachments of those who work not at all have, by this time, become seriously injurious to the rights of others, there are many thinkers and persons of learning who are driven over the line, and become hand-workers; for which they, as they usually afterwards declare, can never be sufficiently thankful. There is no drowning the epithalamium with which these two classes celebrate the union of thought and handicraft. Multitudes press in, or are carried in to the marriage feast, and a new era of society has begun. The temporary glory of ease and disgrace of labour pass away like mountain mists, and the clear sublimity of toil grows upon men's sight.

"If in such an era, a new nation begins its career, what should be expected of it?" That was the question she asked of America.

Carlylean, yes, at times almost Marxist: feudalism breeds its opposite, the intellectuals go over to the proletariat, from each according to his ability, to each according to his needs—the ideas are all present in Harriet Martineau, that presumed high priestess of political economy! She shared with the socialists the moral indignation at the society around her and believed that the problem could be solved by the creation of a new society which would obey the great principles of human nature. The alienation of a class-ridden, competitive society had to give way, and she never doubted that men somehow, sometime, would be brought to perfection—that revolutionary faith which has produced such frightening combinations of self-sacrifice and enormity. Policy was always secondary to principle, the actual to the potential, the present to the future.

America stood mid-way between ancient barbarism and enlightenment. She could not stop still but had to move, to be goaded on, and Miss Martineau's attitude to America right to the end of her life was one of hectoring, urging, ordering progress to the goals she saw inherent in the working of natural law. In Cincinnati, which she so much admired as a place for people of ambition to live, someone said to her: "Yes, we have a new creation going on here; won't you come and dabble in the mud?" If only, she said, they will remember that they have a new creation going on and not a fortuitous concourse of atoms, if only they will remember "that the human will is, or may be, the presiding intelligence; that centuries hence, their posterity will either bless their memories with homage like that which is paid to the Pilgrim Fathers, or suffer the retribution which follows the indulgence of human passions, all petty jealousies will surely subside, in the prospect which lies before every good man. . . . They can foresee the future, if they please; and shape it, if they will. . . ."

CHAPTER VI

London: Interlude

ONCE back in her house in Fludyer Street, Miss Martineau led the same active life she had enjoyed before she went to America. To be sure, the contacts with the Cabinet were no more. Brougham was out of office and out of her good graces too. Drummond was in Ireland and Durham in Canada; both were to die in 1840. But if she was not quite so close to the centre of affairs as she had been or had imagined herself before, her political interest was as strong as ever, and she remained a figure to reckon with in London. She saw Fox no more, because of the dubious domestic arrangement, but she no longer needed the Unitarian crutch. Macready could always get a box for her at Covent Garden. The Carlyles were intimate friends, notwithstanding reservations on both sides. Charles Buller, Monckton Milnes, Albany Fonblanque of the *Examiner*, Robertson of the *Westminster*, H. F. Chorley, the music critic of the *Athenaeum*, Eastlake, Browning (whom she much admired), and practically everyone of note came to dinner, called, and wrote letters. The most charming recollection I have seen comes from Charles Darwin, writing to his grandmother. He had just returned from the zoo, where he had seen a remarkable orang-outang.

> So much for Monkey, & now for Miss Martineau, who has been as frisky lately as the Rhinoceros. Erasmus [his brother] has been with her noon, morning, and night; if her character was not as secure as a mountain in the polar regions she certainly would loose [sic] it. Lyell called the other day & there was a beautiful rose on the table & she coolly showed it to him & said "Erasmus Darwin" gave me that. How very fortunate it is she is so very plain; otherwise I should be frightened. She is a wonderful woman: when Lyell called he found Rogers [the poet], Lord Jeffrys [sic] & Empson calling on her;—what a person she is thus to collect together all the geniuses. Old Rogers seems to [be] a warm admirer

> of hers. He says her laugh is so charming, it is like "tickling a child in the cradle". Was there ever such a simile—a pretty little baby indeed. She is very busy at present in making arrangements about her new novel. One bookseller has offered 2/3 profits & no risk, but I suppose that is not enough.[1]

They may have laughed at her a little, they must have wished occasionally that she would be quiet, but somehow they always came back for more.

She was nearly as busy with writing as she had been when she first came to London. There were the American books and *How to Observe* to be done. She wrote the *Guide to Service* for Charles Knight, now publisher to the Poor Law Commission—three little books for the housemaid, the lady's maid, and the maid of all work—and followed them up with an article on domestic service for the *Westminster Review*; the subject was one to which she was often to return. Writing for the *Westminster* was an old ambition fulfilled—though Mill was far from happy about her contributions.[2] Then there was the usual charitable activity: the Polish orphans had to be taken to the pantomime or entertained to dinner; Norwich ladies had to be put into positions; young men wrote for advice and had to be answered. She was always open to pleas to serve causes. The Lord Advocate, Lord Murray, urged her to write some articles for *Chambers's Journal* on penal administration, since he had lost his bill on the subject and wanted to get public opinion in Scotland worked up.[3] Bulwer-Lytton asked her to draw up a petition in favour of Poulett Thomson's copyright bill, and she went to work collecting signatures for a petition to Congress to urge action against piratical American publishers. Miss Aikin thought more might have been done if the Government had intervened, doubting whether Miss Martineau's influence at Washington was as great as she imagined, but the effort could do no harm, and of course Miss Aikin was one of the lady signers collected.[4]

[1] April, 1839, Nora Barlow, *Charles Darwin and the Voyage of the Beagle*, p. 148.

[2] M. St. John Packe, *Life of John Stuart Mill*, p. 236.

[3] *Chambers's Journal*, December 1, 8, and 15, 1838.

[4] Webster and Colonel Preston, she told Brougham, had moved for a law when she was in Washington, and wanted only to be backed by English authors. "I rather think both Houses will fall on their knees on the receipt of our Petition." HM to Brougham, three letters of November, 1836, UCL. HM to Edward Everett, November 8, 1836 and March 21, 1837. Bulwer to HM, and HM to Lady Maria Graham Callcott, November 9, 1836, Harvard. Lucy Aikin to W. E. Channing, December 10, 1836, *Corr.*, p. 269.

She talked incessantly about America. Crabb Robinson found her accounts of America highly interesting, "and not at all offensive by any assumption on her part—Tho' she speaks like one who is conscious of having a right to speak and form a judgment". High praise this, for Crabb Robinson and his brother had investments in American state bonds which were not very sound propositions in 1837 or indeed for a good many years afterwards. It took all of Harriet's skill to reassure him; she told him in 1842 that she was sure that the state stocks would all be paid and expressed her enthusiasm for Wordsworth's sonnet on repudiation with its hope that in time the Americans would come out right. She was full of anti-slavery enthusiasm too: the South, she told Robinson, would be weak in war; separation was no longer so odious, and some abolitionists (among whom she was soon to be ranged) considered disruption better than compromise with the sin of slavery. Then there was American gossip: Calhoun wanted secession so that he could become sovereign of the South; Mrs. Trollope was admitted to no decent society in Cincinnati; Fanny Wright was beautiful but not very wise.[1] She kept up a flow of correspondence across the Atlantic, and she was hostess to a steady stream of American visitors who must have found her house a welcome oasis of sympathy. In fact, she thought seriously about going back to America to settle and to take up the anti-slavery fight in earnest, but family obligations postponed, and eventually her illness terminated, any such possibility.[2]

"I have surveyed my experience, and told my tale," Miss Martineau wrote at the end of *Retrospect of Western Travel*, "and though often visiting America in thought, can act no more with reference to my sojourn there, but must pass over into a new department of inquiry and endeavour." But what were the new exertions to be? She was wonderfully excited by an offer from Saunders and Otley to set up a periodical to deal with economics. It could tap Knight's circulation, she wrote, and that of her series; it could do such good; it could show what a periodical

[1] Crabb Robinson Diary, October 22, 1837; Crabb Robinson to Mrs. Wordsworth, August 27, 1842, DWL.

[2] *Auto.*, i, 390–91. Gannett, *Memoirs*, pp. 176–77; HM to George Bancroft, July 7, 1838, MHS, Bancroft; HM to Clay, May 15, 1837, Colton, *Clay*, iv, 413–14; HM to Edward Everett, March 21, 1837, MHS, Everett; C. M. Sedgwick to C. M. Sedgwick (aunt to niece), March 8, 1837, MHS, Sedgwick; Weston papers, BPL, *passim*. Macready, *Diaries*, i, 355–56.

"with a perfect temper" might be; it could help in setting women forward at once "into the rank of men of business". Though the risk of failure and the very heavy work seemed real personal hazards, she set herself to drawing up a list of articles; Saunders and Otley seemed prepared to grant all her conditions. But when James turned out to be dead set against the idea, she wrote to them at once to decline.[1]

Another possibility was held out for a journal devoted to the cause of women. "In a very merry little female circle," Miss Aikin told Channing, "we hailed Harriet Martineau as our champion, between joke and earnest, and she then told us of the scheme of a periodical devoted to the good of the sex, of which she was to be the editor." Her journal contains excited references to the "Women's Friend scheme"; even though she decided that she could not take full editorial responsibility for the paper, she would certainly write for it.[2] Though this particular plan came to nothing, the "woman question" remained among the most important causes of her life; and her views on it never really changed.

It is significant that Miss Martineau made her first appearance in print on the subject of women. In October 1822, over the signature "Discipulus", the *Monthly Repository* published the first of her two articles on "Female Writers of Practical Divinity". Why that subject? Because some of the most useful and important English works on practical divinity were by women; to point to them might excite "the emulation of those of their sex who are capable of imitating such bright examples". But she did not want simply to perpetuate the blues; the bluestockings could never have paraded their pedantry had women been really valued as they should have been.

Her opinions on the status of women were expressed at considerable length in *Society in America*. The political non-existence of women in the United States was one of the worst violations of those democratic principles by which she so rigorously judged American pretension and performance. There was half the nation's population governed without their consent. And she made short work of the usual arguments against granting the

[1] This is based on journal entries, *Auto.*, ii, 321–24, and letters to James, December 12 and 21, 1837.

[2] Lucy Aikin to W. E. Channing, October 14, 1837, *Corr.*, 299–300. Journal, September 25, September 30, 1837, *Auto.*, ii, 311.

suffrage. It would not do to plead that consent was given on behalf of women, else laws would hardly be necessary to protect women against husbands and fathers. The argument that women's interests were involved with those of husbands and fathers was sufficiently disproved by women without husbands or fathers. As for the plea of acquiescence, that only proved the degradation of the injured party. Moreover,

> I, for one, do not acquiesce. I declare that whatever obedience I yield to the laws of the society in which I live is a matter between, not the community and myself, but my judgment and my will. Any punishment inflicted on me for the breach of the laws, I should regard as so much gratuitous injury; for to those laws I have never, actually or virtually, assented. I know that there are women in England who agree with me in this. The plea of acquiescence is invalidated by us.[1]

As for a woman's virtual influence, her ruling through the heart, one "might as well try to dissect the morning mist".

Poor Macready simply didn't understand: "I do not see what she would have in point of political power, nor for what." And a good many of her friends found her attitude incomprehensible in whole or in part.[2] They were understandably put off by the shrillness of tone and her deliberately uncompromising stand in the enthusiasm growing out of her American experience and the abortive schemes immediately after her return. When the question of women's rights assumed its proper place in the catalogue of reforms, she was reasonable—though still puzzling to some—and remarkably consistent.

Certainly she was not the obvious sort of advocate. She told Florence Nightingale that she had tried to give her "air and space and liberty" by keeping off the Women's Missionaries. She was with them insofar as they wanted to help people to find out what they could do and to do it; but she detested "all setting up of idols, Proclamations of Rights, & all unnecessary divisions of men's and women's work".[3] She repudiated all abstractions of rights, she told Reeve, all *a priori* arrangements for giving women a position, and she thought it would be disastrous if the pedants got hold of the movement. But if the Rights of Women were bad enough, the sentimental novelists were worse, who

[1] *SA*, i, 152.

[2] Macready, *Diaries*, i, 398–99, June 5, 1837. W. E. Channing to E. P. Peabody, September 1, 1837, Peabody, *Channing*, pp. 395–96.

[3] HM to Florence Nightingale, December 3, 1858, BM.

N

looked on women as made to sit beautifully dressed in a drawing-room, with nothing to do but be agreeable to their husbands. Talk about educating women to improve their usefulness to someone else, or to make them fit companions or mothers of heroes did not go very far.

She had discussed education for women in an article in the *Monthly Repository* for February 1823, to which the two earlier articles were really introductory. A proper education, she insisted, would give to a wife the sensible mind she needed, to single women the liberal pursuits necessary to save them from the faults of old maids, and to both the knowledge to transform narrow, selfish charity into intelligent benevolence aimed at the permanent improvement of mankind. Though acquirements would vary with station and circumstances, in general she felt that no Englishwoman above the lower ranks should be ignorant of the evidences and principles of her religion, sacred history, the outline of general history, elements of natural philosophy, and philosophy of the mind, and such living languages and accomplishments as circumstances might direct. In short, she wanted the women of England to be educated as she had been.

Norwich produced her youthful programme, and as it altered, one can detect the influence of W. J. Fox and Eliza Flower. This influence was reinforced by the teachings of the Saint-Simonians who came to England in 1831 on a mission which strongly impressed the Unitarians and which made Miss Martineau at least a temporary convert. They are noticed favourably in her history, and their advocacy of a new position for women must have attracted her attention.[1] But her view, as it matured, leaving aside the occasional strident outburst, remained single. She did not want to have her cake and eat it too; what she wanted was real equality and a chance to show what could be done—a fair field and no favour.

When she read *The Taming of the Shrew*, the fun and cleverness were spoiled by the intolerable pain she felt at the treatment of Katherine: "Such a monstrous infringement of all rights, leading to such an abominable submission, makes one's blood boil, as if it were not a light comedy, but a piece of history."[2] But she was discriminating about the ways to equality. She opposed

[1] On the Saint-Simonians, HM to James, March 24, 1831; *MR*, v, 82–88, 181–89, 279–81 (1831); Mineka, *Dissidence of Dissent*, pp. 213–15; *Hist.*, ii, 141.

[2] Journal, November 20, 1837, *Auto.*, ii, 325.

admitting women to the Commons' galleries to hear debates; that would have meant a descent on the House of silly, frivolous women with time to waste—a nuisance to M.P.s and a disadvantage to the wiser women who knew that a serious cultivation of political interests was better done at home. Again, she defended the bastardy provisions of the Poor Law of 1834, so widely denounced for cruelty because they put the whole responsibility on the woman and let the seducer (responsible under the old law) go scot-free; but she saw only advantage in woman's being made "even through apparent hardship, mistress of herself —the guardian of her own mind and morals, instead of the ward of Man".[1] Though she dissented from his opposition to the Infants Custody Bill, she could welcome Brougham's exposition of the cruelty of the whole of English law relating to women; and she was always ready to agitate for effective changes in the law or to do anything that might improve the position of women. She hoped for a periodical to advance their cause; she wanted to write a novel to redeem women; she wrote leaders about the mistreatment of women by brutalized husbands; and she had some other ideas too. Here is one—affected perhaps by a combination of Saint-Simon and the Lowell Factory girls in Massachusetts— with a characteristic conclusion:

> I should like to see the economy of association made use of by women; to see them living in a sort of club-house, enjoying comfort and luxury, rather than dispersed in poverty among boarding-houses and schools; but there must be no royal patronage, no distinction between rich and poor, no ostentation about schools attached. Simple living without other restraints than as to hours and one or two other particulars. It strikes me to write on this.[2]

The broad and true view of woman's sphere was bounded only by the powers God had bestowed; only that question remained to be proved. Let one hundred women, she said, be educated up to the highest point that education could reach, and it would soon be seen what would be the sphere of each of that hundred: it might be science or medicine; it might be investigating the laws of social relations or active social work; it might be a household and family. But if intelligence was to be worth anything, it had to issue in action; and if all the actions of human life were

[1] *Hist.*, ii, 86, 335–36.

[2] Journal, October 12 and November 11, 1837, *Auto.*, ii, 315–16, 321. *DN*, September 8, 1853 (Brutality), June 28, 1854 (Divorce).

so tainted as to be unfit for women, then they must be equally bad for men, "and we ought all to sit down together to let barbarism overtake us once more". It was already a great gain that so many women—from the Queen down—were working and proving their capacities, not only for labour in hitherto unaccustomed fields but for full responsibilities of citizenship as well; and no one did more for the cause than Miss Nightingale. The images of women on woolsacks had nothing to do with the question. Kings, she had said pointedly in *Society in America*, once laughed at the idea of a commoner stepping into the throne of a nation; but who dared to laugh when Washington addressed the New World from the presidential chair and the Old World waited to catch the echo?[1] The movement was in train, its success as sure as progress; and she stood ready to do what she could to help.

A miscellaneous life, then, with a number of false starts to find some major concern. But when schemes fell through or diminished to proper size, she found her consolation in the thought that she would no longer be kept from writing a novel. It was an idea she had had for a long time. Fox had discouraged her from it when she first began to write for him, but her success with the political economy tales and the pleasant things said by reviewers about her description and characterization must have led her to wonder a good many times whether she had the power to carry off a full-scale novel. Not that she ever expected to rise into the class of geniuses who could convey the true spirit of an age or a people, but perhaps, working within the lesser compass of Jane Austen (as Miss Martineau saw her) or Cather-

[1] This summary is based on a letter to Frances D. Gage, January 2, 1852, Huntington Library; a letter to Henry Reeve, November 19, 1858; a message to the Women's Rights Convention in the United States, written at Cromer, August 3, 1851, and printed in the *Anti-Slavery Standard; Once a Week*, August 10, 1861, v, 175–79; *DN*, February 29, 1856. The subject of women's work was a favourite; there are a number of leaders in *DN* and an important article in *ER*, vol. 109, pp. 293–336 (April, 1859). It is interesting to compare the view of Mary Estlin of Bristol, who told Mrs. Chapman that the American agitation for women's rights would never be understood in England, because the oppressions of women were so merged in others where men were fellow sufferers. "I find very few people who are aware that with you all *white men* are on a legal equality & that consequently our class restrictions, religious disabilities, landed property monopolies, etc., & all the host of oppressions under which we groan resolve themselve with you into distinctions of sex or of colour. If the English public had this key to the enigma they would be a little more merciful to the transatlantic Amazons as they suppose the advocates of Women's Rights to be." January 10, 1853, BPL, Estlin.

ine Sedgwick, she could give a true picture of manners and say some things that needed saying.

The problem was finding a subject. Early in January, 1838, she saw in the *Quarterly Review* an article on Haiti, and it flashed across her mind that her novel should be about Toussaint L'Ouverture.

> Was ever any subject more splendid, more fit than this for me and my purposes? One generally knows when the right idea, the true inspiration, comes, and I have a strong persuasion that this will prove my first great work of fiction. It admits of romance, it furnishes me with story, it will do a world of good to the slave question, it is heroic in character, and it leaves me English domestic life for a change afterwards.[1]

She began reading about Toussaint, but a friend discouraged her, and the idea was dropped for a time. Another subject was suggested by a paragraph in a police report, but deferred, lest newspaper readers should remember the outcome; it was never taken up again, she said in her autobiography, because "I have seen more and more the importance of dwelling on things honest, lovely, hopeful and bright, rather than on the darker and fouler passions and most mournful weaknesses of human nature". Finally, she lighted on a situation—later found to be untrue—in which a family friend was supposed to have been forced by a matchmaking lady to marry a woman whose sister he loved. She began to write *Deerbrook* in June, 1838, and finished the first volume by the end of August. She then went north to Newcastle and to Scotland, took up the novel again in November, and finished it in January.

Briefly, the story is this. Hester and Margaret Ibbotson come from Birmingham to the village of Deerbrook to stay with their cousins the Greys, while their father's estate is being settled. Mrs. Grey at once sets about bringing Hester together with Edward Hope, the local physician, who finds he prefers the stronger mind and personality of the less beautiful Margaret. Mrs. Grey, however, forces Hope's hand by telling him that Hester is in love with him; and Hope, believing rightly that Margaret is in love with Philip Enderby, the brother-in-law of Mr. Grey's partner Rowland, decides to marry the woman he does not love, and Margaret comes to live with them. Then enters the villain, Mrs. Rowland, Mrs. Grey's social rival, who

[1] Journal, January 15, 1838, *Auto.*, ii, 334.

cannot forgive the capture of Hope by the Grey connection and accordingly sets about to ruin him, by spreading rumours that the Hopes are not happily married, by encouraging the prejudice of the ignorant rustics against the doctor's alleged body-snatching, and by driving her brother Philip and Margaret apart. Her activities, together with the resentment of the local squire at Hope's vote cast in an election, bring the Hopes with remarkable suddenness—"arithmetically impossible" said *Spectator*—into poverty. Adversity brings out the best in everyone's nature; Hester's jealousy and suspicion are resolved in the trial; and the marriage emerges successful. The hostility against Hope is put an end to by his services in a plague that strikes the village; Mrs. Rowland is put to rout and confesses her evil machinations; and the extraordinary virtue of the family in the house on the corner is rewarded with happiness.

Reviewers were reminded at once of Jane Austen; a reader would be reminded of her today—at a distance; and that is no accident. Miss Martineau was a great admirer of Miss Austen and put herself through a re-reading of her novels before she went to work on *Deerbrook*. But she saw that Miss Austen could do many things that she could not, and that is true enough. There are some fine things in *Deerbrook*. The *Athenaeum* reviewer was perfectly correct in pointing to the impressive picture of a small, ingrown society (the "village tone" of Deerbrook). Some of the minor people are hit off well; and some of her characterization in the major figures is good. The contrasts between Hester and Margaret are drawn with an insight one might not expect—the *Edinburgh* reviewer could remember no portraits of sisters better done. Mrs. Rowland and Mrs. Grey are striking embodiments of their types. With the men, however, she was a dismal failure. Edward Hope, modelled, Miss Martineau tells us, on the character of Dr. Furness, the Unitarian minister in Philadelphia, is impossible in his high-mindedness; and Enderby is contrived. She never could write dialogue well; she was much too concerned with ideas and idealization. The plot is simple, but hardly strong enough to bear the length. The *Spectator* reviewer hit the core of this problem neatly: the novel was planned as a tract and expanded to the requisite three volumes by her disposition to philosophize, her taste for home scenes, her skill in painting them, and her bias for setting out (as she had done in the political economy tales) her feelings and opinions in dialogues. "Very ligneous," said Carlyle, "very trivial-didactic, in fact very absurd for the most part," but Miss Martineau was pleased with it. And of course it is the didacticism that counts. The *Edinburgh* reviewer saw this impressively in comparing her to Miss Austen. Both showed

> the same microscopic observation of foibles—the same quick sense of the ridiculous, especially as displayed in affectation and pretension; both avoid the leaven of romance; and both draw their scenes among country society of the middle classes. Both have displayed a very uncommon knowledge of human nature; but Miss Austen is like one who plays by ear, while Miss Martineau understands the science. Miss Austen has the air of being led to right conclusions by an intuitive tact—Miss Martineau unfolds her knowledge of the principles on which her correct judgment is founded.

Deerbrook has two purposes. First, its social complexion, as the *Athenaeum* called it. We have already seen the importance which Miss Martineau attached to the middle classes; to convey this in fiction was a dubious enterprise at best in the thirties, when high life, romance, and melodrama filled the circulating libraries. An "unromantic and unpicturesque portion of the community," said the *Edinburgh* reviewer, and Sydney Smith had a grand time as usual. No "'poticary," he said, could be a hero in fiction: if he took his mistress's hand, he would feel her pulse by force of habit; if she fainted, he would have only Epsom salts; he would put cream of tartar in her tea and flower of brimstone in her bosom—no, a "medicinal lover" would not do. But, for all his jokes, the middle-class setting was vital to Miss Martineau. She had criticized Scott for the narrowness of his range of society; all the passions and the "natural movements of society" that he found in the higher ranks existed in the lower, magnified and deepened proportionally as reality prevailed over convention and as the adventitious was less mixed with the true. The time had come, she said (in 1832), for less picturesque but graver themes:

> We have had enough of ambitious intrigues; why not now take the magnificent subject, the birth of political principle, whose advent has been heralded so long? What can afford finer moral scenery than the transition state in which society now is. Where are nobler heroes to be found than those who sustain society in the struggle; and what catastrophe so grand as the downfall of bad institutions, and the issues of a process of renovation? Heroism may now be

found, not cased in helm and cuirass, but strengthening itself in the cabinet of the statesman, guiding the movements of the unarmed multitude, and patiently bearing up against hardship, in the hope of its peaceful removal. Love may now be truly represented as sanctified by generosity and self-denial in many of the sad majority of cases where its course runs not smooth. All the virtues which have graced fictitious delineations, are still at the service of the novelist; but their exercise and discipline should be represented as different from what they were. The same passions still sway human hearts; but they must be shown to be intensified or repressed by the new impulses which a new state of things affords.[1]

This view was characteristic of a radicalism dedicated to a new society which art had to serve. *The Economist* in 1846 insisted that "high art" become low art, that it appeal to the understandings and interests of the people who counted, that it serve the public, in its real interests, not its presumed ones, and certainly not the artist himself. Hogarth had acquired popularity by his pictures of the rake and the harlot, subjects the people knew.

A follower of Hogarth . . . might find the progress of a Rothschild, or the fate of a needlewoman . . . equally fit subjects for historical pictures. . . . Surely our high artists might find in the death of Huskisson, at the opening of the first great railway in England, to which the building of the Pyramids was an uninteresting event—a Hargreaves dying in a workhouse, and an Arkwright or a Peel building up a colossal fortune by the help of his inventions—a Watt presiding at the forging and putting together his first steam engine—the meeting of those seven gentlemen who formed the League, which has become the type of a great change of the commercial policy of the world;—historical painters might in such subjects as these find fit and proper themes for their skill, which would win for them, though even crude in colouring and grouping, the admiration of their countrymen.[2]

It is a view not very far from the "socialist realism" of which we have heard so much: and the purpose, in the creation of a society, was precisely the same. Miss Martineau's mission is beyond question. In one foolishly self-conscious entry in her journal she noted a disagreement with her mother about the quality of their friendships. The important thing for her was to enlarge her acquaintance among the middle classes, among people below rather than above her; and if "the high quit me on that account, let them. They will not be worth the keeping. . . . I *must* keep my mission in view, and not my worldly dignity."[3]

[1] "Genius of Scott", *Misc.*, i, 40 ff., 54.
[2] July 4, 1846.
[3] January 13, 1838, *Auto.*, ii, 333.

If the class of her characters was justified by her political principles, what was her second purpose? *Deerbrook* is a simple village tale, where political or economic triumphs as subjects would not seem to belong. But principle—in its broadest sense—is operative anywhere. The aim, as *Spectator* summarized it, was to teach "suffer for the right, and all will come right at last". Here the figure of Hope is especially important. He embodies central and permanent principles in action, however incredibly. He is a man of science, who has to stand against and suffer for the superstition and folly of popular ignorance. "Now, as to this present duty," he says, "it seems to me very clear.

> It is my duty to offer moral resistance to oppression, and to make a stand for my reputation. When it pleases God that men should be overwhelmed by calumny, it is a dreadful evil which must be borne as well as it may; but not without a struggle. We must not too hastily conclude that this is to be the issue in our case. We must stay and struggle for right and justice,—struggle for it, by living on with firm, patient, and gentle minds. This is surely what we ought to do, rather than go away for the sake of ease, leaving the prejudices of our neighbours in all their virulence, because we have not strength to combat them, and letting the right succumb to the wrong, for want of faith and constancy to vindicate it."[1]

This principle holds not only for the medical superstition of the mob—always a concern of Miss Martineau's—but for politics as well. Hope courted danger by the vote he gave in opposition to the squire's interest and against all the advice of the trimming Grey. To stand for principle and to suffer for it; the two decisions were inevitably linked in Miss Martineau's mind, and the reward beyond them was certain.

Evil, to be sure, was a power. So Enderby to his sister, the diabolical Mrs. Rowland:

> "They will be happy with their greatness and loveliness, sister; for it is Heaven's decree that they should. Why will not you let yourself be happy in witnessing it, Priscilla? Why will you not throw off the restraint of bad feelings, and do magnanimous justice to this family, and, having thus opened and freed your mind, glory in their goodness,—the next best thing to being as good as they? You have power of mind to do this:—the very force with which you persist in persecuting them shows that you have power for better things. Believe me, they are full of the spirit of forgiveness. Do but try——"
>
> "Thank you. I am glad you are aware of my power. If they forgive me for anything, it shall be for my power."[2]

---

[1] *Deerbrook*, ii, 291–92.

[2] ii, 277.

But principled and right action was *in itself* a power greater than Mrs. Rowland's. *Spectator* objected to the plague which brings Mrs. Rowland's defeat by killing her child and vindicating Hope. "No moral in fiction, when the author undertakes to exhibit the *whole*, can ever be pointed by accidents or extrinsic circumstances, but must spring from a conjunction of character and conduct strictly producing legitimate consequences." But the reader who would wonder what might have happened without the intervention of providence would be wasting his worries, for the plague was a merely adventitious addition to provide a climax which fails to come off. The tension that Miss Martineau builds up so well at the end of the second volume in the opposition of Mrs. Rowland and Hope is not artistically resolved; but it is equally certain that the whole burden of her intention was to show that right action itself, good necessarian morality, will triumph. It was a demonstration central to a belief in progress and for the liberal creed.[1]

It seems to have been a woman's book. Mrs. Jameson recommended it to Ottilie von Goethe, warning her that it had long dreary stretches, but that it was "very *English*": it gave an "exquisite picture of English *provincial* life in the middle classes"; it was a book not to make one feel, but to make one think, and it filled her with admiration. Mrs. Carlyle may have agreed with her husband, and Mrs. Macready may have had her doubts, but Miss Barrett liked it, and Mrs. Emerson was "for these two days past petrified to a water dropping stone by the novel of Deerbrook".[2] The novel sold reasonably well, going into three editions, though it was never a great popular success, and certainly did little to secure a reputation for its author. The moral demonstration was lost on most of her readers. People had read the political economy tales for their stories and had let the doctrine go—the ever-present danger of didactic fiction. So it was with *Deerbrook*. Despite its many virtues, it had too many weaknesses to carry the lesson.

Miss Martineau was scornful enough about the novel, as she

[1] Miss Martineau's own discussion of *Deerbrook* can be found in the *Autobiography*, i, 411–16, ii, *passim* in pp. 317–39. The reviews which I found particularly perceptive are in *Athenaeum*, April 6, 1839; *Spectator*, April 13, 1839; and *ER*, lxix, 494–502 (July, 1839).

[2] *Jameson-Goethe Letters*, pp. 111–12. Jane Carlyle, *New Letters*, i, 75. HM to Elizabeth Barrett, [April 15, 1845?], Yale. *Carlyle-Emerson Letters*, pp. 232–33. *Emerson Letters*, ii, 319.

deprecated most of her early works, in her autobiography. She rejected the "laborious portions of meditation" intruded into it, and if she were to do another novel, she said, she would require more simplicity and a far more objective scheme. But it was faithful to her principles and sentiments at the time, and she believed it useful "not only in overcoming a prejudice against the use of middle-class life in fiction, but in a more special application to the discipline of temper". She was glad she wrote it, but did not want to be judged by it at any later period. Again the incidentals of her "conversion" blinded her and led her to severer judgments than were warranted, either by the novel itself or by what happened to her after it was written. *Deerbrook* is not a major work, but it is a revealing one; the themes of the twenties and early thirties are embodied in it, and its chief contentions appear again in some of her later writings.

Deerbrook then, had as its message the importance and certainty of the necessarian morality; the abolition of slavery and the potentiality of the Negro were the most vital concrete applications of that morality. "Harriet Martineau is coming," wrote Carlyle to Emerson, "with beautiful enthusiasm for the Blacks and others."[1] When *Spectator* published an article suggesting that the abolitionists had hurt the position of the Negro, Miss Martineau wrote two letters to the paper in reply.[2] When the World's Convention of the British and Foreign Anti-Slavery Society was held in London in 1840, Miss Martineau, though an invalid in Tynemouth, was named a delegate from Massachusetts, a typically Garrisonian assertion of principle, for the Convention refused to seat women.[3] From her sickbed in Newcastle and Tynemouth she directed fund-raising to benefit Oberlin College in Ohio—that hotbed of antislavery enthusiasm which she always called "the Oberlin"—and she was hostess to John Keep of Oberlin when he travelled to England in 1839 to raise money for that most radical of institutions and the first college to admit women and Negroes.[4]

The two most important contributions to the cause in this period were an article and another novel. The article was "The Martyr Age of the United States", which appeared in the

[1] November 15, 1838, *Carlyle-Emerson Letters*, i, 199–200.

[2] Journal, October 6, 12, 19, 1837. *Auto.*, ii, 314, 316–17. *Spectator*, October 14 and 21, 1837.

[3] *Life of Garrison*, ii, 353, 379.

[4] J. A. Collins to Mrs. Chapman, December 3, 1840, BPL, Weston.

Westminster Review in December, 1838. In substance it is a short history of the abolition movement in America from Garrison's first efforts to the murder of Lovejoy and the new Congressional career of John Quincy Adams. The actual history need not be summarized here: it is familiar enough. Naturally, she wrote a thoroughly Garrisonian history, though other workers in the field than the Bostonians are given recognition—Lydia Maria Child, the Grimke sisters, Weld, and the college at Oberlin. The inferences for her British audience are worth setting down. (1) The struggle for abolitionism cannot subside until it prevails, so yielding to it by its opponents would save "a world of grief and woe". (2) Other sorts of freedom will come in with freedom for the slave—the aristocratic spirit is being purged, and for every black slave liberated, a white one will be freed also. (3) Republicanism is not answerable for the disturbed state of America, whose tyranny and turbulence come from the persistence of an old-world feudal spirit. (4) Finally, the coloured people have a "promising *morale*" on which to ground their civilization.

As to the abolitionists themselves, her peroration is a sincere one:

> Nowhere but among such, can an array of countenances be beheld so little lower than the angels. . . . They are living fast and loftily. The weakest of them who drops into the grave worn out, and the youngest that lies murdered on his native republican soil, has enjoyed a richer harvest of time, a larger gift out of eternity, than the octogenarian self-seeker, however he may have attained his ends. These things, as branches of a general truth, may be understood at the distance of half the globe. Let us not, therefore, wait, as it has been the world's custom to wait, for another century to greet the confessors and martyrs who stretch out their strong arms to bring down Heaven upon our earth; but even now, before they have stripped off care and sorrow with their mortal frame,—even now, while sympathy may cheer and thanks may animate, let us make our reverent congratulations heard over the ocean which divides us from the spiritual potentates of our age.[1]

The article was widely circulated as a pamphlet, both in England and America, the Garrisonians being convinced for some unfathomable reason that representations from England were potent weapons in America. H. B. Stanton told the World Convention in 1840 that the article excited so great a sensation that the publishers were forced to apologize for its insertion; "still the article was read, and read in the Southern States. . . ."[2] Its

[1] *WR*, xxxii, pp. 31–32.

[2] *Proceedings of the World Convention*, p. 125.

importance in England was undoubtedly much greater, for it was the first full-scale introduction for the general public to the work of the abolitionists, a stimulus not only at the time it was written but in the fifties too. Bright in 1867 paid tribute to Miss Martineau as "a very noble woman who taught the English people much upon this question by introducing the names of the great Americans to the English public". And when Garrison called at Fox How, Matthew Arnold told him how deep an impression was made on him in his childhood by his father's voice as he read "The Martyr Age" aloud to his wife.[1]

The novel she gave to anti-slavery was *The Hour and the Man*, a revival of the Toussaint idea. It was written after she returned, an invalid, from a European tour which had taken her to the fortress in the Jura where Toussaint was imprisoned and had died. The book was much admired. Channing told her he knew no grander conception of heroic character; Crabb Robinson thought it her masterpiece, despite its faults; and Florence Nightingale called it the finest historical romance in any language.[2] It seems, today, a poor and nearly unreadable book. A great deal of research went into it, the same techniques that she had used to such good effect to summon up picturesque scenery for the political economy tales,[3] but the faults of *Deerbrook* are magnified fantastically. The characters are impossible, and their conversations even more so, if one insists on any relevance to fact or possibility. Toussaint, said the *Spectator* reviewer, is neither a Negro, nor an emancipated slave, but a philosopher and a philanthropic statesman, or Miss Martineau's *beau ideal* of one. In a letter to Empson, Lord Jeffrey said he supposed Toussaint really was an extraordinary man, though he doubted he was such a combination of Scipio, Cato, Fenelon, and Washington as she made him out to be.[4] And, one might add,

[1] Louisa Chick to Miss Estlin, n.d., BPL, Weston. *Life of Garrison*, pp. 200, 227.

[2] Crabb Robinson Diary, December 15, 1840. *Channing Memoirs*, iii, 236. Florence Nightingale to Jane Martineau, June 29, 1876, and to Mrs. Chapman, September 29, 1876, *Auto.*, ii, 578, 581.

[3] HM to Elizabeth Pease, July 13, 1840, MHS, Norcross.

[4] *Spectator*, December 5, 1840. Carlyle's comment is worth quoting: "You saw her *Toussaint l'Ouverture*: how she has made such a beautiful 'Black Washington', or 'Washington-Christ-Macready', as I have heard some call it, of a rough-handed, hard-headed, semi-articulate gabbling Negro; and of the horriblest phasis that 'Sansculottism' can exhibit, of a Black Sansculottism, a musical Opera or Oratorio in pink stockings. It is very beautiful. Beautiful as a child's heart,—and in so shrewd a head as that!" To Mrs. Emerson, February 21, 1841, *Carlyle-Emerson Letters*, pp. 317–18.

Cromwell and Chadwick; for Toussaint not only frees the Negroes of Haiti from French rule, not only works in obedience to the voice of God within him, but presides over a quite automatic reform of the island in which morals become pure, labour is honoured, inventions are made by ingenious labourers able to work for themselves, and every cottage has two rooms! Of course, a criticism on the grounds of probability is beside the point. Artistic success to Miss Martineau was secondary to moral considerations, and the moral considerations of this book had considerable impact at the time.

Like everything she ever wrote, *The Hour and the Man* was concerned to demonstrate a truth, here the great potential of the Negro. This had impressed her in America, and to the abolitionists Haiti was a crucial experiment in which they were prepared to see what they wanted; it disproved for them the scepticism of slaveholders about what Negroes could become—not simply in fifty years or so, as *Spectator* suggested, but immediately. The contention that there is no better way of educating for responsibility than giving it—was here applied with a vengeance. The whole conduct of the Negroes, she said in "The Martyr Age", "affords evidences of generosity, patience, and hopefulness, from which fine results of character may be anticipated, wherever the unfortunate race shall have leave to exert their unfettered energies under circumstances of average fairness". So of course Toussaint's family had to talk like Europeans and could show no sign of the effects of generations of conditioning as slaves. It seems an odd, though understandable, violation of her Hartleianism; but perhaps the paradox is resolved by her idealism, which rarely stopped for logic, and by the nature of her didactic view of fiction: to show not actuality, but potentiality. Saints and martyrs could scarcely concern themselves with less.[1]

The period between Miss Martineau's return from America and her journey to the continent in 1839 was an interlude in which the old impulses worked automatically in changed situations, but without a central core or an outstanding accomplishment. Her years in Tynemouth, though at first they might seem even more an interlude, were in reality immensely important. The central fact was that she fell ill in Venice and returned to England an invalid.

[1] Jeffrey's letter is reprinted in *Auto.*, ii, 351–52. The reviews I have cited are in *Spectator* and *Athenaeum*, December 5, 1840.

CHAPTER VII

Tynemouth: The Uses of Suffering

MISS MARTINEAU was a celebrated medical case. Her highly publicized mesmeric cure in 1844 posed a challenge which was eagerly taken up by the doctors, who, in some sober reports on the autopsy, were able to have the last word. Moreover, her brother-in-law, T. M. Greenhow, who attended her, published a pamphlet describing in detail her case and its treatment. We are then in a position to know a pretty fair amount about her physical condition. The problem is more complex, however, and its complexity must carry us into speculations about that morbid realm of Victorian illness which is likely to escape modern understanding entirely.

It should be said at once that Miss Martineau was really ill. Her invalidism was not simply hysteria or hypochondria or an excuse to escape, however much all of them may have entered into the situation. She had begun to feel unwell in 1838, periodically suffering from loss of strength and "great failure of nerve and spirits".[1] Somewhat similar interruptions had troubled her before, but her condition was not allowed to interfere with her plans to travel on the continent. In Venice, in June 1839, she collapsed. She had been suffering from sharp abdominal pains, disturbing discharges, and severe nervousness. She was unable to stand or walk, and pains in the back shot down into her legs. A Venetian physician, consulted but not permitted to examine her, from a description of her symptoms at once concluded that the difficulty was prolapse of the uterus and polypous tumours. She and her friends then went on to

[1] James's abstract of her letter of July 30, 1839, refers to the failure of spirits and notes also (quoting) "Apprehensiveness, anxieties, and self-contempt", which are characteristic responses to a prolapse. Miss Martineau's own accounts of her illness are almost hopeless, for reasons which will become clear enough in time. I am relying here on T. M. Greenhow, *Medical Report*, and articles by Greenhow and T. Spencer Wells in the *British Medical Journal*, April 14 and May 5, 1877.

Lucerne; movement had become all but impossible and she found little relief from the measures suggested by the Venetian doctor or by Dr. Greenhow, who had been consulted by letter. On returning to England in October, she went directly to Newcastle to her brother-in-law, and the diagnosis was confirmed. It was a matter for later medical debate how this condition was related to the growth of the ovarian cyst which finally, if indirectly, killed her. The tumours were removed, but the uterine condition could be corrected only by then rather risky surgery, which was not considered, so Greenhow had to do what he could medically to relieve her.

She took small morphine doses regularly, much too small for addiction. An iodine ointment suggested by Sir Charles Clarke, the famous gynaecologist, she refused to use, but Greenhow substituted an iodine tonic, which she found helpful. Her situation was aggravated, however, by other ailments—severe digestive troubles and an abscess in the throat. Still, the prolapse is enough to explain the discomforts of which she complained: back-ache, depression, nervousness, and lack of energy. She was able to move about a little: it was not until 1842 that she stopped going out into her garden finally. But most of her time she spent on a couch which, because of her back, was arranged that she might lie on it prone. At times she suffered severe pain, probably connected with the growth and movement of the ovarian cyst; at other times she felt only a kind of *malaise*. But the physical situation remained virtually without change until 1844.

After a short stay in lodgings in Newcastle she moved into the Greenhows' fine house in Eldon Square, where she remained until March 1840, when she moved to lodgings in Mrs. Halliday's house in Front Street, Tynemouth. The Greenhows had one of the happiest homes in the world, she told Carlyle,[1] but when the difficulty showed no signs of clearing up, she wanted to avoid dependence. The new room was a tiny one, up a short flight of steps from the ground floor. It was later enlarged by the addition of a room in the house next door, with a door cut between. She grew plants, decorated the room with casts and prints, received gifts of fresh flowers and fruit; she read, and wrote, and drew, and studied Euclid, and looked out of her bay window. The window was a great resource, and Mrs. Reid

[1] November 2, [1839], Princeton.

gave her a stand telescope through which she could watch the ordinary occurrences at sea and along the river and keep herself in touch with life outside. The window looked (and still looks) out upon gardens and across the mouth of the Tyne to South Shields. It was a remarkably varied prospect—sea, river, town and country—its only fault that there were no trees except one wretched little sycamore. The sea offered not only the drama of storms and wrecks, but the beauty of its subtler changes; the gardens and river-banks showed people at ordinary tasks or amusing themselves; and there was a fascinating exercise of the imagination to be found in watching people in action or conversation, or in gazing at flags, on the castle, on ships, or in the towns.[1]

She had a maid to take care of her; her doctor was twenty minutes away by rail; and in the intervals when she was well she worked. She wrote *The Hour and the Man*, the four tales which comprise *The Playfellow*,[2] and *Life in the Sickroom*, and of course the usual voluminous correspondence. But this was nothing like the quantity of work that she was able to turn out during the thirties or after 1845. Visitors were limited in number and in time; sometimes she was not well enough to see callers at all. Yet in her better periods she held court, and there was a steady stream of distinguished visitors. The local aristocracy—Lambtons and Ravensworths—were within easy reach; her friends Elizabeth Reid and Julia Smith would come up from London and stay for weeks, visiting her in the evenings. Lady Byron, Mrs. Jameson, Crabb Robinson, Lord Morpeth, Monckton Milnes, Carlyle, the visiting Americans all found their way to Tynemouth. She had always been a good person to visit, and illness changed that not at all.

Nor did illness stop her benevolence. When she could not write, she could knit and do woolwork; her pieces went to Boston to the anti-slavery bazaars organized by Mrs. Chapman and were sold locally to help a barrack library she had organized for the soldiers and their families attached to the local garrison—

[1] There are a great many descriptions of her quarters and activities. *Life in the Sickroom, passim.* HM to Mrs. Macready, December 29, [1840], NLS. HM to Crabb Robinson, January 8, 1841, DWL. HM to Miss Estlin, February 25, 1844, NYHS. HM to Elizabeth Barrett, [March 8, 1844], Wellesley. Crabb Robinson to Thomas Robinson, July 7 and 15, 1842, DWL. Anna Jameson to Lady Byron, 1842, in *Anna Jameson: Letters and Friendships*, pp. 206–18.

[2] *Settlers at Home, The Peasant and the Prince, Feats on the Fjord, The Crofton Boys.*

to buy them the books she most wanted them to read. She fed materials and ideas to Greenhow for lectures which he gave—on slavery and education—to the Popular Lecture Society in Newcastle, a body whose meetings "had not only been duly appreciated by the working classes for whose benefit the society was more especially established, but had also been patronized by the presence of many of their more wealthy neighbours". The success of penny postage touched off another enthusiasm. She wrote and issued a handbill at Shields and Newcastle to support the testimonial fund for Rowland Hill, and sent out her maid with a large ruled sheet of paper for names and a china basin for the sixpences of grateful servant maids and soldiers. families. She did what she could for education and "town problems", in part with the hundred pounds that Lady Byron sent her annually for the charity she could no longer support from her own earnings. She was following her own rule: if everyone made his property available for the happiness of others, the world would be much more pleasant to live in.[1]

Wrote Carlyle:

> As for poor Harriet . . . I found her confined to a sofa, dangerously ill, I believe, though not in immediate danger; for the rest, brisk, alert, invincible as ever. There is a kind of prepared completeness in Harriet, which does honour to nature and the Socinian formula. In my travels I have met with few more valiant women. Poor Harriet! She was absolutely affected, amiable, almost sublime to me there. *Sunt lachrymae rerum.* How are all human souls crushed in by this formula or that, by this good fortune or that; and hardly any formula supportably fits a man, and the most are not coats, but straight-waistcoats; very lamentable! [2]

Had Miss Martineau seen that letter, the first part would have pleased her very much, particularly the word "sublime". And the "prepared completeness" which Carlyle saw was true and, I think, Socinian. Mrs. Woodham-Smith has recently suggested that Miss Martineau took to her sofa to escape domestic responsibilities; much more she emphasizes that Miss Martineau belongs among those Victorians who found in the invalid's life "a climate in which they could work".

[1] HM to Mrs. Chapman, August 25, 1843, Harvard. HM to Mrs. Romilly, March 9, [1844], Bodleian. *Newcastle Chronicle,* January 25 and April 18, 1840. *Fifty-second Year's Report of the Literary and Philosophical Society of Newcastle-upon-Tyne.* HM to Elizabeth Barrett, [March 8, 1844], Wellesley.

[2] Carlyle to Milnes, July 19, 1841, Reid, *Milnes,* i, 265–66.

There is no question but that life in the Fludyer Street house had become difficult. Her mother was going blind. Her brother Henry continued to be a problem. After the failure of the firm in 1829, he had begun to drink and to stay out so late that he had to be threatened with locking-out. His sister carefully reported each sign of improvement to James, and assured him that Henry continued popular in the town. In 1834 she interceded with Lord Durham, unsuccessfully, to get Henry appointed an assistant poor law commissioner. Finally, in 1838 he had to be brought to London and added to the household. He went to work as a clerk at Somerset House, but his improvement was only apparent and so, following a suggestion of James, the family financed Henry's emigration to New Zealand. To get away from depressing and difficult entanglements like these was a great release. But work, even though a considerable amount of writing was done at Tynemouth, was certainly not her main object.[1]

Miss Martineau, as we have seen, was really ill, though not so ill as she insisted, and she looked upon that illness in a peculiar way. At times she could hint that the disease would be fatal; at other times simply incurable. To any suggestion that she might get better she responded with absolute disbelief. She was determined, of course, to give her friends no trouble—the same principle she had enunciated in her *Letter to the Deaf.* She saw them only when she was at her best and pleasant and stimulating. But she also demanded certain things of her guests, among them the avoidance of the usual consolation. It was, she wrote in *Life in the Sickroom*, "purely irritating to one who was not feeling better, nor believing that he should ever be better, nor in a state to be cheered by any speculation as to whether his pain would, or would not become more endurable with time!" Nor did she want to be told how useful and honourable a life she had led—a sheer absurdity in a condition when suffering magnified all one's moral shortcomings. "Everything but truth becomes loathed in a sick-room." And she insisted on the truth.

> Then the question arises, what sort of truth? Why, that which is appropriate to the one who administers. To each a separate gift

[1] Cecil Woodham-Smith, "They Stayed in Bed", *Listener*, February 16, 1956. HM to James, July 14, October 21, December 28, 1830, June 6, 1832, March 6, 1838, December 5, 1839, October 2, November 19, 1840, June 28, 1841. HM to Durham, December 18, [1834].

may be appointed. Only let all avoid every shadow of falsehood. Let the nurse avow that the medicine is nauseous. Let the physician declare that the treatment will be painful. Let sister, or brother, or friend, tell me that I must never look to be well. When the time approaches that I am to die, let me be told that I am to die, and when. If I encroach thoughtlessly on the time and strength of those about me, let me be reminded; if selfishly, let me be remonstrated with.

Her brother-in-law knew perfectly well that there was no malignity; he always believed that in time she would "take up her bed and walk". However, "she never willingly listened to my suggestions of the probability of such prospective events, and seemed always best satisfied with anything approaching to an admission that she must ever remain a secluded invalid. This state of mind, perhaps, may be considered as an additional symptom of the morbid influence over the nervous system, of the class of diseases in which this case is included." Poor Greenhow! He was, she told Miss Barrett, the perfect specimen of the sanguine man, beating the man in the *Rambler* all to nothing. At first he predicted that she would be well in a month, then in the autumn, then in the spring, and finally in ten years—he thought the menopause a likely time—but ten years was as near giving up as he would go. She always knew it was hopeless, she said, and his going so far saved talk. "There is always such a sunshine of hope in his eyes that he cannot see far before him for the dazzle."[1]

Several factors enter into this attitude. Greenhow spoke of the "morbid influence over the nervous system", and there is no doubt that, psychologically, the attitude is common enough. There are, I think, other considerations. She was, to begin with, medically superstitious and highly suggestible; and, as we shall see, she had a great distrust of physicians which is odd, considering her family background or even Edward Hope in *Deerbrook*. But, most significantly, suffering was necessary as a moral probation and a badge of martyrdom. An operation, Lucretia Mott reported to Mrs. Chapman, would kill or cure Miss Martineau; as a philosopher and Christian, she expected the former. Miss Barrett wrote to a friend that she was told by Miss Martineau that the disease was gaining, but that only made her serenity and elevation of mind more triumphant. And Carlyle, in a moment of exasperation, commented that her book sounded as if "she

[1] [March 8, 1844], Wellesley.

were a female Christ, saying, 'Look at me; see how I am suffering!' "[1]

In writing to Milnes about her illness in 1841, she stressed its difficulties—the conviction of deterioration, a morbid introspection, loss of self-respect, increasing reliance on human opinion—but, on the other side, it was the trial appointed to make havoc of small complacencies and to reduce life to its essentials. Perhaps, she thought, in a few years she would reach the elevation Milnes had complimented her on. By 1842 she was commenting to him on the intensity with which she felt the realities of life, an attainment which made bodily pain and mental conflict as nothing if they were conditions of such experience. "It matters little that the straightest road to such conviction is sometimes terribly rough."[2]

At this juncture she read Bulwer-Lytton's new novel, *Zanoni*, which deals, in highly mystical (and rather loose) terms, with the self-sacrifice of Zanoni, who consents to lose the immortality conferred by his attainment of ultimate knowledge by marrying Viola, an opera singer, and dying in her stead in the last days of the Reign of Terror. The reviews, she wrote to Bulwer-Lytton, were perfectly insensible to the doctrine of the novel. Although an admirer of his early work, she did not expect from him anything so remarkable, indeed, any book in English so worthy of Schiller's meditations. Then, finding her friends mystified over something that seemed as obvious to her as that a map of Norfolk was not intended to show Cornwall, she drew up a scheme for their guidance; she was anxious to make the steps to the conclusion as clear as the conclusion itself for readers without German and unfamiliar with the "language of the Ideal region". She sent the scheme to Bulwer-Lytton who evidently felt it sufficiently accurate and helpful to be appended to the 1845 edition and to all subsequent editions of the novel. The marriage, as she saw it, is the linking of instinct (Viola) to idealism (Zanoni), and the climax is the fulfilment of that union, in which the laws of the two natures become one. Faith extorts the saving truth from Fear itself, "the inestimable Proof wrought out by all labours and all conflicts", that only beyond the grave can exemption be had from mortal conditions, that "the Universal

[1] Lucretia Mott to Mrs. Chapman, n.d., BPL, Weston. Elizabeth Barrett to Mrs. Martin, September 4–5, 1843, *Letters*, i, 151. Wemyss Reid, *Milnes*, i, 435.
[2] December 4, [1841] and June 22, [1842].

Human Lot is, after all, that of the Highest Privilege", a privilege wrought out in self-sacrifice and death.[1] Thirty-five years later, W. R. Greg, in his obituary, caught the Stoicism in her attitude and the "force of conviction akin to that of the fanatic and the martyr".[2]

When Harriet Martineau was a child, a neighbour child underwent an amputation.

> I was naturally very deeply impressed by the affair. It turned my imagination far too much on bodily suffering, and on the peculiar glory attending fortitude in that direction. I am sure that my nervous sytem was seriously injured, and especially that my subsequent deafness was partly occasioned by the exciting and vainglorious dreams that I indulged in for many years after my friend E. lost her leg. All manner of deaths at the stake and on the scaffold, I went through in imagination, in the low sense in which St. Theresa craved martyrdom; and night after night, I lay bathed in cold perspiration till I sank into the sleep of exhaustion.

The recollection of this incident found its way into one of the children's tales she wrote while an invalid, and out of scruple she wrote to Emily Cooper, her childhood friend, to apologize. She received in reply "one of the noblest and sweetest letters that ever was written, not a trace of pedantry or formality, but a letter flowing, frank, calm, Oh! most touching, from one [so?] silent on the subject of her infirmity."[3] How gratifying it must have been!

The strain is apparent in transmuted forms throughout her adult life; the high calling of the martyr and the blessedness of suffering for principle are recurring themes. Nor is this attitude simply Christian: it is Unitarian. "If ever we are conscious of a breathing of the Godhead in man," she wrote in 1838, "it is in the sanctified presence, actual or ideal, of martyrs to truth." Most martyrs are liable to peculiar faults, which men are more likely to forgive because, of all men, martyrs most extensively command sympathy. "As truth is the one eternal good, the single pursuit of truth is the one eternal virtue which wins and elevates all human souls." Priestley was precisely such a martyr, a man without stain, driven for his beliefs to America, where he still had much to suffer. "My trials," he wrote, " . . . are as great as I can bear, though I doubt not that a wise and good

[1] HM to Bulwer-Lytton, July 2, August 8, 22 and 28, [1842].
[2] *Nineteenth Century*, ii, 102 (August, 1877).
[3] *Auto.*, i, 34. HM to James, January 17, 1842.

Providence overrules all events, and I have daily a more habitual respect to it. Nothing else could support me. . . ."[1]

She found examples of martyrdom everywhere: in principled politicians who died carrying out their beliefs, like Drummond; in Grace Darling, who rescued five men and a woman from a wrecked boat; and of course in the abolitionists. Unquestionably some of the abolitionists suffered severely and Lovejoy was murdered; equally certainly they sought martyrdom, exaggerated their sufferings, and gloried in them.[2] She told Crabb Robinson that she was no fit companion for her American friends, who heroically, gently, and patiently went back to first principles of anti-slavery morals, while she found herself recoiling from the labour of arguing the matter with a temporizing correspondent.[3] She called her account of them "The Martyr Age of the United States".

To espouse the primary principles of Christianity, she wrote in the twenties, was still dangerous in some Christian countries: the days of difficulty and trial were not over, and the obligation to confessorship was as great as ever. But while the supports of martyrdom can be realized, it is not so easy to recognize its trials: the most god-like of martyrs found the cup almost too bitter to be tasted; the conflict with nature and man was not easy to bear.[4]

> To suffer is as important a part of obedience as to act; and the more enlarged our views of the purposes of the moral government of God, the less rebellious will be the struggles of our will. Those who know how the passions grow by indulgence, who are taught by science as well as by experience that counteraction is as necessary as stimulus to the perfect vigour of the mind, find a substantial relief in sorrow in the conviction that their suffering is conducive to their ultimate good. A yet higher satisfaction arises when self is no longer explicitly regarded, and the energies of the sufferer are directed to the investigation of the Divine purposes in the afflictions which have befallen him, and to an earnest endeavour to co-operate in the fulfilment of those purposes. To submit to inevitable misfortune with humble acquiescence, is the common duty of all: to struggle, without repining, while the issue of events is doubtful, is lawful for all; but to welcome the dispensations of Providence,

---

[1] *RWT*, i, 109–17.

[2] Hazel C. Wolf, *On Freedom's Altar*, is woefully deficient in ideas, but it at least catalogues the sufferings of the abolitionists.

[3] November 27, [1843], DWL.

[4] "On Moral Independence", *Misc.*, i, 189.

> whatever they may be, to derive spiritual vigour from every alternation of joy and sorrow, to perceive the end for which those alternations are appointed, and to aid in its accomplishment, are the privileges of the few; and those few are as much distinguished by rectitude of understanding as by purity of heart.[1]

Believing this, how could she do otherwise than reject friends or doctors who would dash the cup of sorrow from her lips and deprive her of the purification of suffering? There lay the real reason why she wanted to be alone in Tynemouth: she was working out the necessarian metaphysic.

The visitors came in summer. For the long months of winter she was usually alone. Sometimes the trumpet would lie untouched on the table for days, and the repose, she said, was more delightful to her than her friends could imagine.[2] Carlyle thought that the forced silence of her confinement would do her good.[3] It certainly gave her time to read and think. She told Miss Barrett that she had stopped being a reader in her girlhood; she had *studied* since, but within a narrow range. In the forties she was reading more widely again.[4] She could also criticize what she had done before her illness.

The dangers of a situation like this were evident enough to her at the time; and, as one might expect, had been anticipated in the twenties. In an article in the *Monthly Repository* in 1827, she had set down the dangers of adversity: that the soul might become calloused or timid; that timidity might lead to despondency, ingratitude, insensibility, and atheism; that living in a dreamy world of sentiment and imagination would bring listlessness in the performance of irksome duties; that sincerity and ingenuousness were endangered. What could result from such a course

> but daily increasing selfishness; morbid feelings which, instead of retaining or deepening their intensity, must induce insensibility; a gradual forgetfulness of God and disregard of duty; a growing craving for sympathy, the approbation, the applause of others; a paramount desire of being interesting, and the sacrifice of one thing after another, of *all*, for the sake of being so.

Some minds are naturally equipped to overcome these perils; some find it easy; but the solution is attainable by everyone.

[1] "Art of Thinking", *Misc.*, i, 118–19.
[2] HM to Elizabeth Barrett, March 6, [1844], Yale.
[3] Carlyle to Emerson, December 8, 1839, Slater Edition.
[4] [October 16, 1843], Wellesley.

> The grand rule is to look to *principles*, and to leave feelings to take care of themselves. This rule includes everything. Principle will lead the mourner to refer all to God; principle will oblige him to forget himself, and will suggest to him continual occasions of doing good to others. Principle will teach him that affliction is not intended to set him apart from others, but to enlighten his views of his relation to them, to exalt his affections towards them, to animate his efforts in their behalf. He must, sometimes, notwithstanding his endeavours to forget himself, feel what an aching void sorrow has left in his heart; but, instead of turning his views inwards to behold the desolation there, he will look abroad with a searching eye to the varied aspects which life presents to him. . . . He does not desire to shroud his mind in mystery; it is there, clear and transparent, for all to look into who choose: he only wishes that the gusts of passion should not ruffle, or the clouds of despondency overshadow it. His regard to duty imposes on him the care of his health and of his tranquillity. The works of God are his study abroad; the word of God employs him at home.[1]

What were the moral dangers, she wrote to a friend in 1844, "but a call to try how they may be overcome?" The counsel, helpful in her bereavements in 1827, was applied to the adversity of the forties. There were the dangers of becoming too abstract, of losing sympathy with passing emotions, once withdrawn from society; hence her concern for proper arrangements of the sick-room and her systematic use of the view from her windows. The danger of selfishness and morbidity she conquered—or, one cannot help feeling, fell into—by the demands she put on her friends for "the truth" and by such expedients as the letter she sent to Miss Barrett (who was very upset by it) upbraiding her for flattery.[2] An invalid, she said, was unfit for doubtful moral enterprise, being unable to put up with recurring doubts or to take cheerfully the conviction of a moral mistake: these things loomed too large when one had only to brood on them. But happily, one may add, doubtful moral enterprise was a rare thing for Miss Martineau, and where the case was clear, she thought moral enterprise was the best medicine.

She re-examined her intellectual positions; indeed, she considered writing a deeper and more comprehensive volume than Bailey's, on the proper methods to reach and serve truth. But faith remained her firm foundation. Crabb Robinson said he knew of no orthodox sufferer, Calvinistic, Roman, or

[1] *MR*, n.s., i 558–63 [August, 1827].

[2] Miss Barrett to M. R. Mitford, September 28, 1844, *Barrett-Mitford*, pp. 222–23. HM to Miss Barrett, [August 21, 1844], Wellesley. See above pp. 13–14.

Anglo-Catholic who seemed more intensely convinced of his scheme of hope; the Unitarians, he thought, could be proud of her.[1] One's misdeeds rose up, she told him; every foolish thing one had ever said recurred to mind; these questionings of the past were the real trial of illness, but they drove one out of one's self for interests and helped in other and "perhaps holier" ways.[2] To realize that what seems evil is really appointed for a greater good which will one day become clear; to rise above one's self; to win the moral victory: these were the injunctions of necessarianism as Priestley taught it. And out of this she formulated an idea of more potential to the sufferer than any other: that what we *do* matters infinitely less than what we *are*.

> If we cannot pursue a trade or a science, or keep house, or help the state, or write books, or earn our own bread or that of others, we can do the work to which all this is only subsidiary,—we can cherish a sweet and holy temper,—we can vindicate the supremacy of mind over body,—we can, in defiance of our liabilities, minister pleasure and hope to the gayest who come prepared to receive pain from the spectacle of our pain; we can, here as well as in heaven's courts hereafter, reveal the angel growing into its immortal aspect, which is the highest achievement we could propose to ourselves, or that grace from above could propose to us, if we had a free choice of all possible conditions of human life. If any doubt the worth of the thought, from the common habit of overlooking the importance of what is *done* in its character of index of what the agent *is*, let him resort at once to the fountain head of spiritual exemplification, and say whether it matters most what Christ was or what he did.[3]

"It was a turning point in my life", she wrote later to a young man whom she was advising, "when I got not to care in the least what became of me,—otherwise than morally. *That* is in our own power; & therefore a proper object of care—though by no means of anxiety."[4] The Tynemouth experience reinforced belief.

Conviction of course led her into print. The *Playfellow* tales for children are a startlingly morbid collection, likely, one would guess, to produce trauma in any child who read them. But their purpose is clear. *The Settlers at Home* deals with the Linacres, who had emigrated from the continent to escape religious persecution, only to be persecuted in their settlement in the newly

[1] Crabb Robinson to Thomas Robinson, July 7, [1842], DWL.
[2] October 29, [1842], DWL.
[3] *Life in the Sickroom*, p. 162.
[4] HM to Arthur Allen, December 31, [1851], Yale.

drained fens. The continental protestants, observes Oliver, suffer for their religion and feel that they are martyrs.

> "Do you think there is comfort in that thought, [asks the minister] —in the pride of martyrdom,—to the son who sees his aged parents perish by the wayside,—to the mother whose infant is dashed against the rock before her eyes?"
>
> "How *do* they bear it all, then?"
>
> "They keep one another in mind that it is God's will, my dears; and that obedient children can, if they try, bear all that God sees fit to lay upon them. So they praise his name with a strong heart, though their voices be weak. Morning and night those mountains echo with hymns; though death in one form or another is about the sufferers on every side."

In the last of the tales, *The Crofton Boys*, which she thought would be her last printed work and which she intended to be highly instructive,[1] Hugh suffers an accident which results in the amputation of a foot, but his bravery in overcoming so dreadful an accident leads to the fulfilment of his happiest dream—to be sent to a career in India. "An exquisite little thing," George Eliot called it; she wept over it and insisted that two or three lines would feed one's soul for a month. She was particularly impressed when Hugh's mother says, "They soon had a new and delicious pleasure which none but the bitterly disappointed can feel—the pleasure of rousing their souls to bear pain, and of *agreeing with God silently*, when nobody knows what is in their hearts." [2] These pointed and grisly little stories were constructed, said R. H. Horne, to suit the minds for which they were intended, being founded on the emotions and actions of children and breathing "a spirit of noble fortitude, endurance, energy, and self-control, which make them healthy reading for old and young".[3] They are a far cry from present-day conceptions of children's tales, but it is conceivable that such hard themes—the stories were universally admired—were a useful preparation for a hard world.[4]

The full expression of her views was, however, still to come.

[1] Crabb Robinson to Thomas Robinson, July 15, 1842, DWL.

[2] George Eliot to Mrs. Charles Bray, [May 25, 1845], *George Eliot Letters*, i, 192.

[3] R. H. Horne, *New Spirit of the Age*, p. 235. Miss Barrett helped Horne with this book, and the section on Miss Martineau is undoubtedly hers. See her commendation of the tales in almost the same language and a reference to their "fine heroic child-spirit" in a letter to Browning, January 26, 1836, *Browning Letters*, i, 428.

[4] This suggestion is made with considerable force in an amusing article by Miss Marghanita Laski in the *Observer*, February 4, 1951.

"It was not because I was destitute of kind nurses and visitors that I needed to pour out what was in my mind," she said in her autobiography, "but because the most perfect sympathy one can meet with in any trial common to humanity is reached by an appeal to the whole mind of society." [1] The result was *Life in the Sickroom*, written at white heat between September 19 and November 4, 1843. She would never repent this work, she wrote to Moxon, when she sent him the manuscript, because "it must be right to communicate an experience which is *true in every line*. . . ." [2] Such a book would have been invaluable to her, and must be to other people.

The book was published anonymously and immediately discovered, for there was no attempt at disguise other than the title-page. She insisted she could take no money for it, though Moxon later sent her £75 and another £50 on a new edition.[3] Most people had some reservations about it—"rather exaggerated and overwrought," said Miss Mitford—but it was received generally with deep respect, by Miss Barrett, by Wordsworth, by Maurice.[4] A lawyer wrote to ask her prayers, saying that the book had made him weep and pray as he read it in the Reform Club. Letters came, in quite a new tone, from Puseyites, Evangelicals, bishops, and clergymen, not to mention all the sufferers who wrote about their spiritual troubles. "It makes me ask, in mournful wonder, why we do not oftener gather light & life from each other by speaking the truth in faith & love." [5] The response to the book revealed a new truth, or a new formulation, to Miss Martineau: her business in life was to suffer for other people's information—

> to be a sort of pioneer in the regions of pain, to make the way somewhat easier,—or at least more direct to those who come after. If you knew what a continued series of disappointments & troubles my life has been, & how directly whatever I have been able to do has arisen out of this, you wd agree with me.—But how slow we are in learning such lessons. Though I had had such long experience before, I never discovered this truth,—never perceived this

[1] *Auto.*, i, 457. [2] October 31, 1843, PHS. [3] *Auto.*, i, 460.

[4] Mitford, *Life*, ii, 286; Kemble, *Records*, p. 505; *Elizabeth Barrett Browning Letters*, i, 169–70; Crabb Robinson Diary, December 6, 7, 9, 12, 1843; Maurice, *Life of Frederick Denison Maurice*, i, 364–65.

[5] HM to Crabb Robinson, January 3, [1844], DWL. HM to Miss Estlin, February 25, 1844, NYHS. Monckton Milnes collected opinions of the sick about the book; the two letters I have seen divide on the subject, one being highly laudatory, the other calling it morbid, exaggerated, and untrue to experience.

aspect of my present condition till within a few weeks,—my eyes being opened to it by the eagerness with wh my experience . . . has been received. . . . It will be dastardly if I ever again feel my condition a heavy one. At present I find it all lightened & raised by this last discovery. . . . So do we stumble & grope onwards, (through gloom enough at times) to the clear issues of our lives! [1]

I am afraid that Miss Martineau conquered only parts of her morbidity and pride; and if the important thing was what she *was*, it was something not much to our taste. Yet the impulse to communicate her experiences and convictions—already noted so many times—is here put more strongly than ever, and carries over into her next publication, one not received so politely. Moreover, this concern about the meaning and place of suffering is only one result of her moral concern. The old impulses, newly fired, carried her into other demonstrations, some foolish, some admirable. Jane Carlyle was disgusted:

Poor Harriet seems to me to be got into a dreadful state of "*self-consciousness*" of late—to be fancying always that the world has nothing more important to do than to occupy itself with her "*principles* of action"—that affair of the *pension* having subsided—& full time that it should!—she has got up a new *excitement* for herself [demanding that her letters be burned]—and this she calls —not what it really is, a diseased anxiety about her future *biography* but "her protest *against the laxity of society in the matter of letters*". She feels it her *duty* (varnish!) to set this example, etc., etc.—I felt it *my* duty (without varnish) to tell her that I considered the whole uproar "*unworthy* of her"—to tell her a great many very sensible things, which have been entirely thrown away—"she perceives that I think her a little *mad*—morally," but the only inference she has drawn from that is that *I* must be a little mad—morally—and so she goes on exciting this letter-conflagration as if it were "the burning-up of all the sins of the world".[2]

When John Worthington lay dying, Miss Martineau had written urgently to his family to have her letters to him returned; she felt bound to rescue what she had said about others from possible misuse. Now she was to generalize and enforce that concern. Injunctions about her letters went out to all her correspondents: they were either to return them to her or suffer excommunication, and she did what she could to prevent any publication of her letters after her death. A few of her friends sympathized with her views, but most of them gave in to the

[1] HM to Mrs. Romilly, March 9, [1844], Bodleian.
[2] To Jeanie Welsh, January 26, 1843, *Family Letters*, p. 84.

destruction with bad grace matched only by the annoyance of writers since. But, as always, Miss Martineau descried a general principle: that letters were written speech, and the privacy of speech was inviolable. If she knew her letters would be printed, she would be unable to write freely, and she preferred silence to that.[1]

Her decision about a pension was equally principled. Having presumably given up writing after 1841, Miss Martineau was in some financial difficulty, since the deferred annuity in which she had invested her savings, wisely as it seemed at the time, was not to begin payment until 1850. Her income in 1842 was £120. It was quite natural that she should again be offered a Civil List pension. There had been talk of one in the thirties, when she was inclined to accept with misgivings, and she had flatly refused an offer after her return from America. Now she was to refuse again. She could not, she said, accept public money from an unjust system of taxation, "levied afflictively upon those, among others, whom I have made it my business to befriend, (however humbly)—the working classes". The correspondence about the proposal was published in the newspapers, and a radical meeting in London, chaired by Perronet Thompson, voted thanks to her for her action in upholding a great principle—a tribute that must have been a great gratification to her.[2] But her decision was not without its critics: the Wordsworth household thought she was "considerably damaged in the upper story," and Crabb Robinson was relieved to see no pointed comparison in the papers the next year when Wordsworth accepted a pension, although Thomas Robinson told him that some radicals had drawn the contrast. Mrs. Austin, when she accepted a pension of £100 in 1849, told Guizot that she was not disposed to "*faire effet*" like Miss Martineau and talk about robbing the people. "On the contrary, I told Lord John that though I could not have taken it on the score of *want*, I accepted it with pride and satisfaction, as a proof that my humble labours have been thought useful." [3] Miss Martineau saw the matter differently—

[1] HM to James, May 14, 1827. Her views are given clearly in the introduction to the *Autobiography*.

[2] HM to Charles Buller, August 21, 1841, *Auto.*, i, 591. The resolutions of the meeting are in *Auto.*, ii, 364–65.

[3] E. Quillinan to Crabb Robinson, November 28, 1842; Thomas Robinson to Crabb Robinson, November 9, 1842; Crabb Robinson Diary, October 29, 1842, DWL. Mrs. Austin to Guizot, July 27, 1849, Ross, *Three Generations*, p. 235.

and quite sincerely. She had probably never forgotten Fox's gibe at the time of the poor law tales about her involvement with the Whigs.

Her worsening financial situation was saved by a testimonial fund, managed by Erasmus Darwin and some friends in 1843. A sum of £1,358. 8s. 10d. was given to her. She had insisted resolutely on not being involved in the planning, but after the subscription was taken, she intervened to demand that £100 of the money be invested in plate, to the great annoyance of Darwin and his friends. They flatly refused on the grounds that nothing had been said about plate in the solicitations; and they left it to Miss Martineau herself to make the investment in a superb tea service with a suitably worded engraving. It is not an edifying passage.[1] But the fund brought her an additional two hundred pounds a year, and as Lady Eastlake said in her journal, it seemed to justify Miss Martineau's confidence in the mob, for that was more than the Government had proposed in their name.[2]

Foolish as all this brooding was, Miss Martineau was not wholly absorbed in her "dreadful state of self-consciousness". As usually happened when she got off the subject of personal morality, she did some remarkably acute and characteristic thinking about politics. Like all the Radicals, she had little but contempt for the Whigs who had so long held on to office while the country drifted into an alarming economic and social situation. She very quickly saw in Peel the man she was looking for, the successor of Canning. When Peel became prime minister in 1834, she was all for turning him out; indeed, she was sure the Tories would go out for ever.[3] But Peel came into office in 1841 with an effective programme and an imaginative financial policy with strong free-trading inclinations; and he soon showed that his administration was going to try to do something for Ireland and against O'Connell's demagoguery. By the summer of 1842 she was priding herself on her moderation and freedom

[1] Erasmus Darwin to Crabb Robinson, March 15, 1843, DWL. Jane Carlyle to Thomas Carlyle, July 17, 1843, *New Letters*, i, 119–20. A printed report of the fund is in the Barrett letters at Wellesley.

[2] *Journals and Correspondence of Lady Eastlake*, i, 37.

[3] HM to Charles Brooks, Washington, January 25, 1835, LC.

from party spirit; by 1843, she was convinced that a new era had begun.[1]

As she saw it, liberalizing forces were operating irresistibly. Never had society been so able to dispense with a political hero, for never had society been so markedly controlled by principles "clearly and strongly compelling their own adoption, and working out their results". The question was not what point the ship of state was to be steered to next, but how best to manœuvre amid the perils of an ordained course. The important ability for a statesman in such an age of transition was to live and learn. One kind of man who all his life believed that certain principles were for the good of society now learned to extend his faith to measures he once thought dangerous. Another sort of man, wishing that the old state of affairs could be preserved, nevertheless saw that it was impossible, and made timely concessions rather than endanger the peace. But the Whigs were merely crying, "Hands Off—that is my truth". Did the old Christians attack the new converts in the same way? It was clearly a time for the breaking up of parties, to be reconstituted on a new set of principles.

Best of all, the situation of the working classes—which had so depressed her in the late thirties and early forties—seemed by 1843 to be improving rapidly.

> We see that large principles are more extensively agreed upon than ever before—more manifest to all eyes, from the very absence of a hero to work them, since they are every hour showing how irresistibly they are making their own way. We see that the tale of the multitude is told as it never was told before—their health, their minds and morals, pleaded for in a tone perfectly new in the

---

[1] Lord Stanley she did not much like. For Gladstone, at this time, she had an enormous respect, though she wished he could live without language for a time or with a foreign one or that somehow he could make his thinking more precise, for he was always being led astray by the ambiguity of language. Peel was no hero, but an able man with a clear view of his business and of the tendencies of the time. "I wish he may remain in power long enough to repeal the Corn laws,—establish national Education, establish & increase a good Income tax, making it a substitute for a huge burden of bad taxation,—make sundry currency reforms,—& O! if he cd cause a comprehensive Law reform, that wd crown all." To Monckton Milnes, May 28, [1843]. On her income of £120, she had to pay £6. 10s. income tax. Mrs. Jameson thought this "monstrous", but Miss Martineau was "entirely in favour of the tax, notwithstanding, & of opinion that when the details are amended & the manner of collecting it better arranged, that it will work well and that it will, if continued, render other taxes unnecessary". Mrs. Jameson to Lady Byron, 1842, *Anna Jameson, Letters and Friendships*, p. 207.

V. The View from Harriet Martineau's Sickroom at Tynemouth

VI. Harriet Martineau, 1849

> world. We see that the dreadful sins and woes of society are the results of old causes, and that our generation has the honour of being responsible for their relief, while the disgrace of their existence belongs, certainly not to our time, and perhaps to none. We see that no spot of earth ever before contained such an amount of infallible resources as our own country at this day; so much knowledge, so much sense, so much vigour, foresight, and benevolence, or such an amount of external means. We see the progress of amelioration, silent but sure, as the shepherd on the upland sees in the valley the advance of a gush of sunshine from between two hills. He observes what the people below are too busy to mark: how the light attains now this object and now that—how it now embellishes yonder copse, and now gilds that stream, and now glances upon the roofs of the far-off hamlet—the signs and sounds of life quickening along its course. When we remember that this is the same sun that guided the first vessels of commerce over the sea—the same by whose light Magna Charta was signed in Runnymede—that shone in the eyes of Cromwell after Naseby fight—that rose on 800,000 free blacks in the West Indies on a certain August morning—and is now shining down into the dreariest recesses of the coal-mine, the prison, and the cellar—how can we doubt that darkness is to be chased away, and God's sunshine to vivify, at last, the whole of our world? [1]

This optimism must be investigated more deeply.

Her ideal solution to the labour problem was set out in essence in the political economy tales: enlightened factory owners like Mr. Wallace and clear-sighted, sober working-men, hand-in-hand. In 1838 she published an important article on domestic service, the implications of which run far beyond housemaids and cooks. Though little was said in general society on the spirit of the poor, she saw symptoms of disturbance and fear in every house in the country. The disease was called rick-burning one year, trade unions another, while a corrupt domestic service was an endemic form. Dorchester labourers were transported and recalled; the trades marched to the Home Office; vitriol was thrown, systematic assassination was planned, emigration was forced. Whatever the occasion of such outbreaks, they would never have occurred if the temper of the poor had not been exasperated. Both parties to the struggle were short-sighted in blaming particular individuals for this temper; men on both sides were heirs of a long tradition which in good radical fashion she traced back to the exploitation of the Saxons by the

[1] *Life in the Sickroom*, pp. 78–79. The whole passage, pp. 72–79, is borne out in her letters to Crabb Robinson, April 27, July 20, and November 27, [1843], DWL.

Norman conquerors. It was the Saxons who burned ricks, collected assassination funds, broke stocking-frames, and threw vitriol—or squabbled in the nursery.

> These are all outlets of the same volcano, which may leave off puffing in this or that place, but is not likely to become extinct till it has discharged itself of its "perilous stuff". There is such a volcano in the centre of every society where feudalism has crusted itself over the central fires of humanity. But there is a real giant stretched beneath on the molten lake; sooner or later he finds his day, arises, and shivers the crust to atoms. The world was much amazed at the breaking up in France. It would be folly in the world to be ever amazed at such a thing again.

This historical tension was aggravated in England by the ascetic tradition which touched the rich lightly or not at all while it ruined the poor and ignorant by forcing them to give up their pleasures, leaving them only degrading and clandestine means of escape—cheap penny theatres, stealthy dances in pubs where no music was allowed, country beershops. Further, the commercial spirit, however much it may have accomplished collaterally, was immediately unfavourable to free mutual trust—of classes as much as individuals—hence an increased alienation. The reserve and unsociableness of the national character was a bar to reconciliation; tracts said nothing about reciprocity of duties.

> It is commonly said that Education is the remedy for this, as for other social evils. This is true; but the education must begin with the master. What is commonly called education is a great good; but if it has failed to teach employers the truth which lies at the bottom of social reform, it will probably fail to impart it to the employed. This great truth is, that *mutual service is honorable, and not disgraceful.* Reading and writing, the study of history, science, and art, have not yet enlightened the aristocracies of the earth upon this matter; and they may be sure that no charity schools will of themselves make the labouring classes wise upon the point.[1]

Chartism she looked at through the eyes of Carlyle; she saw it passionately and more wisely than many modern historians.

> And what were these stirrings? What was it all about? The difficulty of understanding and telling the story is from its comprehending so vast a variety of things and persons. Those who have not looked into Chartism think that it means one thing—a revolu-

[1] *WR*, xxxi, 218–32 (July, 1838).

tion. Some who talk as if they assumed to understand it, explain that Chartism is of two kinds—Physical Force Chartism, and Moral Force Chartism—as if this were not merely an intimation of two ways of pursuing an object yet undescribed! Those who look deeper—who go out upon the moors by torchlight, who talk with a suffering brother under the hedge, or beside the loom, who listen to the groups outside the Union work-house, or in the public-house among the Durham coal-pits, will long feel bewildered as to what Chartism is, and will conclude at last that it is another name for popular discontent—a comprehensive general term under which are included all protests against social suffering.[1]

Young England had little enough to offer. Operating on the assumptions of an outworn system of society, they were making philanthropy ridiculous, doing good at every cost but their own, "running after every little wheel of the engine, to turn it, & throw[ing] cold water on the fire under the boiler". It was good to see the educated take an interest in the less educated and men of pleasure play with men of toil; but it was pernicious to hold out old hopes of protection and dependence when the essential thing for the working classes to realize was that they held their condition in their own hands.

As truly as the Reformation took men from under the dictation of priests, and gave every man's conscience into his own charge, had the growing up of manufactures in our country taken the working-classes from under the no longer practicable protection of the landed and moneyed capitalists, and compelled them to protect themselves or perish. If they have enlightenment enough to see and rule their own destiny, they are raised to a condition far above that of the serf-like working-men of old. If they have not that enlightenment, they perish.[2]

But until that enlightenment was attained, some things had to be done, and doing them raised the problem of the proper province of legislation.

The situation of labour in Britain, as Miss Martineau saw it, was highly complex, and the difficulty of finding the right path overwhelming. A free market for labour had been attained, but the free admission of food was still denied. The labouring man was free, but he had been denied the education to teach him how to make the best use of his labour or to show him what his responsibilities were. Everywhere one saw degraded human

[1] *Hist.*, ii, 262–63, followed by a lengthy quotation from Carlyle's *Chartism.*

[2] HM to Monckton Milnes, September 6, [1844]. *Hist.*, ii, 519–20. Cf. J. S. Mill, *Principles of Political Economy*, ii, 345–46.

beings, selling their children perhaps, or looking on them only as breadwinners. Men spent the money they earned on themselves and denied to their families what might otherwise be a decent maintenance; women had no conception of proper housekeeping or child-rearing.[1] Humanity demanded action. Yet what could the legislature do that might not in the long run be worse than useless? How successfully could the law interfere in the relationship between parents and children, or with the operation of the great natural laws of the economic system?

> It is impossible to admit that, under a representative system it is the proper business of government to regulate the private interests of any class whatever. It is impossible, under the far higher constitution of humanity, to refuse attention to the case of the depressed, ignorant, and suffering, of our people. The only course seems to be to admit that, as we have not been true to our representative system (being at this day far from having carried it out), we cannot be harshly true to its theory. Having permitted a special misery and need to grow up, we must meet it with a special solace and aid. As to how the solace and aid are to be given—this is the point of difficulty. In the absence of all theory which can command agreement, men must bring themselves into agreement as well as they can under the one guiding principle that nothing must be done to impair any one's rights as a citizen under a representative system. Every man who is now practically excluded from the benefits of the representative system is to be regarded as destined to inclusion under them; and nothing that is done for his mind or his fortunes by the grace of the state is to lower him from his position of theoretical citizenship under a constitution which presumes every man's condition and interests to be in his own hands.[2]

Humanity demanded action about child-labour, even though the effectiveness of the law in interfering between parent and child might be questionable. Moreover, in the appalling report on mines in 1842 she saw a case both special and extreme: it was a great thing to have put a stop to the employment of women in work wholly unsuited to them and to have broken in upon a system of child-slavery, unrealized because hidden underground.[3] But with adult labour in general the case was different. Even

[1] From her window, she told Chadwick, she saw more of life in one respect than ever before; the lives of three families went on under her eyes, "& it deeply impresses me that *all* the trouble & sorrow I have witnessed among them for three years,—(& it is not a little) has proceeded from their own ignorance or folly. A chronicle of their sufferings wd be not a little melancholy, but very instructive." November 27, [1843?], UCL.

[2] *Hist.*, ii, 552. See also *Hist.*, ii, 90–92.

[3] *Hist.*, ii, 555. See also a letter to Crabb Robinson, May 11, [1844] and James Pope-Hennessy, *Monckton Milnes: The Years of Promise*, pp. 187–88.

though she felt long hours in themselves were not necessarily evil, she was not inhumane. Hours of labour were simply not the concern of the state. She welcomed the early closing movement in shops, which would bring that exhausting labour within "endurable limits". She told Milnes in 1844 that among all the gratifying things that were happening, nothing pleased her more than that the "workies" were trying to get a shortening of labour by compact instead of law.[1] But for the state to interfere was precisely to lower the working-man from the theoretical position as a citizen which presumed his condition and interests to lie in his own hands.

She deeply admired W. R. Greg's essay reviewing Arthur Helps's *The Claims of Labour*, in which he distinguishes sharply between the claims of man on fellow man from those of employer and employed. In a modern situation where the rule should have been bargain and mutual arrangement, both sides tended to borrow the claims of the old position of subservience and protection without admitting the corresponding obligations: there lay the origin of current problems. The true claims of labour, as he saw them, were on justice, not charity: for full education, for freedom from legislative restriction on labour or enhancement of prices, for equal freedom or equal restriction in combination. But if labour demanded more, it had to give an equivalent. If an employer gave protection, kindness, and assistance in hard times, then he could expect respect, obedience, and confidence from his work people—indeed Greg would have preferred to see the broader relationship rather than a narrow construction of contract. But any relationship had to be correlative. Miss Martineau emphatically agreed and sent copies of the article to her most important friends.[2]

To maintain this view is not merely to owe a blind allegiance to the doctrines of political economy; to hold it is to believe in something more fundamental, in a particular interpretation of human nature and of the political and historical process, an interpretation by no means crabbed and narrow. With Miss Martineau, as with Greg, a high sense of the potentiality of every man ruled all conclusions in politics. She was convinced that men could, after a certain stage, be taught to use freedom properly

[1] July 29, [1844].
[2] The article is in *WR*, xliii, 445–60 (June, 1845), reprinted in his *Essays on Political and Social Science*, ii, 252–302.

only by using it, not by keeping them in tutelage until some vague time when they might be ready for it. Her assurance about the feasibility of immediate emancipation of Negroes was based on this assumption, and she could hardly deny the same generous view to English working-men. She did not, therefore, reckon with the disparity in power between employer and individual labourer. Her idealistic and demanding views extended to employers as well. They were expected to be fair and benevolent; indeed, theirs was the primary responsibility. Nothing was so appalling to her as irresponsible power, but ultimate decisions of policy should hardly be grounded on aberrations, for irresponsible power was doomed to ultimate defeat, as clearly as Mrs. Rowland was defeated in *Deerbrook*.

The humanity of men lay in their potential; only when they lived up to that potential could their claims be fully considered, except as they challenged society to enlighten them. But, ever sanguine, she tended to see men not as they were but as what they could become. In her views on policy—and in her criticism of practising politicians and administrators who had to deal with what they found—she foresaw and sometimes saw a world of clear-sighted men, hard-working (for work would be honourable), dedicated to ideas, unalienated—and even living, in some cases, under the principles of association, in dormitories as in Lowell or in the model lodging houses she so much admired for their devices of "domestic socialism".[1] The vision may or may not seem attractive today, but she shared it with some great contemporaries with whom she is not usually linked.

Given views like these, she found Lord Ashley's agitation to provide legislative protection for working-men in cotton factories wrong-headed, especially the drive for a Ten Hours Bill. Lord Ashley was benevolent, no doubt, but not very wise. Understanding nothing of the factory districts, he had to rely on informants of, at best, doubtful reputation; while to a manufacturer's daughter, like herself, his statements had "an indescribable and ludicrous air of mistake", such as might pervade her own description of life at court or the pictures of high society in the novels of the "silver fork" school. The Lancashire opera-

[1] *Hist.*, ii, 561. And see below, pp. 273–74, 349–50. In an article in *Once a Week*, April 26, 1862, "What May Come of the Exhibition, 1862", she launched an attack on archaic methods of lighting, heating, writing, dress, and building—and expressed hopes not irrelevant to what she expected to see result from association.

tives were, she maintained, among the best paid of English working-men, and the most able to take care of themselves; in concentrating on them, trying to deprive them of the very freedom they were so fortunate to have, he completely ignored the agricultural labourers, the most helpless and degraded class of English workers. With scientific principle and facts both against him, he should either have turned over his leadership to someone from the factory districts or have gone to live there long enough to learn the truth. And her condemnation of Ashley took in his lieutenants, including her friend Monckton Milnes whom she scolded unmercifully for attacking Sir James Graham on the basis of superficial knowledge, while himself guilty of maintaining the corn laws.[1]

Such stringent opposition to legislative interference did not, as we have seen, extend to Ashley's efforts to protect women and children, and she was an enthusiastic supporter of state intervention in sanitation and education. The evils which Ashley and his friends ascribed to the mills were in reality to be blamed on the towns. She had been deeply impressed by the Lowell factory girls in Massachusetts, who read, danced, wrote poetry, listened to Emerson's lectures, and in general lived what seemed to her an ideal existence, though they worked seventy hours a week. Again, drawing on her authority as a manufacturer's daughter, she knew that the best of the millhands were the healthiest and happiest of the working classes, "while the woes of others are attributable to ignorance, bad dwellings, crowding—in short *town* and not mill evils".[2]

On this score, Edwin Chadwick was, in her opinion, one of the most effective friends of the people. The new poor law had succeeded beyond her wildest dreams, and his great Health of Towns Report, which was promptly sent to her, kept her up so late that she was too ill to write next day to tell him how fascinating she had found it. But once she recovered her strength, she did what she could to get him support and to second his efforts. "Those who wish for the salvation of the people," she wrote to the editor of the *Norwich Mercury*, "must petition & petition & petition." She had written to the Bishop of Norwich to get him to stir up his clergy to stir up their flocks, and she wanted Bacon to do what he could to rouse the town about it. She hounded her relatives in Newcastle to do something about drainage and

[1] HM to Milnes, April 21 and June 12, [1844]. [2] *Ibid.*

the terrible smoke nuisance; she had long discussions on town-planning with Richard Grainger, who had rebuilt the centre of Newcastle; and she wrote articles on his work to show what might be done.

In Tynemouth itself, she found herself up against obstruction from the Duke of Northumberland and his bailiff and ignorance from the people. Her own landlady looked on a sink in the kitchen as a terrible evil and threw down all the waste water into the garden which sloped regularly to a cottage containing nine to fourteen persons. All the water was carried on girls' heads from the back of the village, two streets away, until she had a well dug in the garden, which not only served a whole row of houses with water but also "kept the maids from bad company"—for Tynemouth was a garrison town. Operating as best she could from her sofa, she persuaded the duke and his bailiff to drain from the church to her side of the bailiff's premises, while she had a drain dug down the main street to the harbour—with bricks from her landlord, and money from Sir John Walsham, an assistant poor law commissioner, and others; her own contribution of twenty pounds—from the money made available to her by Lady Byron for charity—was reserved for house drains. The work went slowly at first, partly from ignorance, partly from waiting for a cheaper season for labour; but she hoped that the well-drained houses would sufficiently prove the benefit to bring others in. Voluntary effort and amateur enthusiasm—she doubted that the Tynemouth drainage would satisfy an expert—were her chief resource and recommendation; but she welcomed the Boards of Health and public health legislation, and was a continual advocate, for agricultural and sanitary reasons, of a nation-wide system of drainage carried out under auspices of the state.[1]

The most important step to ameliorate the condition of the working classes was precisely the most difficult to take—national education. While a great many people were committed to the idea of national education, religion bedevilled the whole issue. Churchmen and dissenters had been opposed on schools from the foundation early in the century of the competing National

[1] HM to Edward Moxon, January 31, [1848], Bodleian. HM to Chadwick, n.d., November 27, December 25, [1843], UCL. HM to R.M. Bacon, November 14, [1843], Cambridge, Add. MSS 6247 (87). *Auto.*, ii, 364, *Penny Magazine*, September 5, 1838, *Once a Week*, October 5, 1861. There are many leaders on the subject of drainage in *DN*.

Society and British and Foreign School Society. Even within these two camps, divisions were overcome only when it was necessary to oppose demands of the radicals for a completely non-religious education or for what in effect amounted to the same thing, non-doctrinal education such as Lord John Russell came to advocate.[1] Through this jungle, the small group of inspectors of schools and the secretary of the Committee of Council on Education, James Kay-Shuttleworth, had to find their way in administering the grants which the state had begun to make to the school societies in 1833.

In the forties, the issue was precipitated by the educational clauses of the Factory Bill of 1843. Sir James Graham proposed to use the time secured by the limitation of hours for factory children to educate them—an original intention of the factory acts—in a rudimentary national system, with compulsory attendance. The schools were to be in the hands of the Established Church, but dissenting parents were allowed to have their children excused from religious instruction. The proposal created a furore among the dissenters who came together in defence of "voluntaryism"—and to an extent in justification of it, for they redoubled their efforts to found and maintain schools and to take away the lead of the Anglicans. Petitioning against the educational provisions of the bill was so voluminous that Graham had to give in and, after some futile attempts to amend them, withdrew the offending clauses. There was no subsequent attempt to provide a national system until Forster's act in 1870.

The Factory Bill came at a time of unparalleled religious excitement: to the long-standing problem of Catholicism, especially in Ireland, had been added only a few years before the Tractarian issue, and from 1842 the unbelievably intense quarrel over Scottish Disruption—"the triple pope", as Miss Martineau had it, of the pope in Rome, Pusey, and Chalmers. We have seen how firmly committed she was to the separation of Church and State, that cardinal principle of Dissent. She considered that the parson was the evil genius of English life, and she fought clergymen over social reforms in both Tynemouth and Ambleside. But on the educational question, Miss Martineau parted company with the dissenters.

Her activity on behalf of the Factory Bill was enormous. She

[1] These competing views are analysed by G. F. A. Best in the *Cambridge Historical Journal*, xii, 155–73 (June, 1956).

wrote herself "sick & weary", she told Milnes, and all in vain. She wrote a letter for circulation and possible publication answering the dissenters' case. She wrote directly to the Queen to put the case to her, since she had heard that Queen Victoria was concerned about the plight of the factory children. She hammered at all her friends in any position of political power.

In effect, her argument was one of emergency. She never wavered in her allegiance to the principles of the dissenters; she supported them warmly in their fight against church rates, and thought they were right to refuse compromise on a marriage bill. But they had forgotten that education was a case where delay was impossible, where the voluntary principle would not work because the very people most in need of education were those least capable of demanding or wanting it, or even of conceiving it. The religious struggle was approaching the great war for opinion, but the factory children could not wait until the principles of the Reformation were fought out. Their lot was compulsory, and she thought compulsory education was certainly preferable to compulsory perdition.

Some details of Graham's bill she did not like—the most disagreeable being the entire exclusion of dissenting schoolmasters who were in general superior to Anglicans—but she could see no intent on the part of the framers to proselytize: indeed she thought them remarkably liberal in proposing to start the national education scheme in the towns where the dissenters were strongest rather than in the country where the Church would have no check to its power. Certainly there was no prospect of getting anything better. If, as the dissenters argued, the bill should wait a year, or five years for a new parliament, a whole generation of children would be condemned to ignorance and degradation; and even at the end of five years there would still be a country half Anglican and a government and parliament almost exclusively so. The only course was to accept what could be got and fight to amend the system afterwards. Even if there were proselytizing, would it matter? Surely the dissenters had not lost their faith that the human mind, once awakened, would ultimately come to the right and good? Her own faith, she said, was so great that no dread of error could for a moment compare with her fear of vice and darkness; better that the children should be raised as Mohammedans or even as pagans than deserted or left to chance. Christianity would certainly have an easier access to disciplined minds than to savage ones.[1]

There is no doubt that part of her desperate insistence on any kind of education at once was inspired by what we might call police motives. The period was so disturbed, the spectacle of the lower classes so appalling, that something had to be done if society was to survive, if its energies were not to be diverted from the main struggle for liberty in the world to police actions at home. But her vision was broader than that, broader even than the undeniable advantages that education would confer in an industrial society where it was the primary stimulus to mobility. She wanted everyone to share in the conviction she felt with more intensity than ever, once she was confined to her couch: "How all is changed by the ministering of an idea!"[2] It was horrible, she said in *Life in the Sickroom*, to think of the savage poor, suffering every privation "without the respite or solace afforded by one inspiring or beguiling idea. . . .

> A glimpse into this hell ought to suffice . . . to set all to work to procure for every one of these sufferers, bread and warmth, if possible, and as soon as possible; but above everything, and without the loss of an hour, an entrance upon their spiritual birthright. Every man, and every woman, however wise and tender appearing and designing to be, who for an hour helps to keep closed the entrance to the region of ideas—who stands between sufferers and great thoughts, (which are the angels of consolation sent by God to all to whom he has given souls,) are, in so far, ministers of hell,—not themselves inflicting torment, but intercepting the influences which would assuage or overpower it. Let the plea be heard of us sufferers who know well the power of ideas,—our plea for the poor,—that, while we are contriving for all to be fed and cherished by food and fire, we may meanwhile kindle the immortal vitality within them, and give them that ethereal solace and sustenance which was meant to be shared by all 'without money and without price'.[3]

With Graham's bill defeated, her only hope for political action on education lay in an increase in the parliamentary grant to the Committee of Council. Meanwhile, she tried to do what she could for education by indirect action. In the process of "virtual

[1] HM to Buller, June 15 [1843], MHS, Washburn. Crabb Robinson to Wordsworth, December 4, [1843], HM to Crabb Robinson, March 8, [1844]. HM to Milnes, all of the letters of 1843, especially the open letter inscribed "To Mrs. A.B.C."

[2] HM to Milnes, June 22, [1842].

[3] Pp. 163–65.

education",[1] she continued to be, as she had always been, intensely interested. Seymour Tremenheere, the mines inspector, came to her early in 1844 to enlist her help in improving the temper of the miners of the North-east; the principal proposal she made was a Newcastle periodical to combat the *Miners' Advocate*, William Daniells' excellent working-class paper. She was not physically able to undertake the whole task, and for one reason or another the scheme fell through. But she expressed a strong and wise view on the subject of that kind of writing, which deserves repeating here. The managers could tell her the answers to certain questions, correct her on fact or verbal style, but she would accept no hardening or sharpening of what she said.

> My sympathies *are* with the ignorant and misled; and I *am* on their side, as far as their general *human* claims go. I have not the least doubt that these gentlemen are so too, in the abstract: but I *must* harp upon the men's own favourite terms and ideas, which I know are wearisome and nauseous to their employers; and what I say must stand. For one illustration "Union is strength" they say:—but every viewer quivers at the word Union. I shall adopt the saying,—enforce it, urge it home: and *then* show that Union of all the necessary parts to an achievement is the thing meant: and that "Union" to set one element against another is truly "division". (All in the most familiar mode, of course). Now if these gentlemen take me for a mouthpiece, they must let me supply the *morale* of the matter. About the *doctrine* they and I are agreed; and I thankfully abandon the *facts* to them.[2]

She turned from this abortive project to another which called out for a time her highest enthusiasm, "the great enterprise which has filled my mind, & occupied my days". She was worried, as always, about the effect of the vile reading matter that was finding its way into the hands of the lower classes; and Tremenheere's reports on the mining districts, with their mass of information on reading habits, reinforced her concern.[3] But a more practical problem had increasingly come to her attention. As she was a recognized authority in this area of social improvement, a great many people who were interested in combating

[1] The phrase is hers. *Hist.*, ii, 713.

[2] Letters from HM to Tremenheere, January 25, February 14, 19, and 23, 1844. See a discussion in R. K. Webb, *British Working Class Reader*, pp. 155–57. HM to Elizabeth Barrett, March 6, [1844], Wellesley. HM to Crabb Robinson, March 8, [1844]. Cf. her reflections on such writing, *WR*, xxxi, 226 (July, 1838).

[3] See her comments on the contribution of degrading reading to making men into criminals, *ER*, vol. 122, p. 347 (October, 1865).

pernicious reading by something better asked her to recommend books for libraries. This set her to finding out what books were most popular with members of cheap book clubs. The choice struck her as so odd, and the resources were so small, that she concluded that the literature was in effect uncreated.

If only, she thought, she could bring together all the people who were troubled by the lack of good cheap books, she could provide either a guarantee against loss or an assured circulation to supply precisely what commercial publishers had not tried—"penetrating with the light of knowledge many dark places, where political discontent & many bad passions are now working in minds whose activity has been excited, without due intellectual employment being provided". The Society for the Diffusion of Useful Knowledge, launched with such enthusiasm by Brougham, was on its last legs, killed by whiggism, inefficiency, and lack of support; other efforts, commercial or otherwise, had simply not done what was necessary. She and Lady Mary Lambton put their heads together. Lady Mary was sure that the Sutherlands and others of her friends would help; and Miss Martineau thought she could get the approval of the chief manufacturing firms. She wrote to Charles Knight, the Diffusion Society's publisher and probably the best-equipped and most experienced man in the field, who received her idea enthusiastically; he put it to some manufacturers at Manchester and to the James Marshalls, the flax manufacturers at Leeds, then went to visit her in Tynemouth, and the plan was settled.

The proposal was to print a volume a week on the subjects most appealing to the readers they wanted to capture; the price was to be a shilling for about 300 pages. A library of about two hundred volumes was anticipated. The guarantee needed for success was four thousand copies, leaving the rest to natural demand; a hundred large landed proprietors taking forty copies each would do it, she said, while humbler folk could start village book clubs—twenty members at a shilling a quarter. Long letters went to all her friends asking for support and publicity. She got warm support; royal patronage was granted (she hoped it would quiet some ridiculous opposition from the gentry); the government was to be a principal customer, choosing these books for supply to ships, barracks, prisons, and workhouses, instead of the "infamous" contracting for books which had been the rule.

One great difference between this library and other ventures was to be the respect they would pay to copyright; Miss Martineau was particularly scornful of the Chamberses who lived, she said, almost entirely on the property of living authors, while Knight could not bear to use books whose copyrights had expired without making some payment even to heirs. She made over her own *Traditions of Palestine* to the series and wrote a prefatory letter for a republication of the *Lowell Offering* (by the Massachusetts mill-girls) under the wonderful title *Mind among the Spindles*. Lamb's *Tales from Shakespeare* was on the list, with extracts from the plays added for illustration. A volume of travels was to present the travellers' own accounts, from Marco Polo to Stephens in Central America, "well arranged and entire as far as necessary and desirable". When Tremenheere asked for heroic models for the working people, Professor Long responded with a new Plutarch; when Tremenheere complained of ignorance about the human body and about natural theology, Knight turned out Paley and some books on health. The worst deficiency was in fiction, far and away the most popular type of reading in cheap books clubs, and especially in good historical fiction, to which Miss Martineau looked for some very effective instruction leading to social peace; she did her best, without result, to persuade Bulwer-Lytton that he was precisely the man to do it for her.

Launched in late spring, the scheme was, as she saw it, an immediate success. The desire for books among working people was enormous: they trampled tracts underfoot and rushed to Shakespeare and the Bridgwater treatises. Her answer to Ashley's objections that tired working-men wanted to sleep, not read, was triumphant:

> Instead of this, we find the mothers & sisters of the hardest working young men in the pits, alleging & almost complaining that the said young men become careless of supper, talk & everything, & if they can get into a loft, a chamber, a tree, or any corner, there is no getting them away from their books. Ld. Ashley will learn that tho' they want rest, they find more of it in pleasurable, intellectual recreation than in brute sleep.[1]

It is a characteristic response, full of idealism and enthusiasm.

[1] HM to Elizabeth Barrett, July 11, [1844], Wellesley. HM to Morpeth, April 19 and 26, [1844]. HM to Bulwer-Lytton, April 27, [1844]. HM to Milnes, June 12 and September 6, [1844]. HM to Crabb Robinson, May 11, and August 25, [1844]. HM to Mrs. Leonard Horner, June 4, [1844], NLS. Charles Knight, *Passages of a Working Life*, ii, 312–22.

To call something into existence was to accomplish it; to find a few coveted responses was to find them everywhere. Her silence about the failure of the scheme is characteristic too. Not even twenty of the one hundred and forty of the *Weekly Volumes* reached a sale of ten thousand; the average sale was short of five thousand. The books were welcomed, said Knight, by "those anxious for the enlightenment of the people", but he became convinced that no associations for recommending books or forcing their sale could be successful. People read what they wanted to read, and no adult would read a solid book when an exciting one was available. Nor did the poor buy "furniture books", but only a few books they wanted to read and read at once.[1] I have seen no sign that Miss Martineau ever learned this realistic lesson. She had originated the scheme, but Knight had to attend to its winding-up. By that time other enthusiasms filled her mind and occupied her days.

[1] His highly sensible comments are in *The Old Printer and the Modern Press*.

CHAPTER VIII

Tynemouth: Mesmeric Wonders

THE comedy of doctor and patient had reached an impasse by the beginning of 1844. Greenhow was as convinced as ever that Miss Martineau would one day recover; she was even more convinced that her case was hopeless. By spring of that year, however, Greenhow had reason for encouragement. He had noticed for some time past the greater ease and freedom with which his sister-in-law moved about her room; in April she was talking about recovery herself: she was freer from sickness, she wrote, than she had been for many months, and was amazed at her returning appetite. The improvement was real but, of course, she was convinced that it was temporary.[1]

Some time before, Bulwer-Lytton, who had a genius for absorbing each of the latest rages in turn, had written to her suggesting that she consult mesmerists in Paris. The suggestion appealed to her, for she was already "far from despising" their accomplishments, but knowing that Greenhow and members of her family were hostile, she kept her peace, and was content to await developments.[2] By 1844 the popular excitement about mesmerism had nearly reached its peak, and within a fortnight in May she received three letters urging her to try the experiment. Among these correspondents were the Basil Montagus, who mentioned the mesmeric successes of their young friend Henry Atkinson; while her medical brother-in-law in Liverpool had successfully operated on a mesmerized patient. At this point, Greenhow changed his mind.

Popular enthusiasm for mesmerism was frequently stirred at this time by itinerant lecturers; of these the most famous and successful was Spencer T. Hall, a Sheffield man. On May 25, Hall was in Sunderland, performing his experiments on two

[1] Greenhow, *Medical Report.* HM to Mrs. Romilly, March 9, [1844], Bodleian. HM to Thomas Wentworth Higginson, April 21, [1844], BPL.

[2] HM to Bulwer-Lytton, August 22, [1842].

boys who travelled with him and four young men from the vicinity. The following week he lectured in South Shields, and in June, trailing a cloud of press notices, he moved to Newcastle. He lectured on the history of mesmerism and its various forms from ancient Egypt to the present; he expounded his own discoveries and assured his listeners that mesmerism was not opposed to the Scriptures; he pointed to its curative effects; and of course he demonstrated mesmeric phenomena. It was customary to try to get a physician to take the chair at these meetings. For example, at South Shields, a Dr. Meggett presided and offered his watch to a mesmerized boy who was unable to pick it up, to the surprise of the "highly respectable and numerous" audience. (In fact, two of the members of that audience fell so much under mesmeric influence that they had to be taken out and revived by Hall himself.)[1] In Newcastle, Greenhow took the chair and was sufficiently impressed by what he saw and by Hall personally to decide that it might be worth an experiment with Miss Martineau. Mesmerism, as all doctors knew, was particularly effective with nervous or hysterical persons; so perhaps, he thought, it might relieve the nervous symptoms his sister-in-law displayed. The time had arrived, he wrote later, "when a new and powerful stimulus only was required to enable the enthusiastic mind of my patient to shake them off"—an unexceptionable and highly intelligent medical opinion.

Miss Martineau was amazed and delighted that she would have a chance to test the truth of something she had long believed in. Hall was brought to her—"a true, simple-minded man"—and in twenty minutes she felt a new and strange sensation, the closing in of a clear twilight, while objects directly before her disappeared. That she was susceptible to mesmeric influence was unquestionable, but Hall did not seem to be able to produce great effects, and twice he made her sick. Then, once when he was unable to come, her maid tried the passes she had so carefully, if ignorantly, watched; within a minute Miss Martineau was relieved and spent seven hours feeling perfectly well, her first feeling of entire comfort, she told Milnes, for five years. Hall was unable to stay on, because of the demands of his tour, but he urged that she use any "strong & well-convinced" mesmerist she could find.

[1] *Newcastle Chronicle*, May 25, June 8, June 22, 1844.

The prospect so deliciously opened then seemed to close. If she could have gone to London, there were many offers to help; but that was out of the question. So she and her maid did what they could; she ordered a copy of Deleuze's manual of instruction to help them make the practice something more than a mere mechanical act, but it did not seem to help. By the end of July she was protesting that she had had enough experience to be convinced of the reality of mesmerism and that she wanted no inferences drawn from her failure. At this point, probably through the help of the Montagus, Henry Atkinson intervened with advice, and soon sent his friend Mrs. Montagu Wynyard. But by that time Miss Martineau was already on the way to recovery, with only her maid's ministrations. And one passing remark must carry large significance. She asked to visit her maid to see her room to plan a new cupboard, and the girl refused. Never before had the maid objected to anything suggested by her mistress, who at once yielded the point because, she said, she wanted so very much to have the girl's will uppermost.[1]

If, as I suspect, the real agency in her cure, apart from the undoubted physical change, was the submission to another will, Mrs. Wynyard was precisely the person needed. She had been married to an abominable husband, a clergyman in York, whose debts she had twice paid, refusing a third time only to be much abused by his family. After his death, she had got into wretched health—presumably a nervous breakdown—and was cured by Henry Atkinson. She then became a practitioner herself, doing remarkable things like mesmerizing her laundress in Cheltenham (where she had gone from London to live), so that the girl could describe Mrs. Wynyard's posturings and taste a bun her mistress had eaten. When Mrs. Wynyard arrived in Tynemouth, she received a piece of mesmerized leather from Henry Atkinson to put them into communication. Armed with this talisman, she began to mesmerize her patient so intensely that Miss Martineau became frightened, ran away, and locked herself in her room.[2]

[1] The authority for this paragraph is a series of letters to Monckton Milnes, hampered only by the lack of dating of two of them. The account of the early stages, including Greenhow's attitude and the comparative insignificance of results in the early mesmerizing, is borne out exactly in Spencer Hall's *Mesmeric Experiences*, pp. 63–75.

[2] Lord Morpeth's Diary, December 11, 1844, and January 4, 1845. *Zoist*, iii, 90–92 (April, 1845).

The mesmerist soon established her ascendancy, becoming an indispensable part of the little household. By September Miss Martineau had given up her mild opiates, her appetite and spirits had returned (continuing the improvement, that is, that had begun at least six months before), her hearing improved, and the "hopeless symptom"—the prolapse of the uterus—had partly given way. On fine days she ventured out to the grass plot behind the house; by the end of the month there was a daily walk of half a mile and back; and by mid-October she had got up to five miles, and began to regain her figure, had bought some new clothes, and had re-arranged her furniture "to break sofa habits". "I have a Bonnet now! Yea & a Parasol!! Shoes, Gloves, & Shawls I had happily not given away. My mesmerist here proposes that my Bonnet be exhibited on the Flag staff of the Garrison, like the cap of liberty on a pole, in glorification of her art." [1]

But more extraordinary things were to be done by Mrs. Wynyard. More than the cure, Miss Martineau told Milnes, she wanted to be found capable of clairvoyance, to obtain the knowledge of her condition her doctors could not give her.[2] And now the higher phenomena were found in her own house. Jane Arrowsmith, the nineteen-year-old niece of her landlady, was mesmerized for her head and eyes—she was suffering apparently from hysterical partial blindness—and proved herself "a somnambule & 'unconscious revealer'". In a trance, she described her own and Miss Martineau's internal structure and pronounced "some awful spiritual dicta"; then on one fateful night she turned these remarkable clairvoyant powers to predicting the safe return of the crew of a wrecked ship. It was easy enough for opponents later to demonstrate that Jane could have heard about the rescue before the seance, but that made no difference to Miss Martineau, who devoted her wonderful energy and loyalty to the defence of the ignorant girl. Indeed, Jane's ignorance was essential: to find these powers in a "simple, truthful, conscientious" girl, who knew nothing of either mesmerism or her own powers, proved the truth of mesmerism beyond a doubt.[3]

[1] HM to Elizabeth Barrett, September 16, [1844], Yale. HM to Mary Howitt, September 27, 1844, PHS. HM to Elizabeth Barrett, October 21, 1844, Yale. HM to Elizabeth Barrett, September 28, 1844, Wellesley. HM to Mrs. Jameson, [1844], *Memoirs of Anna Jameson*, pp. 205 ff.

[2] June 13, 1844.

[3] HM to Elizabeth Barrett, October 21, 1844, Yale.

It then became necessary to inform the world. In her autobiography, Miss Martineau sniffed at charges that she had "rushed into print": she waited, she said, until the evidence was complete and until a careful scientific account was made necessary by unwarranted and inaccurate discussion of the case in the newspapers. But her intention to go into print was present, as one might expect, almost from the outset. In early October she wrote to Crabb Robinson that as soon as the evidence was complete, she would throw the whole weight of her character, intellectual and moral, into her testimony to the truth of mesmerism.[1] Her carefully kept journal, the improvement of the "hopeless symptom", her remarkable activity, all carried conviction for the curative effects, and Jane's insights and transparent ingenuousness clinched the argument for the higher phenomena. She chose the *Athenaeum* as her outlet rather than a mesmeric paper like the *Zoist*, because she wanted to offer her account to unbelievers as well as to the converted. Not that she hoped for a single case to convert the sceptics. What she wanted was to encourage others to tell their experiences—that way truth would be mightily aided. Her task was to sacrifice taste to something higher, to summon up the courage to give full details about herself in order to deal with the "morality of the matter". In her testimony to truth, she was as much the martyr as ever:

> I took my part deliberately—*knowing privacy to be impossible*, and making up my mind to *entire* publicity as the only course faithful to truth and human welfare. I cannot tell you how the thought of *Godiva* had sustained and inspired me. Her century was not the only time, nor Coventry the only place for the exercise of her spirit.[2]

One can only be grateful for her sake that the letter did not fall into the hands of another Croker.

The letters appeared in the *Athenaeum* in late November and early December; the initial response was gratifying, to say the least. Six issues of the paper were carried through three editions, and, reprinted in a pamphlet (with an appendix to do justice to phrenology), the articles sold out in four days.[3] The *Zoist* reported happily that mesmerism was the topic of the day, so

[1] October 6, [1844], DWL.

[2] HM to Elizabeth Barrett, December 10, [1844], Yale. HM to Milnes, December 15, [1844]. HM to Bulwer-Lytton, November 27, [1844].

[3] HM to Mrs. Liddell, Carlisle Papers.

much talked about that even Thomas Wakley, the violently anti-mesmeric editor of the *Lancet*, was running a series of articles on it, preparing himself to jump. The cause of it all was the case of Miss Martineau, though even the *Zoist* wished that she had consulted Atkinson before publishing, since one false step from an enthusiastic friend could be more damaging than all the Wakleys and Forbeses.

Prince Albert said at a Palace party that medical men were conducting themselves improperly in refusing to investigate the facts of mesmerism. The Queen Dowager's court were interested —Miss Martineau hoped that would remove much prejudice. One of the maids of honour was in correspondence with her, and Lord and Lady Barrington (she was one of the Queen Dowager's ladies) came to see Mrs. Wynyard and to go away impressed. A succession of such visitors came to Tynemouth, and the volume of the post must have recalled the days immediately after the publication of the political economy tales, with business "most like a Prime Minister's." Doctors wrote to report successes, so she set herself up as a clearing house for information which she hoped would impress the Faculty. Truly she could write, "I am in all the calmness of my strength now,—a new experience to me. Nothing ruffles or tries me."[1]

She wrote that phrase in December, but by the new year she was sorely tried. In the *Athenaeum* of December 28, the editors had offered "a string of comments . . . insulting and slanderous to the last degree"—actually a very intelligent commentary and critique of the letters. They called into question, she said, the characters of Mrs. Wynyard and Jane, and set loose shocking efforts to undermine their assertion of Jane's powers, a controversy which expired "in the sheer inability of the honest party to compete with rogues who stuck at no falsehoods". She was furious with Charles Dilke, the editor, and his associate, her old friend Henry Chorley. Even worse was the publication by Greenhow early in 1845 of a shilling pamphlet, "not even written in Latin", setting out all the facts of her case. She had thought he would publish in a medical journal, and, with considerable justification, she resented the form of publication, although it seems equally certain that, had he been less clinical, more sympathetic to mesmerism, and less conclusive, she would have

[1] *Zoist*, iii, 86, 96–97 [April, 1845]. HM to Elizabeth Barrett, December 10, [1844], Yale. HM to Crabb Robinson, December 12, [1844], DWL.

welcomed his public testimony. As it was, though there was no quarrel, she refused to see him again.[1]

Amid the general excitement provoked by the case, people who knew Miss Martineau had particular reasons for concern, although their reactions varied. Edward Everett considered it the most important case to come before the public, and, believing as he did that there might be occult powers or capacities (an explanation she would strenuously have rejected), he was sure she would render a great service to science "& to its best part viz. practical philosophy if she forces this question as she bids fair to do, to a solution". Crabb Robinson was overwhelmed with comment from his many correspondents.[2]

One doctor told Crabb Robinson that if water had the effect of brandy on Miss Martineau because the mesmerizer willed it, he wished she would try brandy while the mesmerizer willed it to be water. Macaulay dismissed the whole cure by saying, "Oh, it's all my eye and Hetty Martineau!" Elizabeth Sedgwick concluded that her former friend "could not get ill—or get well—without some special fussification". Macready was led to ask in his diary if she was in her clear senses, and Carlyle announced that the adherence to mesmerism, added to refusing a pension and burning her letters, conclusively proved her mad.[3]

A good many people took a more just view of her position. It could be maintained that Miss Martineau's case for clairvoyance rested not on facts—for the loopholes in Miss Martineau's account are enormous—but on her belief in the character of her witnesses; an unshakable conviction of their trustworthiness pushed her to extreme statements. Miss Pease found much explained by Miss Martineau's "fine imagination", so prone, as we have seen, to enthusiasm. J. B. Estlin, a Bristol physician and ardent abolitionist, put his views particularly well—and he

[1] *Auto.*, i, 475–76. *Elizabeth Barrett Browning Letters*, i, 225–26. HM to Elizabeth Barrett, [April 4, 1845], and May 15, [1845], Yale.

[2] Edward Everett to Mrs. Davenport, February 28, 1845, MHS. Mrs. Arnold to Crabb Robinson, November 27, 1844, Mrs. Clarkson to Crabb Robinson, March 24, 1845, Miss Fenwick to Crabb Robinson, January 29, 1845. *Barrett-Mitford*, December 14, 1844. Elizabeth Barrett to Mrs. Martin, November 26, 1844, to James Martin, December 10, 1844, *Letters*, i, 217–20. M. R. Mitford to Elizabeth Barrett, November 27, 1844, to Miss Jephson (*c.* July, 1845), *Life*, ii, 272–73, 287.

[3] Crabb Robinson to Thomas Robinson, December 14, 1844, DWL. Dering, *Memoirs of Lady Chatterton*, p. 95. Elizabeth Sedgwick to W. E. Sedgwick, May 18, [1845], MHS. Macready, *Diaries*, ii, 276. Elizabeth Barrett to R. H. Horne, [December 3, 1844], *Barrett-Horne Letters*, ii, 173.

was a man not unsympathetic towards the more reasonable claims of mesmerism:

> I have no hesitation in saying I believe her recovery has been accelerated by Mesmerism. Her local disease had begun to subside before she had recourse to Mm: her faith in this influence inspired her with *hope*, gave courage to her efforts to leave off opiates, use exercise, & surmount invalid habits, & greatly aided in her restoration. But with the recovery of bodily health, she has extensively lost the credit of having a sound mind. The rapidity with which she believed, & published her convictions of the mesmeric performances of J. was most lamentable. To many of her best friends, her *fall* in public estimation is grievous, especially to those who had seen her powerful mind command respect & attention from persons most opposed to her political & theological views. Her admirers & defenders of former days can now say nothing when the present example of her weakness is pointed at in proof of their former exaggerated appreciation of her intellectual powers.

He was convinced that she had been imposed upon by Mrs. Wynyard and Jane, who, without intending to deceive at first, were caught up in the publicity and excitement produced, and in their self-delusion carried Miss Martineau with them.[1] Certainly the speed with which Atkinson sent Mrs. Wynyard is suspicious, although it is not necessary to impute conscious deceit to either of them. The opportunity of gaining support for what they truly believed from so important a person as Miss Martineau was not to be missed.

But how can her ready response be explained? Miss Barrett saw that this was a crucial case: not that of a weak-minded woman,

> but of the most manlike woman in the three kingdoms—in the best sense of man—a woman gifted with admirable fortitude, as well as exercised in high logic, a woman of sensibility and imagination certainly, but apt to carry her reason unbent wherever she sets her foot; given to utilitarian philosophy and the habit of logical analysis; and suffering under a disease which has induced change of structure and yielded to no tried remedy! Is it not wonderful and past expectation? [2]

Miss Martineau thought she had been cured by mesmerism, but

[1] Crabb Robinson had liked Jane and was "almost prepared to be a compurgator", but from the first he disliked Mrs. Wynyard, though without any specific reason. To Miss Fenwick, July 16, 1845. E. Quillinan to Crabb Robinson, March 23, 1845, DWL. Elizabeth Pease to Mrs. Chapman, November 7, 1845, BPL, Weston. J. B. Estlin to Samuel J. May, March 2, 1845, BPL, May. See also *Life of M. R. Mitford*, ii, 272–73, and *Letters of George Cornewall Lewis*, pp. 137–41.

[2] To Mrs. Martin, [*c.* Sept., 1844], *Letters*, i, 196–97.

her eagerness to push beyond simple curative effects needs more explaining than gratitude or credulity can supply. The mesmerists themselves could see nothing but conversion, while no one else knew enough about mesmerism to see how perfectly it fitted her broader commitments and limitations, how thoroughly prepared she was to believe, and how fully mesmerism could promise her a clear road to the most important of her goals. To explain these circumstances must take us on a long digression into one of the most curious and revealing byways of early Victorian intellectual history.

In 1774 Franz Anton Mesmer, a Viennese physician, heard of cures worked by applying a magnet to the body of the patient. Quickly concluding that the cause was a magnetic fluid, he soon found that the same results could be obtained by dispensing with the magnetized iron and using passes, by means of which the magnetism flowed directly to the patient from the operator's fingertips. Mesmeric treatment became the rage, first in Vienna, and then after the profession had driven Mesmer out, in Paris, where he arrived in 1778. The cures which he obtained were, of course, the same as those produced by relics, faith healers, or medicine men. For certain classes of diseases the cures were unquestionable; for others it was perhaps enough that the patients thought themselves cured. The Academy of Medicine, alarmed by the practices, appointed an investigating body which condemned mesmerism in 1784, but the craze continued to spread. Mesmer's pupil, Count de Puységur, carried his investigations into somnambulism or sleep-waking, in which a subject in a trance would respond to suggestions of the operator, even long after the trance was over and without any recollection of the command. Mesmer, Puységur, and the other mesmerists were dealing with phenomena which have become commonplaces of modern psychology and psychiatry; but their explanations and methods merely confirmed the prejudices of the medical profession, prejudices which seemed perfectly justified in the light of contemporary knowledge, however misguided they may seem today.

The enthusiasm for mesmerism crossed the Channel from Paris to make its impression on English society and pamphlet literature just before the Revolution,[1] and after the war interest

[1] E.g., [John Pearson], *A Plain and Rational Account of the Nature and Effects of Animal Magnetism*, an ironic spoof of 1790, with an appendix of denunciation. On

revived. It was discussed in books and articles and talked about in society—Crabb Robinson's diaries are an excellent barometer of English interest—and reactions varied widely. Some people were worried about the religious implications; others found it morally disgusting that beautiful expressions which should have come from moral or intellectual activity were produced by the pressure of the thumb on the skull. The sensation-minded saw all sorts of immoral possibilities inherent in the mesmerizer's position; the more sober confined their worries to uncertainty about the scientific basis of mesmerism.[1]

Mesmerism was only one of several similar enthusiasms in the thirties and forties. Of the others, phrenology was most closely connected with mesmerism, but public interest ran impartially to hydropathy, homeopathy, vegetarianism, and ultimately spiritualism. Converts to mesmerism could forsake it for the others or hold any of them concurrently. There were, of course, mesmerists and mesmerists. For most of the public, mesmerism was a fad, taken up for a time, played with while it was fashionable, and forgotten. But to a few people, it was a cause and a life's work. Harriet Martineau was one of these; she belonged to a particular group within the mesmeric fraternity, a group with an unshakable devotion and certain very special characteristics.

The central figure in this circle was Dr. John Elliotson, one of the most remarkable medical men of his generation.[2] Born in 1791, the son of a Southwark druggist, Elliotson studied at Edinburgh and Jesus College, Cambridge. Beginning his stormy career as physician to St. Thomas's Hospital, he became a popular lecturer on medical jurisprudence and medical aspects of criminology, and his lectures were published (with his approval) and widely circulated by Thomas Wakley, the enterprising, unscrupulous, radical editor of *The Lancet*. Besides his unorthodox taste for publicity, Elliotson held some novel medical theories: he was among the first in England to use the stethoscope and

Mesmer generally see Gardner Murphy, *History of Psychology*. There is also an overdrawn but informative popular account in Stefan Zweig, *Mental Healers*.

[1] Besides Crabb Robinson's diaries, *passim*, see Elizabeth Barrett to Mrs. Jameson, December 1844, and to Henry Chorley, April 28, 1845, *Letters*, i, 227–28, 257–58. Mrs. Clarkson to Crabb Robinson, July 28, 1845. *Diaries of a Lady of Quality from 1797 to 1844* (Frances Williams-Wynn), pp. 329–35. Mrs. Poyntz in Bulwer-Lytton's *A Strange Story*.

[2] There is an excellent popular account of Elliotson's life and career in J. H. Harley Williams, *Doctors Differ* (London, 1946), to which this section owes much.

auscultation; he was converted to the phrenological theories of Gall and founded the London Phrenological Society in 1824. An immensely popular teacher, and a sought-after consultant, he shocked older members of the profession not only by his radical medicine, but by his preference for eminently sober and utilitarian trousers instead of knee-breeches, It was a perfectly natural choice when in 1831 he was made Professor of Medicine at the new radical University of London (now University College), whose hospital he helped to found. Dr. Harley Williams rightly makes the point that Elliotson, coming to medicine before anaesthesia, the germ theory, or psychosomatic medicine, was a man frustrated by limitations but without the genius or the patience required to bring about a real advance.

Elliotson's first contact with mesmerism had been through an Irishman named Chenevix, but it was not until the experiments of "Baron" Dupotet at Middlesex Hospital in 1837 that he was converted. He saw in the new technique not only an anaesthetic and curative power, but, because of the apparent ability of somnambules to see and pronounce on the internal condition of themselves and others, a new means of diagnosis. He repeated the classical experiments of Puységur and others with two sisters named Okey—perfect hysterical types—saw in their reactions the possibility of discovering new physiological laws of human nature, and actually used one of them to predict the deaths of patients. Of course Elliotson came up against strenuous resistance from the profession and his own colleagues. Perhaps even worse, he made his friend Wakley into an enemy, and the *Lancet* launched a full-scale attack in its best style against Elliotson's experiments. The notoriety presented a serious problem to the Council of University College who finally ordered Elliotson to stop the practice of mesmerism in the hospital. Elliotson replied by resigning. In 1843 he founded *The Zoist.* And in 1846, as if to make amends, he was invited to give the Harveian Oration at the Royal College of Physicians. The lecture was a temperate appeal to study the phenomena of mesmerism; the experience of Harvey was dutifully and effectively invoked, and, characteristically, Elliotson was the first Harveian Orator to lecture in English instead of Latin.[1]

[1] Harley Williams, *Doctors Differ. Lancet*, May–September, 1838. Crabb Robinson Diary, March 29, May 3, May 26, December 20, 1838, DWL. *Zoist*, i, pp. 89–94 (April 1843), and iv, 113 (April, 1846).

Elliotson helps to explain Harriet Martineau. Her friends were puzzled that what seemed a logical, masculine mind could be led astray by *post hoc* argument; it would seem more puzzling that a number of medical men, some of them very distinguished, were the most prominent of the significantly large number of respectable, educated believers. The answer lies, faddism aside, in a certain quality of mind. A Manchester surgeon, writing on the mesmeric puzzle in a professional paper, pointed this out. Certain errors, he said, are peculiar to men of talent.

> The reason of which fact may probably be found in the ardour of imagination which characterizes some individuals of high mental endowment. Enthusiasm, inquisitiveness, and eagerness for novelty, hurrying such persons to premature conclusions, they seem to cling to these, as sources of wonder and delight, with most affectionate tenacity. But, indeed, in all ages, a love of the marvellous has originated follies without number; follies which are the peculiarity of no one class. They are often conceived by the able, curious, and imaginative minds, and the multitude receive them on trust. . . . Hale for Witchcraft, and Wiseman for the Royal touch, were authorities in their day, certainly equal to Elliotson and Townshend at the present time. Why should we yield assent to the latter, and not to the former? We know that it has been the fashion to claim for the nineteenth century a comparative freedom from the folly of credulity; but we very much think that our superiority in this respect equals not the vaunt; we suspect that, however the objects may change, the *disposition* remains but little diminished.[1]

Now, what were the elements of this enthusiasm? In the first place, for persons of a radical bent—and the group of devoted mesmerists with whom we are concerned were all more or less in that category—the extraordinary changes which they had witnessed during their lives predisposed them to accept marvels. As one of them said, geology had opened a new world to human inquiry, chemistry in a lifetime had become a new science; what that the mesmerists said was more astounding than universally admitted facts, such as the electric telegraph? In 1837, a considerable flurry was raised by Andrew Crosse, an amateur scientist who claimed to have produced animal life (*acarus crossii*) in a caustic solution by electric current, a discovery, said Miss Martineau in her *History*, of "unbounded philosophical significance". In a society soon to be shaken by the *Vestiges of Creation*, some enthusiasts were quite prepared to accept such

[1] *British and Foreign Medical Review*, xix, 470 (April, 1845). The writer was a Mr. Noble of Manchester. See John Forbes, *Illustrations of Modern Mesmerism*, p. 95 n.

pronouncements as Crosse's as proved, and from there move on to new discoveries.[1]

Naturally, minds which welcome change, particularly if they have some particular end in view, are impatient and intolerant of anything that stands in the way of change. There is something wonderfully symbolic in the paper which Henry Atkinson read to the London Phrenological Society in April, 1843, analysing Lord Eldon's head. It is nothing less than a diatribe against a reactionary, its contentions confirmed in the jargon of the phrenologists. Elliotson was a convinced penal reformer and opponent of capital punishment, and the *Zoist* is full of demands for national education and other radical programmes. A phreno-mesmerist of Southampton urged phrenology as a guide in the choice of a parliamentary representative.[2]

A stand against conservatism and reaction was especially exciting when the enemy could be identified, not merely with ignorant and unimaginative individuals, but with the power of an organized, selfish and obscurantist interest. A good radical, by no means convinced of the doctrine of the mesmerists, saw that much good in them:

> Still, there must be *something* in mesmerism—it cannot all be delusion. At present its advocates have to suffer persecution in its defence, & this in itself inclines me to listen with candour to all they have to say upon it. The professions, of course, are loudest in its condemnation—the medical from self-interest & "esprit de corps"—the clerical in accordance with their general character, as the opposers of every reform.[3]

Thomas Robinson told Crabb Robinson that he thought some of the discoveries of the mesmerists might be claimed in support of religion, since the sects were so fond of collateral arguments; and there were both ministers to do so and mesmerists to stress the religious contributions their science could make. But the men around Elliotson tended to be free-thinking materialists. To an enthusiast like Dr. King, who thought the ministry were paid to tell lies, or even to good Unitarians like Crabb Robinson and Harriet Martineau, the explanation which mesmerism offered for the miraculous nature of Christ's healing powers was potent

[1] Joseph W. Haddock, M.D., *Somnolism and Psycheism; or the Science of the Soul and the Phenomena of Nervation*, pp. 1, 3. *Hist.*, ii, 451–52.

[2] *Zoist*, i, 277–84 (October, 1843), iii, 399–416 (January, 1846), and *passim*.

[3] Elizabeth Pease to Anne Weston, November 7, [1845], BPL, Weston.

and liberating.[1] The clergy, however, were secondary. The medical profession was the real enemy. In rejecting the mesmeric work of Dr. Esdaile in India, said Elliotson, the doctors revealed an utter absence of moral principle that reminded him of the mob shouting for Barabbas. Or again:

> You stigmatize Mesmer as an empiric. In what do you differ from him? He performed wonderful cures for money, so of course do you: and you will die a far richer man than Mesmer. If he often failed to cure, so do you every day of your life, receiving ample fees without bestowing benefit. He employed means without knowing more than the fact of their power; so do you. You cannot tell why a single medicine you employ acts as it does.[2]

The profession was cowardly, morally weak, selfish, blind; and Elliotson was not the only person to refer to Harvey. The opposition to Harvey, Galileo, and every other great innovator was a major forensic device of all the mesmerists.

To be sure, the medical profession deserved some of the attack. Doctors scoffed and sneered and brought down Prince Albert's rebuke; they boycotted mesmeric meetings or tried to break them up.[3] But when serious consideration of the claims of mesmerism led to rejection, the denunciation by the mesmerists was just as fervent. A physician like J. B. Estlin, already referred to, was quite willing to grant the success of mesmerism in effecting certain cures, through its operation on nervous states or by providing rest so that the body itself could effect a cure, a view expressed in the best medical commentators. But even so sympathetic an observer and practitioner as James Braid, the Manchester surgeon who stands at the beginning of the modern history of hypnotism, was criticized by mesmerists for stopping short of a belief in the magnetic fluid or the higher phenomena or whatever was the particular enthusiasm of the critic.[4]

To the convinced mesmerist the medical profession was partly a straw man of his own creation, but he was fighting a good

[1] The most vocal religious opposition to mesmerism was led by the Rev. Hugh MacNeill of Liverpool who called it the instrument of the Devil. *Zoist*, 1843, *passim*, and *Phreno-Magnet*, *passim*. On King, see Crabb Robinson's diary, December 7, 1851. Henry Robinson to Crabb Robinson, January 14, 1845, DWL.

[2] *Zoist*, iv, 144 (April, 1846), *Mesmerism in India*, pp. 18–19.

[3] *Phreno-Magnet*, i, 163 (July, 1843).

[4] J. B. Estlin, *Mesmerism in 1845*. Estlin to S. J. May, March 2, 1845, BPL, May. Braid, *Neurypnology*; and *Magic, Witchcraft, Animal Magnetism, Hypnotism, and Electro-Biology*. On Braid, see J. Bramwell Milne, *Hypnotism*, pp. 21–29. *Zoist*, ii, 281–84 (July, 1844), contains an answer to Estlin.

radical fight. The principal effort of radicalism in the past fifty years had had to be devoted to tearing down old institutions and blasting out entrenched interests. One mesmerist, amid references to Harvey and Jenner, cited that good radical theoretician, Samuel Bailey:

> There are few things more disgusting to an enlightened mind, than to see a number of men—a mob—whether learned or illiterate, who have never scrutinized the foundations of their opinions, assailing with contumely an individual who, after the labour of research and reflection, has adopted different sentiments from theirs, and pluming themselves on the notion of superior knowledge, because their understandings have been tenacious of prejudice.[1]

The trouble with a commitment to attacking entrenched interests is that it easily spills over into attacking all interests and all groups. Certainly with the mesmerists anti-professionalism is a major force, as it seems to have been to so many earnest Victorian intellectuals, concerned to root out vested interests, to open the arcane, to salvage beliefs, and, above all, to protect the vast and cloudy claims of Victorian amateur presumption. One writer, in a notable departure from a basic contention of Adam Smith, ascribed the moral cowardice of the medical profession to its specialization and subdivision, so great that the most mediocre talent could rise to success by "detached hackwork" which

> shall cheat the public out of reverence and throw into the shade that of some less bustling contemporary whose original mind imparting new light to every subject it approaches, shall cause the name of its possessor to live in futurity as long as that of one of the chosen few who have imported new *principles* to science.[2]

And where could mesmerism take hold when rejected by such selfish interests? Why,

> out it would burst, and that in quarters least expected—among the humble and unconventional masses of the country—those whose only facilities for receiving or dispensing information were the passive faculties with which Nature herself had furnished them for the purpose. . . . It remained for a Mechanics' Institution to be the first large conventional body that would dare to have its name identified with Phreno-Magnetism.[3]

---

[1] [Lang], *Mesmerism: Its History, Phenomena, and Practice*, pp. 232–33.

[2] *Zoist*, iv, 435–41 (January, 1847).

[3] S. T. Hall, *Phreno-Magnet*, i, 65–66 (April, 1843). The Mechanics' Institution was in Sheffield. "It is an odious, disgusting, and impious business, and is worthily

As the radical temper led to vituperative attacks on vested interests and professionals,[1] another radical characteristic, or defect, became readily apparent: that the mesmerists themselves fell into camps and sects who abused each other soundly. Hall in the *Phreno-Magnet* attacked the *Zoist* for dogmatizing and arrogating to itself the right to speak on the subject of mesmerism. Henry Atkinson demanded that the *Phreno-Magnet* recognize his claim to discoveries of new phrenological organs by mesmeric means. The *Zoist*, in a generally unfavourable review, attacked Professor Gregory especially for not giving due credit to others, i.e., Elliotson and the *Zoist*. Newnham regretted that some magnetizers ascribed their anti-religious views to magnetism, and when Dr. Engeldue, Elliotson's associate, gave an address in which materialism was made a necessary consequence of phrenology (with loud approval from Elliotson and Atkinson), some members of the Phrenological Association, including James Simpson, Professor Gregory, and James Silk Buckingham, drew up a declaration against such a necessary link, pointing to the lack of evidence for such a contention.[2] These divisions were felt intensely and pronounced in unmeasured terms. It is not accidental that they are reminiscent of the internal quarrels of the abolitionists.

The intelligent medical writers observed the distinction made by the mesmerists between the ordinary and higher phenomena. Trance, catalepsy, suggestion, a certain range of cures, and—though here there was uncertainty—anaesthesia, they accepted as fact and were suitably modest in offering explanations. It is on the observance of this distinction that Braid could rest his claim to be heard and respected. But the crucial test of mesmeric claims rested in the higher phenomena. Here again the intelligent critics did not deny many of the things claimed by mesmerists and somnambules; they did, however, insist that all of the claims could be explained by ordinary means—heightened

---

advocated by women without principle, and lectured upon by men who drop their *h*'s." *Journals and Correspondence of Lady Eastlake*, i, 152.

[1] "If, therefore, those who descend to be sweeps and scavengers *will* run against a decent man as he passes along, he should not be blamed for making in return a little dust when shaking himself clean of them." *Phreno-Magnet*, Advertisement, xii.

[2] *Phreno-Magnet*, i, 99–100 (May, 1843), 220–22, 238–40 (August and September, 1843). *Zoist*, ix, 201–6 (July, 1851). Newnham, *Human Magnetism*, pp. 84–87. *Zoist*, i, 143–56 (July, 1843).

faculties, coincidence, or collusion. And their most telling attack lay in the area of proof and method.[1]

Certainly, reading the mesmerists on the higher phenomena is a strain. Here is Spencer T. Hall on his phrenological discoveries: "It was little more than a fortnight ago that we discovered a most important class of mechanical faculties, as to the existence of which theretofore we had not received the slightest hint." On a moment's notice, as it were, he discovered in the eyebrows the faculties for walking, riding, swimming, diving, sailing; and he kept on discovering faculties, even down to the organ for Love of Pets.[2] Atkinson's discoveries by mesmeric inquiry were similarly sweeping and casual. The publication of Professor Gregory's translation of Reichenbach's work on magnetism brought a devastating review in the *British and Foreign Medico-Chirurgical Review*,[3] aimed at the mesmerists' "inductive method". Reichenbach was found highly hypothetical and credulous as to his own powers. In receiving subjective for objective phenomena, he was negligent of proper precautions to guarantee scientific accuracy, and incompetent from his ignorance of his principal instruments of research—the human brain and the senses of touch and vision. And, said the reviewer, Gregory had to share the blame, indeed bear it more strongly, for his insistence on Reichenbach's perfect adherence to proper rules for investigation, while Gregory himself relied on even flimsier proofs. One's doubts about the professor of chemistry at Edinburgh must be seriously reinforced on reading his conditions for conducting experiments in the higher phenomena. His two most telling requirements are that "no one who is already convinced, without enquiry, and therefore with prejudice, that the patient is an impostor, should either be present or in any way concerned with the experiment", and that "failure is not to be held, as it cannot logically be held, to decide the question of truth of lucid vision".[4]

It is an idle occupation, wrote one mesmerist (a doctor) to try to use demonstrations to satisfy "stiff and superficial thinkers"

[1] So, J. B. Estlin in his *Mesmerism in 1845*, or *British and Foreign Medical Review*, xix, 428–85, esp. p. 470 (April, 1845).

[2] *Phreno-Magnet*, i, 34 (March, 1843).

[3] viii, 378–431 (October, 1851), esp. pp. 405 and 390.

[4] *On the Theory of Imagination, as explaining the Phenomena of Mesmerism.* This pamphlet is a magnificent example of vagueness in assertion, statistical weakness, and evidential problems. Cf. Miss Martineau: "Failures are only the supervention of other conditions than those you are seeking; and they cannot invalidate their antecedents." *Letters*, p. 44.

who cannot yield "their inflexible and guarded habits of trained reflection".

> It is a common observation that, for the most part, those persons who are by mesmeric treatment put into a state of somnambulism, exhibit sincerity and truthfulness. With them rank has no existence. Equality of station is established, and nature is supreme. . . . Even then when the sleep-waker has returned to a knowledge of this artificial world, and tastes of the fraudulent practices which govern mankind in their daily intercourse, the exceptions to a love of candour and sincerity seem to be dependent upon the existence of an unusually large size of those cerebral organs which in the wide-awake state determine the habit of loving falsehood better than truth. It would be useless to enlarge upon this point to experienced mesmerists, and the objection that deceit has frequently been met with in sleep-wakers would apply with far greater force, if statistics could be resorted to, against a large majority of persons wide awake.[1]

His criteria of testimony, he admitted, might not satisfy a sceptic, but that was not a very important matter. Dr. Ashburner's attack against the habits of the trained mind is paralleled by the Reverend George Sandby's attack on a lay critic, George Cornewall Lewis, with the additional (if contradictory) indictment that Lewis presumed to apply his method to everything under the sun. But that was what one might expect from "a well-known character in the *bureaucratic* world", an M.P. "who has been for some time in the habit of 'laying down the law', *with* or *without* a reason." [2]

The shield of the mesmerist against attack was laid out by one writer as consisting in "full unswerving belief" coupled with a knowledge of the subject based on long, private, practical investigations; in prudence, or the ingenuousness which leaves unfilled gaps to further experiment; and in independent principle, that is, moral courage to stand up in dignity to maintain truth and to bear every imputation rather than to allow his patient to be tampered with by the sceptical. "Forgetting that scepticism and ignorance, (being negative principles,) have no positive rights, there are men pluming themselves most magnificently on

[1] *Zoist*, iv, 125–26 (April, 1846).

[2] *Zoist*, vii, 203–11 (July, 1849). The work in question is Lewis's *Essay on the Influence of Authority in Matters of Opinion.* It is interesting that Sandby sneered at Lewis's having held the position of poor law commissioner, "one of that formidable triumvirate at Somerset House, whose dicta decided such momentous questions as pauper diet and discipline. . . ."

their professional acquirements, who attack all belief in Phreno-pathy as groundless and absurd, simply because they are not acquainted with its nature." Another writer laid the burden on Hume himself, whose requirement for testimony to a miracle was far greater than for natural phenomena. The sceptics persisted in regarding the higher phenomena as miracles; whereas they were only imperfectly known results of natural laws.

> If then we show, that the nature of human testimony is so great that a *small number of competent witnesses* will establish the truth of *a miracle*, which is assumed by the great sceptic to require a more than ordinary array of evidence,—it will follow *a fortiori* that *a like number of* competent witnesses will establish the truth of magnetic phenomena beyond the possibility of any reasonable doubt.

And he went on to show that hundreds of thousands of educated and honourable men and women had testified to mesmeric phenomena.[1]

The means of proof on which the mesmerists depended are revealing. Like most of the early Victorians, they had a passionate faith in statistics, but a very weak sense of statistical proof. The faults of amateurishness which so exasperate the historian trying to work with many inquiries made by local statistical societies are present in the mesmerists in heightened form—vagueness, carelessness in observation and recording, lack of definition, unintelligent categorization, and an absolute disregard for possible alternative explanations.[2]

It is amusing to read the criteria of competence in witnesses. Can we expect, asks one writer, that Elliotson, Braid and Simpson could be parties to deception, or "that individuals of character and standing in society . . . should also have become participators in the wretched fraud?"[3] Respectability and "just in-

[1] *Phreno-Magnet*, i, 161–62 (July, 1843). Newnham, *Human Magnetism*, pp. 25–27. The demand for proof in the *British and Foreign Medical Review*, xix, 431–32, is Humean.

[2] A particularly flagrant example is the great fuss made in the *Zoist*, e.g., vi, 380–84 (January, 1849), about Major Buckley's patients who were able to read the mottoes enclosed in nuts bought at sweetshops. Nuts containing mottoes were apparently good Victorian party fare. Harriet reported to James (August 9, 1819) that at a family meeting, a dish of walnuts, with original mottoes, was passed at supper.

[3] Lang, *Mesmerism*, pp. 236–37. It is worth noting that Braid put great stress on the quality of his witnesses: "At a conversazione a few days after, in the presence of Lady S., Sir Thomas Arbuthnot, Colonel Arbuthnot, Major Wilbraham, John Frederick Foster, Esq., Chairman of the Quarter Sessions, D. Monde, Esq., stipen-

fluence" were the criteria, not knowledge. A fact was the same fact to whoever observed it; it never seemed to cross their minds —or crossed only in condemnation—that a great many facts can be recognized only by those who have been trained to see them. But early Victorian culture was resolutely amateur. What specialization there was was largely below the surface, and a true professionalization of society was a considerable distance in the future. The amateurishness was reflected in a number of ways— in the reviews and magazines, in the enthusiasm for the British Association, the National Association for the Promotion of Social Science, and the local statistical societies. Having demolished entrenched interests to liberate the individual, they let him have free rein: every man his own historian and scientist and doctor and philosopher and poet. And if that amateurishness had its virtues in a unified, culturally concerned society where knowledge could still be considered one, it also had its defects in the poets of the Spasmodic school and in the wilder flights of mesmerism. It is worth noting that the greatest exponent of Victorian amateur presumption, Herbert Spencer, made some of his earliest appearances in print in the *Zoist.*[1]

Testimony, proof, and method were, however, the rhetoric of the movement, not its core. There remained one overriding factor which captured their imaginations and carried conviction. Mesmerism was only a means to an end: it was an engine to create a perfect society.

In the prospectus of the *Zoist* there is a marked Comtean strain. Most men, it says, rest content with the first principles and leading facts of any science, but a mere array of facts cannot give men "the least idea of the power of the mighty engine they possess to push them onward in the race of human improvement". What they must do is to study the science which will compel them to study themselves, to learn its philosophy, its regenerating powers, its practical application to the affairs of men and society, "in fact to all that appertains to humanity". Mesmerism presents the only avenue through which the intricate phenomena of the nervous system and of life can be revealed. A few years

diary magistrate, and many others, both gentlemen and ladies. . . ." *Neurypnology*, p. 137.

[1] i, 367–85 (December 1843), ii, 186–88 (July, 1844), 316–25 (October, 1844). Sir Henry Holland, the eminent physician, noted as a major change in his lifetime the boldness of modern scientific hypotheses, but with it an increasing insistence on rigorous proof. *Recollections of Past Life*, pp. 260–64.

earlier it would have been considered madness to conjecture the lessening of pain; yet it was done—and for beneficent purposes. Now, let what is probable concerning the higher phenomena be established, that is,

> that this state of increased activity can be rendered permanent and carried into the natural state, and who does not catch a glance of a mighty engine for man's regeneration, vast in its power and unlimited in its application, rivalling in morals the effects of steam in mechanics.

The path will be rough, but

> they look for their reward in the plentiful harvests of the future, rather than in the reapings and gleanings of the present or the past. "Glorious, heroic, fruitful for his own Time and for all Time and all Eternity, is the constant speaker and doer of Truth." The assertor of truth may be crushed and we may breathe a sigh over the martyr as he passes from the field of his labours,—ignorance and prejudice may for a time reign triumphant, and the abettors of sloth and selfishness be considered the great, the good, and the wise,—but Time rolls on, and Reason will assert her dominion.[1]

Elliotson, in his appeal for the study of mesmerism, was similarly visionary:

> Let us never forget these things: never allow authority, conceit, habit, or the fear of ridicule, to make us indifferent, much less to make us hostile, to truth: and thus, being single-hearted lovers of truth, and prizing it above everything else, we shall all love one another.[2]

The mesmerists had hold of a partial truth. Their plea for the investigation of phenomena was admirable, but by conducting their investigations in a questionable manner, they may well have postponed the limited results they had a right to demand. They were not men who could brook limitation or sit patiently and wait. When so much had been done, so much more remained to do. In their activity they espoused many good causes: national education, prison reform, a new treatment of the insane, rational hygiene, among others; all of these subserved the new society. But was it science they preached, or something old in the trappings of science? Turning to a slovenly account of clairvoyance by William Newnham, Dr. Estlin found the fatal weakness:

> The story is mentioned incidentally by Mr. Newnham as nothing

[1] *Zoist*, i, 1–4.

[2] *The Harveian Oration*, p. 66. Miss Martineau comments on the oration in *People's Journal*, ii, 52 (July 25, 1846).

> out of the common, and he simply asks in reference to it, *What good* can arise from producing these effects of mesmerism? Others would be more disposed to ask, What *truth* there was in such a marvellous narrative? Mr. Newnham, as a philosopher, has no right to dismiss such a case with a "cui bono". It is either all true or all false.[1]

But to radicals in a sea of change, unexampled and uncharted, *cui bono* was ship, chart, rudder, and anchor. Without its security, they might have foundered and gone down.

Having said so much about a group of devoted mesmerists, it is hardly necessary to go into detail to demonstrate why Miss Martineau should have given them her allegiance. In 1830, apparently at James's suggestion, Harriet's head was "read" by a phrenologist. The results were dismissed as absurdities, but two years later, she and the celebrated Indian visitor, Rajah Rammohun Roy, were studying phrenology together. Still, her remarks about Spurzheim's American tour, which touched off the craze for phrenology there, were mildly amused and sceptical, and the other pseudo-sciences were treated similarly.[2] A phrenological lecturer, she wrote, could captivate Boston, but before five years have gone, he "will find himself superseded by some professor of animal magnetism, some preacher of homeopathy, some teacher who will undertake to analyse children, prove to them that their spirits made their bodies and elicit from them truths fresh from heaven." [3]

Her conversion to phreno-mesmerism dates precisely from the outburst of mesmeric enthusiasm in Britain in the late thirties. She met Elliotson at dinner at the Macreadys, and of course she must have followed the affair at University College closely, with remarks about the Faculty which one can easily imagine. Then came the experience of friends. Among Elliotson's principal supporters were Sir Isaac and Lady Goldsmid; their governess, Miss Rankin, was a cousin and close friend of Miss Martineau's and accompanied her and Mrs. Reid on the continental trip in 1839. Being ill, Miss Rankin was mesmerized without effect; then, leaving her companions in Switzerland, she went under Elliotson's instructions to Paris, where a mesmeric patient dictated

[1] *Mesmerism in 1845*, pp. 13–14.

[2] HM to James, May 5, 1830, March 2, 1832. John D. Davies, *Phrenology, Fad and Science*, deals with the American crusade and has provided some suggestive parallels for this entire section.

[3] *RWT*, ii, 188–89.

remedies; and after five months in the Goldsmids' house, she was cured. The Goldsmids denied any medical interference in the case at all.[1] The apparent cure must have impressed Miss Martineau, by this time herself an invalid, very deeply. And with the growing excitement about the subject which came into her room with nearly every visitor,[2] by 1843 she was ready to proclaim her conviction. How could mesmerism be revived again and again, she asked, unless there were something in it? Whatever the quackery and imposture, "it seems impossible but that some new insight must be obtained by its means, into the powers of our mysterious frame. . . ." And she included in her blessing the water-cure and homeopathy.

> Are we not growing sensibly more merciful, more wisely human towards empirics themselves, when they cease to be our oracles? Are we not learning, from their jumbled discoveries and failures, that empiricism itself is a social function, indispensable, made so by God, however ready we may be to bestow our cheap laughter upon it? To us retired observers of life there is too much of this easy mockery for our taste, or for the morals of society.[3]

She was prepared to love the mesmerists for the enemies they had made. It was surely her Norwich manufacturing background (her uncle and brother notwithstanding) that led her to write in 1861 of the contempt shown to the commercial occupations by the professional classes. She had fought vested interests with political economy and was to fight them again. As a dissenter, she needed no prodding to believe in the obstructionism of the clergy, and her distrust of the medical profession has already been referred to. The mistaken kindness to which they were given meant that one must cross-question a physician "and hold him to it till he has told us all". It is interesting that her article in 1834 on Salem witchcraft centred on professional obscurantism and the pious fraud so abhorrent to her: a physician first suggested witchcraft in Salem and the clergy took up the cry.[4]

[1] Crabb Robinson Diary, November 19, 1844, DWL.

[2] Cf. Anna Jameson, *Letters and Friendships*, p. 213.

[3] *Life in the Sickroom*, pp. 82–85. Cf. the opening of ch. 6, book 2, of *Zanoni*, where Bulwer-Lytton wonders whether the marvels of alchemy and mysticism might not lead to more noble discoveries.

[4] *Once a Week*, August 17, 1861. *A Tale of the Tyne* and *Sowers not Reapers* in *Illustrations of Political Economy*. *Hist.*, *passim*, e.g., ii, 185. "Letter to the Deaf", *Misc.*, i, 252. The witchcraft article is in *Misc.*, ii, 396.

The same obscurantism she could still find in her own time:

> When scientific men, and those whose profession pledges them to the pursuit of physiological science, are open-minded and earnest enough to admit and study mysterious facts which occur before their eyes, popular fanaticism about sorcery and inspiration may give way; but, till this happens, not even the widest spread of popular education will give more than a check to the cruel follies of superstition.[1]

To her, the scientific claims of mesmerism, the insistence that its phenomena were fragments of an undiscovered general law of nature, and the elaborate folderol of her friends Atkinson and Gregory, were part of its attraction and the burden of its proof. It was not empiricism now, but science.[2]

By the same token she was appalled by the widespread enthusiasm for and belief in spiritualism. In 1834 she had written of Salem witchcraft as a tragedy arising from ignorance and pious fraud, chiefly of the clergy. In 1868, without remembering that she had written a review of an earlier book by the same author, she came out of retirement to write an intense and urgent article on the same subject. This time the relevance of the episode was directed (in Comtean terms) to the nineteenth-century form of the tendency to ascribe one's own consciousness to external objects. The spiritualist circles of the eighteen-sixties were to her precisely the same as the gatherings in Mr. Parrish's parlour in Salem, and with so much less excuse.

> We are very far from true explanations—i.e. being able to refer facts to natural causes, but we know that for all facts there *is* a natural cause and that those causes are bound to become known to us. Moreover, in this instance we are on the right track as the physiologists and psychologists discover more and more. The multitude may be deluded with Spiritualist marvels, but the scientific physiologists are proceeding, by observation and experiment, to penetrate more and more secrets of our intellectual and moral life.[3]

What she has to say about the state of psychology and, even more, what she has to say about a proper scientific attitude is

[1] *Hist.*, i, 408. Cf. her comments on the rejection of Esdaile's work, *EL*, p. 235.

[2] Compare, *SA*, i, 184 and 294–95, on American empiricism, with her comments on Hallam's belief in mesmerism, *Biog. Sketches*, pp. 81–82.

[3] "Salem Witchcraft", *ER*, vol. 128, pp. 41–47 (July, 1868). Cf. the classification of opposition in *Zoist*, iv, 435–41 (January, 1847). For the reminiscence of Elliotson, see above, pp. 55–56. Also on spiritualism, see HM's opinion in *ASS*, May 29, 1860, and a letter to Mary Carpenter, April 17, 1866, *Auto.*, ii, 531.

remarkably wise, just as what she had had to say in the twenties about the art of thinking was wise. Yet neither Miss Martineau nor her mesmeric associates followed out her injunctions. In her early writings, she cautioned against taking too simple a view in cause and effect analysis, against jumping to conclusions, against remaining wedded to conclusions which might be disproved by one exception, in short, she warned against *post hoc* argument.[1] But while this warning might be thrown at the medical critics of mesmerism, it was not applied to her own faith in mesmerism. She sounds like Hume, but when he drew close to her dearest beliefs, she drew back—his analysis of miracles was irrelevant. To begin with, she rejected the very notion of miracles, assuming that everything could be explained by natural law. But for natural events, one could rely, had to rely, on qualified testimony. On the testimony of one man she would not believe that ice when heated retained its solidity; but if five men of "science, sagacity, caution, and integrity" declared the fact, she would believe them.

> It may easily be admitted that a case of false individual testimony might occur which should be wholly unaccountable to us; but when a number of men (say five or ten) qualified to bear testimony, and acting under an ascertained system of motives, (as the apostles in the promulgation of Christianity,) agree in asserting facts which we should have previously supposed impossible, the probability is that unknown physical causes operated in one instance, rather than unknown moral causes in five or ten.[2]

The question was who had the science, sagacity, caution, and integrity? Fifteen years later her passionate belief in mesmerism relied on the qualifications to bear testimony of Atkinson, Mrs. Wynyard, and Jane Arrowsmith, along with a host of other amateurs; while the reasonable objections of the professional judges were stormed at and rejected. Miss Barrett put it very well, referring to Jane's prediction in trance of the safe return of the crew of a wrecked ship:

> The "Athenaeum" has done quite enough to *disprove the proving* of the wreck story, and no more at all. The disproving of the proof of the wreck story is indeed enough to disprove the wreck story and to disprove mesmerism itself (as far as the proof of mesmerism depends on the proof of the wreck story, and no farther) with all doubters and undetermined inquirers; but with the very large class

[1] *Misc.*, i, 82–83.

[2] *Misc.*, ii, 190–92.

> of previous *believers*, this disproof of a proof is a mere accident, and cannot be expected to have much logical consequence. Believing that such things may be as this revelation of a wreck, they naturally are less exacting of the stabilities of the proving process. What we think probable we do not call severely for the proof of. Moreover, Miss Martineau is not only a believer in the mysteries of mesmerism . . . but she is a believer in the personal integrity of her witnesses. She has what she has well called a "communicable confidence". And this, however incommunicable, is sufficiently comprehensible to all persons who know what personal faith is, to place her "honour", I do maintain, high above any suspicion, any charge with the breath of man's lips.[1]

Harriet Martineau believed that she was cured by mesmerism alone; that was the most obvious reinforcement of her belief in the new science. She had found release, indeed almost ecstasy, in submitting herself to the will of a powerful woman like Mrs. Wynyard or to the transparent innocence of her maid or to Jane, that plain, clumsy girl "who now might have passed for Ly Hamilton, or the Madonna . . . with a cushion which she treated as a baby." [2] She could not in consequence deny them their prerogatives. But, at bottom, we are dealing with a religious faith which has borrowed the trappings of science. She assured Mrs. Jameson that the subject was very serious and solemn to her and always had been, for she saw in mesmerism "an agency by which human transactions will be as extensively modified in the future as outward modes of living will be by such discoveries as Faraday's." [3] Through its insights and predictions, and I think one dare add its means of control, the perfection of man and society could be attained. It could not be done by piece-meal reforms. An administrative reformer like Huskisson might open his hand a finger at a time; this was excusable if not wise. But the moral reformer could find no room for compromise; he had to commit himself completely.[4]

In fully committing herself she found an intensification of her earlier convictions. She hoped, she told Bulwer-Lytton, that one day men might penetrate into the life of brute animals; mesmerism seemed to offer a way to do it—she mesmerized at different times a cow and a bear—and "who shall say what analogical instruction may not arise as to the life above us. . . ?" [5] Under

[1] To Mr. Chorley, April 28, 1845, *Letters*, i, 255–57.
[2] Lord Morpeth's Diary, January 4, 1845.
[3] Anna Jameson, *Memoirs*, p. 208.
[4] "George Combe", *Biog. Sketches*, pp. 142–44.
[5] January 26, [1844]; before the mesmerizing began.

Mrs. Wynyard or even more the remarkable double mesmerizing tried by W. R. Greg in Ambleside, she thought she saw into the ultimate state and penetrated to the very laws of life, pouring out her visions in beautiful rhapsodies which Crabb Robinson said would have forced Wordsworth into a dilemma—she had either preternatural powers or a poetic gift no one had suspected. But he saw rightly that it was akin to the delirium of liquor or fever, and Lord Morpeth, a convinced believer in mesmerism, thought what she said only "a highly-wrought reflex of her ordinary turn of thought".[1]

What did she see in these states? She repeatedly described the crushing and amputation of her left arm—her childhood friend and martyrdom, if nothing more. She talked a great deal about suffering, about pressing ahead without stopping for it. "You can see further from a prison cell than the top of a mountain." "Look at the shadow of a birch tree on a sunny lawn, you can hardly separate the light & the shade; mix them together, & you would only leave it all grey; it is much better to have both the light & the shade." In other words, precisely what she had been meditating about in Tynemouth—"the universal human lot is, after all, that of the highest privilege". Or again, she saw the march of the whole human race, from the beginning and extended into the future, and their finding the source of life. Another time she saw all the idolatries of the world worshipping at an ascending series of connected "life-fountains", each flowing into the one below, so that, in actuality, all men were adoring the single source. It was what she had imagined in 1831, in her essay for Mohammedans. The Moslem says to the Christian that men collect water from many places, but it is all water and it quenches the thirst of everyone. "The time may come when we shall see the abyss whence it flows in so many forms, and know that there is but one source, and that it is dispensed by one hand over all the earth.—Thus is it with the truth of God." "Even so," replies the Christian, "and thus it shall be at length with the love which cannot but spring out of this truth. Then men shall not reproach one another as infidels, or refuse to worship side by side." [2] Her visions were all old. They summed up rhap-

[1] Crabb Robinson's Travel Journal, January 4, 1846. Lord Morpeth's Diary, July 22, 1845.

[2] Lord Morpeth's Diary, July 22, 1845. HM to Milnes, October 27, [1844], and February 22, [1845]. *The Faith as Unfolded by Many Prophets*, pp. 6–7. "Opacity ceases, the one great Agent will swallow up all others—all others dissolve into this

sodically her childhood fantasies, her Priestleyan optimism, her sense of suffering, and point the way as well to the frankly syncretic position of *Eastern Life*.

Yet mesmerism meant more than personal morality to her, more than cloudy metaphysics. It must have been a thrilling and uplifting experience for her when she read the first volume of the *Zoist*. Elliotson and his friends left no doubt about where they stood; phreno-mesmerism was unequivocally radical. They rejected the separate existence of mind, as Priestley had taught her to do. To mesmerists of this school, the belief in mind was "an exemplification of the tendency in uncultivated man to personify all the actions of nature . . . a barbarous recognition of the manifestations of a property resulting from a peculiar molecular arrangement of matter, and which arrangement *necessitates* the exhibition of the property". This conviction recalls Priestley and (for her) anticipates Comte. The phreno-magnetists were materialists; they were also necessarians. In that belief, they called for a national movement of reform and regeneration, to assert the moral and intellectual supremacy of man. Their philosophy offered a new view of criminology and saw in national education the instrumentality to the remodelling of society. It was a philosophy necessarily opposed to the principles and practices of all governments and to almost all laws and institutions. Above all, it was a philosophy whose adherents stood on principle and proclaimed the truth, whatever they might suffer. Anti-clericalism, scientific method, materialism, necessarianism, radicalism, education, humanity, and martyrdom—every major concern of Harriet Martineau's life was caught up in this new crusade. It was the penultimate step to positivism.

one. Now it comes clearer.—Oh, when can we get the true flow of mind into mind! . . . Time was not created for us, but we are created to suit it—but what relation the future bears to us I cannot solve. The great thing wanted is a collision of spirits:—if we could bring mind to bear upon mind in the mesmeric state—that will come, & then time & space will not divide us; we shall stretch out from pole to pole. Now we are like a dispersed multitude, wandering without a home. We shall invent new laws of being; or at any rate discover those which already exist. One agency wh we now think much of will be as nothing. Agency beyond agency, each modifying the other,—higher & yet higher state. The old polytheism was beautiful—God rising above God—but the worship of the heroes, of the Good, all presented to us with faces radiant, will be far finer. We admire our earthly sunset, where the horizon melts into the clouds & the glorious effulgence lightens both; but such a sunset is as nothing compared to what I see now,—men dissolved into a new state—powers exercised we know not of now; not newly conferred but newly developed—development is our work." (From a transcription in Caroline Bray's commonplace book, Coventry Public Library.)

CHAPTER IX

Ambleside: The Compleat Laker

ONCE her recovery seemed assured, Miss Martineau began to travel, partly to see members of her family, partly to get away from the stultification (and the treelessness) of Tynemouth. She was invited to spend some time on Windermere by Mr. and Mrs. W. R. Greg; Greg, the Manchester manufacturer whose article on labour she so admired, was an early believer in mesmerism. But once she had taken rooms in a house at the head of the lake, it was not long until she decided to settle. After some attempts at househunting, she realized that it would be more practical to build a house. She bought and rounded out a piece of land, which had belonged to an unsuccessful dissenting minister, and engaged a builder for £500 on condition that he break through local custom and pay his men weekly. Whether it was this aspect of her dealings or sheer force of personality, the local residents were amazed at the speed with which the house went up; with the walls roof high in a week, commented Mrs. Wordsworth, Miss Martineau must have mesmerized her workmen.[1]

She quickly became the "compleat Laker". That lovely area had no stouter advocate—she wrote a best-selling guidebook—yet few could have so completely subdued the district to their own patterns. In her autobiography she dealt shortly with the friends who had received her decision to live in the country with incredulity and headshaking. No woman, married or single, she said, can be happy without a domestic life, without being responsible for someone's happiness. At Ambleside she could have her idea of an innocent and happy life—pure air, a garden,

[1] Mrs. Wordsworth to Crabb Robinson, September 16, 1845. The account of the housebuilding in the *Autobiography* is very pleasant. And I cannot resist a remark of Miss Barrett's: "I wish I had the least news to tell you in the world, but none comes near me—except that I heard of the digging of the foundations of Miss Martineau's cottage the other day, and of her descanting on Magnetism without any foundations at all." *Barrett-Mitford*, September 1845, p. 258.

leisure, solitude when she wanted it, freedom to work in quiet, superb natural scenery and, most significantly, young servants whom she could train and attach to herself, and poor, improvable neighbours. If there was anything she liked better than writing, it was running a house—making and mending clothes, making preserves, gingerbread, and custards, cleaning pictures, and the like. She did her gardening herself—"I can't afford to pay gardeners, at rail road rates"—and used her money to provide the planting, although on her walks she kept an eye out for plants that might be transferred to her terrace. In time she imported a Norfolk man and his wife to run her little farm—she wrote a book about that too—and they lived in a stone cottage at the bottom of her two acres.[1] It is still a pleasant place to wander about, even in its present unimaginative (if appropriate) use as a school by proprietors who do not seem quite to realize what they own.

The unwritten law of the Lakes, she said, was never to work unless the weather was bad; and, although that ungrateful district could, under such a canon, be conducive at times to phenomenal amounts of labour, it could also be wonderfully enticing. Miss Martineau's guide to the district was not written from her study, but from her hiking and climbing.[2] Like all the Lakers, she was a target (a willing one) for guests, and, once her working periods were over, the guests were led a merry chase. Nephews, nieces, writers, actors, commissioners, and politicians were introduced to the most distinguished neighbours, put to planting trees in commemoration of their visits, and herded over fell and down dale. Seymour Tremenheere, the inspector, turned the first spade of earth for her house and was introduced to Wordsworth. Macready was taken for walks and views and continual conversation—and strained his back planting a couple of oaks. Invariably visitors had a good time: the house was charming, they were astonished at her brown-complexioned health and remarkable energy, while over all there lay the spirit of their hostess—"the

[1] *Auto.*, i, 497–98. HM to Elizabeth Barrett, February 8, [1846], Yale; HM to Crabb Robinson, May 21, [1846], DWL.

[2] When she became an invalid again, she relied on her niece Maria for information for later editions. "She will take an infinity of little excursions, to gather up the latest views of things. Her sister, Susan, who arrives today, will be her companion for half, & her brother Frank by & by for the other half. *She* does it for my credit, as to the 'Guide': but *I* promote it as holiday for her, & I am sure she enjoys the idea of it." To Florence Nightingale, June 25, 1860, BM.

tonic in the shape of Harriet Martineau", wrote George Eliot, "with her simple, energetic life, her Building Society, her winter Lectures and her cordial interest in all human beings".[1]

Mrs. Wordsworth called her new neighbour "a model of household economy", making her servants happy and setting an example of activity to others. Jane, who had relapsed into blindness after Miss Martineau's departure from Tynemouth, was brought as a cook and maid; eventually she emigrated to Australia. Martha, another servant, married the master of the Bristol Ragged School. There was a succession of girls in this pleasant, immensely competent establishment, and except for one who came highly recommended from Birmingham only to go "melancholy mad", all were happy, all fervently loyal. Then there were the remarkable nieces. Jane and Harriet, who stayed with their aunt in the sixties, paled only when compared to the incomparable Maria who served as secretary and protector, confidante and friend through most of Miss Martineau's Ambleside days. From Maria's death in 1864, she never really recovered. At The Knoll, Miss Martineau created the ties of affection that she wanted to create—through kindness, benevolence, and the good humour which kept the young people flocking there. But she taught too. During the Crimean War she was much concerned, as she had been forty years before, to explain the news to the servants, "to give these intelligent girls an interest in the interests of freedom, and a clear knowledge of the position and duties of England in regard to the war".[2]

The forties were the period of the emergence of the Lakes into their modern function; the "rash assault" of the railway on Windermere brought, besides an indignant sonnet from Wordsworth, floods of tourists from towns to the south, now that Liverpool was only four hours and a short omnibus ride away. At the height of the tourist season, the only thing to do was to let the house and flee to Birmingham, to Mrs. Turner's near Nottingham, to a farm house near Bolton, or to London. But, in a way, Harriet Martineau was herself a "rash assault". Everyone in the

[1] Letters and comments to and from visitors make pleasant reading. E.g., HM to Emerson, July 2, 1845, November 5 and 13, 1847, February 25, 1852, Harvard. George Eliot to Charles Bray, September 18, 1852, and to Bessie Parks, October 30, 1852, *George Eliot Letters*, ii, 56, 64–65. Macready, *Diaries*, ii, 330–31.

[2] *Auto.*, i, 60. Her article on "Modern Domestic Service", *ER*, vol. 115, pp. 409–30 (April, 1862) indicates her attitudes towards servants and her views on running a household.

district very soon realized that a phenomenon was in their midst. Her activity created something of a stir—not only the benevolence and the activity, but the regimen. She rose at six, Crabb Robinson reported, walked out by moonlight, bathed and finished breakfast by half past seven, then went to work at her writing until two. That must be the germ of one of the local legends about her moonlight bathing. The cigar or cigarette-smoking of her later years added to the legend.[1] I have already cited the case of the bull, a token of her war with the squire. And the war with the parson was never-ending. She told Reeve that he protested against races, and in reply the young gentlemen, or the Squire, would ask him for a subscription to improve the breed.

> Meanwhile, the "worky" sort sneer at his zeal, saying that he, with his vast house, & his dozen servants, & carriages, & capital cook, has every luxury in life that he cares for, while he wants to deprive them of their evening beer & pipe, and their annual race. What a novel one might write from 20 years' observation of a place like this,—its Church & its churchyard,—its mushroom squire & helpless parson,—its feudal Flemings, buried in the old park, & its bran-new millionaire Wrigley, flaring out by the lake side,—its prim, prudish, pattern Quaker lady picked up drunk in the road, & its Dr. Davy, J.P. offering blows to the old squire on the bench,—& with all the tragedy & comedy of humble life, wherein the "antique statesmen" are rotting out, & the primitive labourers speak out their notions of new-fangled people & ways! A retreat like this is a far better post for the study of life than any home in a town; & the consistent unrolling of the scroll, from day to day, & from year to year, has an almost too strong interest for me. The Suicides alone, since I settled here 20 years ago, have been more than I took any note of in my whole life before.—But Westmoreland heads the list of all the counties in the United Kingdom for suicides,—from one census to another.[2]

Here was a woman with her free-thought and building societies and an extraordinary knowledge of what went on, but who was always withdrawn and a little mysterious. When the wife of one of her "desperately evangelical" Kendal bankers asked W. E. Forster if Miss Martineau was saving her soul, he, recalling Wilberforce's remark about Clarkson, replied, "O, dear! she is

[1] Crabb Robinson to Thomas Robinson, December 31, 1847. "Still using the solace of 'the labouring classes', about wh you used to quiz me when I came from the East. But don't tell, of course." HM to Monckton Milnes, May 8, 1862. BPL, Weston, v, no. 111, contains Mrs. Chapman's notes on her smoking.

[2] October 18, 1866.

far too busy doing good to think about her own soul, or anybody else's"—an answer which did little to relieve the good lady's perplexity and which probably sent her back to more careful study of Miss Martineau's cheques to find out what she was up to.[1]

Although Miss Martineau kept aloof from ordinary Ambleside society, she became very much a part of the little group of intellectuals who lived there—that "flower garden of ladies", in which Miss Mitford detected a lamentable want of the "manly intellect and manly spirit" so indispensable in the country. This little society revolved around two poles: the Arnolds' house at Fox How was the headquarters of Whiggery, the Wordsworths' at Rydal Mount the seat of high church Toryism. The Arnold ladies were particularly close to her, and, while Matthew Arnold had strong reservations about his famous neighbour, he wrote a poem about her, sent her messages, and once commented amusedly that he had been talking "to Miss Martineau (who blasphemes frightfully) about the prospects of the Church of England, and, wretched man that I am, promised to go and see her cow-keeping miracles tomorrow—I, who hardly know a cow from a sheep". Miss Fenwick and Mrs. Davy were the principal ladies satellite to this household, and except for Miss Martineau's loudly expressed admiration for Peel, all tended to go well.

The Rydal Mount household posed more of a problem—one which they anticipated with some uneasiness—though in the event things worked out beautifully. Wordsworth was so intolerant, said Crabb Robinson, that only Miss Martineau's tolerance made intercourse possible. Maynooth, the Dissenters' Chapels Bill, America, slavery, Texas, and repudiation were all forbidden subjects at the Mount, but at least the two agreed on the publication of letters, and they agreed in not being Arnoldite, though "precisely what the one prizes & tolerates is what the other tolerates & prizes". Edward Quillinan, Wordworth's son-in-law, found her manner so pleasing and friendly that "if I disliked some portions of her writings ten times more than I do I could not help liking *her*". But Mrs. Wordsworth felt differently, at least by 1851. When Miss Martineau returned home that year from one of her jaunts to the South and announced that she would call at Rydal Mount, Mrs. Wordsworth went out of doors every day after two o'clock (when it was not raining) to

[1] HM to Reeve, October 18, 1859.

avoid her. "She is a pest," exclaimed the poet's widow, but I suspect that Miss Martineau's determination won out.

Her closest friend, at first, was W. R. Greg, thanks to mesmerism and their common radicalism. But the Gregs—Mrs. Greg finally hopelessly insane—moved away, and in time Miss Martineau found his attitudes on slavery, politics, and women repulsive. Wordsworth died in 1850; others died or moved away. When, after 1855, Miss Martineau no longer went out, for fear that she would drop dead in the street, she saw little of her neighbours. James Payn used to visit, and of course there were visitors from outside the district; but even they were restricted in the sixties, and the Arnolds were almost the only local residents who could see her.[1]

Mesmerism was the chief awkwardness. Tolerant of unbelievers, she nevertheless lectured everyone in sight, with wonderful disregard for tender susceptibilities; Mrs. Wordsworth, for instance, was made very uneasy by her insistence that the "miracles" of the mesmerists were as great as those of Christ and the apostles. Amid rumours that she had relapsed into illness or had given up mesmerism, she held steadily to the faith and tried to make her contributions. For a time she was an active practitioner, her lodgings strewn with sleepers to whom she was giving relief. Mrs. Wynyard came briefly, then disappeared forever, replaced as a force in Miss Martineau's life by Henry Atkinson himself. Professor Gregory of Edinburgh wrote to introduce himself and came to visit. Greg lived nearby. With "these three Magi" as operators and Jane and herself as subjects, she was sure they would "pick up something in the Reichenbach track". And she wrote in great excitement to the *Zoist* about her success in curing her cow Ailsie. It proved, she wrote, the nonsense of saying that the results of mesmerism were "all imagination", for, fond as she was of her cow, she could scarcely boast of Ailsie's imaginative faculty. When the local cow-doctor learned of the treatment, he was furious and used some forms of abuse she had heard before.

It is a striking instance of the likeness of human nature everywhere,

[1] M. R. Mitford to Boner, February–March, 1846, *Correspondence*, pp. 48–49. Crabb Robinson to Thomas Robinson, January 16 and 24, 1845, December 29, 1848; to Miss Fenwick, July 16, 1845; Quillinan to Crabb Robinson, July 30, 1846, August 17, 1849. Mrs. Wordsworth to the Thomas Hutchinsons, October 11, 1851, *Letters of Mary Wordsworth*, p. 334. Arnold to Miss Wightman, [December, 1850], *Letters*, i, 15. Her review of Greg's *Essays* in *DN*, January 27, 1853, indicates her mixed feelings.

in similar circumstances of stimulus or temptation. I should be glad if any medical man should be struck with this, and (if he deserves the mortification) should see himself reflected in the case of this cow-doctor. The cow-doctor's case is the baldest, because he is cut off from the commonest resort of the opponents of mesmerism,—imputation upon the patient. He cannot say that the cow is an impostor; so he gives us the plain truth, declares his rage to be because we think there is something better than his craft. As he cannot blame his patient, he quarrels with nature and those who study nature and use her benefits. I am sorry for the poor man's passion: but we are obliged to him for thus making himself a mirror of professional nature.[1]

She was deadly serious.

Miss Martineau presented much less of a problem to her poorer neighbours, although at times their looks of gratitude must have been mildly stunned. She liked, she said, a little talk on Sundays with the gardener or workmen or cowherd's wife on their notions of the proper treatment for body and mind, and of right and wrong in morals.[2] But, whatever their response, she was immensely concerned about them and knew what she was talking about. Wordsworth amazed her.

I, deaf, can hardly conceive how he, with eyes & ears, & a heart wh leads him to converse with the poor in his incessant walks, can be so unaware of their moral state. I dare say you need not be told how sensual vice abounds in rural districts. Here it is flagrant beyond any thing I ever cd have looked for: & here, while every justice of the peace is filled with disgust, & every clergy[n] with (almost) despair at the drunkenness, quarrelling, & extreme licentiousness with women,—here is dear good old Wordsworth for ever talking of rural innocence, & deprecating any intercourse with towns, lest the purity of his neighbours should be corrupted. He little knows what elevation, self denial & refinement occur in towns from the superior cultivation of the people. The virtues of the people here are also of a sort different, we think, from what he supposes. The people are very industrious, thrifty, prudent, & so well off as to be liberal in their dealings. They pride themselves

---

[1] *Zoist*, viii, 300–3, 333–34 (October, 1850, January 1851). Elizabeth Barrett to Miss Mitford, December 8, 1847, to Mrs. Jameson, December 1847, *Letters*, i, 352–53, 355. *Zoist*, iv, 276–77 [July, 1846]. *Browning Letters*, i, 112. HM to Elizabeth Barrett, February 8, [1846], Yale. Crabb Robinson to Thomas Robinson, January 24, December 25, 1845, January 8, 1846; Travel Journals, December 31, 1845, January 4, 1846; Diary, June 13, 1847. Mrs. Fletcher to Crabb Robinson, February 25, 1845; Wordsworth to Crabb Robinson, August 7, 1845; Mrs. Wordsworth to Crabb Robinson, May 20, 1846; HM to Crabb Robinson, May 21, [1846]. HM to R. D. Webb, September 22, [1845], BPL. HM to Lord Morpeth, July 4 and August 1, [1845], March 4, [1846].

[2] *Letters*, p. 4.

on doing their work capitally; & in this point of honour they are exemplary.[1]

She knew too about their medical superstition, about the quacks and the bone-setters, about their filth and utter innocence of hygiene. Yet, for all their ignorance, they were so much more persuadable than the gentry—"the same credulity wh makes them the prey of quacks makes them docile to us." [2]

The usual kind of philanthropy would simply not do. The upper classes were generous with visiting, baskets, prayers, and reproof; but they did not go very far. She reported in amusement to Reeve that Grace Davy had offered to sing a hymn to a sick old woman who later complained of the infliction to the doctor, objecting that the young lady had never paid her for it after all. The important thing was "to cut off the sources of disease, sin and misery by a purer method of living".[3] Ordinary generosity and kindliness the poor certainly experienced from her: as soon as she was in her new house, she gave a "bun-and-tea festivity" to the boys and girls of the Methodist Chapel; and on Christmas day there was always open house in the kitchen, "full of odds & ends of people, from 80 years down to 1, with a vast dinner, tea & supper, & such amusement as we can devise".[4] But her two great projects were vastly more important and useful.

One was a housing scheme, organized in her kitchen, in imitation of similar plans at Birmingham and elsewhere, whereby families paid into a common fund added to subscribed capital, which in this case came from Mrs. Reid, among others. A piece of ground was bought in 1848 and ultimately fifteen cottages were erected. Even to this scheme there was objection. Her

[1] HM to Elizabeth Barrett, February 8, [1846], Yale. She reports that when Wordsworth died, one of his rude neighbours, proud of the poet and devoted to his widow, said of Mrs. Wordsworth: "She's a gay [fine] clever body, who will carry on the business as well as any of 'em." HM to Reeve, March 14, 1859.

[2] There is an excellent long letter on this subject to Florence Nightingale, June 25, 1860, BM. The good sense of these letters makes an extraordinary contrast with her own medical distrust and gullibility.

[3] *Auto.*, ii, 8. HM to Reeve, March 14, 1859. She and Maria made their educational efforts very practical. Maria went about teaching the use of the sewing-machine, and whenever anything went wrong—usually when the machine stopped for want of cleaning—they sent for her at once. The sewing-machine agent was so impressed that he sent Miss Martineau a £20 machine to replace the £10 machine she had. HM to Reeve, July 10, 1863. Cf. her views on the proper kind of beneficence, *Once a Week*, viii, 397–401 (April 4, 1863).

[4] E. Quillinan to Crabb Robinson, July 30, 1846. HM to Reeve, December 25, 1861.

agent in the land negotiation refused to have the land remeasured and finally admitted that he did so to avoid arousing the suspicions of the parson, who, if he knew that cottages were to be built near him, would at once raise the price and buy up the land. Another objection was that building good cottages would attract people from outside to live in them and so drive down the price of labour. There was disagreement in her governing board —possibly treachery. And there were the usual difficulties brought on by the death or emigration of prospective cottagers. On the whole, however, the scheme was a success, though the cottages were occupied by fewer working-men than she had hoped. Finally in 1864, after Maria's death, to avoid overburdening Jenny, she sold the land and cottages to a "humane and honourable man", who was proud of his cottages and their "choice tenants". They were choice tenants by design. In a most interesting letter she turned down an intercession on behalf of a doubtful case:

> You see, it is all-important to the welfare of Ellerrigg that only unexceptionable tenants shd go. Suppose Ewington's family shd come down because I put some doubtful people next them! What a pity that wd be! And I don't wish to begin with tenants so doubtful that they have to pay their rent weekly. However, there is nothing in that.—But as you say, the whole thing must be a mere matter of trial; & it is a very serious sort of trial in the case of house-transactions, as it is impossible to get people out of a house, unless they choose to go;—that is, without taking the roof off, as we see done in Ireland, & as I by no means desire to see done in Ellerrigg.—I fear I must say, "No", unless the poor man can offer some security for his rent, & some good testimony to the respectability of himself & family.[1]

The housing scheme, then, could work in only a few cases directly, and to some extent by example. It was otherwise with her lectures. She wanted to do for the children of Ambleside what Lant Carpenter had done for her image of the Holy Land when she was a child—to show them that a "sort of fairy land was a real and substantial part of our everyday earth". The first lecture was given to the pupils of the National School, but when the parson's wife objected that a dissenter appearing in

[1] HM to Jane Claude, August 21, [1852], London School of Economics, Letter Collection I, 41. Crabb Robinson's Travel Journals, December 31, 1848; Diary, December 18, 1851. HM to Kingsley, November 16 [1848], NYPL. HM to Reeve, May 6, 1864. *Auto.*, ii, 8–9.

the school caused discontent in the parish, the series was transferred to the Methodist Chapel. When she was petitioned to lecture to the older people, she expanded the scheme and gave a series of lectures, to a working-class audience, every winter but two from 1848 to 1854. The course on the Holy Land was followed by one on sanitary matters, partly as an encouragement to the building scheme, but as well to point out the virtues of temperance and cleanliness. Another series covered the history of England, still another the history of the United States to the death of Washington, and in 1854 she lectured on Russia and the war. Her illness put a stop to the lectures and to a project dear to her—a course on the modern history of the United States "with a special view to recommend the Anti-Slavery cause".

Clearly it was history (or hygiene) with a purpose. She was delighted to see the boys, men, and women "devouring good King Alfred", and getting some notion of what a serious affair a parliament is. Naturally, in talking about the housing scheme, she made no reference "to the form of tyranny exercised by the owners of land and houses". "My business was to preclude the tyranny, by showing the people that their own interests were in their own hands, and by no means to excite angry feelings about grievances which I hoped to mitigate, or even extinguish." It was radicalism in action, no doubt about that, and a fine example of "informal education" too. "My object," she said, "was to give rational amusement to men whom all circumstances seemed to drive to the public-house, and to interest them in matters which might lead them to books, or at least give them something to think about." Quillinan told Crabb Robinson that he had heard that the lectures were very good. They must have been so, for a partition had to be taken down to throw two schoolrooms into one.[1]

Local benevolence, said Robert Browning, was all very well as amusement, just as her gardening and housekeeping were good for a change. But if they were to figure as of equal importance with bookmaking, "*then* I respect Miss M. just as I should an Archbishop Canterbury whose business was the teaching A.B.C. at an infant-school—he who might set on the Tens to instruct the Hundreds how to convince the Thousands of the propriety

[1] *Auto.*, ii, 4–10. HM to Kingsley, November 16, [1848], NYPL. Quillinan to Crabb Robinson, June 6, 1848.

of doing that and many other things." Making Jane happier and wiser should be incidental to the day's progress "towards the 'novel for next year' which is to inspire thousands, beyond computation, with the ardour of making innumerable other Janes and delicate relatives happier and wiser. . . ." He need not have worried. Miss Martineau could afford to indulge her idleness for a year or so, because she knew that "the need to work will recur quite soon enough".[1] It did, very quickly.

At first, Miss Martineau distrusted the Anti-Corn Law League, because she thought its members wanted discipline; but her opinion was soon revised. In June, 1844, she told Milnes (whom she was scolding for his support of the corn laws) that Cobden and his friends had never been proved wrong, while the League was doing an educational job of the greatest importance—teaching the people to understand public affairs and to apply to them the same faculties and means they used in their private business. The farmers were being made a new set of men, beginning to think for themselves and to react against the despotism of landlords; this, she thought, would mean not only greater production of food but moral advancement and political independence.

Early in that year—how closely this is connected with her newly favourable opinion of the League I cannot say—Cobden, Moore, and Perronet Thompson had come to see her at Tynemouth; she used the *Miners' Advocate* to show them the kind of opposition the League had to overcome. As the little group saw it, the central problem was to teach the truth about determining wages; since she was the acknowledged expert on this subject, they offered her any aid they could give. Presumably she was thinking about her projected periodical for the miners, but her work for the League was done in the event for a quite different purpose.[2]

In August, 1845, she wrote to John Bright, whom she had not met, to say that some country gentlemen she knew had suggested that she write a tale or some tales on the game laws, the concern of a select committee of Commons, chaired by Bright. The subject was too upsetting, she said, for fiction; nor was fiction appropriate, for fact was more important in this case than doc-

[1] Browning to Elizabeth Barrett, [Feb. 16, 1846], *Letters*, i, 477. HM to Elizabeth Barrett, [April 15, 1845], Yale.

[2] HM to Milnes, June 12, [1844]. HM to Tremenheere, January 25, 1844, LC, Hales.

trine. She asked Bright to send her the report of his committee, from which she could draw a set of true stories to expose the system from end to end. Bright was delighted, and she set to work on August 28, the same day that the builders started her house. How pleasant it was to begin "to pull down a bad thing & build up a good one on the same day". Her busy, happy "indolence" was put aside, her study was filled with documents and parliamentary evidence, and before long the Arnold household were reduced to tears amid their praises, as she read aloud the little stories—illustrating the game laws from the middle ages to the present—before they were sent off to Moxon.[1]

The attack on the game laws was made not simply because they were an injustice or because of impending famine; rather it was a tactical move in the anti-corn law agitation. In the game code, undoubtedly, farmers had a grievance which the League saw as a wedge to drive between the two wings of the protectionists—farmers and game-preserving landlords. The apparently impartial law of 1831, which provided for licensed shooting and gave a lessee the right to take game on his own land, was "utterly unavailing", since it was possible for landlord and farmer to agree to game preservation—a bargain, to say the least, unequal, given the existing competition for farms. The discovery of the League seems to have been remarkably politic, for as soon as the repeal of the corn laws was secured, Bright lost interest. His committee's report resulted only in a timid half-measure, and effective reform was postponed until 1880.

Miss Martineau was not, however, a politician. Enthusiasm, as usual, underlined conviction. It was a tremendous subject, she told Tremenheere, which, even though it might be pushed aside by the larger issues of repeal, would have soon to come into its own. It was not simply the enormous loss of produce by game —equal to the imports of food and exceeding the income tax— but the complete demoralization, of which no one who had not seen the evidence could have any idea. Peel, "our oldest & most practical freetrader", had to finish the job, and the "gratuitous labour" of the tales was her contribution to the repeal of the corn laws.[2]

[1] HM to Bright, August 7 and 28, October 11, [1845]. Crabb Robinson to Thomas Robinson, December 20 and 25, 1845. *Auto.*, ii, 521.

[2] *Hist.*, ii, 616. *Auto.*, ii, 522. HM to Tremenheere, December 12, 1845. On the game laws and the League's concern with them, see Chester Kirby, "The English

She did not want the League to appear to have anything to do with the tales, lest they be kept out of the hands of country gentlemen who might read them as hers. But the indirect support of the League was counted on heavily; Moxon naturally assumed a large sale and went to the extra expense of having them stereotyped. The series was a failure. A thousand copies were sold at once, and another thousand later—no more. Miss Martineau explained the failure by the political excitement of early 1846, when no publication could be successful. Moxon told Crabb Robinson that Miss Martineau's mesmerism had kept the trade from subscribing. Whatever the reason, the author at least did not mind; her conviction about the power of truth triumphed over figures: "If I could but learn that some of the 2,000 copies sold had gone into the hands of the farmers, and had put any strength into their hearts to assert their rights, and resist the wrongs they have too tamely submitted to, I should feel that the result deserved a much greater sacrifice." [1]

The radicalism which lies behind that remark is more clearly evident—surprisingly so, given the usual stereotype of Miss Martineau—in the writing that she began to do, now that she had come back into action. Sometime early in 1846, Tremenheere sent her a head-shaking complaint about a paper similar to *Chambers's* called *The People's Journal*. The sight of the prospectus caused in her "a certain stirring" to do something. Then her old uncle sent her a portrait of herself taken from the *Journal* with a memoir by William Howitt not exactly to her taste. She soon had a letter from the Howitts (William having just become part proprietor) asking that she permit her name at least to be connected with the paper. She replied that she wanted to do something more than merely lend her name. This decision brought her into touch with John Saunders, the founder and co-editor, "the ugliest little man alive", for whom she developed a great respect and affection. [2] She undertook several tasks for

Game Law System", *American Historical Review*, xxxviii, 240–62, (January, 1933), and "The Attack on the English Game Laws in the Forties", *Journal of Modern History*, iv, 18–37 (March, 1932).

[1] *Auto.*, i, 521–22. HM to Bright, August 7, [1845], January 30, [1846]. Crabb Robinson Travel Journals, December 28, 1845. This is the period of her "only political plot", in which she was instrumental in reconciling Peel and Cobden. *Auto.*, i, 523–27. The exchange of letters between HM and Peel is in BM, Add. MSS, 40,585, ff. 287–95b.

[2] Saunders, a Barnstaple man, came to London in 1840, worked with William Howitt, then with Charles Knight. He edited the *Illustrated London News* in the

the journal, including the department of "household education"; a series of surveys of current events called "From the Mountain": and a set of "Lake and Mountain Holiday" papers. She enjoyed the work immensely. For Saunders she had nothing but admiration; her old friend and guide W. J. Fox wrote for the paper; and although she had reservations about the Howitts, she sympathized with "their warm & sedulous humanity, & in such of their leading opinions about social matters as I know". Above all, the circulation of the paper was rising, and she could not miss an opportunity to reach some hundreds of thousands of readers.

Actually, Tremenheere's complaint was no minor one. He was appalled, and he told Miss Martineau as much. To him, hostile as he was to democracy, the paper was radicalism of the worst kind, with ultimate consequences which could be only disastrous. It was not the style and temper that annoyed him, he said, or the subordinate opinions of writers like Fox and the Howitts, but "the principles which gave birth to those 'subordinate' opinions", and, in joining the paper, Miss Martineau had made herself responsible for giving currency to those principles. She replied that he had completely misunderstood her and the paper. The principles of the *People's Journal* were principles she had long held: its views about property were her views in *Society in America*. Everything that could be said to reprobate her opinions had been said (a bad prophecy), so she could scarcely be concerned when ten years' strength was added to her opinions, and "10 years more regard on the part of those who wish to hear what I have to say". The paper was not, as he thought, an enemy of all existing institutions; it aimed at building up, not destroying. But the building up was clearly viewed as educating the crucial middle and lower parts of the population to their responsibilities, social and political. In short, the *People's Journal* was democratic, and if Tremenheere was unwilling to accept democracy at her hands, he had to suffer what others suffered who ran foul of her principles. He did. They never met or corresponded again.[1]

---

fifties, wrote novels, tales, and some plays which attained considerable repute. *The People's Journal* had W. J. Linton to do the engravings, and some of Sidney Dobell's earliest verses appeared in it.

[1] HM to Tremenheere, July 6 and 10, [1845], Tremenheere to HM, July 13, 1846. Tremenheere was not the only reader disturbed by the tendency of the paper. Mary Howitt's sister and her husband criticized some articles to which Mary replied: "What canst thou mean by thinking *The People's Journal* is not Christian in

It is easy to understand Tremenheere's feelings. About half of the paper was made up of material similar to that in the *Penny Magazine* or *Chambers's*; Samuel Smiles wrote on recreation and women's work; a series called "What is Being Done" dealt with progress in various towns; there were articles from self-educated working-men and, of course, the usual pieces on art appreciation and other topics of general interest. But the rest of the paper—strong stuff on politics and society—certainly set the tone. A writer on mechanics' institutions insisted on the importance of their being organised democratically and not under middle-class domination. Cobden's stand on the short-time question was criticized. There was a favourable review of J. F. Bray's socialist tract *Labour's Wrongs and Labour's Remedy*. William Howitt himself not only wrote in condemnation of military flogging but in a dithyramb on Peel's resignation speech referred to the deference Peel had shown to that public opinion which had knocked down the aristocracy left standing after 1832. Most striking of all was a series of articles by Mazzini on democracy, including attacks on Bentham, Saint-Simon, and Fourier, to which Saunders published replies by Communists and Fourierists, while he himself appended a note disagreeing with Mazzini's depreciation of the socialists.

Miss Martineau too took a strong line. In one article—obviously influenced by Greg's article on the claims of labour[1]—she tore into the Duke of Richmond for having said at a sheep-shearing that a man who showed a deep interest in the welfare of his employer was worth a hundred who worked "for the sordid considerations of their daily pay". No longer, she said, did a master have a right to the attachment and devotion from his employees, for no longer did he maintain his labourers. But it was worse than the ignorance of a duke to find Archdeacon Manning saying the same thing, a Christian clergyman putting affection for a duke higher than a working-man's affection for his family. These were the Christians too, she said, who talked about missionary activity when there was so much to be done at

spirit?—there is no attempt to set the poor against the rich, but on the contrary, to induce them to be prudent, sober, independent; above all to be satisfied to be workers, to regard labour as a privilege rather than a penalty, which is quite our view of the case." Amice Lee, *Laurels and Rosemary: The Life of William and Mary Howitt*, pp. 171–72. Howitt was in his most radical phase in the mid-forties. See his *The Aristocracy of England—a History for the People*, written in 1846 under the pseudonym John Hampden, Jr.

[1] See above, p. 215.

home; and she then turned to pillory the Bishop of Chichester for his efforts to stop Sunday trains. "While there is among us such a low kind of fear of God, and such a narrow strictness about holidays as would affect our brother's Christian liberty, we are hardly qualified . . . to take upon ourselves to rebuke and extirpate the superstitions of the heathen."[1] She felt herself clearly at one with Saunders in an article he had written the year before in *Jerrold's Magazine*: The spirit of the age, he had said, aware of the enormous evils which humanity was suffering, and seeing the insufficiency of ordinary processes of reform, had turned society into one huge workshop and had set out to destroy whatever was not useful to its ultimate purpose of a new, harmonious, and nobler state. His aim for the *People's Journal* was to temper the destructive tendencies by infusing a love for all humanity, and to make the rebuilding go on as fast as the demolition, to bring about the new society before the old one disappeared.[2]

Miss Martineau's contributions were interrupted by her trip to the East, but, unhappily, there was no paper for her to come back to. Its financial affairs were in sorry shape—Saunders was apparently no business man—and Saunders and Howitt fell out in a violent quarrel that took them into the bankruptcy court and an unedifying battle in the press. It was another of those almost incomprehensible fights that punctuate the history of intellectuals. Partly personal, partly financial, it must also have involved some deep conflict about policy; for a comparison of the paper under Saunders' editorship with its successor under William Howitt is to contrast hard-hitting radicalism with a milk-and-water reversion to the pabulum of the *Penny Magazine*. Or perhaps William Howitt was frightened by 1848; if so, he was not alone. Miss Martineau stood firmly by Saunders and never forgave the Howitts. But, if her radical journalism had to go elsewhere, she had at least got a start on the household education papers which, after her return from the East, she was to expand into one of her most successful books.[3]

Household Education—a subject originally suggested by Saunders —is an interesting and significant amalgam of several strains in Miss Martineau's concerns. To begin with, it falls into the

[1] This article appears in ii, 19–21 (July 4, 1846).

[2] *People's Journal*, iii, 3–4 (1847).

[3] HM to W. L. Garrison, November 1, 1853, BPL. HM to Reeve, October 8, 1859. Carl Ray Woodring, *Victorian Samplers: William and Mary Howitt*, pp. 127–29.

pattern of guidebooks for raising children so widely produced among the more enlightened elements in society. Lant Carpenter had written a couple of ancestors to this book; and, like Carpenter's and the others, Miss Martineau's book bears a strong impress of Hartleian psychology, reinforced by some of the psychological implications of phrenology—a conviction that, properly guided, the child can be moulded, his faculties developed and brought into proper balance.

A second, associated concern is of a piece with her interest in mesmerism and the other pseudo-scientific enthusiasms of the forties. Dr. Samuel Brown, writing in the *Westminster Review*, lumped all of these enthusiasms together as "physical puritanism"—a turning away from drugs, an emphasis on natural foods, freedom of movement, fresh air, and cleanliness. This was the creed of the Combe brothers; the Owenites were working in the same direction; while the very atheism of the enlightened artisan emphasized bodily virtue. "Cleanliness and temperance", Brown wrote, "are the very religion of the materialist, and should be the complement of religion for all." [1] Edwin Chadwick had as his ambition, it has been said, to wash England all over; he found, as we have seen,[2] an enthusiastic assistant in Harriet Martineau.

In her travels she had paid a great deal of attention to the way in which children were raised. Although she was critical of the health of American women, she saw in the United States what she thought the best specimens of human development she had encountered; and she was particularly impressed that every man, however learned, could ride, drive, take care of his horse, and roof his house; while women (except, of course, in slave states) could do all their own housework. In the Near East, she found a freedom and grace in children which contrasted strongly with the "ungainly and unnatural inexpressiveness of childish manners in England".[3] The importance of diet, of proper dress, of ventilation, of affection and understanding are continual themes of her periodical writing; the rational care of children is the theme of *Household Education*.[4]

In the third place, the book is radical, radical not only in its

[1] *WR*, lvii, 409–19 (April, 1852). See HM's opinion on the hygiene of George Combe in *Biog. Sketches*, pp. 134–35.

[2] See above, pp. 217–18.

[3] *SA*, *passim*, and *EL*, pp. 59–60, 478.

[4] See reprinted articles in *Health, Husbandry, and Handicraft*.

psychological foundations but in its religious and political implications. She wrote it, she told Holyoake later, with perhaps a little foreshortening, from her final convictions in free-thought. Education had to be put on a philosophical basis, free from the usual dogmatizing and preaching about conventional religion; this book was intended for "the Secularist order of parents". Jesus appears as the great exemplar—a natural legacy of her Unitarianism—but He is no figure of Christ on the Cross. Too much has been made, she says, of His suffering and sorrow; instead we should turn reverence and sympathy to His abounding joy, to His promise of the earth to the meek and disinterested and of satisfaction to the earnest. With all the conflicting images of Christ, one method only appears absolutely safe, wise, and worthy of Him.

> Each of us has a frame, "fearfully and wonderfully made", with such a variety of powers, that no one yet knows them all, or can be sure that he understands the extent of any one of them. It is impossible that we can be wrong in desiring and endeavouring to bring out and strengthen and exercise all the powers given to every human being. In my opinion, this should be the aim of education.[1]

To reach secularist parents, she wanted to sell the book cheaply. She had heard of working people who said they would walk twenty miles to see the writer of the book, of others who could not read but who got their children to read it to them bit by bit so that they could study how to apply it. It sold first at six shillings, in numbers at three; once the original Moxon edition was sold off she wanted to arrange a very cheap edition, perhaps at half a crown. Negotiations with Holyoake fell through, but the book was republished by Smith, Elder in 1861 and subsequently to 1876, and it ran through a number of American editions.[2]

An even more significant aspect of the radicalism of the book lies in what she called its great point of ignoring rank. She thought it could be used in Buckingham Palace or in any cottage where life was decently conducted,[3] but it was the artisan who attracted her most—his kind were not only the crucial element in English society in a disturbed period, but its greatest potential.

Certain occupations, she had written in the thirties,[4] produce

[1] *HE*, pp. 18–19, 25–26.

[2] HM to G. J. Holyoake, November 13, [1851], January 2 and April 7 [1852], December 18, [1855], BM.

[3] Ibid., November 13, [1851].

[4] *How to Observe*, pp. 151–52.

persistent general characteristics, however circumstances might modify particular instances. As landlords and tenants might sometimes be liberal, but find a point beyond which they cannot go, so the occasional Tory artisan could turn in a single step to ultra-radicalism, showing his Toryism to be spurious. Above the degradation of the pauper, without the conventional restraints and selfish interests of the upper classes, this middle position seemed to her most favourable "for making the most of a human being, and best fulfilling the purposes of his life". Hardworking and close to nature, yet able, with awakened minds, to check and reinforce the one with the other—the artisan and his children had the privilege of double instruction. Children would toil like their father and share his respect for learning; out of such a busy home must grow the most natural and the best discipline.

> The children learn that it is an honour to be useful, and a comfort and blessing to be neat and industrious—And how dearly prized are the opportunities for book-study which can be secured! . . . They thus obtain that activity and enlargement of mind which render all employments and all events educational. The powers, once roused and set to work, find occupation and material in every event of life. Every thing serves—the daily handicraft, intercourse with the neighbours, rumours from the world without, homely duties, books, worship, the face of the country, or the action of the town. All these incitements, all this material, are offered to the thoughtful artisan more fully and impartially than to such below or above him as are hedged in by ignorance or by aristocratic seclusion: and therein is his condition better than theirs. After having come to this conclusion, it is no small satisfaction to remember that the most favoured classes are the most numerous. So great a multitude is included in the middle classes, compared with the highborn and the degraded, that *if they who have the best chance for wisdom will but use their privilege, the highest hopes for society are the most reasonable.*[1]

This is conviction, not flattery, and a conviction central to an understanding of Miss Martineau's position and activities. Inherent in her radicalism from the beginning, tied to her belief in democracy and her faith in the intelligent and unconventional middle orders, this view was based on Hartley's epistemology and optimistic necessarianism. It led her to a remarkably intelligent understanding of working-class movements—for her time, class, and limited experience.

[1] *HE*, pp. 45–49. Italics mine. She returns to the same theme in a letter, "American Notions of English Reform", signed "An English Traveller in America", *DN*, March 11, 1859.

In the great debate on socialism in the forties, she was far from associating herself with the usual hostility of the respectable classes. To her, socialism and communism were not aggressions, but, like Chartism, social symptoms pointing to a very different future. Changes in the fundamental constitution of society, she wrote in 1850, could come in time only from the ripened will of society as a whole. Until that will ripened "under the light and warmth of conviction", the inevitable transition period would be full of trials and experiments by those who were, or believed themselves, ready to begin the new, organic era—and the more experiments the better, so long as they were carried on with patience and earnestness by men and women who knew what they were about.[1]

In America she had seen the Rappite and Shaker communities. She declared then, and continued to do so, that they were both rich and miserable—miserable because they ignored human nature by insisting on impossible rules like celibacy; but rich because of their communism. Though Robert Owen's special schemes failed, though there was much in his system thoroughly compatible with arbitrary government, even though she had written against home colonies in the dogmatic enthusiasm of her political economy tales, she knew that Owen "is, and will sooner or later be admitted to be, the father of the great social changes which are preparing, and already going forward, as the evidence of the Economy of Association becomes more clear". Associations with an agricultural basis were the most promising; she had seen her own little farm—"some digging and weeding, done under the guidance of earnest thought and a hearty will"[2]—create subsistence for and revolutionize the lives of two people and set an example for a neighbourhood; surely that could be generalized. Consumers' co-operatives on the Rochdale principle, another offshoot of Owenism, claimed her fullest support to the end of her life.[3] She did not, however, have much hope for the producers' co-operatives of the Christian Socialists, which excluded the

[1] "Land and Social Reforms", *Leader*, August 24, 1850.

[2] *Leader*, September 21, 1850.

[3] See below, pp. 349–50. It is not entirely fanciful to refer to a leading article in the *Globe*, the paper the Martineaus took in Norwich, for October 6, 1825. Owen's difficulties, it said, were with human nature, and it was a question whether present society were not productive of more happiness to the mass of men; though if feeding, sleeping, and health were all man's happiness, no doubt his societies would be preferable. Still, it goes on, a perfect education might bring about the things he suggests; and certainly there is no objection to people trying communities.

employing capitalist and had to face competition with an outside world organized on a different principle.

Another important factor in this sympathy is that by the mid-forties she had come to share the free-thinking assumptions of the socialists. She knew or knew of sober, dedicated working-men committed to her ideals, and she saw no reason why their kind should not become universal. The only requirement was that working-men conduct themselves as intelligent and aware individuals. To one so individualistically oriented the pressure to solidarity and the constraint of a limited and very different kind of ambition were inconceivable. The passion which could from time to time seize (and seriously damage) parts of working-class movements she could neither accept nor understand; she could not abide dictation or the demagogue. But at least it must be laid to her credit that she showed a sympathy far in advance of most of her contemporaries and an intuitive grasp of the need —however much she over-dramatized and idealized it—for the thoughtful, unique individual who must be the basic building block of liberalism.[1]

In this spirit she made her brief contribution in the crisis of April, 1848. *The Voice of the People* was a government scheme, confided to the management of Charles Knight. Knight at once called on Miss Martineau, who was already excited by seeing the announcement of the plan in the papers. Foolish as a sugar-plum thrown to a mad bull, Emerson called it,[2] but Miss Martineau came to London anxious and determined to work. She contributed two parts of a story for a projected series on "Life in Many Lands"—explaining how Mustafa, an Egyptian peasant, though seemingly ideally situated for farming, given regular inundation and continual sun, suffered through government exactions and his inability to own or accumulate property. But the paper did not survive for a third issue, and it is easy enough to see why. It was a steady appeal against organic change demanded by Chartists in England and Repealers in Ireland; it was full of invocations of political economy (here called social economy), corrections to the working-class press, answers to O'Connor, and the quietist preaching that crisis had produced since the French Revolution—including the beginning of a history of England designed to show how things had improved.

[1] *Hist.*, ii, 444. "Robert Owen", *Biog. Sketches*, pp. 276, 278.
[2] Emerson to Mrs. Emerson, May 4, 1848, *Emerson Letters*, iv, 67.

She knew at once that the paper would fail. The Whigs, she said, wanted to dictate its management, they had no ideas to speak of, and what ideas they had were perverse and insolent.

> They proposed to lecture the working-classes, who were by far the wiser party of the two, in a jejune, coaxing, dull, religious-tract sort of tone, and criticised and deprecated every thing like vigour, and a manly and genial tone of address in the new publication, while trying to push in, as contributors, effete and exhausted writers, and friends of their own who knew about as much of the working-classes of England as of those of Turkey. Of course, the scheme was a complete and immediate failure. On the insertion of an article by a Conservative Whig, (which was certainly enough to account for the catastrophe,) the sale fell to almost nothing at all; and Mr. Knight, who had before stood his ground manfully against the patrons of the scheme, threw up the business.[1]

She had learned a great deal, as had Knight, about technique; she learned again, as Knight had learned in the S.D.U.K., that caution and social insulation were fundamental disqualifications. It was no accident that shortly after 1848 Miss Martineau was in touch with G. J. Holyoake.

The impact of 1848 on England was wide and deep. For Miss Martineau the uprisings posed the problem of power which had always concerned her and seemed to presage the resolution of the conflict in an enormous bloody struggle. Her radicalism called mere human authority into question, whether in the pretensions of the priesthood or the "obscurantism" of the medical profession. Irresponsible power, whether in the slave states or in English households or in the village of Deerbrook, was the great enemy. To force there was no answer but force; usurpation of authority by brute force must be put down by the force of reason. "Knowledge is power, and wisdom confers authority; and if we really believe . . . that . . . the highest knowledge and the purest wisdom have been placed within our reach, we must accept the office connected with their possession, and fulfil the conditions on which they are communicated."[2]

The early nineteenth century was a period suffused with the

[1] *Auto.*, ii, 2.

[2] The quotation is from an article on slavery in *Misc.*, ii, 382. On the problems of authority and irresponsible power, see *Misc.*, i, 182–83, *SA* ii, 120–21, *WR*, xxxi, 221 (July, 1838), and *RWT*, ii, 26–27: "Moral power has begun its long series of conquests over physical force and selfish cunning, and the diviner part of man is a guarantee that not one inch of the ground gained shall ever be lost."

idea of impending catastrophe.[1] Canning had crystallized this sense in political terms in his prediction, which Miss Martineau never forgot, that the next war in Europe would be one not so much of armies as of opinions. The lines were drawing up, and 1848 was the starting signal. The slave power in America would be one combatant, Russia another. Then in 1851 Louis Napoleon clarified the situation, happily, as Miss Martineau saw it, for this "more substantial than *papal* aggression" seemed likely to bring about national unity and to keep the country out of that most obstinate and hopeless class of quarrels, those in which all sides are untenable.[2] Against these forces of evil, all good men must fight.

In October, 1849, Miss Martineau sent to Boston a long letter for publication in *Liberty Bell*, an abolitionist annual, which put her view of the matter with great incisiveness. The war of opinion that was preparing she said, was a war between the further and nearer centuries, between Asia and Europe, between despotism and self-government, a war long in coming. Runnymede and the Wars of the Roses were preparatory; the Italian republics, the French Revolution, the voyage of the *Mayflower*, the Swiss League, the Zollverein wrought well for the side of freedom. Now the issue was joined: the first principles of social liberty had to be fought for. The whole force of the free world was needed, she felt, for fighting the enemy; yet much of it had to be diverted to overcome the faults in patchwork governments, discontent, and struggle within the ranks of freedom. Representative government was a mere beginning; nowhere was the principle of human brotherhood practically asserted; nowhere were the principles of civilization declared and made the basis of action. But sooner or later the forces of the West would be prepared for victory.

> If on the one side, the soul comes up to battle with an imperfect and ill-defended body, on the other, the body is wholly without a soul, and must, in the end, fall to pieces. The best part of the

---

[1] The perpetual fear of revolution was, of course, a central factor in creating this atmosphere. Catastrophe was a standard theme in literature and sermons. The enormous popularity of the apocalyptic views of the Rev. John Cumming in mid-century is an important cultural phenomenon which must have been fed heavily by the sense of dissolution in and after 1848.

[2] HM to Emerson, February 25, [1852], Harvard. Miss Martineau had met Urquhart in 1838 and shared strongly in the growing fear and loathing of Russia. *Auto.*, i, 433, and ii, 331 (Journal, January 5, 1838). On Canning's opinion, *Hist.*, i, 303–4, ii, 368.

> mind of Western Europe will make itself a body by dint of action, and the pressure which must bring out its forces; and it may be doubted whether it could become duly embodied in any other way.

What forms society might in the future take could not be foreseen, but if some of the most cautious observers of social movements were saying that England could not stop short of "a modified communism", then the result would very likely be a wholly new social state, if not "a yet undreamed-of social idea".[1] Here was a blueprint for her entire activity, inherent from the beginning, formulated at last; its completion coincided with her writing a book with incontestable claims to greatness, the *History of the Thirty Years' Peace*.

In 1846 Charles Knight, impressed by the amazing accomplishment of English industry and commerce and convinced of the certainty of improvement beyond what anyone could have imagined twenty years before, decided to write a history of the thirty years between Waterloo and the repeal of the corn laws. Because of the withdrawal of his partner from the publishing business, he found he had no time to continue writing; so the history was turned over to G. L. Craik, who very shortly died, leaving Knight with a series of numbers begun—an obligation to his purchasers as well as to his own interest in the subject. When he suggested that Miss Martineau finish it, she had to delay starting in order to complete some other books—*Household Education* and a book on the Lakes—but began finally in August, 1848. Getting started was difficult; it was at this time that her mother, now very old and blind, died in Birmingham; and to judge from Miss Martineau's comments, her mother's illness caused her considerable mental strain, probably with feelings of guilt added to the natural anxiety. Moreover, she was by no means certain that she could write history. But once she had come to a passage about Canning's eloquence, her enthusiasm was fired. The manuscript of the first volume was delivered to Knight in February, 1849; the second in the following November.

The book was published in thirty monthly numbers, for which she received forty pounds each. Her part of the history began in 1820, from Book II, except for a chapter on the South American republics in the first book. By summer, 1849, the sale had

[1] *Auto.*, ii, 115–18. The MS of this letter is in the Gay Collection, Columbia University Library.

doubled and was still increasing. In 1850 Knight proposed that she extend the history at both ends, to make a history of the half-century. The volume covering 1800 to 1815 was published as introductory to the others, but Knight lost interest in the project at that point and the last four years were not finished. With Knight's withdrawal from active publishing, the history passed into the hands of the Chambers firm in Edinburgh, who reissued it, proposing in 1854 that she bring the history down to the war; but her illness prevented that. Then, ten years later, in 1863, the American firm of Walker, Wise, and Company in Boston proposed to republish the history, and she suggested that she write a short introduction. When she came to think it over, she decided it would be worth twice as much if her addition appeared at the end of the history, so she dashed off a concluding chapter to cover the period from 1846 to 1854, writing it, she said, as if it were written in 1855 instead of 1863. It is interesting to note that the American republication was done at the suggestion of some bankers and business men who hoped it would do good in teaching the Americans something about finance, currency, and free trade.[1]

In England the history was well received, adding praise and reputation to its author's already substantial store, said Mrs. Jameson, notwithstanding the blaze that Macaulay's first volume was making. Some, though, had reservations, among them George Eliot. She found the history instructive and parts of it—for example, the narrative of the reform movement—fascinating, but she was put off by what struck her as a "sentimental, rhetorical style". Worse, the book was not really history; it was a badly proportioned compilation by a tyro, no story of England but a series of review articles partly narrative, partly reflective. In spite of these faults, she still considered it was one of the most valuable books to appear in a long time. It is neither a just nor perceptive criticism, although it is certainly not as

[1] She asked Walker, Wise for fifty pounds which would be what she would get from an English publisher for the chapter; the rest of the work, of course, they were getting for nothing. She assured them, however, that she never quarrelled about money with a publisher. But a subsequent letter acknowledging the receipt of £25 is rather pointed in its hopes that another £25 is forthcoming. The negotiations surrounding the publication of the history are to be followed in *Auto.*, ii, 4, 15–18, Knight's *Passages*, iii, 74–76, and the following letters: HM to Milnes, June 4, [1849], HM to Crabb Robinson, June 8, [1848], HM to Reeve, May 6, 1864, five letters to Walker, Wise and Company in the Princeton University Library, and HM to Helen Martineau, July 5, [1848]. MCO.

foolish as Miss Barrett's regret that Miss Martineau was wasting a fine imagination on a history.[1]

Writing contemporary history is no easy task. If it is to survive among generations without contemporary knowledge, it must have pace and an intelligible point of view; if it is to be useful it must be written from a nearly infallible sense of the significant. All of these qualities, Miss Martineau, as a superior journalist, was able to provide, and she could add a considerable amount of inside knowledge from her own contacts with the men who were making the history. I know no finer tribute to it than that it was extensively used as a source by Elie Halévy in his great history; it should be used more widely now than it is.

Her sources were the obvious ones—the *Annual Register*, articles in journals, Hansard, memoirs and letters of public men. The style, though once in a while it becomes pretentious, seems well within the boundaries of early Victorian taste and in general is superbly adapted to its purpose. The organization is exemplary and the development beautifully modelled—climaxes effectively built up and points driven home. There is real feeling and passion too—the intensity of the analysis of Canning or the very personal account of the crash of 1825 are examples—and there are some fine artistic effects. For example, she uses Lord Eldon alternately as villain and clown; but in spite of this calculated artifice (it is worth recalling Atkinson's phrenological diatribe against the old Lord Chancellor), she treats him with remarkable judiciousness. For me, the literary high point of the book is her description of the funeral of the Duke of York. The great are gathered about the open grave in a cold, damp St. George's Chapel. There are Canning and Huskisson, wondering perhaps, about their destinies but hardly foreseeing their tragic ends, while Eldon, who was to survive all the mourners, was worried only about catching cold and trying to avoid it by standing on his hat. It may not be scientific history, that passage, whatever scientific may be, but it is a grand set piece in a style that can justly be called Churchillian.

[1] Mrs. Jameson to Ottilie von Goethe, April 17, 1849, pp. 165–66. George Eliot's Journal, February 2–3, 1858, *George Eliot Letters*, ii, 430, comments on the style on a re-reading of the new edition of 1855; her comments on the first appearance of the *History* are in a review in the *British Quarterly Review*, xi, 355–71 (May, 1850). The review in the *Leader*, April 6, 1850, says exactly the same thing, so must be either by George Eliot or Lewes. Miss Barrett's comment was made to Miss Mitford, October 10, 1848, *Letters*, i, 387.

Halévy used the *History* as a source for history; we must use it in a way equally valuable, as a phenomenon in itself. It is no mere chronicle but a sustained study from a consistent point of view. To her the history of ideas was the only true history, and, while she believed that biography was the best way to accomplish what needed doing, she was no mere biographer nor a partisan of Carlylean interpretation. Indeed, she was anything but Carlylean in history.[1] Individuals were important as representatives of ideas and stages in the progress of civilization; they were to be studied—and judged—in those terms. When a nation is young, she wrote, it admires, like a young person, accounts of wars, conquest, and adventure. But when it becomes mature, a stage in civilization is more important than an extension of territory; institutions and laws are seen to be the central concerns; and the general mind opens to a sense of the qualities necessary to attain the higher good. The big historical questions then become the origin of political amelioration and who brought it about.[2]

When she started to write in 1848, she was uncertain of her ability as an historian, but that was not for want of having thought about history. One of her earliest essays was on the use of the retrospective faculty. The past is likely, she said, to distract our attention to an insignificant measure of time from the foreshortened because baffling eternity of the future. But it is wrong to fall back on the familiar, simply because it is familiar. "What chance has the helmsman of steering his course aright, if he contemplates only the shore he has left, the breakers he has traversed, and the clouds which have blown over?" He may see no limits ahead, no familiar object on the horizon to help in measuring distance; but he knows that more than mere waste lies ahead and that he must try to reach it by the shortest and safest track. It was the future that was important to her; the past was an aid to charting the course—as true in individual restrospection (she was contemplating autobiography at the very beginning of her career) as in wider concerns. To examine the past in such conditions is neither injurious nor enervating be-

[1] She admired the attack on Froude's *History* in *ER*, vol. 108, pp. 206–52 (July, 1858).

[2] *EL*, p. 194. She wrote a striking introduction at the very end of her life to Una M. Goodwin's translation of Reinhold Pauli's *Simon de Montfort* (London, 1876), on which this paragraph is largely based. See also her preface to *Biog. Sketches* and the comment on her view of biography in *Nation* (New York), June 17, 1869.

cause, in doing so, we are instituting vigorous present action.[1] This is Whig history with a vengeance.

Within a few years she had absorbed an interpretation of history which made sense of the past and certainty of the future. One order after another had grown into indispensability only to be replaced by still others—chieftain and priest; the lawyers, the merchants. Aristocratic wars and feuds left the middle and lower classes space and time to rise and grow into strength until the forces of society shifted and its destinies assumed new form—and one could see the triumph of moral force over physical. Able to rely on this view of the past and prone to extrapolate from it the future of mankind, she was able, she said in the forties, to take a calmer view of politics, to realize that single questions and separate measures, by which she had set so much store, were relatively unimportant compared with higher, more philosophical developments. Popular interests were undoubtedly progressing, and some of the greatest questions seemed on the way to settlement; one could rise above the battle to watch.[2] Not that she ever became quietist, not that she ever spared denunciation to the short-sighted in politics or ceased her advocacy of single questions and separate measures; but she was prepared with a comprehensive view which made the interrelation of the events she saw more apparent and her canons of judgment more nearly infallible. Her interpretation of history was not derived from her study of Comte's *Positive Philosophy*, the historical sections of which John Stuart Mill thought one of the French philosopher's greatest contributions; what Comte did was to sharpen her formulations—and her historical views are among the few areas in which, in the last two decades of her life, she appeared as a true disciple of the great positivist.[3]

History was not, however, a mere aid to understanding; it was, as she had indicated in her youthful essay, an impetus to action. Consequently, the true view had to be disseminated. If everyone, she wrote in 1858, could study the history of the English constitution, could understand the rise and success of their various orders, could see the regular progress of freedom and the clearness and decision of popular aims as they had been embodied

[1] *Misc.*, i, 221–22.

[2] *Life in the Sickroom*, pp. 68–71, developing a passage in *How to Observe*, pp. 38–48, especially interesting for its proto-Marxist interpretation. Cf. George Eliot's similar, Comtean interpretation in her review of HM's *History*, *British Quarterly Review*, xi, 365–67.

[3] See below, pp. 305–309.

in the great struggles of the past, then men able to govern effectively would be brought forward. Then, too, ordinary men and women would see what was possible and impossible in the realm of politics, would come, as she had herself, to set less store by single questions and separate measures.[1] One of the things she most wanted in the *Weekly Volumes* was good historical fiction. It could do "more than any other means whatever to turn polit[l] discontent into sound polit[l] knowledge and views". And, of course, that was what her *History* was intended to do. The book was planned, "not for the fastidious aristocracy, but for the great middle & operative class of readers". And she started writing it in 1848.

With all this burden of philosophy, faith, and urgency laid on her volumes, it is comforting to be able to say that Miss Martineau was a good historian in spite of herself.

[1] *DN*, October 11, 1858. HM to Bulwer-Lytton, April 27, [1844]. HM to Morpeth, April 19, [1844]. HM to Milnes, June 4, [1849].

CHAPTER X

Ambleside: The Logical Conclusion

WHAT happened to Harriet Martineau in the religious sphere was in various ways happening to a good many Unitarians. The diary of Crabb Robinson, himself a Unitarian, offers notable documentation to the straits in which the sect found itself, the old, respectable congregations at any rate. Older members were falling away, and in 1851 Robinson was told by Richard Martineau, Harriet's cousin, that the sect could attract no promising young men. Some ministers openly proclaimed themselves anti-supernatural; Fox had left to found the South Place Ethical Society; and, in noting the conversion of one lady, who had been befriended abroad by Roman Catholics, Robinson asked pointedly: "Who can deny that U[nitarianism] is mostly cultivated for its negative qualities?" [1]

Unitarianism served as a religion for radicals or as a half-way house for those abandoning more dogmatic faiths, but precisely the compromise character which made it a resort for souls adrift made it unsatisfactory to the intellectually demanding. They could go in a number of directions: F. D. Maurice, like Coleridge, had begun as a Unitarian. Others went over to a secular ethicalism and what must be called agnosticism, though the term was not yet invented. Harriet Martineau insisted that her brother was an unfortunate choice as professor at Manchester College, as he was no longer a true Unitarian, "skipping the nonsense", apparently, as easily as he had done when a boy. Her remark, to be sure, was made after their quarrel, but the difficulties Dr. Martineau had in holding on to his chair seem to indicate that there were Unitarians to agree with her. [2]

[1] Diary, December 17, 1846, August 31 and September 6, 1851, May 4, 1852, DWL.

[2] See the comment by Lucy Aikin about her discontent with the Lockean, necessarian tradition, above p. 84; it illustrates the quandary of some sensitive Unitarians very neatly. On James, HM to G. J. Holyoake, [March, 1857], BM. See also above, p. 95 and below, p. 300.

Miss Martineau's sectarian loyalty began to crumble fairly early. She was annoyed with Mr. Madge, at the Octagon, for his ignoring the religious instruction of the young people of the congregation and shocked when she found he had been preaching sermons written by someone else. He and a good many other Norwich Unitarians resisted her advocacy of necessarianism. She wrote to James from Shields that she could make no headway talking necessarianism to the Unitarians whom she met there and that she was upset by the sophistry of the minister and disgusted with the hymns. She thought her brother James's congregation in Dublin guilty of trimming and timidity when he quarrelled with them over his refusal to accept the *Regium Donum*, the government grant to Irish Presbyterian ministers. She found the picking and choosing among Scripture texts, the elaborate and ingenious apologetics, distasteful. So when she was told in one place in America that there was but one atheist in the state, she replied that she wished there were a thousand brought out of the depths of their concealment and suffering; and she was delighted to hear a Unitarian clergyman comment, when someone was eulogized as a man and a Christian, that it was much more to be a man than a Christian.[1]

Religion, she wrote, in its widest sense is "the tendency of human nature to the Infinite", manifested in the pursuit of perfection in any direction; under this canon some "speculative atheists" had been deeply religious men, even though unable to personify their conception of the Infinite. In a narrower sense, religion is "the relation which the highest human sentiments bear towards an infinitely perfect Being". To narrow it further, to provide any system of reward or punishment is to degrade religion into superstition.[2]

So liberal a construction of the claims of religion is characteristically Unitarian and rationalist. Within this liberal commitment, however, Miss Martineau displayed all the signs of an active Christian faith. She remained a devoted reader of the Bible, putting herself through a course of it in America and confiding to her journal in 1837, "Especially let me fill myself full of the gospel. How one thirsts for it, after a busy interval."

[1] HM to James, January 8, February 22, July 15, 1822, January 6, 1823, November 14, 1824, April 4, 1825. *Auto.*, i, 28–29 shows the kind of argumentation used by men like Madge and Belsham. *Auto.*, ii, 263. *SA*, i, 346.

[2] *SA*, i, 314–15.

She continued to look on the necessarian scheme as the dictate of an all-wise Father.

> While the world and life roll on and on, the feeble reason of the child of Providence may be at times overpowered with the vastness of the system amidst which he lives; but his faith will smile upon his fear, rebuke him for averting his eyes, and inspire him with the thought, "Nothing can crush me, for I am made for eternity. I will do, suffer and enjoy, as my Father wills; and let the world and life roll on!" . . . This universal, eternal, filial relation is the only universal and eternal refuge.[1]

Man's probationary state in this world, she told Milnes, was one lighted by an unseen glory, and consciousness of that same unseen glory pervaded *Life in the Sickroom*, which made Maurice comment on the real faith which the book showed.[2]

In 1844 her belief in immortality—she had never believed in bodily resurrection—was still firm. She believed in a future life, she wrote to Bulwer-Lytton, because, under a benignant Providence, any aspiration so natural as to be nearly universal must be true. She believed in the reunion of those whose love was truly great, who had found that intense and pure intellectual sympathy which could survive any change or development of separated persons on earth or in the hereafter. On such a question one had to abandon reason as a guide and reject it as a barrier, relying on the "life of the heart" and the affections. She was writing a letter of condolence, to be sure, but the tone rings true.[3]

Within three years, however, she had abandoned these remnants of theological orthodoxy—the belief in God as a Father (and with it its corollary, the argument from design, on which Priestley had laid such stress), and belief in life after death. Within a further three or four years she had worked out a positive faith to replace the discarded one. She began in other words, to define religion only in its second, narrower sense. At the same time, her loyalty to its broader meaning became more

[1] *Deerbrook*, iii, 1–6.

[2] *Auto.*, ii, 319. HM to Milnes, December 4, [1841]. *Life in the Sickroom*, pp. 110–112. Maurice to Mr. Strachey, March 13, 1844, *Life*, i, 364–65.

[3] HM to Bulwer-Lytton, January 26, [1844]. She returned to the subject in another letter to him on February 8. Lytton had said that Newton disbelieved in reunion, to which she replied: "As to Newton,—if he was so indifferent about union here, I don't want to force reunion on him hereafter. He is well enough, no doubt, for he will find Mathematics wherever he can go." She was being more naïve than funny.

intense, and for that she found new secular and scientific formulations. It was a pilgrimage similar to that made by a great many thoughtful people at about the same time, a dozen years before Darwin made the Victorian crisis of faith obvious.[1] What was involved in her "conversion", and what brought it about?

Some credit must be given to her pushing further the traditional anti-clericalism of Dissent. The bibliolatry so abhorrent to Unitarians seemed increasingly ridiculous, indeed shameful,[2] witness her steady attack on Sabbatarianism. The bigotry, conventionalism, conservatism, and stupidity of the clergy which she had so often attacked as a dissenter, she encountered in very concrete form in the clerical obstructionism she had to face in Tynemouth and Ambleside—and in Dissent as well. The fate of the educational clauses of the Factory Bill of 1843 had its effect. Worse, the timidity of American clergymen (including some Unitarians) in politics and especially in abolitionism had shocked a dissenting conscience prepared to find across the Atlantic all the advantages of a voluntary system; instead she found that "the yeomanry of America, those who are ever in the presence of God's high priest, Nature, and out of the worldly competitions of a society sophisticated with superstition, are perpetually in advance of the rest of the community on the great moral questions of the time, while the clergy are in the rear".[3] Again and again in her later writing she comes back to the theme that churches do not make religion; religion makes churches. She was opposed to church-building programmes and to missionary activity which took attention away from secular reforms that needed doing. She welcomed the shock of the religious census of 1851 because it might lead to an inquiry into the "form of godliness" that was so rapidly superseding Christianity in England.[4]

Policy considerations could hardly in themselves have brought about the change without an intellectual shift. Here she put great emphasis on the Tynemouth period. She was not yet capable of a wide philosophical survey, she recalled, or morally

[1] Cf. Howard R. Murphy, "The Ethical Revolt against Christian Orthodoxy in Early Victorian England", *American Historical Review*, lx, 800–17 (July, 1955).

[2] *EL*, p. 355–56.

[3] *SA*, i, 350, 356–57, 364–65. The entire chapter on religion in America is revealing in its implications for the conscience of an English dissenter.

[4] E.g., "Results of the Census of 1851", *WR*, n.s., v, 323–57 (April, 1854), esp. pp. 354–56, and *DN*, June 28, 1852.

bold enough for deep investigation of things she had always taken for granted. But when the old questions of divine government, future life, and the origin of evil, were raised acutely, she had the leisure for thought and "abundance of material for that kind of meditation which usually serves as an introduction to a higher". There was a succession of deaths among her friends and relatives, many of them carried off in the prime of life by some accidental or violent means; there was, of course, her own suffering. Both burdens reinforced her old contempt for the orthodox solution of ascribing justice to God and mercy to Christ. Long repelled by the necessary consequence of that view —the tyranny and cruelty of God—she took refuge in the conclusion that we cannot understand the scheme of the universe and that no revelation can truly explain such events because men have no faculty for understanding things beyond humanity.[1] It was a rigorous extension of a commonplace of eighteenth-century theology to be found in Priestley and in her own early periodical writing—that only through revelation or in the next world could men understand God's plans.[2] A new concentration on its implications helped to reveal the unsatisfactory nature of these traditional comforts, however closely she may have clung to them as late as 1844. But if the traditional groundings of security were crumbling, at the same time her increasing conviction, in political and social matters, that things were inevitably coming right helped to provide a bridge to a new, and absolutely necessary, security. She concentrated the ferocity of her Priestleyan optimism on this world, not the next.

The final demolition of the old structure of faith was provided by her trip to the East and, more particularly, by the reading and thinking that surrounded it. Egypt had long fascinated her,[3] and, of course, the Holy Land held a very special spot in her affections from the days of Lant Carpenter and the *Traditions of Palestine*. In the forties a great many Englishmen travelled to the East. It did not, therefore, take much urging to make her put aside some publishing commitments for a journey. She was invited by Mr. and Mrs. Richard Yates, of Liverpool, who were ˙oined later by J. C. Ewart, the member for Liverpool. Both

[1] *Auto.*, i, 466–71.

[2] There is even a tract of Hannah More's to enforce the lesson for the poor. *Turn the Carpet* gave them, said Bishop Porteus, "Bishop Butler's Analogy, all for a halfpenny".

[3] HM to Monckton Milnes, May 28, [1843].

men were wealthy, so the journey was done with every advantage, and Mr. Yates met all Miss Martineau's expenses. They left London in October, 1846, accompanied by Henry Atkinson as far as Boulogne, made a wretched crossing of the Mediterranean, spent ten weeks on the Nile, journeyed by caravan through Sinai into the Holy Land and Syria, and returned to London in the summer of 1847, whereupon a book was forthwith written.

Eastern Life, Present and Past suffers from the same fault as *Society in America*. It is both descriptive and didactic, a book of travels and a torrent of philosophizing. The criticism of this uneasy marriage of types which met the publication of *Eastern Life* in 1848 was partly an expression of discomfort about the unorthodox conclusions,[1] it was also a complaint of real literary substance. There was so much to say. Climbing Sinai or the Pyramids seemed no effort at all, and she was disappointed that the intense heat prevented her climbing Mount Tabor. She was wonderfully excited by the voyage down the Nile, by her amateur archaeology, by her visit to a harem, by the experience on the desert—mirages and all—and by her conviction that the cures and oracles in Egyptian religion were mesmeric. She was incensed by the ignorance and superstition of the Christians she saw and by the degradation of the Holy Places. Above all, in seeing the Holy Land, her Unitarian conception of Jesus as a man and teacher was reinforced. If Jesus had come to England in the nineteenth century, he would have talked about rural cottages and town alleys, robins, dog-roses and brambles; instead he talked of rock and sand, of ravens and lilies of the field—and now she had seen them. His lamentations for the cities of Galilee became as real as if he had cried "Alas! for you, Liverpool—alas! for you, Bristol."

> To my apprehension, on the spot, and with the records of his life in my hand, and the recollections of Egypt and of Sinai fresh in my mind, nothing could be simpler than his recorded words, and

---

[1] Mrs. Clarkson to Crabb Robinson, October 29, 1851, and Robinson's Diary, November 22, 1848, commenting on the review in the *British Quarterly Review*. Emerson to Margaret Fuller is charming: "There is much of interest for the public who have not read Egypt at the first sources. The vice of the book is that of the position, namely, the running to Egypt because other people do, & then writing of it with the air of Bur[c]khardt or Herodotus. Inspired travellers are good as all inspired things are, but who the deuce are you?" April 25, 1848, *Emerson Letters*, iv, 63.

nothing less like what is superstitiously and irreverently taught, as coming from him, in most of the churches of Christendom.[1]

All this, as an enthusiastic traveller, she had to communicate—not only because she enjoyed it so much, not only for the enjoyment of her readers, but as a guide to those who might follow—hence the recommendations about clothing and travel and wall-washing in the tombs.

The main burden of the book, however, was something else. Did she dare, she wondered, tell what she had discovered? Would it be presumption to declare that she dissented from the statements of authorities like Heeren and Warburton?[2] Would it be rash to say that the theology of almost everybody in the civilized world was baseless, to state it before she knew that her faith was enough for her own self-government and support?

I know, as well as I ever knew any thing, that for support I really need nothing else than a steady desire to learn the truth and abide by it; and, for self-government, that it is enough to revere my own best nature and capabilities: but it will require a long process of proof before I can be sure that these convictions will avail me, under daily pressure, instead of those by which I have lived all my life.

All these fears she wrote to Atkinson, confessing that they made her sadly isolated; he replied with a typically diffuse and condescending letter, supporting and pressing further her new convictions, sympathizing in her loneliness, and urging her to say what had to be said.

It is well that men feel loneliness in advancing in truth, for it holds them back to instruct and bring others forward, and gives them a mission to perform, to save their fellows from that to which they cannot return. For knowledge, to the truthful and earnest, is a mistress to whom you are wedded for life: and in confidence and constancy must you seek your self-respect and happiness, whatever may be the peril and disaffection of the world. . . . I see no pleasure in martyrdom: but I feel it necessary to die if it must be, in maintaining what I believe—earnestly, and in reason and faith believe, to be true; to sacrifice friendship and every other thing to maintain this predominating impulse and want. You feel, nevertheless, a sense of loneliness now; and so do I; and have done more than I

---

[1] *EL*, p. 440.

[2] Arnold Hermann Ludwig Heeren (1760–1842), historian of the ancient world. Bartholomew Elliott George Warburton, author of *The Crescent and the Cross*, 1844, a traveller, and a friend of Milnes.

> do now. But this is passing away, and one friend in truth is a host against the world assembled.

And on and on, quite sincerely touching every chord in her nature.[1]

She published the book, though Murray who was committed to do it backed down when he saw a manuscript "of infidel tendency" which undermined the authenticity of the Bible. But Moxon took the book at once. The sale was small at first, she said; she hoped it would increase, as usually happened with forbidden books. And forbidden her book was in some families, though the reviews denied her the full benefit of banning by treating it largely as a book of travels. But whatever its fate, she had cleared her mind, and the book could cheer and enlighten the free. Their numbers, she knew, were rapidly increasing, while the spirit of orthodoxy, "the opposite to the spirit of power & of love & of a sound mind", was losing its grip.[2]

Her contentions can be fairly simply stated. She had travelled to Egypt, Sinai, and Palestine, each of which had produced a distinctive faith; and to Syria where all the modern faiths were in conflict. As she looked back on her travels, she was happy that she had taken the countries in that order, for it made more strikingly evident the genetic connection between them that she, along with some leading scholars of the time, believed to exist. In other words, she was making a study in what we would call comparative religion. She was infuriated at other English travellers in Egypt who rejoiced that western Christians had found the true faith in contrast to the barbarism and idolatry they saw in the tombs. There was barbarism and idolatry enough in the Christians to drive her to unfavourable comparisons; moreover, she insisted that religions be judged by their highest exemplars and not by popular credulity. She would ask as fair a consideration for Christianity five thousand years hence, when its existing forms would be forgotten and its principles expanded into something yet unknown. Would these Christians want a gargoyle on a cathedral to be taken as an indication of their idolatry?[3]

Amid the popular superstitions, amid the symbols and myths repeated in one religion after another, she saw something else—

[1] This important exchange of letters is in *Auto.*, i, 539–49.

[2] HM to Emerson, April 5, [1848]. HM to Crabb Robinson, June 8, [1848]. HM to Monckton Milnes, June 4, [1848].

[3] *EL*, pp. 89–91. HM to Monckton Milnes, off Gebel el Elredeh, January 31, 1847.

the great governing ideas of mankind as a source of unity. In her mesmerized ramblings at Ambleside she had seen a connected series of life-fountains with all the nations worshipping the source —a conception that goes back at least to 1831; the boundary line there between personal God and Ideas is faint enough. Now she saw these "guiding lights of the human intellect" in their proper role. "The great Ideas of Moral Obligation and strict retribution, of the supreme desirableness of moral good, and the eternal 'beauty of holiness', pass from system to system, immortalizing all with which they assimilate, and finally annihilating all else, dispensing the best blessings that men have ever received, and promising an increase of them in all time to come." [1]

The higher Egyptian priesthood, whatever errors they may have made in deluding the common people, served these ideas and arrived, ultimately, at a monotheism. From them Moses derived his monotheism, with the addition of something vital: seeing that his people had to be removed from the influences which made them what they were, he also saw that they had to be educated into an independent social life.

> In following out this course of speculation, he was led to perceive a mighty truth, which appears to have been known to no man before him;—a truth so holy and so vast that even yet mankind seem scarcely able fully to apprehend it;—the truth that all ideas are the common heritage of all men, and that none are too precious to be communicated to every human mind. It was his clear apprehension of this truth, and his intrepidity in bringing it into practice, which made Moses the greatest of men, and the eternal benefactor of the world.

In short, Moses embodied the dissenter's rejection of a priesthood, the Hartleian or phrenological doctrine of conditioning, the liberal's faith in education; and he was, withal, a necessarian.[2] Add to it the reinforcement of her impression of the humanity of Jesus by seeing the places where He taught, and the Unitarian basis of her interpretation of the East is clear.

It is confirmed by her views of Mohammedanism. Mohammed was right (i.e., Unitarian) in refusing to rely on miracles and in rejecting a priesthood; he was wrong in imposing a religion based only on precept. It might be said that the Arabs were mere children who had to be ruled by precept; but a children's religion could never be universal. Mohammed failed, and his religion

[1] *EL*, pp. 194–95.

[2] *EL*, pp. 262–63, 296–300 ff.

must fail, because he did not recognize the governing power of principles. The Egyptians, at their best, had known that; Moses gave it to the Jews; and Jesus directed his whole teaching to detaching men from preceptive guidance and introducing them "to the prerogative of their own reason, conscience, faith, and affections. . . . He who so well knew what was in man, knew that men can do anything that they see; and Christianity therefore gives the light, instead of offering a hand to guide men through the dark. It gives the light, calling upon men to find, train, and exercise their powers of sight." It was what she had said in her attempt to convert Mohammedans in 1831.[1]

In abandoning a personal God and immortality, she let herself be ticketed an infidel. Actually, she never denied a first cause; she denied only that we could ever know its attributes. And her yielding of immortality, though ultimately complete, was gradual: in 1847 she was still willing to allow the possibility of life after death—not as a scriptural promise but as a still hidden phenomenon of nature which some curious mesmeric accounts made one wonder about. She had, however, given up the presumption in favour of it when she came to question the universality of the desire for immortality on which her presumption was based.[2] The rest, culminating in the joyful stoicism of the last chapter of the *Autobiography*, was a matter of course.

To turn from belief to disbelief in these two immense conceptions was not easy; she recalled how unprepared she was at her first meetings with Henry Atkinson in 1845 to take in the boldness of his talk.[3] Consequently, in looking back at her earlier, "selfish" views, even more in looking about her at the beliefs of others, she readily saw the change as a major break. It was in the light of this appearance that she was so critical of her early works and youthful convictions. But she had for years been dependent on only a few dogmatic beliefs, and they were subject to the powerful corrosives of her rationalism and her view of development or juggled with her two definitions of religion.[4] Her vaunted freedom from dogma came from cutting away inherently incompatible survivals in her Unitarian inheritance.[5] Forcing them out left stronger than ever the central

[1] *EL*, pp. 468–69. *The Faith as Unfolded by Many Prophets*, pp. 10–11.
[2] *Auto.*, i, 548. [3] *Auto.*, i, 489–93. [4] See above, p. 284.
[5] It is worth recalling that the French *philosophes* considered Priestley a puzzle, when they met him, because he combined, illogically as it seemed, enlightened

intellectual and emotional concepts which Unitarianism had brought to her from the eighteenth century. In the new dispensation she had a firmer because more consistent security. She had become ashamed, she told Atkinson, of the enthusiasm with which she had formerly acquiesced in God's will when she came to find "a much higher ground of patience" in herself. As for morality, never had she felt more desirous of doing right or more discomposed when she realized she had done wrong. With this strength in herself, largely found in Tynemouth, generalized by her Eastern experience and reflections, she was ready to move on. Not in education alone did it remain to be seen what could be done "by a direct appeal to our noble human nature".[1]

A good many years after Miss Martineau's visit to Egypt, Anthony Trollope turned a knowing eye on the broad churchman and wrote movingly about the challenge that the new learning posed: one had to cut the ropes and put out in the little boat, not knowing where one was bound, for the learned man who beckoned had nothing to offer but doubts and a subrisive smile.[2] It is still a compelling statement of the conflict of inevitability and nostalgia, of security no longer tenable and a threatening future. In that sense Harriet Martineau never faced a crisis in her faith, or faced it only for that brief instant when she turned to Atkinson for advice which she would shortly have given herself. She never doubted that she had a faith to substitute, and she was quickly reassured as to its potency. She proclaimed it to the world in 1851 in what surely must be one of the strangest books to carry the name of a reputable writer, *Letters on the Laws of Man's Nature and Development.*

Atkinson's letters make up most of the book, with Miss Martineau confining herself largely to comment and to drawing him out. Atkinson was a man who had a good many projects in the talking stage, and this expression of his views would never have been printed had it not been for Miss Martineau's insistence and her editing. But if most of the words are his, the doctrine is hers as well, for she accepted everything he said with an enthusiasm which is nothing short of embarrassing. "I do not like to say anything after your last letter," she wrote, "I do not like to touch it, or the state of mind it produces in me. Yet it is

principles with a lively Christian faith. Basil Willey, *The Eighteenth Century Background*, pp. 171–73.

[1] *Auto.*, i, 546–47.

[2] *The Clergymen of the Church of England*, pp. 128–29

right to tell you that it does so work upon any one mind as it does upon mine.—What an emancipation it is,—to have escaped from the little enclosure of dogma, and to stand,—far indeed from being wise,—but free to learn!" Or, in a letter bridging two of his windy phrenological accounts of the physiology of the brain: "Now for the cerebrum! Where do you begin?"

Miss Martineau gushed and Atkinson ranted. In a brilliant, if ill-advised, review of the book, James Martineau made Atkinson a target for devastating sarcasm. In his mixture of materialism, necessarianism, and "science" derived from mesmerism and phrenology, Atkinson had referred everything to his own convictions and so forced his critics to look to his qualifications; consequently, James Martineau not only made great play with the slovenly use of words, inconsistency, disorganization, and intense conceit of the book, but with malicious accuracy he went to Atkinson's contributions to the *Zoist* to reinforce his attack and to tease him for his violence to English grammar. That, at least, Miss Martineau had spared him this time! James's only extended reference to her was to express his regret that she had forsaken her faith to follow such a master, to "glory in the infection of his blind arrogance and scorn, mistaking them for wisdom and pity; and meekly undertake to teach him grammar in return. Surely this humiliating inversion of the natural order of nobleness cannot last. If this be a specimen of mesmeric victories, such a conquest is more damaging than a thousand defeats."[1]

James Martineau was a superb controversialist; he had an easy target, and he made the most of it. And yet, for all the nonsense and inanity, for all the ignorance and constriction of the *Letters*, there was something in what they had to say. The assumption which underlay the jargon and rodomontade was that which Miss Martineau was to find so compelling in Auguste Comte, and which according to John Stuart Mill formed the basis of all scientific advance—that we can know nothing but phenomena and the laws which govern them. Like the scientists, when they were acting as scientists, from Galileo down, Miss Martineau and Atkinson called for the rigid separation of science and theology, put their faith in the former, and presumably asked "how" not "why". However confusedly, they were on the wave of the future, and much of what they said (about free will, for instance)

[1] "Mesmeric Atheism", *Prospective Review*, vii, 224–62 (June, 1851).

seems commonplace to our psychologically oriented, relativistic age.

One must convict them, however, of failing to understand a good many of their implications.[1] Although materialism was a good Priestleyan inheritance, Miss Martineau never bothered to reconcile it with her faith—as strong after 1851 as before—in the governing power of great ideas. While their doctrinaire necessarianism produced a scathing denial of free will and individual moral responsibility,[2] James Martineau saw perfectly clearly that probably neither of the two enthusiasts, certainly not his sister, could act in accordance with their teaching. A daughter of Elizabeth Rankin Martineau far gone in relativism and abstaining from judgment? Hardly. Again, although they were apostles of science, they continually thought in ways and talked in terms borrowed from their old commitments—incessantly moralizing, resolutely teleological. In short, neither of them ever really understood what science was about. Their proudly flaunted new convictions were little more than a change of rhetoric in the preaching of old concerns.

Take first Miss Martineau's enthusiasm for science. We have already seen that science played a large part in her inherited intellectual positions—it is enough to be reminded of the hero-worship of Newton among the Unitarians. But in *Society in*

[1] "For my part I should not have called it by so hard a name [as 'atheistical']. I should rather have doubted whether either the lady or the gentleman quite knows the exact thing that the letters do mean. I am sure I do not, and I suspect that many other of their readers will be in the same predicament." M. R. Mitford to Boner, April 17, 1851. *Correspondence*, p. 186.

[2] "Will is the echo and act of the majority and strongest power: as clearly so as the weathercock points to the wind, and the ship follows the impress of the rudder and the sails, and is carried along by wind and tide. If it could think, it would imagine that it slid away by its own impulse and will, or undetermined force. . . . Free will! the very idea is enough to make a Democritus fall on his back and roar with laughter, and a more serious thinker almost despair of bringing men to reason,—to experience the advantages of knowledge, and the calming influence of a recognition of universal law and necessity." Pp. 194–95. "All that a judge and jury have to ascertain is how a man has behaved: but it remains for wiser men than judges and juries at present are to say what treatment will be the best check upon inferior natures. We must remove the gallows, and no more use the rod; for these are not instruments of reform and civilization, but the instruments of barbarism, and the cause of brutality." Pp. 243–44. These are both by Atkinson. Cf. Priestley, *Works*, iii, 518: ". . . a Necessarian who, as such, believes that *nothing goes wrong*, but that everything is under the best direction possible . . . cannot accuse himself of having done wrong in the ultimate sense of the words. He has, therefore . . . nothing to do with repentance, confession, or pardon, which are all adapted to a different, imperfect, and fallacious view of things."

America she made a sharp disjunction between science and the practice and spirit of religion, the latter for all, the former for only a few. Even then she thought that the day might come when all would have the breadth of mind to deal with science, but for the foreseeable future, most men could not aspire so high and would find their guides in the true spirit of Christianity freed from the corrupting influences of dogma.[1] In her analysis of *Zanoni* in 1842 she seems to have taken a less favourable view. Science, embodied in the aged Mejnour, was "less fallible than Idealism, but less practically potent, from its ignorance of the human heart . . ., ever striving to carry the most gifted beyond ordinary conditions—the result being as many victims as efforts, and the striver being finally left a solitary—for his object is unsuitable to the natures he has to deal with". Science was blind, that is, to the great message of the novel, that "the universal human lot is . . . that of the highest privilege". Her view of science, then, was high but limited. What made her regard it later as the basis of all that was valuable to man?

The scientific excitement of the time had much to do with it. Miss Martineau had attended the meeting of the British Association in Newcastle in 1838 and followed all its activities with interest. She was fascinated by what Faraday was doing and equally by the *acarus* of Mr. Crosse, that presumed production of life by means of an electric current. The great geological controversies had pushed back the history of man and, of course, she accepted the findings,[2] while the publication of Robert Chambers's *Vestiges of the Natural History of Creation* in 1844, the first popularization of evolutionary views, was a wonderfully exciting event to her. It not only prepared her for Darwin's revelations, which she received with great enthusiasm as "overthrowing (if true) revealed religion on the one hand, and Natural (as far as Final Cause & Design are concerned) on the other"; it brought science into closer relation with the moral concerns which meant so much to her.[3]

The main impulse to her new scientism was, I am sure, her belief in mesmerism. Here was a field for the discovery of new laws of nature of unbounded significance for the welfare of

[1] *SA*, i, 329–31. [2] *EL*, pp. 73–74.

[3] HM to G. J. Holyoake, Friday, n.d., probably late 1859. *ASS*, January 28, 1860. Atkinson told her that the *Vestiges* was by his friend Hewitt C. Watson, former editor of the *Phrenological Journal*; she believed him and passed on the information. HM to Crabb Robinson, June 24, [1845].

humanity and society and one in which she had herself made and seen great contributions.[1] With Professor Gregory's reputation as a scientist and Atkinson's transparent goodwill to back her up, she responded emotionally to the prospects the mesmerists offered; and with such seemingly incredible results all but attained, it must have seemed possible for her to move up her timetable, either to turn everyone into a scientist or to make them aware of the claims of science to demonstrate conclusively, as she had done in a limited field with political economy, the dominion of the laws of nature and the futility of opposing them, whether from wilfulness or ignorance.

The first task was to clear away the theological debris which cluttered the ground; hence the attacks on dogmatic Christianity, freewill, and the vested interests of the clergy. Hence too the repeated references to Bacon. Bacon, to be sure, was something of a hero to the radical admirers of science,[2] but it was not merely his method (the faults of which the amateurs would hardly see) or his publicizing that endeared him to Atkinson.

> We must profit by Bacon's admonitions, and not mix up theology with science. We must not see ourselves reflected,—see the ghosts of ourselves in Nature, and imagine we recognize design, or a human origin of things. We must follow our great master Bacon, and make a stand against the fallacy of natural theology, and that exceedingly weak argument of Paley's about the watch. . . . Science must be wholly cleared from theology, or we shall be stopped at the very entrance of the temple. . . .[3]

It was a nineteenth-century view of a seventeenth-century dilemma.

Science, however, was a means to an end. On the positive side there was the zeal for reform and perfection of society.

[1] "Mr. Atkinson and I shall be happy to hear of any new facts, bearing on our doctrines, pro or con.—I dare say you have seen the accounts of Mr. Rutter's 'Magnetoscope,' at Brighton. I have written to inquire whether the investigation has been really sound and well conducted. The Reports are in the 'Homoeopathic Times' for October 18th and 25th." HM to Mr. Stark. November 30, [1851], inserted in a copy of Forster's *Life of Dickens*, Cornell.

[2] Robertson, the editor of the *Westminster*, introduced to Arthur Stanley by Miss Martineau at the British Association meeting in 1838, told him that the New Testament and the *Novum Organon* were the only two books he knew thoroughly—the first giving the sublimest morals, the second the best training of the intellect. Prothero, *Life of Stanley*, i, 203–4.

[3] *Letters*, pp. 139–40. James Martineau in his review accused Atkinson of perverting Bacon by misinterpretation and quoting out of context.

> From the recognition of universal law, we shall develope a universal love; the disposition and ability to love without offence or ill-feeling towards any. We shall see that no one can be a true friend to us who is not a friend to all. We shall learn that dirt is beauty unformed; that evil is undeveloped good; or rather, that we judge the universal in reference to ourselves, not ourself in reference to the universal.[1]

I do not know what he means by the last clause, but the drift of the whole is clear. And it is easy to see how Atkinson influenced Miss Martineau. He was not her master; there was nothing insincere or diabolical. Both had long held an intense if woolly vision of the future, a future in which alienations from society (their own included) would be undone, yet more, in which every evil of society would dissolve into perfection. The highest prospect for society, she wrote in the thirties, is that all men should live as brothers. That fraternal principle, the ground of Christianity, the inspiration of the poets and philosophers, was beginning to appear in the working of society. Charity was no longer done from mere compassion, but more abstractly, from a spiritual interest in the welfare of other classes. With missions, abolitionism, and care of the unfortunate, the great day had dawned and would soon brighten into noon.[2]

But the most charming and in some ways remarkable expression of this view by Miss Martineau was purely unconscious. In writing *Eastern Life* she recalled the ugly unison singing of the crew on their Nile boat—always in the minor key, man's natural expression until he is taught otherwise.

> I often wished that I could sing loud enough to catch their ear, amidst their clamour, that I might see whether my second would strike them with any sense of harmony: but their overpowering noise made any such attempt hopeless.—We are accustomed to find or make the music which we call spirit-stirring in the major key: but their spirit-stirring music, set up to encourage them at the oar, is all of the same pathetic character as the most doleful, and only

---

[1] *Letters*, p. 209 (Atkinson). Or compare what he said in the letter encouraging her to go on boldly with *Eastern Life* (*Auto.*, i, 544): "Let us unindividualize ourselves;—merge our personality in the infinite;—raise the ideal in our mind;—see each as but a part of that ideal;—and we lose the sense of imperfection—the sense of individual opinions and character, and rise into a new life of godlike conceptions—active, practical, and earnest . . ." etc., etc. See also the conclusion to Elliotson's Harveian Oration, above, p. 246, and Atkinson's call for a great poet, *Zoist*, iii, 118–20 (April, 1845).

[2] *How to Observe*, pp. 210–12.

somewhat louder and more rapid. They kept time so admirably, and were so prone to singing, that we longed to teach them to substitute harmony for noise, and meaning for mere sensation.[1]

Action, harmony, and didacticism—the three virtues in that paragraph are leitmotifs of her life.

The publication of the *Letters* brought her the martyrdom she predicted. The book made a great noise, the reviews, almost without exception, were harsh and contemptuous, and Miss Martineau's friends and acquaintances were appalled. "There is no God," ran Douglas Jerrold's witticism, "and Harriet is his prophet." In common terminology the book was atheistic. The offence was compounded by the apparent rejection of any absolute canons of morality and by the tone, which even George Eliot, who gave the book credit for being one of the boldest in the language, called "studiously offensive".[2] Mrs. Reid, Mrs. Arnold, Julia Smith, Crabb Robinson, Macready, most of her old friends were shocked, and some never resumed the friendship. Others who had already quarrelled with her, like Tremenheere or Mary Howitt, found their worst suspicions confirmed: "This is what your strong-minded women come to," wrote Tremenheere. In spite of the disclaimer in the *Autobiography* (a piece of unaccustomed charity that does her credit) Charles Knight wrote to break the contract for the continuation of the *History* and advertised—without mentioning her name—that he was not going on with it.[3] Even the *Zoist* came out against the book. And George Eliot, reviewing it in the *Leader*, while admiring the courage and the nobility, rejected the mesmerism and asked why if reason was not allowed to dictate poetry, it should be allowed to dictate religion.[4]

[1] *EL*, p. 18. Cf. Atkinson, *Letters*, p. 194: "The language of music, when it is a true utterance, is the most perfect of all languages. Would that the mind was always in tune, and all was sweetest melody, and radiant harmony! But alas! for the discord of passions, and the discord of untruth, and the scraping on the instrument in self-considerations,—and the sounding brass and tinkling cymbal in our pride and vanities!"

[2] George Eliot to Charles Bray, [October 4, 1851], *Letters*, i, 364. Crabb Robinson's Diary, February 8, 1851.

[3] Crabb Robinson's Diary, *passim*, 1851. Tremenheere to Mrs. Parker, March 25, 1851. Mary Howitt's Journal, quoted in her *Autobiography*, pp. 68–69. Macready, *Diaries*, ii, 91 (February 2, 1851). *Auto.*, i, 19–20. Crabb Robinson mentions the advertisement in his diary, March 9, 1851. "This will open her eyes if anything will," he said. The letter is referred to in Mrs. Chapman's notes on the quarrel with James, BPL, Weston, vi, no. 3.

[4] *Zoist*, ix, 65–69, 224 (April and July, 1851). *Leader*, March 1 and 8, 1851.

Hardest of all to take, of course, was the attack by James. Relations between the two of them had been strained for some time. He had felt otherwise than she did about the educational clauses in 1843; he had entered a strong protest about letter-burning; he could never accept mesmerism; and reconciliation was not easy to bring about. Yet Miss Martineau was writing cordially to James's wife at the end of 1849 arranging for a visit early in January—preferably mid-week so that she could see more of them, not being herself (she said rather pointedly) a chapel-goer.[1] James maintained that he wrote the review because it fell to his turn among the editors of the *Prospective Review* and none of the others wanted it; but clearly he need never have reviewed it at all, had it not given him an opportunity for letting off a long accumulation of steam. One need pay no attention to the easy allegations of her friends that James was motivated by jealousy, of either her accomplishments and superior intelligence or "her higher social position". These explanations are nonsensical, except insofar as James may have understandably resented the wide publicity his sister got for intellectual views that seemed repugnant to him and religious views that were contemptible.

It is simple enough to explain the review by the intellectual estrangement between the two. James had originally become a necessarian under his sister's urging, and when he broke loose in the thirties, a quarrel was one day inevitable. When it came, it must have been because he felt her ostentatious rejection of religion, on largely fallacious grounds, both a reflection on him and a presumption that had to be put down. It may have been more besides. Perhaps she cut too close to the bone. Crabb Robinson found the whole Martineau family in London very bitter towards her, "perhaps even more than there is occasion for—at least she has only carried out principles which her friends have long avowed".[2] James was fighting to defend and refound his church and must have loathed traitors within. Whatever the motive of his attack, he did it superbly. But apparently even that was not enough: he would have reviewed her translation of Comte, too, if the editor of the *Westminster* had not turned him

[1] HM to Milnes, May 31, [1843]. HM to Crabb Robinson, June 24, [1845]. Crabb Robinson's Travel Journals, December 21, 1847. HM to Helen Martineau, n.d., but 1847 (in which she is still hoping that the clergyman who has rented her house will read James's books), and December 29, [1849], MCO.

[2] Diary, March 11, 1851, DWL.

down.[1] A pretty Westminster quarrel, said Matthew Arnold, like the family of Pelops.[2] But it seems to have issued logically from the concern for ideas which Arnold wanted to generalize in English society.

"She has lost the friendship of nearly all those she most respects," wrote Crabb Robinson, "she affects great happiness & triumph in the sort of social persecution, as she affects to consider the withdrawal of friendship which she now experiences." "My genuine friends did not change," she said, "and the others, failing under so clear a test, were nothing to me." It was very hard for some, like Mrs. Reid, who managed to stand by her; she welcomed the loyalty if she did not fully comprehend the struggle. But she was not without some enthusiastic support; it helped. Holyoake's *Reasoner* gave her a glowing review; a working man wrote to the *Leader* in admiration, and she reported happily to Holyoake in 1852 that the two copies of the book in a Birmingham library used by "thinking men & women of the *lower middle*, & working classes, were always out, & read with extreme eagerness & thoughtfulness".[3]

The best consolation, if consolation was needed, was that at least she had testified to the truth. Her book made a striking contrast, she said, to W. R. Greg's *Creed of Christendom*, which came out at about the same time, or to Francis Newman's *Phases of Faith* of a year earlier; both were weakened by reluctance to follow their premises to logical conclusions. Unlike them, her book did "an immensity of good, by carrying the war into the enemy's camp, and releasing a host of pining captives".[4] So she would always be bold in speaking out. When well-meaning friends or acquaintances wrote to her on the subject, she never held her fire out of any respect for their prejudices or feelings. Those who sent her Testaments, as if she had never seen one, she could sometimes ignore. Whenever complacent Evangelicals wrote to her, "I always take high ground with them, when I answer them at all,—showing them the gross self-regards [*sic*] they exhibit & wd recommend to me, & giving them some hints

[1] Mrs. Chapman's notes on the quarrel, BPL, Weston, vi, no. 3. Atkinson to G. J. Holyoake, March 25, 1877, BM. Upton, *James Martineau*, pp. 14–18, 93–94n.

[2] Arnold to Mrs. Forster, October 10, 1854, *Unpublished Arnold Letters*, p. 26.

[3] Crabb Robinson to Thomas Robinson, September 22, 1857. *Reasoner*, March 12, 1851. *Leader*, March 1, 1851. HM to G. J. Holyoake, April 7, [1852], BM.

[4] HM to Philip Carpenter, January 16, [1853]. HM to Milnes, April 20, [1855]. HM to Crabb Robinson, July 6, 1850.

of aspiration towards something loftier, humbler, holier, purer, & more disinterested." When she was sent *In Memoriam* in the hope that it might counteract her materialism, she replied at once with a long letter making a full statement of her case for "scientific humanism".

When Mary Carpenter, the prison reformer, a daughter of Lant Carpenter, and the brother of one of her regular correspondents, wrote lamenting that Miss Martineau did not have the comforts that she derived from her religion, Miss Martineau sent back a sizzling reply that led Miss Carpenter's brother to intercede and ask that she not be proud with a humble Christian like Mary. The fury redoubled. It was always the Christians who were humble, she sneered; when they stood up for what they believed, it was called zeal for the Gospel; when she stood up for what she believed in, it was called pride and haughtiness. There was too much truckling to the Christians, and now that Mary had insulted her by pitying her, it would be treachery to the truth and cruelty to mankind not to defend the loftiness and breadth of the principles of her faith.[1] I have nowhere seen any letters of hers so violent as these: it was clearly too good an opportunity to miss, to take on the daughter of the man who more than anyone else had confirmed her in her youthful "superstition"; it was, too, I am sure, an indirect answer to James.

There were many other ways of serving the faith. She was a strong supporter of the *Reasoner*, Holyoake's paper, and when W. J. Linton, the radical wood-engraver, attacked Holyoake for using the term secularist instead of atheist—"sneaking" Linton called it—she defended Holyoake in a strong letter to the *Liberator*, the abolitionist paper in which the attack had appeared, and in a covering letter to Garrison she cast a series of not very subtle aspersions on Linton's character. She thought about writing a burial service for secularists. She hoped for a number of years that she would produce a life and letters of Francis Bacon, a project dear to Atkinson's heart, but after her illness came on in 1855, she more or less gave up the idea and hoped that Spedding's life would do as well as Lyell had led her to believe it would. And of course the *Autobiography* itself was aimed at enforcing this last great lesson of her life. W. R. Greg, who

[1] The letter to Furnivall concerning *In Memoriam* is printed in *Auto.*, ii, 392–94. HM to Philip Carpenter, January 7, 9, 11, 15, 1856. Carpenter stood for it, too.

could give her credit as she never could him, commented in his obituary on the positiveness of her convictions, as firmly held as any martyr's. In the certainties of science, she became more and more cheerful; one of the richest lessons of the *Autobiography*, to him, was that joy and comfort were possible under such a belief. She was religious to the end, never a sceptic.[1]

Against such a background of positive if non-theological faith must be seen her enthusiasm for Comte's *Positive Philosophy*. Neither she nor Atkinson knew Comte's work directly at the time of their book, and they came to what knowledge they had through the chapter on him in Lewes's *Biographical History of Philosophy* and the epitome by Comte's disciple Littré. She had no sooner begun to read the work itself in the spring of 1851 than she hit upon the idea of translating it, a scheme which after some consultations became a plan for a free translation and condensation, reducing the six volumes of the original to two, to be published by John Chapman. Learning of the project from Chapman, Edward Lombe, a Norfolk gentleman, resident in Italy, was sufficiently enthusiastic about the realization of something he had once thought of doing himself that he sent a draft to her for £500. She took only a part of it—£200 she says in her *Autobiography*—for her compensation, invested the rest, and had Chapman apply it to supporting the publication.

Shortly thereafter Chapman learned of a similar translation and condensation, already well under way, by a clergyman, W. M. W. Call, who George Eliot thought might well be better qualified than Miss Martineau to do the job. The question in her mind was whether Call's version would be "fitted for circulation among the people"; certainly Miss Martineau's style was admirably adapted to that task, whatever the deficiencies of her mind. And, apparently, that consideration (with Miss Martineau's reluctance to abandon her project) prevailed. Miss Martineau wrote to Holyoake in October that the other version was "not in popular form", so Call gave in to their advantages and offered her the use of his manuscript, on condition that he could claim his portion of credit for introducing Comte to England. She thought that she might send him some of Lombe's

[1] HM to Garrison, two letters, dated November 1, 1853, BPL, Anti-Slavery. The Holyoake correspondence in the BM, and two letters in the Holyoake papers at the Co-operative Union, Manchester. HM to Philip Carpenter, September 29, 1856. W. R. Greg in *Nineteenth Century*, ii, 108–12 (August, 1877).

money if his manuscript was of any use to her; but nothing more was said of him, and the autobiography mentions him not at all.[1]

As is the case with all her books, the speed with which the translation was done must be taken into account in judging it. She first read the *Philosophie Positive* in 1851; she began translating in June, 1852, but did not return to it until December. The final pages went to the printer, who was already at work, in October, 1853, and the book was published in November. Amid a flurry of journalism, she tried to do from twenty-five to thirty pages a day and on one day did forty-eight. As usual, she finished as she went along, not having another look until the proof-sheets came. The earlier portions on mathematics, astronomy, and physics were gone over by her friend J. P. Nichol, professor of astronomy at Glasgow and the husband of Elizabeth Pease, the Darlington Quaker philanthropist; he made no changes except to add some footnote comments. Thanks to Lombe's gift, the price was set at eight shillings a volume, and she was much concerned to get it as widely circulated as possible to serve the "cause of sound knowledge & free thought", though she knew that it could never, from its bulk and difficulty, attract the general reader; its public, said the *Reasoner*, was in the "thinking or self-taught". She arranged for some of the profits to go to Comte himself—Herbert Spencer carried something under £20 to Paris in 1856—and Miss Martineau herself got something out of later editions. "Here is the thing done," she wrote in 1874 of a reprinting by Trübner, "no toil or trouble in prospect, the book at the call of the working classes, & £30 in the Bank already."[2]

The English positivists received the work with rejoicing. Lewes thought it "admirably well done" and saw to it that there was a favourable review in the *Leader*. Spencer, who did not know the original, thought it perfectly lucid. T. H. Huxley reviewed it in the *Westminster* and compared what she had done to what Dumont did for Bentham. Holyoake thought it a complete justification of the secularists by giving them a positive body of faith to oppose to the hackneyed accusations that they were

[1] *Auto.*, ii, 57–59, 66–67. *George Eliot Letters*, i, 360–61, ii, 17. HM to Holyoake, October 6, [1851].

[2] *Auto.*, ii, 70–73. *Reasoner*, November 30, 1853. George Eliot to S. S. Hennell, November 8, [1856], *Letters*, ii, 271. HM to Holyoake, April 9, [1853]. HM to Spring Brown, October 20, 1874, NLS.

negative and destructive. It was everyman's title deed to an estate in the new realms of belief and knowledge, which "not only leaves him in present possession, but promises a further wealth to his remotest posterity". Comte himself wrote flattering letters to Miss Martineau and substituted her condensation (which was translated into French) for his own work in the *Positivist Library*, a generosity scandalously repaid, said Frederic Harrison, by pretended philosophers who elaborately criticized a work the original of which they had never read. Harrison, perhaps the most important of Comte's disciples in England, was no more than tolerant of the translation; he objected not only to errors but to the inevitable omission of much of Comte's elaborate qualification. Within her purpose and for the occasion, the book was adequate, no more.[1]

Harrison's estimate was correct. The haste with which the work was done helps to account for the awkwardness and the fuzziness which occasionally mar a mechanical translation; she was writing too about matters of which her understanding was at best superficial. If she was not as outrageous as she was in the political economy tales, it was because she was only translating and condensing; besides, Comte himself came perilously close to absurdity in his parochialism and passion for systematization. But the great burst of interest in Comte in the forties and fifties is an important symptom in Victorian intellectual life, and Miss Martineau's particular brand of enthusiasm has implications which are more than biographical.

Comte's work was a remarkable achievement, whose importance in the mid-nineteenth century was not at all overstated by the judicious and generally favourable critique of John Stuart Mill.[2] From his encyclopaedic knowledge of the sciences and history (helped on by the fact that he read no more books after he had arrived at his theory), Comte had constructed an evolutionary view of the development of man's intellect and society which is still highly suggestive. Starting from the general assumptions of science, Comte proposed the law of three states, whereby all sciences, all men's thinking on particular subjects,

[1] George Eliot to S. S. Hennell, [November 25, 1853], and to Charles Bray, February 6, [1854], *Letters*, ii, 127, 140. *Leader*, December 3, 1853. *WR*, n.s., vi, 194 (July, 1854). *Reasoner*, May 25, 1853. Frederic Harrison, *The Philosophy of Common Sense*, pp. 325–28, a reprinting of an essay on the republication of the book in Bohn's Library.

[2] *Auguste Comte and Positivism*, 1865.

and indeed by analogy society itself, are seen to pass from theological and metaphysical stages into the positive state. From explaining phenomena by reference to supernatural agency (there is a subdivision into fetichism, polytheism, and monotheism), man progressed to explanation in terms of abstract entities, and finally emerged into the clear light of a scientific, positive approach—an examination of phenomena, not in terms of ultimate explanations but in terms of the laws which can be discovered controlling them. On the basis of this law, Comte constructed a hierarchy of the sciences, according to the order in which they attained (or would attain) positivity, starting with mathematics, progressing through astronomy, physics, chemistry, and biology, to the final crowning science (in his time barely begun), the science of society for which Comte coined the term sociology. Having set his assumptions, he proceeded to an analysis of the sciences, and the book culminates in a philosophy of history (to which Mill could take no exception) and the adumbration of the organic society which would one day succeed when the positive principles of sociology had been discovered.

Miss Martineau was never a true Comtean; that fact underlay Harrison's criticism. She was never able to accept the lunacy of Comte's positive polity, that totalitarian conception of society modelled on Catholicism, with refinements of intellectual dictatorship the Church had never attained, if it had aspired to them.[1] Even to the positive philosophy of the earlier volumes, her allegiance was remarkably spotty.

Much of the terminology and rhetoric she used. The *Autobiography* and her letters are full of references to her own emergence from theological and metaphysical views to positivism. Her interpretation of history sometimes carries a positivist veneer. But it is by no means exclusively Comtean: Comte never drove out the dramatic prospect of the great struggle for opinion which she had derived from Canning, a struggle she conceived in purely English terms.[2] Again, Comte was scornful of political economy, and she was duly scornful when the opportunity

[1] HM to Reeve, June 7, 1868.

[2] She was much more responsive to the general nineteenth-century tendency to "scientific" history which discovered the laws of progress. Comte was only part of this. Marx and Buckle were even better examples, and Miss Martineau was a great admirer of the philosophy of history contained in the now-forgotten *Secularia* by Samuel Lucas. HM to Milnes, August 11, 1862.

offered; but even though she could say that the pretended science was no science at all, she never failed to preach from the gospel of the economists as if they had attained the final truth.[1] Comte's views on the natural subordination of woman and—even though his later religion worshipped woman—on her confinement to her own proper fields were abhorrent to Miss Martineau, so obviously so that she never refers to them, even to refute them, in anything I have seen; her whole tone on the subject of women remained utterly alien to Comte's. And, as we shall see, with her insular pride in British institutions as well as her traditional devotion to Protestantism and Dissent, she could only be amused or possibly annoyed by Comte's almost total blindness to the character and contributions of either.

What, then, was it that attracted her, if only some formulations remain? Surely she could borrow Comte's terminology because he offered an entire system which at one point after another struck familiar notes. Both were necessarians; both were phrenologists. Like her, he insisted on the separation of the spiritual and temporal, on the limits of political action, and on the supremacy of the moral over the political. More remarkably, she had anticipated the law of the three stages years before:

> As the aggregate experience of mankind accumulates, truth is developed, and the faculties of the mind approximate to a harmonious action. The imagination becomes more disposed to exercise itself on forms which have truth for their essence, and are therefore immortal, than on those which are inspired with a capricious and transient life. In the infancy of society, the imagination can find the elements of its creations in nature alone; and therefore its action is, for a time, pure. In a more advanced state, its elements are chosen from the dreams of a preceding age, and its illegitimate exercise gives birth to superstition. But the result of a further discipline of the universal mind is to make the imagination again subservient to truth; while the fuller development of truth expands and exalts the imagination.—Higher and purer excitements are at length administered by truth than ever sprang from delusion, however poetical. The thoughts and feelings suggested by the exercise of the abstract powers on real objects are more influential and permanent than any which originate in superstition. The associations which cluster around realities, in themselves insignificant, afford greater variety of excitements than the machinery of pure fiction.[2]

[1] *Auto.*, i, 512. *DN*, January 27, 1853, a review of Greg's *Essays in Political and Social Science*.

[2] *Misc.*, ii, 114–16; the article dates from 1834. She goes on to talk about the

And for years she had been preaching sociology without the name. Here she is in 1832:

> Such then is the state of inquiry among us. Physical science is advancing steadily, and with an accelerating rapidity, under the guidance of philosophical principles. Moral science is lagging behind, blinded, thwarted, led astray by a thousand phantoms of ancient ignorance and error, which would have disappeared long ago, if the dawn of philosophy had not arisen as cloudily upon this region as brightly upon the other.

She was sure that the time would come when moral science would no longer be the province of the uninstructed, but would be confined to the philosophers who would be as important to the "science of society" as Herschel to astronomy and Beaufort to hydrography. Then, instead of imprisoning philosophers for their discoveries, men would gratefully accept their findings, as now they accepted the discoveries of physical science.[1] This is not to claim priority or originality for Miss Martineau; it is simply to indicate that Comte's ideas came out of the commonplaces of his time, another example of "what oft was thought, but ne'er so well express'd".

There is, however, another consideration of overriding importance in which the singleness of Comte's view, the fact that he collected all of these currents into one book, plays an important role. Frederic Harrison, at Oxford, was appalled by the conflict of opinions in the fifties. "How can the minds of keen young students retain their calm or any fixity of thought, when week by week they are swept by 'every wind of doctrine'—winds that blow in turn from each quarter of the theological compass, which they 'box' with incessant revolutions."[2] To this dilemma, to the increasingly unsatisfactory answers which orthodox religion gave to mid-Victorian problems, Comte provided a solution which was heightened by a belief in progress and a passion for serving humanity. "I never parted with any belief till I had found its complement," wrote Harrison in 1890;[3] neither did Miss Martineau. "We are living in a remarkable time," she wrote in her preface to the translation,

---

way in which ignorant men and enlightened men will look on word of a shipwreck —an interesting passage, considering the *brouhaha* about Jane's prevision concerning the wreck at Tynemouth.

[1] *Misc.*, i, 190–94; *SA*, i, 334–35; *How to Observe*, pp. 14–15.

[2] "Apologia pro fide mea", *Creed of a Layman*, pp. 14–15.

[3] *Ibid.*, p. 1.

> when the conflict of opinions renders a firm foundation of knowledge indispensable, not only to our intellectual, moral, and social progress, but to our holding such ground as we have gained from former ages. . . . The supreme dread of every one who cares for the good of nation or race is that men should be adrift for want of an anchorage for their convictions. I believe that no one questions that a very large proportion of our people are now so adrift . . . The work of M. Comte is unquestionably the greatest single effort that has been made to obviate this kind of danger; and my deep persuasion is that it will be found to retrieve a vast amount of wandering, of unsound speculation, of listless or reckless doubt, and of moral uncertainty and depression.

She had built her new faith on the foundations of her old convictions. It was proclaimed partially from the political economy tales to *Eastern Life* and *Household Education*, stated fully in the *Letters*, and then its analogue given the world in her translation of Comte. As for Comte's deficiencies and errors, they were of as little account to her as the dogma of the economists which she later ignored, or the evidential weaknesses of the mesmerists which she shared, or the fuzziness and arrogance of Atkinson which she never saw or misread as Christ-like. Mill, it will be recalled, commented on her reduction of political economy to an absurdity by carrying it out to all its consequences. Such absurdity never mattered to her when something else mattered more. She was, she told Bulwer-Lytton, a hopeless critic. The only books she could read had one quality in common: they were full of earnest thought. "This provided, I become one with the writer so completely as to be unable to rise to any capacity for judging,—or to any right to compare my likings, (otherwise than experimentally), with those of better trained & qualified readers."[1]

It is a pity that her candour about this defect—which explains so much in her career—did not extend to a candour about her early works, or rather that she misapplied her candour, scoffing at them when she might have seen in them the core of everything she did afterwards. I suppose her pride and belief in progress, perhaps even her quest for martyrdom, made that impossible. Whatever the reason, there is no doubt that after all the reading and thinking and talking and writing, after all the enthusiasm and discovery and rejection, she had found herself—a disciple of Priestley and a manufacturer's daughter—and called the treasure philosophy.

[1] August 28, [1842].

CHAPTER XI

Ambleside: Journalism by Rule

MISS MARTINEAU liked to say that her life began with winter, while spring, summer and autumn crowded together in the ten years after she settled in Ambleside. From 1855 she was expecting death at any moment. She survived for another twenty-one years, a prolongation, I should say, of the briskness and activity of autumn. These years have a unity in remarkable contrast to the episodic nature of her earlier life. It is provided, for one thing, by her work; for another, by the state of her health.

In the early fifties she was often away from Ambleside, visiting her relatives and friends, travelling to collect material for her industrial series in *Household Words*, working in London for the *Westminster Review* or the *Daily News*. Her first appearance in the latter was with a series of letters from Ireland in 1852. But she knew during that journey that she would not travel again; in the next two years appeared the distressing symptoms which took her to London to consult physicians in January, 1855. Short and difficult breathing, "odd sensations at the heart", partial disappearance of printed words could be dismissed at first as results of indigestion, but she was soon convinced that something was wrong with her heart. Referring to his notes made at the time, one of the doctors said, years later, that there were abnormal sounds, but no murmurs; he assured her that all the symptoms could be accounted for by the menopause. "But she plainly distrusted, or rather she disbelieved, my reassurances, looking upon them, I fancy, as well-meant and amiable attempts to soothe and tranquillise a doomed patient"—that is, she treated Sir Thomas Watson as she had treated her brother-in-law fifteen years before. The big question was the ovarian cyst. The doctor's notes mention it, and in June, 1855, she wrote to Atkinson, quoting her Ambleside doctor as saying that the increase in her girth must be due either to dropsy or to an ovarian tumour. But her own account in the autobiography, written directly after she returned from London, was that her disease was enlargement of the heart; she continued to explain all her difficulties by the resulting displacement of internal organs. Of course it was the enormous cyst that did it.[1]

Milnes visited her in the spring of 1855—he saw some of the autobiography—and thought she looked better than he had ever seen her. However, she took her illness seriously, and not without some reason. In July she was suffering fainting attacks and could not be left alone for a moment; she could still sit out of doors but no longer walked or rode in a carriage; it was not long until she never went out again, though she continued to move about the house until the sixties. Largely nerves, Richard Webb thought it, or certainly "something peculiar about the mental as well as the physical constitution of that remarkable woman". And so indeed there was. Ill, yes, beyond a doubt: seriously ill, probably not. As had happened in the forties, there were painful complications. She had influenza and rheumatic pains. In the early sixties she developed a facial tic, but mesmerism—Maria mesmerized her bedclothes unknown to her—helped and so did carrot tea, a remedy she strongly urged on Florence Nightingale. She seems to have suffered more in the summers; winters found her an invalid but quite well. She had got over the pursuit of martyrdom of her Tynemouth days; she had not got over the medical superstition. But she managed to keep going with, at one time or another, oysters, game, champagne, turtle, brandy, and laudanum—and she got a fantastic amount of work done. Too many strangers were intruding, said a letter from Miss Martineau's physician in the newspapers.

> When we have adverted to the fact that, notwithstanding her shattered health, Mrs. H. Martineau devotes every hour in which pain leaves her free to prosecute her labours in disseminating information on the most important economical, political, and social questions—that on the verge of existence her active interest in all that concerns humanity is as genial and comprehensive as ever—we have said enough to show all right-minded persons the absolute necessity of not harassing her by the intrusion of visits of mere idle curiosity.

---

[1] *British Medical Journal*, July 1 and 8, 1876, and April 21 and May 5, 1877. Atkinson to Milnes, June 23, 1855.

Here Mrs. Woodham-Smith's analysis seems to fit precisely: the illness kept her free to work.[1]

Some of what she did, despite her repeated insistence that she never wrote for money, was pure pot-boiling. She had contributed articles to Charles Dickens's *Household Words*, from its beginning in 1849, stories, some articles on health and sanitation, and a highly interesting descriptive series on various industries, which, judging from the invitations she received, were excellent publicity for the firms concerned.[2] Dickens was pleased with her contributions at first, although he commented at one point about her being "grimly bent upon the enlightenment of mankind". But the connection ceased in 1857 when, alarmed by the anti-Catholic bias of the paper, she turned her artillery of principle on W. H. Wills, the editor, while Dickens ran increasingly afoul of her for his crudity, his attitude towards women, and his sentimentalizing about factories in *Household Words.*[3] She also wrote short stories and sketches for the *Leader* in 1850 and 1851, and later for *Once a Week*. During one period of financial stringency, just after the death of her niece Maria in 1864, she refused loans from friends and found herself rescued by having been obliged—"pro bono publico, not for lucre"—to write articles for *Cornhill Magazine* (at Matthew Arnold's request) and the *Edinburgh Review*. She was utterly sincere.[4]

Nevertheless, she had to live, and in general lived well until she had to give up her writing; then when she was hit by inordinate expenses or—worse—by the temporary failure of her dividends, she had to retrench severely and even to count on her family to continue the luxuries of wine and food which helped her feeble health. A couple of contrasting budgets exist, one given by Mrs. Chapman in the *Memorials* for an unspecified year when she was

[1] She began to call herself Mrs. Martineau, an obsolescent practice for elderly single women. Reid, *Milnes*, i, 510. Maria Martineau to Arthur Allen, July 20, [1855], Yale. R. D. Webb to Anne Weston, March 31, 1858. HM to Reeve, May 25, 1860 and January 1, 1863. Maria Martineau to Philip Carpenter, June 14, 1860, BPL. *DN*, August 28, 1856. See above, pp. 196–97.

[2] A good many of these articles are reprinted with others in *Health, Husbandry, and Handicraft*. *Auto.*, ii, 67–70. There is a letter in the Columbia University Library which she wrote to Edward Flower, the Stratford brewer, a Unitarian and supporter of the *Westminster*, suggesting that she stay with him for two days to write about his brewery under his direction. Coming out from Birmingham, she could cover the ribbon industry at Coventry, if Charles Bray could arrange it, on her return. As it turned out, there was no article on brewing.

[3] *Auto.*, ii, 91–95. *Charles Dickens as Editor*, pp. 154, 249–50. *Letters of Charles Dickens*, i, 314.

[4] HM to P. P. Carpenter, August 31, 1864, MCO.

in full work, the other, in Mrs. Chapman's papers, for the year 1871.

				£ s. d.	£ s. d.
INCOME					
Dividends and interest				382 10 5	
Earned. *Daily News.*				280 7 0	
Periodicals				66 0 0	
Old works				30 17 9	
Old papers, etc.				1 0 9	
Farm				42 0 3	
					802 16 2
EXPENDITURE					
House and selves				230 5 3	
Highest sums, beyond wages					
Meat	22	2	7		
Wine and beer	12	4	9		
Fuel	13	8	6		
Postage, etc.	11	2	2		
Gave away				261 4 8½	
Farm				108 6 7	
					599 16 6½
BALANCE					202 19 7½

	£ s. d.	£ s. d.
INCOME		
Dividends	224 12 6	
Annuity	100 0 0	
Interest	2 7 5	
Waggon Company	40 10 0	
Works (Comte's *Positive Philosophy*, last of edition)	55 8 1	
Farm produce sold	38 5 9½	
		470 3 7½
EXPENDITURE		
House and selves	191 2 2	
Given away	170 0 6	
Farm and Man	101 15 8	
Extra (gravel)	2 5 0	
		464 3 4
BALANCE		5 0 3½

It was a well-run household: it had to be. She could continue to give away a third of her income and still refuse a pension, when Mr. Gladstone offered it in 1873.[1]

The serious writing went in a number of directions: *Macmillan's Magazine*, *Cornhill Magazine*, the *Atlantic Monthly* and *Once a Week*. For a period she was writing on America for *Spectator*. But her major efforts were for the *Westminster* and *Edinburgh Reviews*, the *National Anti-Slavery Standard* in New York and, most important of all, the *Daily News*.

The *Westminster* connection was confirmed by positivism. The review was in the hands of John Chapman and George Eliot, who looked on Miss Martineau as one of their most reliable contributors. At one time Miss Martineau lent £500 to rescue the journal for Chapman when he was being hounded by creditors, and it was mortgaged to her; and she did what she could to boost the *Westminster's* reputation by glowing reviews of it in the *Daily News*.[2] For most of the fifties it supplied, she said, a "vigorous, clear, well-informed, and honest liberalism" to fill the gap left by the "rancorous toryism" of the *Quarterly* and the "dull imbecility" of the *Edinburgh*. But in 1858, she switched her loyalties to a larger circulation: her cousin Henry Reeve had become editor of the *Edinburgh*.

Periodical writing, however, merely punctuated her regular work as a leader-writer for the *Daily News*. Edited for a very short period from its start in 1846 by Charles Dickens, the *Daily News* was intended as a Liberal counterpoise to *The Times*. After some difficult passages in its early years, by the 1850's the paper was fulfilling the intention in the hands of an excellent editor, Frederick Knight Hunt, who took Miss Martineau's letters from Ireland and then suggested that she send him two or three leaders a week. She started writing on Australian emigration—a subject she had lectured on in Ambleside shortly before—in May, 1852, and never stopped writing leaders until April, 1866, except for a three-month break in 1855 when she wrote her autobiography. Hunt died young in 1855, to be succeeded by William Weir; he was followed by Thomas Walker and, as managing editor, Sir John Robinson. With all of the editors and officials of the paper she had the warmest relationship, and Miss

[1] *Auto.*, ii, 548–50.

[2] *George Eliot Letters*, ii, 163, 237, 257, 490. The letters dealing with the advance and mortgage are in the Mill Collection in the London School of Economics. *DN*, January 3, 1855, and *passim*.

Martineau is still recalled proudly in the offices of the paper's successor.[1]

At times she wrote as many as six leaders a week, particularly when the office was short-handed in holiday time. She hounded Rowland Hill to get an evening or early morning despatch of mails from Ambleside so that she could write her articles in two or three hours after receiving the news at about 7.30 in the evening and have them in the London office by the following afternoon. After her illness, she confined her writing to the mornings. It was pleasant and easy work: an invalid could do it and be conscious of making an important contribution. Her range of concerns was astonishingly wide; she always had half a hundred topics, she told Lord Carlisle, that she could write on when the occasion offered.[2] A good many of the traditional subjects for leader-writing fell to her—royal occasions, the seasons, and summaries of the year's news. She dealt with her own long-standing concerns, church rates, for example, the position of women, or domestic service. She was an agricultural expert: the need for agricultural statistics, drainage, agricultural shows, cattle plague, harvests. She wrote on every major political subject, not of course immediate comment, but always within a few days of an important development: foreign affairs, colonies, education, parliamentary reform, strikes, factories, cotton supply, free trade.

She spared no one. She wrote as freely on the subject of cousin marriages, she said, as if Victoria had married a grandson of Prester John, especially when Albert laid the foundation stone of an asylum for idiots. She *knew* that the Queen had meddled in the question of the purchase of commissions: she would frighten her. She deplored the manners of the people who surrounded the royal family, who needed to see some of the middle classes. She wanted to get hold of "the indubitable particulars of one, two, or three of the D. of Cambridge's jobs, in order to alarm him, & excite the attention of others,—the 'Daily News' lawyer

[1] Sir John Robinson's recollections, *Fifty Years of Fleet Street*, contain some interesting reminiscences of her importance and accounts of his visits to Ambleside. The *Daily News* apparently was sympathetic to unusual women. Jessie Meriton White (1832–1906), who had been refused as a medical student by fourteen London hospitals, was taken on as *Daily News* correspondent in Genoa; she married one of Garibaldi's officers and returned to England smoking cigars, even as Miss Martineau. *George Eliot Letters*, ii, 379, n. 3.

[2] *Auto.*, ii, 82–88. Her letters to Rowland Hill are in BM, Add. MSS, 31,978, ff. 290, 294, 296. HM to Carlisle, December 7, 1855.

taking care to keep within the verge of the libel law". She was merciless to Palmerston and Malmesbury for their irresponsibility and stupidity in foreign affairs. At every step of the way—indeed, it seemed almost her primary task—she fought "that rotten old oracle", *The Times*. Nor did she spare her readers. She was out to set them right on everything, from the pernicious effect of the peace policies of Cobden and Bright to the importance of learning to swim. Again and again she referred to the difficulty of enlightening the people on complex questions: clearly the *Daily News* gave her the chance to treat the whole country as she treated her maids.[1]

In addition to the leaders she wrote book reviews, special articles, letters over a variety of pseudonyms, and a superb set of obituaries, republished in 1869 to help her out when the Brighton Railway stopped paying dividends.[2]

Her work has relevance, urgency, cogency, and impatience with muddled situations, those characteristics of good journalism which must mark any paper which would form opinion and influence policy. It has too the correlative faults: one leader contradicts another, crisis after crisis is *the* crisis, old issues are dropped for new, and the real difficulties of politicians are ignored to the extent of naïveté. It is also intensely, if not always consistently, dogmatic. She could do so well so far from the centre of affairs, not only because she was free from distractions but because her mind was so completely prepared to deal with any subject that she never needed anyone else to lean upon.

In a sense this whole book has been devoted to describing the preparation of that mind: the concerns and the way they are treated are absolutely predictable, once one knows the radical, Unitarian, manufacturer's orientation which she inherited and matured into her brand of positivism. Everything was tied ultimately to her vision of a new organic society, not sketched in

[1] This impression is derived from a reading of the articles, a good many of which will be referred to below; see also the bibliographical note on the *Daily News*. HM to Florence Nightingale, July 15, 1860, October 9, 1861, May 17, 1863. HM to Milnes, August 11, 1862, on the pernicious influence of the Court. The wonderful comment on *The Times* is taken from a letter to Philip Carpenter, September 29, 1856, MCO.

[2] Many of them were written before the death of the subject. "Think of that drawer of prepared obituaries," Samuel J. May wrote to R. D. Webb, BPL, May. One of the obituaries so prepared was, ironically, that of Florence Nightingale, to be found in the Women's Service Library. On the *Biographical Sketches*, see Robinson, *Fifty Years of Fleet Street*, p. 195.

detail, of course, but clear in its main outlines; and, more immediately, she related the events and outlooks of the period directly or indirectly to the degree of preparedness for the coming struggle with despotism, the great war of opinion which Canning had taught her to look for. In all this she was thoroughly parochial. Again and again she wrote, in the most understanding terms, about the differences of other races or nations or classes; but whenever the issue was really joined, the relativism fell away and she remained loyal to Norwich, Priestley, and England.

The great discovery of her generation, she said, was the philosophy of history, established and proved as a key to interpretation. The despotisms, doomed by the inevitable transfer from a military to a commercial period, were fighting their last old-fashioned battles—Russia, Prussia, France, Spain, the papacy, and the slave states. Mischief of this sort would continue to occur until religion and temporal concerns were entirely separated—a law true in its operation from papal government to the English supremacy in Ireland. Moreover, the despotisms failed from the breakdown of the mixture of the three elements of society. In Russia and France people and sovereign combined against the aristocracy; in the papal states and Germany the king and aristocracy against the people; in the South there was a dominant aristocracy which was both aristocracy and king, with no middle class and an abject people. In contrast, England presented the one example of stability in Europe. An old aristocracy, with real functions, constantly recruited from the people, formed a link between throne and people. Whatever might be the form of the organic society, this arrangement offered the best example. Italy had followed it, Prussia might recover the right track; the important thing for England was to learn to prepare for and undergo change, keeping the democratic element in society in moderation and balance instead of what it is when a despot flatters and betrays it or a stupid aristocracy destroys it and falls in the effort. In other words, Miss Martineau believed as firmly as any eighteenth-century writer in the theory of balanced government, adding only the characteristic nineteenth-century idea of progressive adaptation. She remained proud of England, as proud as she had been when she wrote a jingoistic poem about it in the thirties.[1] Her task was to keep England up to the mark,

[1] "Lion of Britain", to a tune from Marschner's *The Vampyre*. *MR*, vi, 492 (July, 1832).

to make her worthy of the flattery of imitation which would come inevitably from the rest of the world.

In foreign policy the country badly needed shaking up. England's protestantism had given her a principle of life, but, once the need to protest had gone, there was nothing substituted. Improving the constitution by democratizing it was good as far as it went, but not enough. "A man is very right", Miss Martineau wrote, "to improve his health and personal morality; but he is not leading a good life unless he is doing his social duties also." But what had England done except to try to humiliate France—a sad falling-off from the days when Elizabeth and Cromwell were fighting for principle? Palmerston talked liberty and acted against it; the peace societies strengthened the wrong and weakened the right, mingling worldliness and piety in the worst possible taste; the people had no control over foreign policy; England was despised and distrusted. This was in 1854 and a crisis had come: the collective will had to be enforced on parliament; there had to be burning words, cheerful sacrifices, and heroic deeds; and much was to be gained by a virtuous war.[1]

The case of the Crimean War was clear. Russia had long been the object of her deepest antipathy, so she devoted herself to exposing Russian machinations abroad, notably in the United States, and to demonstrating the internal evils (and weaknesses) of serfdom and bureaucracy. The serfs showed signs that, like slaves, the closer they came to freedom the more they valued it; to continue to deny it to them was to drive them into rebellion and murder. With the central weakness of serfdom compounded by the vicious centralization of the bureaucracy, Russia clearly seemed ready to fall of her own weight. The Czar in his ignorance could not read the principles in history, but philosophical students could foretell his future as clearly as prophets. Britain and the West had only to strip away the veil of hypocrisy and to keep completely clear of the taint—even to the extent of sending back with interest the five hundred pounds the Czar had given to finish the Nelson statue in Trafalgar Square.[2]

The war was to determine whether the Asiatic or European principle of government would prevail; it was for the people, not

[1] "England's Foreign Policy", *WR*, n.s., v, 190–232 (January, 1854).

[2] *DN*, December 2, 1853, January 13, 1854. "Emperor Nicholas", *Biog. Sketches*, p. 409. *Once a Week*, July 19, 1862, vii, 92–96. "Prince Dolgoroukow on Russia and Serf-Emancipation", *ER*, vol. 112, pp. 175–212 (July, 1860). HM to Reeve, March 6 and May 25, 1860.

the sovereigns, to decide under what rule they would live, and a resolute campaign for this fundamental principle on behalf of all nationalities would settle once and for all the question which would, unsettled, bring war for generation after generation until the final, terrible conflict. England's task was to strike a heavy blow at the chief aggressor, to keep herself clear of alliances with despots, and if the nationalities should come to the English side, to leave them to their own choice.[1]

For the Austrian alliance she had nothing but distrust. "There can be no radical truth, no genuineness in it; and it can neither last, nor be good while it subsists." But she was able to swallow France as an ally by making a convenient distinction between the emperor and the people; she hoped that audiences at the Crystal Palace would learn to rise and cheer when *Partant pour la Syrie* was played. As for Turkey, her disease had proved to be functional, not organic; she embodied the sound principle of local self-government, as opposed to the modern practice of centralization; and the recent demolition of schemes of civil service and county constabulary seemed pretty strong proof that the lesson had been taken to heart in England.[2] The diagnosis was one of the wilder flights of her ingenuousness.

Indeed, it was at home that the greatest results of the war were expected. It was important for Britain to remain a blessed island amid the storms, "a solitary kingdom where monarch and people may understand and love each other; a lofty platform, where the national honour so shines amidst the surrounding gloom, that any shadow allowed to pass over it would be an eclipse to the nations".[3] But to be that, the house had to be set in order. War would purge the weaknesses of peace. When the use of foreign auxiliaries was attacked, she replied by comparing them to earlier adventurers, Columbus, Caesar, Newton, and Luther; these new adventurers sought not gold or territory, not even science or the spread of civilization, but to prevent the overthrow of civilization, to keep the Czar from driving the nations back to barbarism. The followers of St. George and St. Denis would hardly notice the spatterings of mud along the way. Indeed, they were expected to ignore considerably more than mud: the nation had to go joyfully into the conflict, not to "peep

[1] *DN*, October 8, 1853, July 29 and August 8, 1854.

[2] *DN*, April 22 and July 8, 1854, on Austria. March 2 and September 6, 1854, on France. June 26, 1854, on Turkey.

[3] *DN*, June 24, 1852.

about for cholera in the ditches, or grumble over our food, or treat with bystanders over the hedge, or stand stock still to see how many of the foe will sink without our touching them, but having invoked the right, to conquer". Who dared to talk about disorganization in the army which had fought the Peninsular campaign? To do so was "profane and lying licentiousness".

> If Wellington got over the October and November of 1811, and won his victorious way from Ciudad Rodrigo to Toulouse, we may well expect to get over the November and December of 1854, and advance from Sebastopol to that point, whatever it may be, where the Czar may at length hold up the white flag, and let our gallant soldiers turn homewards. In that day there will be retribution in store for any traitor who, in the first season of adversity from wind and weather, charges our steadfast, long-suffering soldiery with "disorganisation".

It was Miss Martineau against *The Times*; until that paper could show posts unserved, trenches deserted, and duty shirked, there was no need to pay more attention to its doleful prophecies than to its spiteful and treacherous slanders.[1]

Within two weeks she had changed her tune. If military officials refused to have navvies for the laborious work, then the civilians must see it done; the military must watch out or England would send out a corps of women—and Florence Nightingale's work was the subject of some of Miss Martineau's most enthusiastic rhapsodies. By the end of the war she was hammering at the incompetence of ministers, hounding the Aberdeen government. The important thing now was to open public service to talent. The old system of patronage and bribery was intolerable—Russia, France, the United States were all warnings; and under the impulse of war, sustained by the guarantees of a free press, a worthy new profession could be created to administer the state. And administer it in a new spirit: war would substitute reality for sentiment, reverse the trend to centralization, and bring home to the people the folly and inconsistency of that misguided state intervention which damaged constitutional government in all eyes. She was sorry to see the war over so soon; it would have been better for European liberty, for the world's virtue, for improvement at home, if it had gone on until the purgation was complete; but, peace or war, there was nothing to fear. "Our business is to preserve in

[1] *DN*, August 8, 1854, January 4 and 8, 1855.

peace the high and calm spirit which carried us through the war, and to promote at once the freedom and peace of Europe by being wise and happy at home, and by extending commerce abroad. If anything could carry Europe safely through inevitable revolutions it would be an universally free commerce." In the light of this belief she hoped Manchester would be consistent and return Cobden and Bright in 1857; when they were defeated, however, she drew the moral that while they would be missed as reformers, it was good for the world to know that England would never countenance any doctrine of non-intervention, any paltering peace-mongers.[1]

Once the war was over, she could allow her loathing of Napoleon III full rein. The French alliance, she said, was with the people; it would be better to fight Russia alone than in alliance with the Emperor. Napoleon and Eugénie in her letters became Scamp and Scampess. And when the war scare appeared in 1859 there was no more fervent supporter of the volunteer movement. She knew, she told the Americans, that French ships were stealthily taking soundings at night, French visitors went to the coast, winter and summer, "for their health" and carried off sketches and surveys. But a successful attack was impossible as fortifications were expanded and "our higher kind of defence, the vital force of our national manhood, which no foreign army will ever overwhelm, grows in extent and ability from day to day".[2]

This distrust of France carried sharply into her opinions on the Italian war in 1859. Doubtful about the Italians to begin with,[3] she could not forgive an alliance with Napoleon. No doubt, she said, the Italian situation had to come to a head when Piedmont was sufficiently advanced in her liberties to take the lead; it should have been done under an allied England and France. But an alliance with "the most intrusive and absolute despot of his time" (except perhaps the king of Naples) was impossible, and England had no choice but to stand aloof. It was, she had no doubt, the great war for opinion, the great struggle to determine whether Europe would be ruled despotically or

[1] *DN*, January 23 and May 28, 1855, August 14, 1856. On the sphere of legislation, November 18, 1854, January 20, 1855. On peace, April 8, 1856, March 24 and 31, 1857.

[2] HM to Reeve, September 25 and November 20, 1859. *ASS*, May 28 and August 18, 1859. *DN*, November 10, 1855, May 4 and 10, July 5, December 13, 1859.

[3] HM to Reeve, January 13, 1859.

constitutionally; but England could not be a party to substituting a French despot for an Austrian one. Rather, as she saw the cause of civilization and progress endangered by the spread of war, it became more important for her to take up the duties which other states had dropped, to guard the creative and conservative processes of social life, to serve, that is, as the example and defender of the things which other nations were determined to destroy.[1]

Gradually her initial distrust of the Italians began to soften. Napoleon's treacherous peace called out her sympathy for them. She had begun to hope that they might live tranquilly under free institutions. By the end of the year she insisted that Italy had proved herself and deserved the full support of Britain. Dynastic claims had to be rejected and the nation upheld who would copy British freedom and security. She did not think this support would mean war, but if it did, it would be a war ennobled by the common interest of all citizens. The Italians, she told the Americans, were enough to incite all the defrauded peoples to turn out their cheating rulers and settle things for themselves. She flared up at Cavour and Victor Emmanuel for the cession of Savoy; they forfeited all respect for so dishonest an act. That was early in 1860; but by the end of 1860 she was sure that only Cavour was capable of guaranteeing liberty—of steering his way between the reactionary agents and the red republicans; and she was merciless with Mazzini (whom she never had any use for) and Garibaldi for their factionalism.[2]

Small wonder that Matthew Arnold, surprised at her unfavourable review of his pamphlet on the Italian question, called her "a little incalculable". It was partly because the nature of her work made inconsistency inevitable, at least in detail, and partly because she was guilty of an "ideal and unpractical habit of mind", the sin of which she accused Elizabeth Barrett Browning for her "Poems before Congress".[3] The ideal was parochial, the impracticality lay in her conviction that, despite her insistence on

[1] HM to Reeve, March 6 and April 21, 1859. *ASS*, April 30 and May 14, 1859. A very important leader in *DN*, February 18, 1859, her "manifesto" against any French restoration of Italian liberties.

[2] HM to Reeve, July 14, 1859. *ASS*, May 28, June 18, September 3, 1859, [Feb. 27 dated], April 21, October 13, December 29, 1860, May 11, 1861. *DN*, November 3, 1859. *Once a Week*, November, 1, 1862.

[3] The review of Arnold is in *DN*, August 8, 1859. Arnold to Mrs. Forster, August 13, 1859, *Letters*, i, 118. The criticism of Mrs. Browning is in *ASS*, May 5, 1860. See above, p. 14.

VII. The Knoll, *c.* 1850

VIII. Harriet Martineau in old age

The Daily News.

HAYMARKET.

THIS EVENING, THE OVERLAND ROUTE. Messrs. Chippendale, Compton, Buckstone, and C. Mathews; Mrs. C. Mathews.—And PAUL PRY. Messrs. C. Mathews, Chippendale, Rogers, and Villiers; Mrs. C. Mathews and Mrs. Poynter.

PRINCESS'S.

THIS EVENING, MACBETH. Messrs. James R. Anderson, Shore F. Matthews, Weiss, and Bartleman; Miss Elsworthy, Miss R. Leclercq, and Miss R. Isaacs.—And THE FIRST NIGHT. Mr. A. Harris; Miss M. Harris.—Commence at 7.

ADELPHI.

THIS EVENING, JANET PRIDE. Messrs. B. Webster, Toole, P. Bedford, and Selby; Miss Woolgar.—And THE ENCHANTED ISLE; or Raising the Wind on the most Approved Principles. Messrs. Toole and Bedford; Miss Woolgar.—Commence at 7.

OLYMPIC.

THIS EVENING, SOMEBODY ELSE. Mr. F. Robinson; Miss L. Keeley.—A FAIR EXCHANGE. Mr. H. Wigan; Miss L. Keeley.—And SHYLOCK; or, THE MERCHANT OF VENICE PRESERVED. Mr. Robson; Mrs. Emden.

ASTLEY'S.

THIS EVENING, MAZEPPA AND THE WILD HORSE.—And Achievements in the Scenes of the Arena, supported by the Star Riders of the day.—A MID-DAY Performance on SATURDAY, to commence at 2 o'clock.

BRITANNIA.

THIS EVENING, A LIFE FOR A LIFE; or, The Burden of Guilt.—Messrs. Reynolds and Smythson; Mrs. W. Crawford.—THE SPOILED CHILD. Master Roselle; Miss Downing.—And THE BEGGAR'S PETITION. Mrs. E. Yarnold.

HIGH WATER AT LONDON BRIDGE.

THIS DAY—Morning, 0h. 0m.....Afternoon, 0h. 22m.
TO-MORROW—Morning, 0h. 50m.....Afternoon, 1h. 15m.

LONDON, TUESDAY, AUG. 28.

A REVIEW of the Session of Parliament, which this day comes to a close, is a task which an English journalist would gladly decline, if he only might. For the fact is that the country has been insulted with false promises, neglected in regard to its most important business, and left in a worse position, in regard to its essential liberties at the end of the Session than it held before. The Ministers and the Houses will gain nothing by throwing the blame of the loss of this session on each other. If it is usually irksome and humiliating to show how much less has been done than was proposed, it is a grave penance, indeed, to have to show that, so far from mending their own ways and our prospects, our rulers, in the Cabinet and in Parliament, have at once failed in doing the work of the nation, and succeeded in restricting some of the liberties which they are appointed to protect and expand. The QUEEN's Speech presented an array of good measures which it was not unreasonable to suppose would be law by this time; and the CHANCELLOR of the EXCHEQUER emphatically answered us that the session of 1860 would be memorable for its richness in blessings. Yet now we find ourselves without the blessings specially promised, with our work sonably hope that after much controversy, and even confusion, this great measure of the present Government will form a new period in our commercial history, and prevent the session of 1860 from being altogether barren of those popular blessings in which Mr. GLADSTONE promised that it should be fruitful. It was well for the scheme and its authors that no one foresaw what demands would arise in a few weeks, calling upon us for both new taxes and some form of loan, or our commerce with France might have continued to be the example of folly that it was, as between two industrious nations living within sight of each other.

Next in interest to the Budget and the Treaty in the department of Finance were the topics of the Army and Navy—the War-office and the Admiralty. On the 13th of February, Lord CLARENCE PAGET brought forward the Naval Estimates in a speech full of his customary frank avowals, which, as usual, have been of no practical avail, so far as Admiralty Reform is concerned. The enormous supplies he asked for were granted; but there is no evidence that the Admiralty is improving, or that we have our money's worth in effective and well-manned Nothing has been done this session towards that thorough reform of the Admiralty which must precede a satisfactory condition of the Navy. We all said the same thing of the Army last year, and in consequence a commission was appointed to inquire into our military organization. The Report of that Commission was presented late in the session, when it was found that no one of the main points of maladministration was touched upon at all. There is nothing in the action of the Commission to prevent our suffering from the same disasters to-morrow, in case of a new war, that destroyed the first army we sent to the Crimea. The work of reform in our military administration remains not only to be done, but to be designed. The estimates were brought forward by the SECRETARY for WAR on the 17th of February with a frankness worthy of Lord CLARENCE PAGET. They were the largest estimates offered since the Russian war, being nearly two millions in excess of those of last year. In the course of the debate, on the 6th of March, on Sir DE LACY EVANS's motion on the gradual abolition of the purchase system in the army, the SECRETARY for WAR announced that Government was ready to abolish purchase in the case of all commissions above the rank of major—a new indication that the service must soon be opened to qualifications more professional than wealth. Throughout the session the subject of our military defence was incessantly recurring, till, towards the close, the Fortifications Report was presented, and special supplies for new protective works were called for, on the 23rd of July, in a speech of Lord

IX. A LEADING ARTICLE

An extract from a fine example of Miss Martineau's mature journalism, a review of the parliamentary session in the *Daily News* for 28 August 1860.

free choice, the nations of the world should do precisely as she wanted them to do. In that at least she never wavered.

It has been seen that the situation in America was a part of the larger struggle between despotism and liberty; it was, to her, incomparably the most important part,[1] a conviction she had brought back with her in 1836, and which grew stronger with the deepening crisis. The fifties were an exciting and discouraging time: the Compromise of 1850, the Kansas-Nebraska Act, the war in Kansas, a Congress and a country falling apart, and, finally, acts of desperate fanaticism—Representative Brooks' vicious beating of Senator Sumner, John Brown's raid—and war in 1861. Small wonder she talked to her visitors about little else.[2]

A deepening crisis and disaster, as she saw it, were inevitable, a magnificent example of necessarianism in action:

> The opportunity of regenerating the Republic, and regaining the old place of honour among nations is now present and pressing. If our American kindred accept and use it, in cordial alliance with England, their best days are yet to come. If they let it pass, the world will grieve, but the work will not the less be done. It is the "manifest destiny" of justice and humanity to lead the world onward; and no retrograde ignorance, no sordid self-interest, no guile, however audacious or refined, can prevail against them.

The only question was what the punishment would be for resisting historical inevitability—military despotism, break-up of the Union, or a servile war. The one hopeful result, abolition of slavery, was precluded by the moral retrogression of southern society.[3] This moral corruption of the South, issuing in an aggressive foreign policy and contempt for law and order, could be traced to the preponderance, thanks to the Constitutional compromise which allowed three-fifths of the slaves to be counted in apportioning seats, of an aristocracy who lorded it over slaves and "mean whites" without the necessary counterbalance of a middle class. Unhappily, the rot extended to the North; Northern men allowed themselves to be led, dared to compromise

[1] HM to Garrison, February 16, 1855, her farewell letter and manifesto for the abolitionists; a copy is enclosed with a letter to P. P. Carpenter, December 22, 1855. HM to Reeve, May 25, 1865.

[2] Earl of Carlisle's Diary, October 22, 1858.

[3] HM to Carlisle, March 26, 1857. HM, "Slave Trade in 1858", *ER*, vol. 108, p. 586 (October, 1858).

with sin, and too often treated corruption with "ignorant levity". A sad contrast they made to the Hungarians, Poles, and Italians fighting against despots for their liberties.[1]

This view of a declining South and a corrupted nation was based on books like Helper's *Impending Crisis of the South* and Olmsted's *Cotton Kingdom.* But, above all, information and point of view came from her old associates, the Garrisonian abolitionists. She gave them money, she sent wool-work to be sold at their bazaars, she wrote to friends and enemies alike to raise money for the cause; for the "Old Organization" of the abolitionists was the "fountainhead of energy and storehouse of experience in case of prosperity", the one guarantee, could they but prevail, of regeneration.[2] They were the one set of people in America who were "rational, thoroughly informed, of enlarged views & accurate & various knowledge, consistent, & above all disinterested". She was with them in their consciousness of sin, with them in the proliferation of their radicalisms, with them in the violence of their language, with them even in their anarchism, which Mrs. Clarkson could scarcely believe, because it seemed to her as wild as the Fifth Monarchy Men.[3]

Like her American friends, she was adamant against compromise, even for what might seem humanitarian purposes: to her way of thinking it was wrong to raise a ransom for members of a free Negro family sold into slavery. It put money into the hands of slave-owners and induced repetitions of the crime; men of good will should focus their attention only on rooting out the entire institution; they should never be led astray by particulars.[4] Again, like them, she rejected political action. The Free-Soil party was beneath her lofty gaze, and on the eve of the Civil War she urged the abolitionists to refrain from supporting the Republican party. Their task was not to join but to beckon parties to see if they would follow. Theirs was the cause of humanity, not

[1] HM to Reeve, March 9, 1859, to P. P. Carpenter, October 3, 1860. *DN*, January 2, April 26, 1860. *ASS*, July 23, 1859, October 5, 1861.

[2] On Helper's book, "the true agent of the revolution", HM to Reeve. March 9, 1859 and January 28, 1860. HM to Garrison, October 23, 1850. Weston Papers, xx, no. 136. HM to Carlisle, October 25, 1858 and February 21, 1859. *DN*, February 26, 1856.

[3] HM to Reeve, February 15, 1861. Mrs. Clarkson to Crabb Robinson, March 21, 1844, DWL.

[4] There is an attack on Henry Clay for compromising in her obituary notice of him, *DN*, July 13, 1852. "Slave-Trading in England", a letter signed A.Z., *DN*, November 17, 1852.

politics, and, as the politicians began to show signs of following the abolitionist lead, the cause became more important—and contributions more urgent—than ever.[1]

The raid on Harper's Ferry in 1859 by the fanatic John Brown neatly illustrates her abolitionist connection. The action was puzzling to the English, she said, and apparently it puzzled, even disgusted, her. Writing on November 7, she compared Brown with Robert Emmett, who had let passion lead him into rebellion in Ireland without ever inquiring into his chances for success. By contrast Garibaldi was a successful revolutionist; he had waited until Piedmont had abdicated its responsibility; then, having shown that he could obey and co-operate, he could unite the wills of men. Two weeks later, however, she took another view and stuck to it. Brown was a martyr; while his spectre walked, slavery could never again be what it was. He had shown the cowardice of the slaveholders; he had died a magnificent death. She was still doubtful about the defensibility of his scheme, but by January she was proclaiming that history had known no finer death, that Brown was a benefactor to the cause and to humanity.

> The thrill of awakened conviction and resolution is evidently passing through society, and that is bliss, in comparison with the previous thraldom belonging to acquiescence in wrong. The Abolitionists, who have kept their liberty, must be happy to see others entering into it.

It is hardly necessary to have the full transatlantic correspondence to know what had happened.[2]

She was thoroughly involved in the fantastic quarrels within the abolitionist ranks. "So very solemn a cause requires the refining & refining again of its agents. The doubtful, as Mrs. Chapman says, should have a chance periodically to find their

[1] *ASS*, July 9, 1859. HM to Brougham, November 21, 1858, UCL. HM to Carlisle, December 6, 1858.

[2] *ASS*, December 17 and 24, 1859, January 28, 1860. Compare S. J. May, one of the chief Garrisonians, to R. D. Webb, January 10, 1860, BPL: "The John Brown 'raid', as the foolish Republicans call it, is taking up this Nation by the four corners, and shaking it to its very centre. The agitation is tremendous, but healthy. It is developing the diabolism of Slavery as it never appeared before—or, not least, as it was never seen before by any but the handful of abolitionists. John Brown knew a great deal, but he has worked and 'builded better than he knew'. All honour to his Example. 'Tis a glorious one, and wonderful to have happened in this land, so dead in its trespasses and sins—its conscience so seared by its long persistence in cruelty and fraud—so drunk with the intoxicating wine of slavery. This death is proving a mighty teacher of what the human soul can bear and do."

way back to the Church and the World." She denounced Harriet Beecher Stowe to her friends for her sentimentalism and irrationality, for being not quite up to the mark. When Parker Pillsbury or Wendell Phillips fell out with Garrison, she tried to whip them back or to rob them of followers. Mrs. Chapman was overjoyed at the good work she did, though occasionally someone ventured to suggest that Miss Martineau was a bit far away to understand.[1]

This loyalty meant that her view of the American conflict followed a strict party line, that her sources of information bore the *imprimatur*, and that what she said was sometimes considerably remote from reality. But what she said and did was also conditioned strongly by the attitude to America in England. Most of England was either apathetic or hostile to abolitionism. *Uncle Tom's Cabin* aroused enormous enthusiasm for the anti-slavery cause, but it soon evaporated. Politically conscious workingmen and some of the most important radical leaders were supporters of the North; but even there there was ignorance—she had to explain Bright's misinformation to her American readers —and beyond them, in the upper levels of society, there was not only ignorance but viciousness. So many other considerations than the true one of slavery entered into determining British attitudes: dislike of Americans, distrust of a rival, a perverse or snobbish sympathy for slave-owning aristocrats, even a belief in self-determination; and governing it all an almost inexhaustible supply of errors about the Constitution, the state of society in America, and the character of the Negro, not to mention the issues in the conflict.[2] Here again *The Times* was the great enemy. Its sheer ignorance was bad enough, but the paper also did what it could, she told Milnes, under a lure of gentility, to parade everything discreditable and vulgar in the national character. Even the dispatches from the Confederacy of its brilliant reporter, William Howard Russell, she dismissed as "small, shallow & unsatisfactory", for, however good he was in the Crimea or in

[1] HM to Mary Estlin, February 25, [1844], NYHS. HM to Elizabeth Pease, February 27, [1841], BPL. HM to Mr. Shepherd, n.d., BPL. HM to Reeve, October 20, 1861. May to R. D. Webb, August 7, 1859. Parker Pillsbury to May, July 12, 1859, BPL. Mrs. Chapman to S. H. Gay, n.d., Columbia. Oliver Johnson to Mrs. Chapman, August 31, 1859, BPL. *ASS*, June 25, July 9, August 20, 1859.

[2] For two excellent analyses, see *The Journals of Benjamin Moran*, ii, 934–35, and the letters of R. D. Webb in the Weston Papers, esp. to Anne Weston, November 6, 1861 and April 21, 1865; to Mrs. Chapman, January 18, 1865. HM on Bright, *ASS*, April 16, 1859. On the self-government issue, HM to Reeve, November 7, 1863.

India, he did not know enough about American (and particularly Southern) character and corruption to see the real state of the case. "I am still in more thorough possession of the case than other people,—I might perhaps say,—anybody else here," she told Reeve; she had full communication with the United States and had seen the South when it had real leaders.[1]

She did what she could to set her country straight. From April to December, 1858, she wrote American articles for *Spectator*, but resigned when the paper went into bad hands, "not only pro-slavery but disreputable". She didn't like writing about America in *Once a Week*, she said, because Lucas, the editor, was too much of a *Times* man, but any ground rescued from the enemy was good, so she devoted a good many of her surveys of current events to it.[2] The *Edinburgh Review* was a more important outlet. Her first article for it was an attack on the slave trade which she accused Napoleon III of reviving with the connivance of the Liberians, on whom she had written for the *Westminster* in 1857. Her material for these articles was sent to her by the abolitionists, Sidney Gay, editor of the *Anti-Slavery Standard*, among others; and confident in what they reported, she said what she wanted and left Reeve with the responsibility of a possible libel suit. She could prove every statement she made, she insisted, and, as Richard Webb put it, "an action for defamation of the sinners is too good to be hoped".[3] The article, all her friends in Paris told her, was the real cause of the Emperor's giving up his "slave trade"; its very success must have been what made Brougham talk about libel actions for an article "at the instance of abolitionists". Two other American articles appeared in the *Edinburgh* from her pen.[4]

It was, however, the *Daily News* that counted most. Throughout the fifties she hammered at her favourite American themes—an alleged connection between the Russians and the slaveholders, the moral bankruptcy of the South, the disgraceful filibustering and expansionism, the slave trade, the potentiality of the Negro,

[1] HM to Reeve, December 1, 1860, January 27 and May 31, 1861. HM to Milnes, August 11, 1862.

[2] HM to Reeve, January 13, 1859. HM to Mrs. Chapman, March 27, 1862.

[3] "The Slave Trade in 1858", *ER*, vol. 108, pp. 541–86 (October 1858). HM to Reeve, June 24, 26, 27, 1858, March 18, 1859. Mrs. Chapman to Gay, April 8, [1858], Columbia. HM to Carlisle, December 6, 1858.

[4] "The United States under the Presidentship of Mr. Buchanan", vol. 112, pp. 545–82 (October 1860). "The Negro Race in America", vol. 119, pp. 203–42 (January, 1864).

the greatness of the abolitionists, the developing crisis. In all this she had to defend herself against the editors who kept telling her that readers did not want to read so much about America. When the war broke out, she was triumphant; she had said the crisis would come, she had said it would be a revolution, and she was right. She then had even more to do. So did her editor, thoroughly committed to the Northern cause, against the proprietors who were, as Walker told Benjamin Moran, "all rebel in their tendencies".[1]

The Civil War in America was clearly analogous in her mind to the Crimean War, in its potential effect on society. "I am anything but unhappy about America," she told Florence Nightingale.

> It is the resurrection of conscience among them,—the renewal of the soul of the genuine nation. I think destruction will overtake the wicked; & the good,—the best,—are already in the heights of honour & hope. It has come exactly when & as all expected who had a right to an opinion. The details are most moving, but not grievous.[2]

As the Russian colossus was expected to fall of its own weight, so the South would collapse at the first blow. She told Reeve before she knew of the war, to believe nothing in any Southern newspaper, so strict was the censorship: the soldiers were mutinous, the working classes were starving, the planters were overridden by non-slaveholders, the managers were at each other's throats, secret societies of Union men existed everywhere. The Northern defeat at Bull Run upset her, but not nearly so much as the letters she got saying that the war was for Union, not for abolition: that seemed to indicate that the North thought England cared only for cotton or that the North was still as corrupt as ever. When the war dragged into its second and third year, she became very depressed, buoyed up only by the knowledge, after 1862, that emancipation was worth any sacrifice, and by the fervent conviction that, no matter what, the South would be defeated. She was delighted to hear of their defeats, she eagerly repeated all that she was told about internal decay,

[1] HM to Garrison, July 7, 1867. *Moran Journal*, ii, 1851.

[2] May 8, 1861. Miss Martineau, said Mrs. Chapman, was a believer in the *ultima ratio* of the military method; the abolitionists who were, in general, non-resistants "did not hate her for it", however. Mrs. Chapman to Lizzy, February 23, 1864.

she wrote that General Sherman's march had fulfilled all her hopes, and when the war was over, she exulted that at last people would learn the truth about society in the slave states: Johnson's policy was causing the South to show what they were like, and they came out worse and worse.[1] Her leaders not only repeated these contentions, but she regularly answered and savagely attacked Southern emissaries like Yancey and Mason, apologists like Maury and Spence, and their English supporters, *The Times* in particular. Under the guise of giving information and comment, she was acting as a propagandist.

Her role became even clearer in her comments on American politics. When Seward was about to visit her in 1859 she thought he was the obvious choice for the Republican nomination.[2] But Seward apparently did not come out of the visit well. He noted that she spoke almost entirely from the standpoint of the Garrisonians and was very despondent.

> I gave her my own more practical views, and spoke of course hopefully if not confidently. . . . She betrayed or rather confessed an opinion that I was a politician rather than an abolitionist of her school. I explained to her that there was need of organizers of the Anti-slavery movement as well as of disorganizers of the Pro-slavery forces, and that I believed even Theodore Parker and Wendell Phillips were content that I should act in my own way. She readily understood and accepted all these explanations.

She liked him but was shocked by his confession that the fuss about British cruisers in the Caribbean was concocted with the British minister, as Seward believed that the more noise there was about war, the less probable war would be. When the bluster continued to the extent of his urging annexation of Canada, she wrote him off completely.[3]

With Seward out of the picture, she saw no leaders on the horizon at all. Sumner was still suffering from the beating he had received from Brooks, and she had doubts about his ability

[1] HM to Reeve, April 21, May 7, August 6, 1861, July 9, 1862, April 25, 1863, September 29, 1863, December 20, 1865. HM to G. P. Putnam, June 9, 1863, NYPL. HM to ? (unknown corr.), December 30, 1864, NYHS. Leaders in *DN*, *passim*.

[2] She thought he was more able than Sumner, and hoped to see him the first anti-slavery president; her only criticism of him was for his bluster about British cruisers in the Caribbean. HM to Reeve, June 29, 1859.

[3] HM to Reeve, July 6, 1859, February 15, 1861. *ASS*, January 31, 1861. Seward's letter to his wife about the visit is printed in the *University of Rochester Library Bulletin*, vii, 13–15 (Autumn, 1951).

in any event; Everett was beneath contempt; and about Lincoln she remained dubious:

> Will Lincoln and Hamlin . . . then, measure their strength against the difficulty, and extirpate the gangrene which is destroying their country? It is scarcely credible that anybody expects this of such men, chosen at such a time. Their party itself is crude, stumbling in its aims, hazy in its purposes, undisciplined in its work. It is the newest and rawest expression of the disgust and indignation of the Free States at the crises of administration and the decline of the national character and reputation; and some of its best leaders openly lament its probable success, on the ground that four years more would have raised the party into some worthiness of the work it has to do, and strengthened its capacity for action.[1]

It was partly, she told the Americans, their system: they could hardly expect to pick up a great statesman, given the way they chose their Presidents; but at least Lincoln seemed honest, and that was a relief after the succession of traitors and knaves the country had been saddled with. Though sadly hampered by Seward, Lincoln turned out better than she had expected, the first president since Jackson without intrigue, brag, or cant. When Lincoln interviewed some of the abolitionist leaders in 1861, she was overjoyed, yet she could still turn on him: "What a vile message Lincoln's is!" she wrote on Christmas Day in 1861, "Insincere was well as reserved."

She was obviously puzzled by Lincoln. She took into account the divisions within the cabinet and the difficult position in which he was placed; but early in 1862 she was criticizing him for a lack of clearly defined aims. By the end of March he had come out for gradual emancipation; she knew that meant there was no going back, yet she could not understand why he made a speech in September urging emigration on the Negroes. Her leader of October 10, on the Emancipation Proclamation, shows her enormous relief: he had come out at last from vacillation to certainty. "I say as much as circumstances permit," she told Garrison in 1864, "in honour of Mr. Lincoln in "Daily News" & I shall try my best to work in the best possible direction."[2] She was out to set things right in English eyes. And she was sure that, to a remarkable degree, she was succeeding.

[1] *DN*, October 23, 1860. *ASS*, December 29, 1860.

[2] HM to Reeve, February 15, April 21, May 31, July 28, December 25, 1861. *ASS*, April 13, 1861. *DN*, esp. September 2 and October 10, and March 1, 1862. HM to Garrison, August 10, 1864.

It was not enough, however, to preach with some success to the English; she had to hector the Americans too.[1] She had heard, she told Reeve, that there was a great rush to the *Daily News* in America; her labour for their cause entitled her to scold them now. The complete ignorance of cultivated Americans outside the ranks of the abolitionists appalled her,[2] and when she was asked to write for the *National Anti-Slavery Standard* she jumped at the chance. The *Standard* was one of Mrs. Chapman's enthusiasms, and it was through her that the invitation came. The fact that the circulation of the paper was small and only among abolitionists of a particular stripe never seems to have occurred to Miss Martineau. She saw the invitation as a great opportunity to teach the Americans to distrust acting on impulse and to ground their proceedings on some sort of principle. So she lectured them on the ethical bases of their society, she criticized their manners, she said it was difficult to defend them because of the barbarism of the warfare, and she urged them to play cricket and to set up games festivals.[3] Moreover, she saw a chance to supply the link between American and European politics, to show how the national interests and questions of two continents were tied together. In supplying this European link, one tack Miss Martineau took was extensive comment on the developments on the Continent, particularly in Italy, where a successful movement for national regeneration was taking place. But the link also meant speaking for the great laws of nature and (what amounted to the same thing) for England.

The Morrill Tariff of 1860 was an abomination to Miss Martineau, a surrender to selfish and short-sighted interests, contrary to political economy and to English experience. If the regions of the country continued to consider their own interests "instead of regarding the general commerce of the country as an affair of

[1] It was characteristic that she tried to help the war effort. She forwarded to the Secretary of War in Washington a copy of *England and her Soldiers* and the documents embodying the army reforms for which Miss Nightingale and Sidney Herbert had worked so hard. She said, too, that she would have been happy to do the same for the Southern troops, if she had had access to their leaders. HM to Simon Cameron, September 30, 1861, LC. HM to Florence Nightingale, September 21, 1861, BM.

[2] HM to Reeve, July 28, 1861, June 27, 1858.

[3] *ASS*, [July 18, 1859], August 18, 1860, February 15, 1862, December 16, 1859, December 28, 1861. On the European link, HM to Reeve, March 9, 1859. On December 27, 1859, S. J. May wrote to R. D. Webb, asking him to forward £40. 16s. od. to Miss Martineau for the American Anti-Slavery Society; this was presumably in payment for her contributions to the *Standard*.

principle, or as in any way connected with the character and representation of the Republic", retribution was certain, even if the danger might be masked for a time by prosperity. It was a moral question of the first importance.

> Natural laws are usually regarded as "extravagant" and "harsh" till their character of immutability is understood. Probably there have been men in every generation for 1800 years who have thought the declaration extravagant and harsh that "Whatsoever a man soweth, that shall he also reap." One and another may think it does not apply to his case, or that he is strong enough or insignificant enough to escape the conditions; but the law is immutable and universal. So is the law of equal freedom in industry and trade. . . . There is no possible evasion of the law by which the imposition of protective duties is followed, sooner or later, by the impoverishment of both the employing and employed classes. . . .

A right view required education, and on that score the war was not altogether bad: "As the citizen soldiers talk for long hours over their camp fires, let us hope that the topics of the rights of industry and the true principles of taxation may come up in practical shape, so that the commerce of the republic may have fair play, and the honest workers may become too clear-sighted to allow certain orders of manufacturers to help themselves to a large percentage of every man's earnings."

Poor innocent! The Americans resented her. Abolitionists wrote to the paper to denounce her dogmatism; Horace Greeley manœuvred his big guns into position; the editor of the paper himself inserted a leader questioning the sincerity of anti-slavery sentiment that might be alienated by a tariff. And Miss Martineau, protesting to Reeve about the ignorance of the Americans, replied, both in the *Daily News* and the *Standard*.

> You are a little angry with me, I see, for saying this, and as yet you don't half believe it. Well, it is only a question of time. Science always justifies itself; and this is not a matter of opinion. Science always prevails, and all the world will be free traders by and by.[1]

It is doubtful if this assurance mollified her critics.

Before the dust of the tariff controversy had a chance to settle, Commander Wilkes of the United States Navy stopped the British ship *Trent* and removed Mason and Slidell, the two envoys of the Confederacy to Great Britain. Protest in Great

[1] The un-Comtean character of this insistence on the laws of political economy should be noted. *ASS* and *DN*, *passim*. The quotations are from *ASS*, June 1 and August 3, 1861. Replies appear in *ASS*, April 20, June 29, July 29, 1861.

Britain was strong, the representations of Her Majesty's Government to Washington were stern, and Miss Martineau grew hysterical about this insult to the flag. She told her American audience in the most violent terms that they were running a grave risk of war and that the British would be one in supporting their government in avenging the dastardly insult. Could she possibly have expected them to take her rantings submissively? They most certainly did not. Oliver Johnson, the editor, suppressed her second letter and rebuked her in print; subscriptions were cancelled; and everyone was terribly upset. "*Will* you just excuse me for saying I wish I could punch Miss Martineau's head for her?" wrote one irate woman to Mrs. Chapman. "I know that sounds dreadfully vulgar, but I have lost all sense of propriety and lady-like deportment. I have given up my subscription to the Standard, because I will not pay one penny for English insolence to come over here. I think we have enough of it, 'free, gratis, for nothing,' don't you?" "She exceeds her privilege & oversteps the bounds of decorum," said one correspondent. Her "schoolmistress airs", said Samuel May, her domineering, lecturing, and censuring, were quite unbearable. Even Mrs. Reid wrote to Mrs. Chapman to apologize for the "raving". And the *Boston Transcript* commented both on the ingratitude of foreigners and on the futility of paying attention to the "mental exhalations of this excessively conceited and peevish old spinster".[1] The storm, which Mrs. Chapman tried in vain to dispel even in her own family, forced Miss Martineau to resign.

As for Miss Martineau's view of the fuss, she said that at least she criticized the Americans only to themselves, and thought it strange that they should complain that no one in England understood them only to object when someone who did understand them told them where they were going wrong. "I don't *think*," she said, "I am apt to make a point of other people thinking as I do." But it is hard to say what other interpretation to put on this little comedy. The editor of the *Standard* put it well in justifying his decision not to strike out offending passages, but to give her a good supply of editorial rope to hang herself with. "Her blind, dogged John Bull-ism, and her patronizing ways toward America are offensive to me." [2]

[1] The offending articles, and the correspondence surrounding them, are all in the May Collection at Cornell. See also the May Collection in Boston.

[2] HM to Reeve, January 23, 1862, February 25, 1866, November 8, 1861. Johnson to May, December 5, 1861, BPL.

But the lesson was lost on her. She was sent a pamphlet, she told Reeve in 1863, by a Boston citizen who had cut her for abolitionism; now he was complaining that England was not anti-slavery enough to understand America. This to her! So she would tell him what she thought of him. The English attitude, she said, only represented what they had been taught to think by a generation of Americans who were compromisers in corruption ("*You* were helping to stone the prophets when I left Boston"). How could the English be expected to take a wiser view? But what difference did it make anyhow? "I am sure, if we were in a revolution, we shd never spend two minutes in thinking what was said by anybody outside." And then she belaboured him for the American crime of allowing the republic to split over slavery, to the damage of democratic institutions and the liberal cause everywhere.[1]

Miss Martineau displayed a similar combination of dogmatism and parochialism when she turned her attention to Ireland, whose ills were a leitmotif of English politics in the nineteenth century. Ireland was no mere incidental interest to her: James had preached in Dublin for a few years; Thomas Drummond, the great Irish under-secretary, was both friend and hero to her; the forties thrust the problem into the forefront of everyone's consideration; early in the fifties she travelled in Ireland and she wrote about it continually in the *Daily News*. *Ireland*, in the political economy series, was a not unsympathetic tale. She explained rural violence in terms of religious impolicy, lack of capital, uneconomic land practices, and over-population. Rejecting palliatives like an absentee tax or the widely debated Irish poor law, she found the immediate solution in emigration, and the long-range solutions in education and the establishment of a capitalist agriculture on the English model. For the rest of her life, she held to her formula and remained certain that it was working.

There was at least an arguable case for her economic solution to Irish problems: to introduce the English-style capitalist and all his beneficent works was a frequent Radical proposal and one which seemed to promise well. Where she, and most other Englishmen, went wildly wrong was in their inability to compre-

[1] HM to Reeve, January 1, 1863. HM to Charles Greeley Loring, January 2, 1863, Harvard.

hend or appreciate the nationalist force which lay behind Irish agitation. To Miss Martineau, as to most radicals, a recasting of institutions would solve the economic problems and, with the help of education, reconcile men's minds. At stake for her, in Italy, America, or Ireland, were rational political and economic principles; irrationality, emotion, and violence were skew to her assumptions and had to be explained away.

This failure to grasp the meaning of nationalism is nicely illustrated by the case of a young Irishman named Langtree, who came to London full of patriotic fervour. His pathetic letters to Miss Martineau brought him, through her help, a job with Knight and the ministrations of her friends during his lingering death from consumption. She asked Mrs. Reid, in one letter however, to tell him to buckle down to his job and to forget politics, to somehow modify "his absurd and painful nationality". He wrote to her, Miss Martineau complained, expressing pain at reading about a fraudulent Irishman, an historical figure, in *The Hour and the Man*. Is this, he had asked, what you think of the Irish? Was her opinion of Napoleon, she replied in astonishment, to be generalized as her opinion of Corsicans, or her opinion of John Thurtell, the murderer, to stand for her view of Norwich people?

> I never in my life had one transient feeling of dislike or mistrust of the Irish; & I *have* no distinctive national feelings at all,—but, having had to do with a good many nations, am without any belief in the distinctive nationality which quite fills up this poor youth's mind.

Every nation, having all kinds of men, women, and children in it, was no better or worse than any other. To her, the Irish were no more different from the English than the Scots, unless they made her believe that they were. "The worst thing I know of the Irish is their not having prospered better. A people really equal to others commands circumstances with a peaceful resistless force, & cannot be retarded." Given this view, her distrust of Irish oratory and her hatred for the Fenians and the pro-Southern antics of Mitchel and Meagher make sense. So does her loathing for O'Connell.[1]

[1] The quotations are from a letter in the possession of the author. The best account of the Langtree episode is in Chorley, *Autobiography*, ii, 72–76. She herself told the story in an article for the *Atlantic Monthly*, viii, 337–45 (September, 1861): it is discussed in a letter from HM to Ticknor and Fields, March 19, 1861, Huntington Library. On Irish oratory, *ASS*, September 22, 1860, and on the Fenians, *DN*, August 22, 1865.

She believed that O'Connell, whatever his methods, had done a good thing in bringing about Catholic Emancipation; after 1829 his agitation ceased to be genuine. So far as the English were concerned, his lies and abuse were more acceptable than his continuing to live on priest-levied contributions from the poor; and, having promised the Irish everything lumped into Repeal, he was unable to deliver, and his movement collapsed. It was the fate she knew awaited any demagogue who mistook social and economic ills for political ones.[1] The worst thing about O'Connell and the others was that they were believed, not only in Ireland but abroad. She had been shocked when she visited America to find the Americans unable to make a distinction between political misgovernment and personal slavery, "between exasperating a people by political insult, and possessing them, like brutes, for pecuniary profit".[2] And she continued to try to set the matter right for them.[3] To take an example, she told readers of the *New York Evening Post* in 1854 that the Irish were not bound and downtrodden, but had representation and rights in the imperial legislature; the disabilities of Catholics had been removed. But bad as she thought the continued establishment of the Church of Ireland was, fifty years of it was a lesser affliction to the poor Irish than a single day of rebellion.

> The enormous rashness of exciting an ignorant multitude to rebellion, without any clear aim, or intelligible statement of political grievance, we, on this side the water, are accustomed to attribute to ignorance, and the recklessness which is its natural consequence. If the leaders had known anything of history, anything of the principles of social construction, anything of political economy, any of the many things that they ought to have known before leading the multitude to insurrection, they would not have sought a cure for social evils in political convulsions, &c. . . . As for the way in which they were regarded by good men, who did *not* rebel, they were excused—partly on the ground of their manifest ignorance, & partly because the misery of Ireland was really so dreadful, that almost any effort for a change seemed pardonable. But these men forfeited that amount of sympathy . . . by the barbaric tone of the newspapers & speeches. They proposed not only

---

[1] *Once a Week*, December 14, 1861. *Hist.*, ii, 8 ff. *DN*, January 24, 1854.

[2] *SA*, ii, 124.

[3] HM to Mrs. Emerson, April 25, 1848, Harvard. HM to Crabb Robinson, November 27, [1843]. *DN*, December 20, 1858. HM to Jacob Snider, October 6, 1844, Am. Phil. Soc., Madeira-Vaughan Collection. HM to Milnes, November 21, [1844].

> vitriol, molten lead, and hot sand, but iron hoops, red hot, to be dexterously cast from the houses on the soldiers, to pin their arms to their sides, and at that same time, burn them to the bone. Enough of that!

Intelligent Irishmen had always favoured union, she said, and if the Irish would only send good representatives to Westminster they would be safe.[1]

The reason for her optimism was that statesmanship had taken over in Westminster; Peel's policy pointed the way to the solution of all problems. Peel's principal contributions were free trade—the famine would never have occurred had it not been for protection—and the initiation of land legislation, of which the Encumbered Estates Act was the most important and useful. The problem, as she saw it, in 1834 and ever after, was not the fault of absenteeism, but the legal tangle brought on the landlords by the legislation of their predecessors—the inevitable result of laws made in self-interest. By permitting landlords to get out from under debt-ridden lands by selling to improving capitalists and the nascent middle classes, land transfer legislation was bringing capital into the country, and so enabling the land to support ultimately a larger population, though at the time one much reduced by famine and emigration. When she visited Ireland in 1852, she saw all this in train—gradually improving agriculture, longer leases, some sort of tenant right in the offing, a new demand for agricultural products. Agriculture was on its way to becoming an industry, not a means of subsistence, and all because of the flow of capital, every pound of which "represents a particle of a middle class which, thus deposited, will become fruitful,—filling up the wide space between the barren heights of landlordism and the engulphing floods of pauperism".[2] She never lost her conviction of the rightness of this prescription or of the success which attended it.

The Americans could now see, she told them, that Ireland was made one of the most progressive and happy countries in the world, and it had been done through other agencies than political revolution—a rebuke to hasty and superficial impulses.[3] To accept this conviction she had to explain away new outbursts of

[1] The letter is dated March 3, 1854.

[2] The best brief statement of her views is in "Condition and Prospects of Ireland", *WR*, n.s., iii 35–62, (January 1853). It is also the argument, somewhat more discursively presented, in her journalistic tour of Ireland, articles printed in *DN* and reprinted as *Letters from Ireland*.

[3] *ASS*, dated July 18, 1859.

rural violence in 1858; the most she could say was that it was difficult to know the mind of the peasant.[1] But give in to it, never. When John Stuart Mill, rejecting fair leases, tenant right, and disestablishment as mere palliatives, urged peasant proprietorship, Miss Martineau's scorn was overwhelming. She had said, she told Reeve, when Mill went into parliament that within five years he would have cut his throat politically "by his mingled impressionableness, and assumption of a philosophical bearing,—by his womanish temperament, his professional pedantry, his open vanity and latent self distrust together", and now he had done it. Mill's pamphlet was a fitting production for anyone who wanted to hurt Ireland and England in the extreme—to force expropriation on the great minority of landlords and capitalists who were the source of what prosperity Ireland had had, to make Repeal inevitable by such methods, and by the very operation of peasant inefficiency to lead to the abuses of peasant proprietorship in France or back in time to landlordism. It ought to ruin him, and she only hoped the ruin would stop there.[2]

Her contempt for the Catholic priesthood did nothing to weaken her sense that the Anglican Church in Ireland was an abomination. She rejected Milnes's suggestion of a parallel establishment of the two churches, saying that whatever happened, Romanism would one day become the established church, if not by English hands, by English blood. She wanted political relations established with the Pope and a better education provided for the clergy than the meagre one given in Maynooth College. Although she urged on Milnes that his Church give up its privileged status and become missionary in Ireland, by 1852 she was appalled by the missionary Protestants in Ireland who only served to keep old hatreds alive; as she saw it then, the great cry of the next generation would be about the danger of "speculative infidelity". At any rate by 1868, there could be no temporizing—mere compromises, parings and prunings. The Church of Ireland had to be swept away.[3] And, of course, she was particu-

[1] *DN*, November 18, 1858.

[2] HM to Reeve, February 23, 1868. An article in the *Pall Mall Gazette*, February 24, 1868, "Mr. Mill and Ireland", expressed exactly her views, she told Reeve on March 6. It is interesting, though, that she apparently advocated peasant proprietorship in the West Indies as a part and a proof of emancipation. *ASS*, dated August 29, 1859.

[3] HM to Milnes, November 21, [1844]. *WR*, n.s., iii, 35–62 (January 1853). HM to Reeve, August 7, 1868.

larly alarmed by the religious issue in schools. The National Schools continued to use Whately's book on evidences, which flew in the face of Catholic principles; while the priests, faced with a conversion movement in Ireland and with a suspicion that the emigrating flocks would be converted in Australia and America, naturally wanted to get their hands on the schools. The only solution was purely secular education, leaving religious instruction to the competing sects. It was the typical radical way to save the greatest resource of the country.[1]

I have called her dogmatism parochial. It was not, however, the parochialism of the ignorant or unsympathetic, the narrowness of the colonial mentality. It was parochial only in the sense that to her there was, at least ultimately, a known right, and that England had, with all her faults and shortcomings, grasped that right more firmly than any other people. What the whole human race needed was knowledge

> to bring the workings of this great power into harmony all over the world. At present, we see men in one place feeding, and in another place burning one another,—because they think they ought. In one place, we see a man with seventy wives,—in another, a man with one wife,—and in another a man remaining a bachelor all his life; and each one equally supposing that he is doing what is right. The evil everywhere is in the want of clear views of what is right. This is an evil which may and will be remedied, we may hope, in the course of ages. There is nothing that we may not hope while the power to desire and do what is right is common to all mankind,—is given to them as an essential part of the human frame.[2]

She could be particularly stringent in her demands upon Americans or Frenchmen or even Irishmen because they had come so close to right knowledge that it was unforgivable when they still fell short. But the amplitude of her sympathy for the backward becomes strikingly apparent when we turn to her views on the colonies.

As a friend of Lord Durham and Charles Buller, Miss Martineau was naturally sympathetic to the programme of the Colonial Reformers around Gibbon Wakefield and with them in their attacks on English apathy and Colonial Office "stupidity". She believed in intelligent emigration policies, in respect for colonial claims, and in self-government when the time was ripe,[3]

[1] *DN*, July 5, 1853. [2] *HE*, p. 112. [3] *DN*, January 3, 1853.

but, in general, she paid relatively little attention to the future English-speaking dominions. Except for the Durham mission and her natural interest in her friends the Elgins, she was bored by Canadians—"so *very* mediocre,—neither heroic, nor clever, nor gay, nor accomplished,—nor any thing but intensely common place," [1] as she put it in a momentary lapse from her prescription for respect. Australia appeared occasionally in her writings, thanks to her concern for emigration,[2] but New Zealand and the Cape, Maoris and Negroes notwithstanding, appear almost not at all. Her real colonial interest lay with the great dependent empire in the East.

India, like Ireland, was a constant theme in her interest and her writings. The English visit in 1831 of Rajah Rammohun Roy, the famous convert to Christianity, had wonderfully excited the London Unitarians, at precisely the time when Miss Martineau arrived among them. In an article in the *Monthly Repository*, part of which Miss Martineau wrote, the best hope held out for India was that English settlers might go there and raise the value of land and labour by investment of capital. Once the complexity of Indian land tenure was straightened around, no possible contention could arise between Indians and English—precisely the formula that she applied to settlers in Ireland. The idea of English settlement in India is played down somewhat in her later writings on India, but it is still there and in these same terms.[3] The possibility of cotton culture in India to relieve Britain of dependence on slave-grown cotton is one of the steady —and boring—concerns of her leader-writing. But her greatest efforts were called out by the Mutiny of 1857. It produced two books—an admirably done historical sketch of the English in India and a pamphlet on proposals for post-Mutiny reforms. The history appeared as a series of articles in the *Daily News*, and her suggestions about government were dealt with in a number of leading articles as well as in the pamphlet. From that time on, she was the paper's regular commentator on India—finance, public works, personnel, and politics.

There are four principal contentions in her views of Indian policy. In the first place, she had no patience with the contemp-

[1] HM to Philip Carpenter, n.d. [1860?]

[2] Her first leaders for *DN* were on emigration to Australia.

[3] "Rajah Rammohun Roy on the Government and Religion of India", *MR*, vi, 609–15. *Suggestions*, pp. 72–77. *DN*, June 7, 1853.

tuous attitude of so many Englishmen towards Indians or any other non-white people. Again and again, she insisted on the importance of knowing the people, their languages, literatures, and customs. In her generally favourable estimate of Warren Hastings, the most important quality she found was his concern for and knowledge of Indian culture; she was an admirer of Bishop Heber and of the succession of Orientalists whom she thought too much neglected at home.[1] She saw the intense practicality of this recommendation—in the folly of contempt which produced so many rebellions and frontier wars and in the warmth of response of Indians to the civil leaders or military commanders who took the trouble to understand.[2] She believed, moreover, that respect for the Indians must extend soon to the employment of Indians in government service, and the appointment by Sir George Clerk of six Indians to the local council in Bombay called out her warmest support.[3]

A second consideration for the framers of Indian policy was that institutions had deep roots and that reforms took long to adapt themselves. She hammered at that notion after the Mutiny, and it remained a steady subject for her preaching.

> While this object—of helping the people to become wise as they grow easy in circumstances—is kept in view as all-important, there is a danger belonging to it which should be fully understood. It does not follow, because the revenue, and the general wealth grows fast in India, that everything proceeds rapidly in proportion. The people are like the rest of the world in enjoying ease and desiring wealth; but they differ as widely from some other nations as other nations among themselves in the qualities of mind which they bring to their enterprise. They can acquire new ideas; and having once grasped, they retain them; but they are very slow by nature and habit, in learning new ways. There is no use in hurrying them. For instance, the cultivators will give us good cotton, and plenty of it, some day; but we cannot have it today. There is no use in clamouring for it, or in expecting anything but what can be obtained by addressing their interests in a way they understand, and awaiting the results. This kind of caution is rendered needful by two tendencies which may be observed among us—the tendencies to assume that because India may be profitable to us, India is to be governed for our profit; and to imagine that because Indian finance

---

[1] See her stress on learning something about the Japanese before trying to impose an English pattern on the Japanese or borrowing from them, *DN*, November 16, 1858. On Hastings, *British Rule in India*, pp. 134–35.

[2] E.g., *DN*, March 31, 1865, on the Bhootan War.

[3] *DN*, February 13, 1862.

> has been renovated, and Indian prosperity developed with extraordinary rapidity, all Indian business may be expected to move quickly. If we can keep these tendencies in check we may have more and more satisfaction in our great dependency, so that a future generation of Englishmen may grow up without knowing the sensation of dread which lies deep in all our hearts when we think of the unsounded abyss of severance between us and those Asiatics of ours in matters of faith and understanding, of feeling and belief—in the most essential interests—intellectual, moral, and social.[1]

The third consideration is implicit in this long quotation, that India was to be governed for its own benefit, but that benefit was interpreted in terms of the ultimate conversion of the Indians to right principles. Her relativism went only as far as gradualism, not to acceptance of equality of cultures. She made the Irish parallel explicit: Ireland was being governed in the sixties for bits wn benefit, and successfully; the same must be done in India —oy sound investment and public works programmes, by careful finance, by recognition of merit and by education. And, as in Ireland, she saw the improvement taking place. Everything was getting better: the people saw the possibility of rising in the world and worked harder, thanks to the reform of taxation and the introduction of bank-notes; Hindus were qualifying for professions, and the sons and (most important) daughters of merchants were being educated; public works were expanding; native councillors helped to make laws. Characteristically, the issue of all this was to be the rout of priesthood and idolatry, the union of the two races, and the end of wars.[2]

The final consideration concerns leadership. Because the solution to India's problems, as to Ireland's, was ultimately educational in its profoundest sense, the quality and character of the persons to whom that work was entrusted was crucial. This opinion made Miss Martineau a fervent defender of the East India Company. She saw its shortcomings, but, all things considered, felt its accomplishment without an equal in history. She was opposed to the system of double government which had obtained in India from the end of the eighteenth century, in which the Company's servants, knowledgeable and on the spot, and their masters in the Company offices in Leadenhall Street

[1] *DN*, July 28, 1863.

[2] *DN*, January 24, 1860 (on Irish parallel), January 12, 1860 (on government lands), July 10, 1861 (on irrigation works), and a very important summary view, "Old and New Times for the Hindoo", *Once a Week*, ix, 8–12 (June 27, 1863).

were subject to interference and control from India House, which I suspect she must have distrusted in some part because of the presence there of Mill. In her *History*, discussing the Ashanti War of 1824–26, she blamed such wars on the "lack of steadiness, ability, or knowledge in the agents sent from home", and she could cite no more telling example in later times than the antics of Sir John Bowring in China.[1] But the Company sent out trained men—after all she had visited Malthus at the Company's training college at Haileybury—and it could offer the further advantages that it was free from political changes which so adversely affected colonial policy, that it was open to merit and middle-class influence, and that it tried to rule India for the Indians. None of these things could she expect from the frivolity of Palmerston.[2]

When her plea for retention of the Company was passed by, as she expected it would be, she turned her scrutiny to the men who were chosen to rule India. For some administrators at home she had great respect: James Wilson, for one, the founder of *The Economist* and the financial member of the Council for India in the sixties, who introduced paper money; for most of the politicians she had great contempt, particularly for Sir Charles Wood, the secretary of state for India from 1859 to 1866. Her greatest admiration was reserved for the proconsuls, for Sir John Lawrence, for Sir Bartle Frere, and especially for Lord Elgin, who did such magnificent work in Canada, then in China, and finally as viceroy of India. She was a regular correspondent of Lady Elgin, the former Lady Mary Lambton, her close friend from Tynemouth days, and her letters and the *Daily News* are full of panegyrics on Elgin and his administration.[3]

The prototype of all her colonial heroes, however, was Sir James Brooke, that remarkable man who became Rajah of Sarawak, and who was so relentlessly pursued in Commons in the fifties by Hume and Cobden in the interests of their dogmatic anti-imperialism. Brooke, to her, was "one of Nature's Princes", a man of genius whom she compared to Columbus, Raleigh, Cortez, Penn, Pere d'Estevan, Collingwood, and Wellington.

[1] *Hist.*, i, 309, *DN*, January 2, 1855.

[2] This is the argument of her *Suggestions*, esp. pp. 124–53.

[3] E.g., *DN*, October 3, 1860 (Lawrence and Wilson), HM to Florence Nightingale, September 6, 1867 (Frere). *DN*, October 27, 1855, June 16, 1859, August 8, 1861, HM to Florence Nightingale, December 15, 1863 (all excellent samples of her views on Elgin.)

Sir Stamford Raffles had established the fundamental policy, and Brooke carried it out superbly:

> [Raffles'] scheme was conceived in the spirit of our age, and was inspired by its highest philosophy and morality. He never proposed conquest, or any kind of conflict, while, on the other hand, nothing could be further removed from the helpless spirit of sectarian religiosity which makes our missionary schemes so many failures. . . . His method was one which appears to be too wise for the disposers of armies and the magnates of commerce to appreciate, though the public have, on the whole, shown that they know how to value it. Brooke's view, at the outset, was that Great Britain should use and extend her territorial possessions, not for the purpose of pouring in colonists to swamp the natives, but in order gradually to develope native resources, to improve native character and intelligence, and direct that improvement into the formation of a better state of society; leading back the people, in fact, through the stages of deterioration . . . to their ancient industry, enlightenment, and prosperity, on their way to something far higher and better still.

To fulfil this ideal, European policy should be concerned only to "elicit, protect, support, and guide the native human element". With the consequent security, law, and encouragement of industry, operating in accordance with the natives' grasp of the universal principles of justice, everything would come right: commerce under the laws of free trade, and Christianity under the increasing enlightenment of the people.

> By the simple advantage of the good over the evil principle, without any other warfare, a new region of the globe might be opened to enterprise of every virtuous kind, and we might render our century honourably distinguished from all that have gone before by a nobler and wiser method than was ever before used for connecting ourselves with the ends of the earth, and the outlying tribes of the human race.[1]

Miss Martineau's rhapsodizing about proconsuls is important for more than the obvious reasons. She was clearly a liberal imperialist (I am convinced that, had she lived, she would have been Unionist and anti-Boer) a patriot, and a hero-worshipper. But she was all these things because the empire-builders were serving necessity. In doing so they offered an example and a challenge to England. Cobden and his cohorts, in their "ignorance, conceit, prejudice, and temper of anything but peace", stood

[1] The quotations are all from an important article by HM on Brooke in *WR*, n.s., vi, 381–419 (October, 1854). See also *Hist.*, ii, 514–15, and *Auto.*, ii, 455–56.

as a warning to public benefactors "what to expect from the sectarian interests to society; and to such sectarians that, when most confident, they may possibly not know what spirit they are of". The "peace party" opposed the Crimean War, in which Miss Martineau saw the great purgation of the corruptions and effeminacy of peace from English society. At the same time they pursued Brooke, whose heroic example showed the strenuous path England could follow, not in a single crisis but continually.

How could the example be followed? Why, at the time of the Mutiny,

> What a gallant sight it would be if the gentlemen of England would recognize in each other the spirit of the olden time, and go out to India as the flower of European chivalry went out to Asia five centuries ago! . . . It would make the work-a-day world young and merry again to see the English aristocracy and distinctive gentry proving their quality in the eyes of all nations, to the edification of despotic governments on the one hand, and republican on the other, who may have been fancying that nothing will wear in the structure of society that is not theoretically perfect. . . . Here is a great and necessary work to be done—the setting on high the civilization, heart, and intellect of Europe on the Asiatic platform in the very hour when barbarism is hoping to drive them into the sea.

On such heroic action might depend the decision whether Asia would be civilized with Western intellect and morals or wait for centuries for the inevitable result to come about through the kind of violence that the ancient world had had to endure.[1]

England's imperial obligations were clear: Ireland had to be governed for the Irish, India for the Indians; the rights of labour had to be maintained in the West Indies; and all the colonies had to be ruled in a considerate and liberal way. But these policies would come to nothing without purgation and steady high purpose at home: to keep government true to its principles by opening the suffrage to all who could qualify, to give the poor greater and greater knowledge and access to state service when they had acquired that knowledge, to arrange a fiscal system to free not only knowledge but industry and enterprise. "In short, if we are proud and gratified at our national position, and eager for more content, more satisfaction, more prosperity . . . we must 'do the duty that lies nearest. . . .' "[2]

[1] *DN*, October 1, 1857.

[2] This leader is controlled by the great current controversy—the repeal of the last of the "taxes on knowledge", the paper duty; but the argument stands in

A crucial element of that duty at home lay in defining the proper province of legislation. Law could do nothing, or worse than nothing, to correct morals, the pointed example being the attempt in Maine to legislate against drunkenness by prohibiting the sale and consumption of alcoholic drinks. She saw the Maine Law in a somewhat peculiar light, to be sure, as the exercise of the will of a democratic people: something that would be unacceptable and tyrannous in England where prohibition was not wanted, could be tried as an experiment when it was not foisted on the lower classes from above. Yet its repeal in 1855 convinced her of the futility of such legislation and reinforced her attacks on meddling legislation at home.[1] Street-begging could not be put down by legislation; only an enlightened public opinion would stop it. Legislation against adulteration was unnecessary, for the people, if they would learn to buy intelligently, could punish adulterators themselves; and the co-operatives were showing the way. If steam boilers exploded, the right way to avoid the danger was by voluntary organization for inspection; and she could point with enthusiasm to the Association for the Prevention of Steam-boiler Explosions, a spontaneous society

> with its earnestness permitted to work naturally, its passions unstirred, and its connexion with the operative class left in its normal condition of kindliness and harmony. As masters, instead of victims of their inspectors, the manufacturers of the kingdom will guard their workpeople from accident better than Parliament and Secretaries of State could do . . . [acting] as other men do under motives of universal operation.[2]

The best known of her efforts in this direction was her attack on Dickens and other "sentimental" advocates of factory legislation. In *Household Words*, one Henry Morley wrote five articles in 1855 on factory accidents, paying particular attention to the dangers involved in unfenced machinery. To this Miss Martineau replied with a blast so powerful that John Chapman, to her deep mortification, refused it for the *Westminster*. It was published instead as a pamphlet by the National Association of Factory Occupiers. Her case was that the factory acts dealing with these matters were ignorantly drawn and impossible to apply, while inspectors were both rash and changeable, hector-

---

broader terms as the underpinning of all her views on public policy. *DN*, January 24, 1860.

[1] *DN*, March 15, 1853, August 7, 1855.

[2] On steam boilers, *DN*, February 5, 1857; on adulteration, *DN*, March 18, 1856; on street-begging, *DN*, January 12, 1856.

ing manufacturers about doing the impossible and insisting on compensation for accidents due to employees' negligence. Undoubtedly there was something to be said for her case: the early stages of factory laws and inspection brought injustice and difficulties; but her tone was so shrill and her position so clearly dogmatic rather than empirical that it is impossible not to incline to Dickens's opinion that "there never was such a wrong-headed woman born—such a vain one—or such a Humbug".[1]

Still, for all her dogmatism, she could accept "meddling legislation" when it was called for by otherwise incurable situations. When she learned about dreadful conditions on board American merchant vessels, where she said white men and coloured men were tortured by officers, she wondered why the states did not adopt the British practice of precautionary screening for merchant officers. Inspection of collieries to prevent accidents met with her approval, and she wrote sympathetically about proposals for compulsory insurance in collieries. She had abandoned her doubts of thirty years earlier, when the question of extending the factory acts came up in the sixties: there was no avoiding the necessity for the ten hours act or the laws governing the employment of children. And while she was certain that the best guarantee for sanitary improvement was an enlightened and vigilant people working through their localities, she was disturbed by apathy on the question and wanted her readers to tell the government what it should do, not wait for it to act; but that recommendation she intended to issue in legislation: the public health acts must be put into force, and wherever they fell short of the intention of the legislature and the public, they had to be amended.[2] Government intervention in sanitary matters was new, but the most wonderful thing about it was how well it was borne. And why would Englishmen accept this vigilance of an almost continental type? Because their reason was convinced that private arrangements could not provide for public health, that the selfish interests of a few persons could not be allowed to endanger the many,

and if the wrong cannot be kept in check but by the law and its

---

[1] *The Factory Controversy: A Warning against Meddling Legislation.* See also *DN*, February 12 and March 4, 1856. Dickens to W. H. Wills, January 3, 1856, *Dickens as Editor*, p. 198.

[2] *ASS*, February 11, 1860. *DN*, February 27, March 15, 1860, August 4 and 11, 1863. *DN*, June 18, 1852, September 18, 1865.

> agents, the law and its agents must be permitted to penetrate into the last recesses of the Englishman's property,—the damp cellar or mouldy garret of the lodging-house,—the cesspool on the one hand and the pigstye on the other. A sleepy citizen here and there may start at finding anybody daring to meddle with him and his property; but on the whole, the nation has responded very well to the call to admit of a new department of government, instituted to preserve life by a course of action too extensive for individual management.[1]

It was perfectly possible, then, for her dogmatic stands to be qualified or abandoned when facts contradicted them and necessity demanded. But some facts and situations produced greater flexibility in her than others: she could accept mining legislation, state action in sanitation, and even ultimately the regulation of hours of child labour, where once she had thought it at best dubious. She stood fast against inspecting steam boilers and fencing machinery. We cannot isolate all her criteria, but I suspect that the most important of them was that legislation for sanitation or collieries, insofar as it had adverse effects, affected landlords, while boiler-inspecting and machine-fencing affected manufacturers like her father or her brother Robert. Her manufacturer's radicalism remained very nearly pure. She may have given in to humanity on the question of regulating hours for those who were not free contracting agents; but she could never yield an inch, for all her sympathy with the labouring classes, on the actions of the trade unions.

On few subjects was she so violent and uncompromising as on the Builders' strike of 1859 and the following years: this in obedience to her general philosophy about working-men and trade unions. The demand of the Builders for a nine-hour day seemed to her mere pillage. The "Document"—the agreement demanded of workmen to abstain from union membership—she found thoroughly justified. She was all for friendly societies, but she was dead against mixing up friendly benefits with trade regulation. It was, of course, precisely this mixture that provided the solid base on which the "New Model" unions like the Engineers and Builders were based, but, characteristically, she argued (I am sure ingenuously) from the theoretical incompatibility of the two functions and not from the strategy of power.[2]

[1] *England and Her Soldiers*, p. 103.

[2] The best leaders on the subject are *DN*, August 8 and November 29, 1859, but see also August 6, 1861, and *ASS*, October 1, 1859. There are a great many other leaders in *DN*.

Italy and the other liberated countries were watching these developments, she warned the strikers; if they saw in free England the enforced slavery of the working-man, then what would there be left for them to struggle for? Again and again the question was brought back to the conception which underlay the poor law of 1834—the independent, self-sufficient working-man, able to contract for his own terms of labour, sober, industrious, and prudent. She was always upbraiding opponents of a wider franchise for not knowing the people they objected to admitting to the vote, but she knew them little better. It was her girlhood again: "I will rally my personal experiences (in Norwich) & my more recent knowledge of trade oppression," she told Reeve, "to serve as the picturesque & illustrative part of the exposition," suitably laced, of course, with information about violence in Sheffield.[1] For all her correspondence with men who did know the working classes, men like W. L. Sargant and G. J. Holyoake, she remained as ignorant of what they were truly like as she found Wordsworth blind to the reality of his Lakeland peasants. The differing cultural values of the two classes, the ideal of solidarity among working-men, were subjects permanently closed to her imagination.

At one point she was attracted by a proposal of Joseph Hume for an arbitration tribunal. Let a hundred arbitrators be maintained handsomely, to perfect industrial legislation; let them find the facts, for strikes were not over opinions but over facts. Unlike the anarchy of international arbitration, in the industrial field the laws of political economy held firm; the elements could be computed, and the decision would be indisputable. To be sure, employers would have to abandon their taciturnity and tell the truth about their economic position; the men would have to learn that the wages fund was not inexhaustible and concede that wages should not rise and fall with the price of provisions. But these would be trifling adjustments in comparison with the great gain of a scientific way to industrial peace.[2] It was not a scheme to which she returned; rather the solution that truly captivated her was the co-operative idea.

She had found the "economy of association" attractive in the thirties and forties, and the Rochdale adaptation of consumers' co-operation seemed full of promise in the sixties, as indeed it was. But she saw it not simply as an effective channel for marketing

[1] HM to Reeve, July 14, 1859.

[2] *DN*, November 1, 1853.

and supply, nor was it merely an answer to George Potter and the strike leaders. It was the road to a better life, in the fullest sense, for the working classes. By emancipating working people from the tyranny of credit, co-operation would contribute to their independence—the poacher and sot would return to regular lives, the daughter would forsake her mortgaged finery for homelier styles, the wife would have to learn and practice daily thrift; only the publican would suffer: "It is a question of reinstating a spoiled generation in the respectability of its fathers. . . ." But beyond this, beyond the improvement in quality of goods (and the possibility of common co-operative dining rooms), there would be a gain in insurance and benefits, the advantages of trade unions without the tyranny. The co-operatives offered the means of bridging the gap between rich and poor. By teaching through experience the affinity between capital and labour, they could overcome the labour problem cast in terms of antagonism and, in creating a group of men who could appreciate problems of business and government, prepare those men for the franchise.[1]

The central prerequisite for enfranchisement, of course, remained education. We have already seen how insistent Miss Martineau was in the forties on the creation of a national system of schools, to be rammed through if necessary against the protests of the dissenters.[2] She found fault with the system of state-supervised parliamentary grants-in-aid because they supported education already provided without touching the lowest classes whom the school societies did not reach. Only a complete national system could cure that difficulty, and she preferred to have education paid for by a rate rather then through a merely palliative scheme like reclaiming anachronistic charities.[3] But her writing on national education in the fifties and sixties differed from her earlier concerns by emphasizing content rather than system.

She found herself in opposition to the prevailing view among inspectors and officials of the Committee of Council on Education, the supervisory body for the parliamentary grants. She wanted industrial training—on which the Ragged Schools had made a

[1] On co-operatives, see especially her article, "Co-operative Societies in 1864", *ER*, vol. 120, pp. 407–36 (October 1864) and letters concerning it to Reeve, October 8 and 18, 1859, and June 17, 1864.

[2] This is made perfectly clear in a leader in *DN*, August 23, 1853.

[3] *DN*, April 7 and 11, 1853.

start—and the creation of solid citizens trained to their station. Reading, writing, and arithmetic were important, but only a third to a fourth of ordinary school hours were enough to teach them.

> Not the less for this do we believe that the rousing of the intellectual appetites is indispensable to good school instruction; while we deprecate the pedantry and practical uselessness of too many of the devices and suggestions of the Inspectors of Schools, who give grammatical analysis when the children should be learning cooking or carpentering, and ancient history and Asiatic geography while the pupils are unaware what it is to have a country, and why it is a duty and a pleasure to live under a system of law and free government.[1]

But even what training in the three R's was given she found lacking in any real proficiency.

It was for this reason that she welcomed Robert Lowe's Revised Code of 1861, whereby state grants were tied to the success of children in examinations—the system of "payment by results" deplored by educational authorities then and since. She was sure the plan would make parents keep their children in school longer by showing them concrete results; she thought too it would encourage masters by providing the children with a solid basis of accomplishment to build on instead of forcing them to cram children with facts which they had no way of understanding. The opponents of the Revised Code were especially vocal on the danger of driving the best schoolmasters away by so rigid a system, but Miss Martineau drew a characteristic conclusion about that. If they feared losing dependence on government and being thrown on to the mercies of school managers eager to see examination results, the masters had lost their "true English independence and pride", and the state connection had gone too far. The educational aims of the state, as she saw them, were or should be limited and practical—discipline, a solid minimum of intellectual equipment, and manual training. If state payments had to be earned by fulfilling these purposes, no man of honour would want it otherwise. "What a treat Mr. Lowe's Educational speech was!" she wrote to Reeve. "Surely we shall grow reasonable and effective now; for there can be no going back. I have

[1] *DN*, November 17, 1855, March 22, 1853, April 17, 21, 22, 1857. See also in this connection her article "Female Industry", *ER*, vol. 109, pp. 293–336 (April, 1859).

been expecting to hear that the speech killed Sir J. K. Shuttleworth."[1] And once the programme was successful, "whenever we have open day-schools for every wanderer, and industrial feeding schools for the destitute, and reformatory schools for the delinquent, and a sound education provided for all the children of the state, we may put our last gallows in the British Museum as a curiosity. . . ."[2]

Sound views on political economy, a solid discipline, an effective and appropriate system of education—these were the prerequisites for a dependable electorate. This electorate should not be organized, Miss Martineau believed, by classes, for class lines shift and criteria change, making class too unstable a base to allow for security. But while she urged the representation of individuals rather than groups, she was no raving democrat. Simon de Montfort had instituted representation, she wrote at the very end of her life, not mere assemblage or democratic delegation; representation was requisite to the understanding and enjoyment of liberty. She had nothing but horror for the wild social democracy of Australia—unless it was the hope that a strong man would appear to guide the Australian people out of their rapacious, drunken, and disorganized state, out of moral evils imposed by an old set of standards into the kind of true democracy that she wanted and expected to see in England.[3]

To attain this true democracy in England meant, apparently, a gradual and careful approach. "I am for admitting the working men (duly qualified) to the franchise," she told Reeve,

> seeing that it may safely be done . . . that it ought to be done,—& that it *must*,—*will*,—be done. There are endless varieties of cultivation, & there is a long gradation of ranks & orders among the working classes; & there are ranks & classes as superior to these tyrannical doings [of the trade unions] as we are. Moreover, the monopolists are just like, not only whole classes of electors within our own recollection,—but groups of representatives—of corn and "green glass bottles" &c.[4]

She was not, then, for indiscriminate admission; yet one cannot be categorical about this, for at times she spoke with another

[1] *DN*, September 24, 1861. HM to Reeve, February 24, 1862.

[2] *DN*, July 16, 1853, a letter "Transportation and Education", signed "A Practical Reformer".

[3] *DN*, January 14, 1854, "The Coming Reform Bills", signed "A Reformer". Introduction to Pauli's *Simon de Montfort*, p. vi. *DN*, July 1, 1852.

[4] HM to Reeve, March 9 and 14, 1859.

voice and seemed, like Mill, to see the franchise as the means to education, not its product. An extended electorate would put a stop to the prerogative nature of foreign affairs, to take one of her special concerns; it would even solve the labour problem by removing the greatest of grievances of the working-men and by giving the sober and responsible among them the opportunity they needed to take intelligent rather than violent and wrong-headed socialist action. She saw, as Disraeli thought he saw in a different sense, the English working-man as a true Conservative. At worst, the new electors could send up some foolish talkers who would soon learn; the anticipation was rather that the new electors would send up some sensible men who understood their interests and who could instruct existing legislators on working-class views and demands. Small wonder that she welcomed Mr. Gladstone's conversion to reform in 1864.[1] Yet when reform came in 1867 she was horrified. To explain that apparent contradiction requires some attention to her attitudes towards politicians and politics.

She was certainly willing to use politicians—as she did in her work for the repeal of the Contagious Diseases Acts, that great focus of feminist activity in the sixties.[2] She was willing too to hector politicians and to rouse public opinion to force them to take action. It was in this connection that her remarkable and fruitful collaboration with Florence Nightingale is so revealing. In 1859, Miss Martineau published *England and Her Soldiers*, an account of the calamities and inefficiencies of the Crimean War based on information privately communicated from Miss Nightingale. Miss Nightingale read the book in manuscript and got herself firmly put down when she suggested a major change, a suggestion which Miss Martineau noted in the margin of the letter as "Sadly absurd, & at once retracted". She also sent fifty-five pounds to Miss Martineau to make up the difference between what Smith and Elder paid her and the hundred pounds Miss Nightingale thought she should have. Miss Martineau was valuable to the great invalid in London, for Miss Nightingale had a horror of publicity, and Ambleside could provide both power and a necessary façade for the almost demoniacal reforming energy centred in Berkeley Street. Miss Martineau stood

[1] *DN*, August 10, 1853, April 9, 1857, March 8, 1859, July 30, 1864. *ASS*, April 21, 1860.
[2] HM to W. E. Forster (copy), July 16, 1871, NLS.

ready to defend Sidney Herbert against his detractors, to hound the permanent officials at the War Office, to encourage attention to the lot of the common soldier, to demand sanitary reform in the Indian army, or to put sympathetic politicians into office. "Agitate, agitate," said the telegram from Miss Nightingale on April 15, 1863, "for Ld de Grey in the place of Sir G.C. Lewis."

> All I *could* do at the moment was for M[aria] to drop a line to the Ed. of "D. News", asking him to send to the train, the next night. In the evening we heard the full news, were up early next morning, and got the article off by the Coach, so that it appeared on Friday,—in spite of the Budget. It is an immense point gained, —as against the Court & the Horse Guards,—this appointment of Lord de Grey.[1]

There was, of course, no control to this experiment, so we can never know how much effect Miss Martineau had.

It is, however, easy to attack and demand by dismissing from one's calculations the varying pressures to which politicians are inevitably subject. She had made the contemptible position of the politician clear in one of her early essays:

> Little is also to be expected of the office-seeker. There is nothing in the discharge of office which is necessarily unfavourable to moral independence. If the servants of Society could not also be friends of God, we must hesitate to believe society to be a divine ordination. It is the seeking of office which is perilous to freedom. An office-seeker puts himself into a position of dependence upon human opinions. He professedly refers his desires to his brethren, and not his Father; he assures them that his welfare is in their hands; that, in short, he is their property. . . . It is a god-like privilege to do the work of society: it is a reptile degradation to prey upon its honours.[2]

This position led to her attacks on American politicians in general—Jackson, Van Buren, Webster, Everett, and for a time Lincoln. She saw the same faults in England. Thus in 1836, Lord Stanley, opposing the appropriation of surplus revenues from the Irish Church, charged the government with insisting on a mere abstract principle and asked them to come to a practical compromise. A decade later in her *History* she commented:

[1] The whole collaboration is documented fully in the Nightingale papers in the British Museum, Add. MSS 45,788. See also FN to HM, October 24, 1861, NLS, and HM to Reeve, February 6 and April 21, 1859, October 2, 1861, April 25 and July 10, 1863; the quotation comes from the letter of April 25, 1863. The leading article in question appeared in *DN*, April 17, 1863.

[2] "On Moral Independence", *Misc.*, i, 187.

> Often as we are compelled to mourn the moral scepticism, the destitution of faith, which is prevalent in the political world, and which is the just ground of the deep disrepute of legislative assemblies, almost universally, it is not often that we meet, in Hansard or elsewhere, with so open an avowal as this—that principles are "the shadow", and arrangements "the substance"—that it is not practical for the legislature to resolve, by clear implication, that there is a world of morals above and beyond the law, to which mankind must occasionally resort for the regeneration of their laws. To admit this most solemnly and deliberately, in full conclave, with a spectacle of murder and famine before the eyes, and the curses and groans and wailings of a suffering people filling the air, is an unpractical thing for a legislature to do, while they might be busy in ordering a plan of distribution of money—some more here and something less there, the suffering of the multitude remaining untouched. Lord Stanley was so far from understanding that a principle is the most substantial and enduring of relations, that he evidently thought he was speaking loftily and patriotically in making his unphilosophical and degrading appeal.[1]

There had been exemplars of right method in politics: Thomas Drummond, the great Irish under-secretary; Canning, of course; above all, Peel, whose business in life was recognizing necessities a little in advance of others and adapting his course to them, without a sign of political profligacy or levity—"the sincere and devout high-priest of expediency in that province of human life in which expediency is both the obligation and the rule of duty".[2] But such an expediency was no mere snatching at expedients—that would have been the profligacy and levity she so condemned in Palmerston or Disraeli; for her, expediency meant adaptation to principle, not mere adaptation. The Radicals in the thirties had shown the way:

> They were so far removed from influence over the mob by the philosophical steadiness of their individual aims as from influence over the aristocracy by the philosophical depth and comprehensiveness of their views. They were as far from sharing the passion of the ignorant as the selfish and shallow *nonchalance* of the aristocratic. They perceived principles which the untaught could not be made to see; and they had faith in principles when Lord Grey preached in his place that no one should hold to the impossible: and thus, they were cut off from sympathy and its correlative power above and below.[3]

---

[1] *Hist.*, ii, 228–29.

[2] On Drummond, *Hist.*, ii, 288–89. This passage on Peel is from *Once a Week*, July 6, 1861.

[3] *Hist.*, ii, 351.

Too often coming to share power meant a falling-off from this high and impotent state: true of a great reforming but flexible administrator like George Cornewall Lewis; true af an impressionable mind like John Stuart Mill's.[1] True, too, of all the great politicians at mid-century

In a way, the political confusion was Peel's fault—a fault that would come to be seen as a virtue when the future showed how necessary and valuable was the break-up of parties. But in the confusion after the dissolution of old arrangements, organization on principle was impossible; there could be no leadership worthy of the name, nothing but levity and opportunism.[2] Gladstone she thought might do a few great things individually considered, but he was unfit for consistent, general rule; everything she saw—for example the "imbecility" of his sympathetic response to a trade union delegation in 1868—confirmed the prediction. Disraeli was worse, "a source of patriotic shame" to her through his whole career, for his flamboyance, his dishonesty, his "vulgar *charlatanerie*" which so offended her that she refused to suffer the provocation of reading his novels. And the Reform Act of 1867 bore her out: "The most stupid deeds of the worst old Tory govts seem to me innocent in comparison with the reckless, political profligacy of the present set,—that is of Disraeli, —& the cowardly subservience of his colleagues," in carrying through "this sudden, unannounced. . . unprepared plunge into a democratic abyss wh the leaders & drivers regarded as Hell itself not many months ago."[3] Bright was as bad: ignorant, demagogic, invariably pitching his appeals on a ground too low. She thought his career a complete failure in 1861, and when he entered the cabinet in Gladstone's administration, she wondered how ministers could get on with so impudent a colleague.[4] But W. E. Forster offers the best case study of Miss Martineau and the politicians.

[1] On Lewis, HM to Reeve, January 1, 1863, and for an evaluation of his career a master's essay by Richard Helmstadter at Columbia University, 1958. On Mill, again, HM to Reeve, August 8, 1865.

[2] This is a persistent theme. *Hist.*, ii, 517–18, *DN*, May 14 and October 11, 1858. *Once a Week*, September 7, 1861.

[3] On Gladstone, HM to Reeve, August 8, 1865, February 23, 1868, December 30, 1870. On Disraeli, HM to Reeve, August 15, 1867, June 7, 1868; HM to Philip Carpenter, June 2, 1867; HM to Milnes, June 12, [1844].

[4] On Bright, *Once a Week*, December 14, 1861; HM to Reeve, July 9, 1862 and December 10, 1869; HM to Garrison, August 24, 1863, BPL. The article in *Once a Week*, incidentally, has a passage of great good sense about demagogues.

She long thought Forster's queer manners (she explained them as a natural revolt of his honesty against Quaker smoothness) his one drawback, otherwise he was a great hope who could not long be kept out of office. When he accepted the Colonial Office in 1866, she wrote to his sister-in-law, Mrs. Arnold, regretting his loss of freedom and, for herself, the loss of free communication with him, an inevitable result of taking office; but she knew he could handle the great tasks he had to face, and she had no doubt of "his showing the country what a man's work may be under the stimulus of such a conscience and such a heart as his". But by 1872 he was "a lost man for statesmanship", like Gladstone both obstinate and changeable, "gloriously fit" for public service and totally unfit to rule. What had he done? In 1870, he had carried his Education Act (the only one he could get) by compromising on religion. Could he possibly be so ignorant of what every Quaker was supposed to know, or did he merely surrender principle and throw the greatest question of the time to fate?

> He affected to make light of the gravest of difficulties, in order to shirk the treatment of it,—he devolved upon local societies & very various communities the work wh was the proper business of Parliament; & the inevitable consequence will be that our country will be torn with religious strife, from end to end, for a generation,—or two or more generations to come. . . . The new rates—already called (& properly) church rates—will not be paid; & we shall have . . . Well, enough of foreboding!

She was right about the generation of controversy; but Forster hardly caused it—he found it.[1]

It is significant and revealing that at the end of her life she couched her strongest objection to a political measure in the same terms as in her best youthful essays: her doing so makes the nonconformist origin of her insistence on principle clear. How well it comes out, to take an even better example, in her criticism of Dean Stanley, "commonly called 'liberal', amiable, gentlemanly,—but utterly obtuse in regard to the real grievance!" In 1861 she called him "totally devoid of,—not only any personal sense of difficulty about the duty of profession or non profession of opinion, but any instinct wh can lead him to conceive of other people's difficulties". In 1866 he preached his famous "William

[1] HM to Carlisle, January 1, 1859; HM to Mrs. Arnold, in T. Wemyss Reid, *Life of the Right Honourable William Edward Forster*, i, 385–86. HM to Reeve, April 25, 1863, March 15 and December 30, 1870. HM to Mrs. Samuel Brown, January 28, 1872, NLS.

the Conqueror" sermon, in which he argued by analogy from the mixture of English and Norman races that the conflict of ideas might result in a reunion of churches.

> He seemed actually unaware [she sneered] that, while races & tongues may amalgamate, *incompatible opinions* cannot, & that, while an association may be formed among any variety of people entertaining a common *sentiment*, a *Church* requires, as its essential condition, a basis of *conviction*, & precisely in those matters on wh the sects (especially within the Church) differ so vitally.

Stanley was not meanly conciliatory, she hastened to add; he was amiable, generous, and sympathetic, but however picturesque and graceful as a writer, he was superficial and unreasoning, indeed seemed to have no conception of the function of reason or the importance of speculative truth.[1] A greater condemnation than that she was incapable of.

In April, 1866, Miss Martineau retired from the *Daily News*. When the Brighton Railway stopped paying dividends at the end of the sixties, she was in some financial difficulty, and the republication of her biographical sketches from the *Daily News* was arranged to tide her over. But though she came out of her retirement to write an intense and to her terribly important article for the *Edinburgh Review* against spiritualism,[2] and though she took an interested part in Josephine Butler's fight against the Contagious Diseases Acts, her last years must have been deeply distressing. Her poor health really made work impossible.

The generosity of her family and friends allowed her to have the luxuries of game, turtle, and wine, which made her condition more tolerable. But her body was increasing enormously in size, she suffered from dropsy in the legs and a good many other painful complications. The difficulties were without question due to the enormous cyst—the autopsy revealed a pear-shaped tumour twelve inches in the longer diameter, ten in the shorter—which displaced the other organs and added to the strain on a heart suffering from the general fatty degeneration which the physician found in the muscular tissue. In her last years, she was taking opiates again.[3] Yet she remained able to write clear letters to within a few days of her death—the "brain mischief" of which she complained, the "horrid sensations" notwithstanding.

[1] HM to Reeve, May 7, 1861, July 16, and August 7, 1868.

[2] *ER*, vol. 128, pp. 1–47 (July, 1868).

[3] *British Medical Journal*, April 14, 1877 and May 5, 1877.

In 1873 Sir John Robinson of the *Daily News* found her a neat, plump little woman, wearing a white cap with frilled edges, a lace collar, and a blue dress with black velvet trimmings. "How small!" was his first reaction. She was not like her photographs—she had bright, lively eyes and the same pleasant smile we encountered when she first went to America—but the smile, he noted significantly, did not mask a certain look of determination. She was determined to the end. Her funeral was to be a plain, inexpensive one, without the usual additions by the undertakers—plumes and the like—"which are of no use in committing the body to the ground". And to carry utility further (very like Jeremy Bentham), she willed her head to Henry Atkinson, who was, however, no Southwood Smith. She died quietly on April 10 1876, and was buried in the family plot in Birmingham.[1]

But her health must have been the lesser burden. To have seen the world go so wrong and to be able to do nothing must have hurt desperately. America, which had presumably purged itself in abolishing slavery, offered a depressing spectacle of ignorance of political economy, violence between labour and capital, and corruption in government so bad that "I am, like many others, almost in despair for the great Republic,—even in its near future". At home, there was a sense of malaise in society and an utter lack of statesmanship and responsibility. The European war in 1870–71, making a mockery of her usual New Year's greetings, reminded her of Waterloo, "but I seem never to have recognized or felt war till now. It feels like the gates of hell having been opened upon us suddenly; & it almost kills me. And then—there is the shame of being so miserable when one has only the pains of sympathy for one's own share."

The plaintive note in her letters is a comment on a world that had left her behind, that had turned to a sense of reality and conceptions of power to which her dogma were irrelevant. But that she never knew. She thought the chaos temporary, no more than an aberration. At her most depressed, in 1867, she wrote to Florence Nightingale:

> How doleful all public affairs have been looking,—abroad & at home! All those mightily religious Governments & Courts abroad,

---

[1] HM to Milnes, October 13, 1873; HM to Garrison, March 30, 1876, BPL; HM to Spring Brown, June 6 to December 25, 1874, NLS. Robinson, *Fifty Years of Fleet Street*, pp. 200–201.

> —what a temper of heathen barbarism they have been showing, on every possible occasion! And our own hopeless Parliament, & set of public men.

But she was more than hopeful, she was certain: "The regeneration is. . . sure. The worse the disintegration, the helplessness, the laxity now, the sooner will the renovation come; & one begins to see a good head here & there popping up from the chaos. . . . We see the need of a return to correctness, truth & principle growing so urgent that what we want must soon arise." [1]

No millenarian was ever more convinced, ever more willing to recalculate the prophecies. And if worse came to worst, if late Victorian reality made yet more thorough nonsense of early Victorian theory, I am sure I know which side, had she lived, she would have chosen: to close her paper, put down her trumpet, and gaze at the firm eternity of Loughrigg.

[1] HM to Reeve, December 30, 1870, June 26 and 28, 1871. HM to FN, May 13, 1867.

CHAPTER XII

Conclusion

HARRIET MARTINEAU grew up as the manufacturing class to which she belonged experienced its greatest access of confidence and power. She became famous in the year of what members of that class and most historians since have considered its legislative triumph; the Reform Act of 1832 was, as we have come increasingly to see, a limited victory, but there is no denying its symbolic importance, then or now.

For some forty years Miss Martineau was active and famous. Her latest books (there was always a latest book) were topics of dinner-table conversation in polite society; she was a controversial traveller and a celebrated medical case; someone in a crowd being harangued in the thirties thought it worth while to shout her name, so the crowd must have known it. In 1855, when her friend was believed dying, Mrs. Chapman found all England "in a live stir about Harriet's opinions", and she was repeatedly asked for a whole evening of exposition of how Miss Martineau feels & thinks to an azimuth—yes even to an ephigraph [sic] 'because, Mrs. Chapman, *this*, now, *really* interests me' ". And, soberly, Mrs. Chapman recorded that at the end of the sixties, young men were naming their horses after the famous writer on the conviction that "no matter who was the favourite, Harriet Martineau would come in by half a neck". Mrs. Chapman left this tribute out of the *Memorials* because someone had said it did a lady no honour. Mrs. Chapman disagreed: after all, she said, a young nobleman was given permission to name a heifer after the Marchioness of Lorne.[1] Good journalist that she was, Miss

[1] For her "household word" reputation, see Hon. Emily Eden, *The Semi-Attached Couple*, a novel written in 1834, reprinted in 1927, p. 115. On the voice in the crowd, see above, p. 123. Mrs. Chapman's notations are in a letter to Anne Weston, n.d., BPL, Weston, vi, no. 43, and in some scratched notes, v, no. 111.

Martineau took each enthusiasm at its height and made Englishmen and a good many Americans, whether from respect or contempt or merely amusement, aware of her views and prescriptions.

She stopped writing at the time of the Second Reform Act and died shortly after the onset of the Great Depression. In the last decade of her life, the world for which she had such remarkable preparation began to slip away from her. Some writers who had to review the autobiography found her reputation a puzzle,[1] and a good many others, like Greg or Stephen in their sketches or George Eliot in her letters, seem to have been trying to explain a phenomenon to an uncomprehending and, save for a few devotees, an indifferent generation. She has survived, as I said at the beginning of this book, as the eccentric she undoubtedly was.

Although her concern about letters and the tone of her autobiography can be taken uncharitably, one must give some credence to her insistence that she was content to use her limited powers for her own time, that she cared nothing for posthumous fame. If she was so thoroughly imbedded in her society, what light can her life and, more, the cast of her mind throw on it?

Her life was, for all its shifts and enthusiasms, astonishingly consistent. It is a noble thing, she wrote in *Life in the Sickroom*, to apprehend truth early, partly because to do so gives the individual the satisfaction of seeing his belief spread towards universality, partly because an early grasp of truth provided an unassailable ground for action. She never questioned, only developed, her own early dedication to known truth. Is it not the case, she asked Bulwer-Lytton, that men never outgrow the first general truths of which they have become the effective possessors, "that one or two of these are not only the basis of our intellectual acquisitions, but so ramify through—so form part of whatever is afterwards attained as that, if these truths could possibly cease before our eyes to be truth, & become merely matter of conception or fancy, our whole intellectual past would immediately begin to dwindle, & could not be kept from perishing"? [2]

The fundamental grounds of her conviction were two—her manufacturers' radicalism and a superbly adapted analogue, Priestley's optimistic necessarianism. In consequence, she was a

[1] Mrs. Oliphant to John Blackwood, *The Autobiography and Letters of Mrs. M. O. W. Oliphant*, p. 263.

[2] January 26, [1844].

liberal, in the literal sense of one concerned for freedom, a freedom both positive and negative, a goad and sanction to do right as well as an injunction to remove restraints. The referents and ordinances of the free society she envisaged were supplied by natural laws, not yet entirely disclosed, which operated as inescapably as the laws of mechanics or the laws of political economy she did so much to popularize. What evils remained as the attainment of a truly free society drew near were curable by education and the benevolence commanded by necessarian morality, and until they were cured, they were tolerable because the adjustments were sure and progress and perfection certain. "I was always hopeful for the world," she wrote at the end of the *Autobiography*, "but never so much as now. . . . It appears to me now that, while I see much more of human difficulty from ignorance and from the slow working (as we weak and transitory beings consider it) of the law of Progress, I discern the working of that great law with far more clearness, and therefore with a far stronger confidence, than I ever did before."

Everyone called Miss Martineau a Radical, so it is tempting to find the essence of her radicalism in her liberal programme. But there were Conservatives too who were liberals—her admiration for Peel is telling—and there were people called Radicals who were anything but liberal. Indeed, the entire programmatic content of liberalism was changing by the end of her life, as manufacturers deserted their old political allegiances and politicians appealed to the demands and prejudices of a new electorate. Political spectrum-making on the basis of programmes is invariably plagued by difficulties. Shaftesbury, Oastler, and Peel, Newman and Blomfield, Disraeli and Cecil make unmanageable gaps in Conservatism; Owen and McCulloch, Fielden and Bright, Mill and Martineau make a meaningless hodge-podge of Radicalism. What can one do about Cobbett or Feargus O'Connor? One must either suppose a capricious incidence of radicalism or resort to what Professor Hexter in another connection has called "apologetic epicycles"—Tory Radicals, Radical Conservatives, breeds of Chartists—to save the appearances. The polarities of conservative and radical are better used to describe tempers or approaches. To classify (for what is it worth) by approach rather than programme, if it does not solve the problem entirely, at least simplifies it.

The all-embracing challenge to Victorian society was change, not only change itself but a pace of change beyond anything men had known before. An eighteenth-century society so isolated socially that it could afford the luxury of anarchy grew into interdependence, new ramifications of which were constantly and often startlingly revealed. Industrialism, for all its antecedents, was bringing about a new world. The Industrial Revolution may have been less revolutionary economically than we have often maintained, but it demanded a revolution in thought and in the structure of society.

David Hume had provided one way of coping with change, in his reliance on criticism, habit, convention, in a distrust of certain, knowable truths and final solutions. Harriet Martineau shows clearly how impossible Hume's way was for a century after his death. "The most indifferent," she wrote when she was young, "must occasionally shudder at the abyss of uncertainty which is yawning beneath them, at the storms of circumstance amidst which they are lost, if they are destitute of principle to guide, or a refuge to which to betake themselves." The same horror drove her to translate Comte, that young men should not want firm moorings in an age of transition.

The conservative could find his security in the past, in the dogma of religion or the canons of social hierarchy and deference. Armed with such authorities, he could adapt old institutions and brake the speed of change. The radical rejected the past, rejected the authority of men and institutions; they were insufficient for the new dispensation. "What is authority to them," continued the young Harriet, "shipped as it is in the same bottom with themselves. All who are men must feel at times, that as man is made speculative, authority cannot be made his permanent rule, stimulus, and sanction. Better be a dweller in a mud hut, on some hillside of Judea, in the season when the rain descends and the floods are abroad, than spend life in the dark cave where all the winds of heaven are at perpetual war." So radicals welcomed change and tried to speed it on.[1]

English radicals, in looking to the future, were in a unique quandary. Radicals elsewhere, setting or coping with the pace of change in their own industrializing societies, could look for

[1] This whole argument owes much to the uncompleted work of Professor Brebner on the history of industrial Britain and to conversations with H. L. Beales on the grounds of nineteenth-century social policy. The quotations are from "On Moral Independence", *Misc.*, i, 184.

guidance either to the English example or to dogma which, directly or by reaction, grew out of English experience. England, the first industrial society, had no other nation to look to, so her radicals, denying themselves the certainties of the past, had only dogma. They had to create the ideals and principles wherein certainty could be found and which could provide the authority for grounding action. In moving, willy-nilly, from something they could know in a traditional society, to something unknown in an industrial society, the radicals turned from observation to extrapolation. They had to predict in order to act. And because they so often believed their predictions to be truth, not hypothesis, they sometimes turned too from order to ordering and became revolutionaries. Rightness was judged not by conformity or submission to human power or to the weight of tradition, but by congruity to a model not made (they thought) but only discovered by human minds. Gradations in incidence, scope, or pertinacity were possible in this allegiance, but Harriet Martineau stood proudly at the radical pole itself. Self-conscious and concerned about method, resolute in analysing the principles inherent in action or brought to test it, she is a cardinal example of the radical temper.

The radical temper ran to certain assumptions. It is a commonplace that radicals take a high view of human nature and possibility. Priestley's disciple, Harriet Martineau was no exception. In *The Hour and the Man*, Toussaint calls misplaced confidence "a safer and nobler error . . . than unbelief in the virtue of man". Throughout her career, in her views on didactic fiction and the purpose of art, in her hopes for America, in her work for the slave, in her fantastic conceptions of working-men and capitalists, she never lost her faith or made the ignoble error Toussaint warned against.

Again, radicals tended to think in scientific terms. The great accomplishments of the scientists in subduing and explaining nature stood as challenges to other men to subdue and explain society. The particular sciences of society were contradictory, partial, and sometimes chimerical. Their partisans were not very well informed on the true nature of science. But whether it was political economy, mesmerism, positivism, or scientific socialism, the security, prediction, and promise of science were the goals. Harriet Martineau was never an advocate of scientific socialism; had she been born a little later in another place she might well have been; but as it was, she found science enough and hope enough in the other three causes I have given.

The radicals shared that Victorian passion for all-encompassing explanations and all-powerful solutions, one mark of a society confronted with rapid change and emerging from old orthodoxies. Hence the possibility of journalism by rule, the broader implications of mesmerism, and the "prepared completeness" which Carlyle found in the invalid at Tynemouth. And they all moralized incessantly. Some of the Benthamites, some of the Chartists, all of the Owenites, legions of nonconformists, and that most eminent of Victorians, Karl Marx, stood beside Miss Martineau at the radical pole, firm in knowledge, confidence, and simplicity.

Such an interpretation of radicalism explains why Miss Martineau seemed so irrelevant when she died, and her irrelevance says something about the fate of early Victorian radicalism. The temper survived and survives today, but its greatest days were gone not long after mid-century. For one thing, some of the radical ranks collapsed and fell away. Dissenters got most of what they were seeking from society and the state and lapsed into indifference or sterility. Manufacturers and their kind had attained their goals and found the new dictates of radicalism galling and threatening: their desertion of the Liberal Party is testimony enough. But the intellectual basis of radicalism was being weakened too. The professionals, in laboratories, in the new disciplines, in government administrations were forced to deal with complex problems and stubborn facts which would not yield to the incantations of theory. Professionalism, growing in every field, made Victorian amateurism impotent and ridiculous and in pursuing researches more deeply broke up the unity of culture, invented new languages, and created enormous gulfs which the amateurs could neither understand nor bridge.

Perhaps more than anything else, the corrosion was caused by time. Men were getting used to living with change. They made what they could out of the world they found, and did it as often as it proved necessary. They took partial views, then threw them over for others. The gap between Miss Martineau's definition of empiricism as unsystematic floundering amid facts and our view of it as a disciplined method is significant. More and more, men were forced by facts and events to a humility early Victorians could feel only towards God, if there, or to an apathy unknown to the preceding generation.

Priestley and his disciples thought they had beaten the great sceptic. A hundred years later, English society had caught up with his genial but corrosive criticism and began to find it relevant. Harriet Martineau died just two months short of the centenary of the death of David Hume.

Bibliography

THERE have been several biographies of Harriet Martineau. When the *Autobiography* appeared in 1877, Maria Weston Chapman added a volume of *Memorials*, wretchedly edited and completely eulogistic. In 1884, Mrs. Florence Fenwick Miller published *Harriet Martineau*; it appeared in the *Eminent Women Series*, a fact which should indicate its tone, though the praise fell short of what Mrs. Chapman demanded. Theodora Bosanquet's *Harriet Martineau: An Essay in Comprehension* (1927) is a sprightly account which, though superficial, contains more insight into its subject than is to be found in any of the other biographies. J. C. Nevill, *Harriet Martineau*, is an adequate brief sketch, published in 1943. The most recent book is *The Life and Work of Harriet Martineau* by Vera Wheatley, published in 1957, a straightforward biography based on quite wide reading in England (though none in the United States). It is nearly as adulatory as Mrs. Chapman would have wanted, and both as biography and as history it is thoroughly amateur.

The listing of Harriet Martineau's books and pamphlets can be omitted here because of the remarkable bibliography compiled by Joseph B. Rivlin: *Harriet Martineau, a Bibliography of her Separately Printed Works* (New York Public Library, 1937), is a work of reference which was used constantly in preparing this book. To list the many articles in periodicals which Miss Martineau wrote would require a pamphlet of considerable dimensions. Fortunately, some assistance is at hand in the appendix to Francis E. Mineka, *The Dissidence of Dissent*, which catalogues the authorship of articles in the *Monthly Repository*. The important articles in the *Edinburgh Review* and *Westminster Review* are noted in the footnotes, and I have not thought it necessary to list them separately. *Health, Husbandry, and Handicraft* provides the clues to her work for *Household Words* and a few other journals; the *Autobiography* is of some assistance. In the *People's Journal* and *Once a Week*, her articles are signed "From the Mountain". The most important material hitherto unavailable is her work for the *Daily News*. Sir Wilfrid Martineau kindly allowed me to use a collection made by Miss Martineau of cuttings of her articles, arranged chronologically in six-month packets and dated. This collection is not complete. The leading articles on America are missing for most of the Civil War period. But I should estimate that about 1500 of the reported 1642 are in the collection. There are a number of reviews and letters, the latter often signed with a variety of pseudonyms. It is possible that some of these may have come from other hands, but I know that some of them are by Miss Martineau, and even though some may not be, she certainly agreed wholeheartedly with the sentiments expressed, and so they may stand as hers. A hand-list of these articles has been sent to the British Museum Newspaper Library, Colindale, the Boston Public Library, the Library of Congress, and to the *News Chronicle*, London.

Miss Martineau's assiduous efforts to destroy her letters were not entirely successful. A list of surviving papers which I used follows. There are undoubtedly others—a great many single letters turned up in autograph collections—but I believe that I have seen the principal collections, except for the letters to Lady Elgin, which I was not able to see. Some of the collections cited here contain letters about Miss Martineau or to her; the most important of these collections are the Weston Papers and the Anti-Slavery Papers in the Boston Public Library, wonderfully complete and superbly indexed. Only one other collection requires comment. In 1843 James Martineau obeyed, most unwillingly, his sister's request that he return her letters; but before he did so, he made abstracts of them, a remarkable series covering the years 1819 to 1843. The abstracts are in shorthand (Doddridge's version of Rich's) and have been most skilfully deciphered for me by Mr. William S. Coloe. A copy of the transcription is deposited in Manchester College, Oxford. In some places it has proved impossible to transcribe certain words, because of the lack of clarity of James's shorthand (they were obviously written at great speed), or of the photostats from which Mr. Coloe had to work. But the sense of the letters and much concrete detail is made available to supplement and correct the account of the autobiography. In some places James Martineau must have changed the meaning slightly in abstracting, but I do not believe that there has been any substantive damage to the sense of the originals.

MANUSCRIPT MATERIAL

Boston Public Library—Anti-Slavery (Garrison); Estlin; May; Weston.
British Museum—Bright; Holyoake; Nightingale; Place.
Cambridge University Library—R. M. Bacon.
Columbia University Library—S. H. Gay.
Cornell University Library—*Anti-Slavery Standard* (cuttings and correspondence); May.
Dr. Williams's Library Trustees—Crabb Robinson (diary and letters).
Harvard College Library—Emerson.
Manchester College, Oxford—P. P. Carpenter; Helen Martineau; James Martineau.
Massachusetts Historical Society—Bancroft, Everett, Mann, Norcross, Sedgwick, Shattuck, Washburn.
Pennsylvania Historical Society—Deborah Logan Diary.
University College, London—Brougham, Chadwick, S.D.U.K.
Wellesley College—Elizabeth Barrett.
Yale University Library—Arthur Allen, Elizabeth Barrett.

Private Collections:

Bulwer-Lytton (Lady Hermione Cobbold)
Durham (Viscount Lambton)
Carlisle—Morpeth (Mr. George Howard)
Milnes (Marchioness of Crewe)
Reeve (Mr. John Martineau)
Tremenheere (Mr. C. W. Borlase Parker)

Scattered letters in the following collections:

Bodleian; British Museum; Boston Public Library; Chicago Historical Society; Columbia University; Co-operative Union, Manchester; Harvard College Library; Huntington Library; Library of Congress; London School of Economics; Manchester College, Oxford; National Library of Scotland; New-York Historical Society; New York Public Library; Peabody Institute, Baltimore; Princeton University Library; John Rylands Library; Women's Service Library, London.

BOOKS AND ARTICLES

Aikin, Lucy. See Channing.

Arnold, Matthew

Letters of Matthew Arnold, 1848–1888. Collected and arranged by G. W. E. Russell. 2 vols. New York, 1896.

Unpublished Letters of Matthew Arnold. Arnold Whitridge, ed. New Haven, 1923.

Bailey, Samuel. *Essays on the Formation and Publication of Opinion and other Subjects.* 3rd edn. London, 1837. (First published, 1821).

Barlow, Nora, ed. *Charles Darwin and the Voyage of the Beagle.* London, 1945.

Barnes, G. H. *The Anti-Slavery Impulse.* New York, 1933.

Barrett, Elizabeth

Elizabeth Barrett to Miss Mitford. Betty Miller, ed. London, 1954.

Elizabeth Barrett to Mr. Boyd: Unpublished Letters of Elizabeth Barrett Browning to Hugh Stuart Boyd. Barbara P. McCarthy, ed. New Haven, 1955.

The Letters of Elizabeth Barrett Browning. Frederic G. Kenyon, ed. 2 vols. New York, 1899.

Letters of Elizabeth Barrett Browning Addressed to Richard Hengist Horne. S. R. Townshend Mayer, ed. 2 vols. London, 1877.

The Letters of Robert Browning and Elizabeth Barrett Browning, 1845–1846. 2 vols. New York, 1899.

Belsham, Thomas. *The Importance of Truth, and the Duty of Making an Open Profession of It.* London, 1790.

Best, G. F. A. "The Religious Difficulties of National Education in England, 1800–70." *Cambridge Historical Journal*, xii, 155–73 (July, 1956).

Blaug, Mark. *Ricardian Economics: A Historical Study*. New Haven, 1958.

Blyth, E. K. *The Life of William Ellis*. London, 1889.

Bosanquet, Theodora. *Harriet Martineau, an Essay in Comprehension*. London, 1927.

Braid, James. *Magic, Witchcraft, Animal Magnetism, Hypnotism, and Electro-Biology*. 3rd edn. London, 1852.

Neurypnology. London, 1843.

Bray, Charles. *The Philosophy of Necessity*. 2nd edn. Coventry, 1863. (First published, 1841).

Brebner, J. B. "Laissez-faire and State Intervention in Nineteenth-Century Britain." *Journal of Economic History, Supplement*, viii, 59–73 (1948).

Brightfield, Myron F. *John Wilson Croker*. London, 1940.

Brightwell, Cecilia Lucy. *Memorials of the Life of Amelia Opie*. Norwich, 1854.

Brose, Olive J. *Church and Parliament: The Reshaping of the Church of England, 1828–1860*. Stanford, 1959.

Browning, Elizabeth Barrett and Robert. See Barrett.

Bulwer-Lytton, E. L. *England and the English*. 2 vols. London, 1833.

Zanoni, Works. Knebworth edition. London, 1873–75.

Bushnan, J. Stevenson. *Miss Martineau and Her Master*. London, 1851.

Butler, Josephine. *Personal Reminiscences of a Great Crusade*. London, 1896.

Carlyle, Jane

Early Letters of Jane Welsh Carlyle. David Ritchie, ed. London, 1889.

Jane Welsh Carlyle: Letters to Her Family, 1839–1863. Leonard Huxley, ed. London, 1924.

New Letters and Memorials of Jane Welsh Carlyle. Alexander Carlyle, ed. 2 vols. London, 1903.

Carlyle, Thomas

The Correspondence of Thomas Carlyle and Ralph Waldo Emerson, 1834–1872. Charles Eliot Norton, ed. 2 vols. Boston, 1883.

——. A new edition, MS. Joseph Locke Slater, ed. Ph.D. Dissertation, Columbia University, 1955.

New Letters of Thomas Carlyle. Alexander Carlyle, ed. 2 vols. London, 1904.

Carpenter, Lant. *Principles of Education, Intellectual, Moral, and Physical*. London, 1820.

Channing, William Ellery

Correspondence of William Ellery Channing, D.D., and Lucy Aikin, from 1826 to 1842. Anna Letitia LeBreton, ed. Boston, 1874.

Memoir of William Ellery Channing. 3 vols. 6th edn. Boston, 1854.

Chapman, John Jay. *Memories and Milestones*. New York, 1915.

Charlton, L. E. O. *Recollections of a Northumberland Lady, 1815–1866.* London, 1949.

Chesterton, G. K. *The Victorian Age in Literature.* Home University Library. London, 1946.

Chorley, Henry Fothergill. *Autobiography, Memoir, and Letters.* Henry G. Hewlett, comp. 2 vols. London, 1873.

Clark, G. Kitson. *The English Inheritance.* London, 1950.

Cogan, Thomas. *Ethical Questions.* London, 1817.

Colton, Calvin. *The Life, Correspondence, and Speeches of Henry Clay.* 6 vols. New York, 1857.

Creevey, Thomas. *Creevey's Life and Times: A Further Selection from the Correspondence of Thomas Creevey.* John Gore, ed. London, 1934.

Davies, John D. *Phrenology, Fad and Science: A 19th-Century American Crusade.* New Haven, 1955.

Dering, Edward Heneage. *Memoirs of Georgiana, Lady Chatterton.* London, 1878.

Dewey, Mary E. *Life and Letters of Catherine Maria Sedgwick.* New York, 1871.

Dickens, Charles. *Charles Dickens as Editor.* R. C. Lehmann, ed. New York, 1912.

The Letters of Charles Dickens. 2 vols. London, 1882.

Drummond, James. *Life and Letters of James Martineau, D.D.* 2 vols. New York, 1902.

Eastlake, Lady. *Journals and Correspondence.* C. E. Smith, ed. 2 vols. London, 1895.

Eden, Hon. Emily. *The Semi-Attached Couple.* London, 1927. (Written 1834).

Eliot, George. *The George Eliot Letters.* Gordon S. Haight, ed. 7 vols. New Haven, 1954–55.

Elliotson, John. *The Harveian Oration.* London, 1846.

Emerson, Ralph Waldo. *The Letters of Ralph Waldo Emerson.* Ralph L. Rusk, ed. 6 vols. New York, 1939.

Estlin, J. B. *Remarks on Mesmerism in 1845.* Bristol, 1845.

Fellowes, Robert. *Common Sense Truths, proposed for the Consideration of the Working Classes.* London, 1845.

Fifty-Second Year's Report of the Literary and Philosophical Society of Newcastle-upon-Tyne. Newcastle, 1845.

Forbes, John. *Illustrations of Modern Mesmerism.* London, 1845.

Forster, E. M. *Marianne Thornton, a Domestic Biography.* London, 1956.

Forten, Charlotte. *The Journal of Charlotte L. Forten.* Ray Allen Billington, ed. New York, 1953.

Foster, John. *Essays in a Series of Letters.* 11th edn. London, 1835. (First published, 1804).

Fuller, Margaret. *Memoirs of Margaret Fuller Ossoli.* 3 vols. London, 1852.

Gannett, William C. *Ezra Stiles Gannett, a Memoir.* Boston, 1875.

Garnett, Richard. *The Life of W. J. Fox, Public Teacher and Social Reformer, 1786–1864.* London, 1910.

Garrison, William Lloyd. *William Lloyd Garrison, 1805–1879: the Story of His Life Told by His Children.* 4 vols. New York, 1885.

General History of the County of Norfolk. Norwich, 1829.

Godden, Rumer. *Hans Christian Andersen.* New York, 1955.

Green, Samuel. *The Working Classes of Great Britain.* London, 1850.

Greenhow, T. M. *Medical Report of the Case of Miss H—— M——.* London, 1845.

Greg, W. R. *Essays in Political and Social Science.* London, 1853.

Gregory, William. *On the Theory of Imagination, as Explaining the Phenomena of Mesmerism.* Edinburgh, 1852.

Griffiths, Olive M. *Religion and Learning: A Study in English Presbyterian Thought from the Bartholomew Ejections (1662) to the Foundation of the Presbyterian Movement.* Cambridge, 1935.

Haddock, Joseph W. *Somnolism and Psycheism: on the Science of the Soul and the Phenomena of Nervation.* 2nd ed. London, 1851.

Halévy, Elie. *A History of the English People.* Vol. ii. 2nd edn. London, 1949.

Hall, Spencer T. "Memoir of Spencer T. Hall, 'The Sherwood Forester.' " *Glasgow Examiner*, October 5, 1844.

Mesmeric Experiences. London, 1845.

Hammond, J. L. and Barbara. *The Village Labourer.* New edn. London, 1920.

Harrison, Frederic. *The Creed of a Layman.* New York, 1907.

The Philosophy of Common Sense. London, 1907.

Hawkins, C. B. *Norwich, a Social Study.* London, 1910.

Hawthorne, Nathaniel. *The English Notebooks by Nathaniel Hawthorne.* Randall Stewart, ed. New York, 1941.

Helmstadter, Richard. George Cornewall Lewis and the Benthamite Poor Law. M. A. Essay, Columbia University, 1958.

Hints to Radical Reformers. London, 1819.

Holland, Sir Henry. *Recollections of Past Life.* London, 1872.

Holt, R. V. *The Unitarian Contribution to Social Progress in England.* London, 1938.

Horne, Richard Hengist. *A New Spirit of the Age.* New York, 1844. See also Barrett.

Hone, Philip. *The Diary of Philip Hone, 1828–1851.* Allan Nevins ed., 4 vols. New York, 1927.

House, Humphry. *All in Due Time.* London, 1955.

Howitt, Mary. *An Autobiography.* 2 vols. Boston, 1889.

Hudson, J. W. *The History of Adult Education.* London, 1851.

Hutchison, T. W. "Bentham as an Economist." *Economic Journal,* lxvi, 298 (June, 1956).

Jameson, Anna. *Anna Jameson: Letters and Friendships (1812–1860),* New York, n.d.

Letters of Anna Jameson to Ottilie von Goethe. G. H. Needler, ed. London, 1939.

Kemble, Frances Ann. *Records of Later Life.* New York, 1884.

Kirby, Chester. "The Attack on the English Game Laws in the Forties." *Journal of Modern History,* iv, 18–37 (March, 1932).

"The English Game Law System." *American Historical Review,* xxxviii, 240–62 (January, 1933).

Knight, Charles. *The Old Printer and the Modern Press.* London, 1854.

Passages of a Working Life during Half a Century. 3 vols. London, 1864.

Popular History of England. London, 1856–62.

Lambert, R. S. *The Cobbett of the West.* London, 1939.

[Lang]. *Mesmerism: Its History, Phenomena, and Practice.* Edinburgh, 1843.

Lee, Amice. *Laurels and Rosemary: The Life of William and Mary Howitt.* London, 1955.

L'Estrange, A. G. K., ed. *The Life of Mary Russell Mitford. Told by Herself in Letters to Her Friends.* 2 vols. New York, 1870.

Lewis, George Cornewall. *Letters of Rt. Hon. Sir George Cornewall Lewis, Bart.* London, 1870.

Lincoln, Anthony. *Some Political and Social Ideas of English Dissent, 1763–1800.* Cambridge, 1938.

Lipson, E. *The History of the Woollen and Worsted Industries.* London, 1921.

MacPherson, Geraldine. *Memoirs of the Life of Anna Jameson.* London, 1878.

Macready, William Charles. *The Diaries of William Charles Macready.* William Toynbee, ed. 2 vols. New York, 1912.

Macready's Reminiscences, and Selections from His Letters and Diaries. Sir Frederick Pollock, ed. New York, 1875.

Malthus, Thomas Robert. *An Essay on the Principle of Population.* 6th edn. 2 vols. London, 1826.

Maurice, Frederick. *The Life of Frederick Denison Maurice.* 2 vols. London, 1884.

May, Samuel J. *Some Recollections of our Antislavery Conflict.* Boston, 1869.

McCulloch, James Ramsay. *Discourse on the Rise, Progress, Peculiar Objects, and Importance of Political Economy.* Edinburgh, 1825.

The Literature of Political Economy. London, 1845.

McLachlan, H. *The Unitarian Movement in the Religious Life of England.* London, 1934.

McLennan, John F. *Memoir of Thomas Drummond.* Edinburgh, 1867.

Mesmerism in India. London, 1850.

Mill, John Stuart. *Auguste Comte and Positivism.* London, 1865.

The Letters of John Stuart Mill. H. S. R. Elliott, ed. London, 1910.

Milne, J. Bramwell. *Hypnotism.* 3rd edn. London, 1930.

Mineka, Francis E. *The Dissidence of Dissent: The Monthly Repository, 1806–1838.* Chapel Hill, 1944.

Mitford, Mary Russell. *Correspondence with Charles Boner and John Ruskin.* Elizabeth Lee, ed. Chicago, n.d.

Letters of Mary Russell Mitford. 2nd series. Henry Chorley, ed. 2 vols. London, 1872.

Mohl, Julius and Mary. *Letters and Recollections of Julius and Mary Mohl.* M. C. M. Simpson, ed. London, 1887.

Moran, Benjamin. *The Journal of Benjamin Moran, 1857–1865.* Sarah Agnes Wallace and Frances Elma Gillespie, eds. 2 vols. Chicago, 1949.

Mott, James and Lucretia. *James and Lucretia Mott, Life and Letters.* Anna Davis Hollowell, ed. Boston, 1896.

Murphy, Gardner. *An Historical Introduction to Modern Psychology.* Rev. edn. New York, 1949.

Murphy, Howard. "The Ethical Revolt against Christian Orthodoxy in Early Victorian England." *American Historical Review,* lx, 800–17, (July, 1955).

Newman, John Henry. *An Essay on the Development of Christian Doctrine.* New York, n.d.

Newnham, William. *Human Magnetism: Its Claims to Dispassionate Inquiry.* London, 1845.

O'Brien, R. Barry. *Thomas Drummond, Life and Letters.* London, 1889.

"Oculus." *The Tale of "Cinnamon and Pearls" by Miss Harriet Martineau, Examined.* Colombo, Ceylon, 1834. (Copy in Central Reference Library, Manchester.)

Oliphant, M. O. W. *The Autobiography and Letters of Mrs. M. O. W. Oliphant.* Mrs. Harry Coghill, ed. New York, 1899.

Packe, Michael St. John. *The Life of John Stuart Mill.* London, 1954.

Paley, William. *The Principles of Moral and Political Philosophy.* 2nd edn., rev. London, 1786.

Pauli, Reinhold. *Simon de Montfort.* With an introduction by Harriet Martineau. London, 1876.

Payn, James. *Some Literary Recollections.* London, 1884.

Peabody, Elizabeth Palmer. *Reminiscences of Rev. William Ellery Channing, D.D.* Boston, 1880.

[Pearson, John], *A Plain and Rational Account of the Nature and Effects of Animal Magnetism*. London, 1790.

Pope-Hennessy, James. *Monckton Milnes: The Years of Promise, 1809–1851*. 2 vols. London, 1949.

Priestley, Joseph. *The Theological and Miscellaneous Works of Joseph Priestley*. J. T. Rutt, ed. London, 1817–24.

Proceedings of the General Anti-Slavery Convention. London, 1840.

Reid, T. Wemyss. *The Life, Letters, and Friendships of Richard Monckton Milnes*. 2 vols. New York, 1891.

Report of Assistant Commissioners for Handloom Weavers, Parliamentary Papers, 1840, xxiii.

Robberds, J. W. *A Memoir of the Life and Writings of the late William Taylor of Norwich*. 2 vols. London, 1843.

Robinson, Sir John R. *Fifty Years of Fleet Street, being the Life and Recollections of Sir John R. Robinson*. Frederick Moy Thomas, ed. London, 1904.

Ross, Janet. *Three Generations of English Women*. New edn. London, 1893.

Saint, William. *The Life of John Fransham*. Norwich, 1812.

Smith, Adam. *The Wealth of Nations*. Edward Gibbon Wakefield, ed. 2 vols. London, 1843.

Smith, T. Southwood. *Illustrations of the Divine Government*. 4th London edn., 1822, reprinted Philadelphia, 1843.

Spencer, Herbert. *An Autobiography*. London, 1904.

Stephens, W. R. W. *The Life and Letters of Walter Farquhar Hook*. 2 vols. London, 1879.

Third Co-operative Congress. *Proceedings*. London, 1832.

Trollope, Anthony. *The Clergymen of the Church of England*. London, 1866.

Tuke, Margaret. *A History of Bedford College for Women, 1849–1937*. London, 1939.

Upton, Charles B. *Dr. Martineau's Philosophy, a Summary*. Rev. edn. London, 1905.

Van Deusen, Glyndon G. *Thurlow Weed, Wizard of the Lobby*. Boston, 1947.

Webb, Beatrice. *My Apprenticeship*. London, 1950.

Webb, R. K. *The British Working Class Reader, 1790–1848: Literacy and Social Tension*. London, 1955.

Weld, Theodore Dwight. *Letters of Theodore Dwight Weld, Angelina Grimke Weld, and Sarah Grimke, 1822–1844*. 2 vols. New York, 1934.

Whately, Richard. *Introduction to Political Economy*. London, 1832.
Introductory Lectures on Political Economy. London, 1831.

Willey, Basil. *The Eighteenth Century Background*. London, 1940.

Williams, J. H. Harley. *Doctors Differ*. London, 1946.

[Williams-Wynn, Frances.] *Diaries of a Lady of Quality from 1797 to 1844*. A. Hayward, ed. London, 1864.

Wilson, David Alec. *Carlyle, to Three-score-and-ten*. London, 1931.

Wolf, Hazel C. *On Freedom's Altar*. Madison, 1952.

Woodham-smith, Cecil. "They Stayed in Bed." *Listener*, February 16, 1956.

Woodring, Carl Ray. *Victorian Samplers: William and Mary Howitt*. Lawrence, Kansas, 1952.

Wordsworth, Mary. *The Letters of Mary Wordsworth, 1800–1855*. Mary E. Burton, ed. Oxford, 1958.

Zweig, Stefan. *Mental Healers*. New York, 1932.

PERIODICALS AND NEWSPAPERS

Athenaeum
Atlantic Monthly
Bristol Job Nott
British and Foreign Medical Review
British Medical Journal
British Quarterly Review
Chambers's Edinburgh Journal
Charleston Courier
Charleston Mercury
Cobbett's Magazine
Daily News
The Economist
Edinburgh Review
English Chartist Circular
Fraser's Magazine
Globe and Traveller (London)
Herald to the Trades Advocate (Glasgow)
Household Words
Lancashire and Yorkshire Co-operator
Lancet
Leader
Monthly Repository
Moral Reformer (Preston)
National Anti-Slavery Standard (New York)
National Intelligencer (Washington)
Newcastle Chronicle
Nineteenth Century
Norwich Mercury
Once a Week
Pall Mall Gazette
Penny Magazine
People's Journal
Phreno-Magnet
Poor Man's Advocate
Poor Man's Guardian
Prompter
Prospective Review
Quarterly Review
Reasoner
Spectator
Southern Patriot (Charleston)
The Times
Westminster Review
Zoist

Index